THE CHICAGO SCHOOL DIASPORA

The Chicago School Diaspora

Epistemology and Substance

Edited by
JACQUELINE LOW AND GARY BOWDEN

McGill-Queen's University Press
Montreal & Kingston • London • Ithaca

Educ.
HM
463
.C553
2013

ISBN 978-0-7735-4265-5 (cloth)
ISBN 978-0-7735-4266-2 (paper)
ISBN 978-0-7735-8969-8 (ePDF)
ISBN 978-0-7735-8970-4 (ePUB)

Legal deposit fourth quarter 2013
Bibliothèque nationale du Québec

Printed in Canada on acid-free paper that is 100% ancient forest free
(100% post-consumer recycled), processed chlorine free

Publication of this book is generously supported by the Department of
Sociology and the Faculty of Arts, University of New Brunswick, and by
a University of New Brunswick Busteed Publication award.

McGill-Queen's University Press acknowledges the support of the Canada
Council for the Arts for our publishing program. We also acknowledge the
financial support of the Government of Canada through the Canada Book
Fund for our publishing activities.

Library and Archives Canada Cataloguing in Publication

The Chicago School diaspora: epistemology and substance / edited
by Jacqueline Low and Gary Bowden.

Includes bibliographical references and index.
Issued in print and electronic formats.
ISBN 978-0-7735-4265-5 (bound). – ISBN 978-0-7735-4266-2 (pbk.). –
ISBN 978-0-7735-8969-8 (ePDF). – ISBN 978-0-7735-8970-4 (ePUB)

1. Chicago school of sociology – History. 2. University of Chicago.
Department of Sociology – Influence – History. 3. Sociology – Illinois –
Chicago – History. 4. Sociology – United States – History. I. Low,
Jacqueline, 1964–, author, writer of introduction, editor of compilation
II. Bowden, Gary Lee, 1953–, author, writer of introduction, editor
of compilation

HM463.C55 2013   301.0973   C2013-906407-9
                                          C2013-906408-7

This book was typeset by Interscript in 10.5/13 Sabon.

Contents

SECTION V   THE CHICAGO SCHOOL DIASPORA:
NEW DIRECTIONS

THE CHICAGO SCHOOL DIASPORA

The Chicago School as Symbol and Enactment

GARY BOWDEN AND JACQUELINE LOW

A cursory review of the literature on sociology at the University of Chicago reveals its startling magnitude. According to Abbott (2007), one of the tradition's most noted historians, close to 2,000 scholarly items have been written about Chicago sociology.[1] This dwarfs the amount written about sociology at other institutional locations and rivals the volume written about major theorists or theoretical traditions (cf. Abbott 1999; Becker 1999; Bulmer 1984; Carey 1975;

---

1 There is considerable variation in the terms used to discuss Chicago sociology. Thus, in this chapter and in the section introductions to follow, we use "Chicago sociology" (or "sociology at the University of Chicago") to refer to the entire corpus of sociological work done at the University of Chicago. We use "Chicago School sociology" (or "Chicago School") when writing of the ideas, individuals, and practices people associate with a particular subset of Chicago sociology. We use the latter inclusively, to incorporate both individuals and work done within the Department of Sociology and the contributions of scholars, such as G.H. Mead, who were at Chicago but not in the Sociology Department. Moreover, we treat this term as a label that incorporates both a social structural object (i.e., the individuals, ideas, and practices of scholars interacting at the University of Chicago at a particular point in time) and a cultural object (i.e., the meaning imposed onto that social structural object by individuals separated from it in time, space, or both). Finally, we use "the Chicago School tradition" (also "heritage" or "legacy") to incorporate both Chicago School sociology and the ideas and practices associated with scholars who see their work as a continuation of Chicago School sociology.

Chapoulie 2001; Deegan 1988; Faris 1967; Fine 1995; Harvey 1987; Shore 1987; Turner 1988).

In contributing to this literature, we document the intellectual breadth of the Chicago School heritage and its continued vitality among scholars, most of whom are not formally associated with the University of Chicago. All of the chapters in this volume are the product of individuals who see themselves and their work as centrally informed by key thinkers and key insights associated with the Chicago School tradition. The volume is organized to highlight the variety of ways in which these scholars build upon and make use of that tradition. Our aim is to shed light on the paradoxical character of Chicago School sociology, which is conventionally represented as a coherent entity (i.e., "the Chicago School") despite the fact that there is little scholarly consensus about its intellectual core. Finally, via our concept of the Chicago School Diaspora, we contribute to an understanding of the process whereby individuals select from and find meaning in figures and ideas they associate with the Chicago School tradition.

THE DISTINCTIVE CHARACTER OF THE CHICAGO SCHOOL OF SOCIOLOGY

What is the Chicago School of Sociology? Becker (1999, 3–4) lists five elements, some or all of which are characteristically associated with the concept: (1) in the early 1900s, the founders, particularly W.I. Thomas and George Herbert Mead, created a coherent and cohesive scheme of sociological thought capable of guiding research; (2) in the 1920s and 1930s, a second generation at Chicago, fuelled by the energy of Robert Park and Ernest Burgess, undertook a vast empirical research program based on that vision; (3) in the late 1930s and 1940s, a third generation, trained by Park and Burgess and led by Everett Hughes and Herbert Blumer, developed what is now labelled symbolic interactionism; (4) after World War II, a group of graduate students trained by Hughes and Blumer, labelled by Fine (1995) as a "Second Chicago School," used the ideas of symbolic interactionism and the practice of field research to create a substantial body of work that remains vital to this date; and (5) as Becker (1999, 4) notes, the story holds that "all of these people were the carriers of a common theoretical tradition which flowed from the vision of Park and the philosophy of Mead, was nourished by the theoretical profundities of Blumer and the research ingenuity of Hughes, and was responsible for two great bursts of theoretically integrated 'Chicago School' work, first in the late 20s and 30s, and again after the Second World War."

   Three features of the above narrative, features that form the fault lines among various interpretations of the School, require explicit identification. First, the account treats the Chicago School as a social structural object – that is, a specific set of individuals interacting in a particular location and producing a coherently meaningful set of works. Second, the account renders the School as consisting of several generations of scholars associated with the department over a period of half a century. Third, throughout the account is the assumption of an overall coherence that binds the various contributions of these individuals together. Thus, the later generations of Chicago School sociologists stood on the shoulders of giants (the earlier generations) in order to come up with a unifying theoretical/methodological paradigm (symbolic interactionism). However, not all scholars accept this account and instead contest the assumptions of the unity of the Chicago School, the chronological span, the relative importance of particular thinkers or chronological periods, and whether or not the School should be defined solely in social structural terms.

   To illustrate, Abbott's (1999, 4–33) historiography identifies three phases in the writing about the Chicago School. The first phase, beginning with the use of the label by Bernard in 1930 and culminating in the works of Faris (1967) and Carey (1975), condensed the image of the thing to be studied and gave it a name: the Chicago School of Sociology. These works identified the individuals associated with the Chicago School, described their methods and interaction, and generally distinguished Chicago School sociology from other things, such as sociology as a whole, sociology at Columbia, the social welfare tradition, and so on. The second phase, exemplified in the writings of Matthews (1977), Rock (1979), Lewis and Smith (1980), and Bulmer (1984), gave comprehensive, if mutually inconsistent, historical interpretations to the object. For Rock, as for Lewis and Smith, the Chicago School was understood primarily in terms of social psychology and/or interactionist theory. In contrast, the interpretations of Matthews and Bulmer emphasized the study of social organization, particularly in terms of fieldwork and the ecological tradition associated with Park and Burgess, in combination with social psychology. While the fault line between scholars who defined the Chicago School in terms of social psychology and those who emphasized social organization is the most dramatic, there are similar divisions within each stream. Thus, for example, both Mead and Park are virtually absent from Lewis and Smith's (1980) social psychology-tinged rendition of the core of the Chicago School, while Rock (1979) argued that Park, as the conduit of Simmelian formalism, had an important role in the development of symbolic interactionism. Works from Abbott's third historiographical phase, represented in the writings of Deegan (1988; this volume), Smith (1988), and Lindner (1996; this volume), re-embedded the Chicago School in larger traditions: the social reform movement for Deegan, the tradition of social critique for Smith, and the tradition of urban newspaper reportage for Lindner. Abbott (1999, 30) summarizes the trajectory of the historiography as having gone from "they were new" to "they had many precursors."

Significantly, the label "Chicago School" was not a member's concept. The term was not used at the University of Chicago in the 1920s (Cavan 1983, 408), and its meaning was not clearly delineated until decades later. As Abbott (1999, 34–79) has shown, it was during departmental debates in the 1950s over the meaning of the tradition that the concept coalesced into a distinct object among Chicago faculty. Buffeted by a variety of internal and external pressures (e.g., tensions between the department and upper administration; the emergence of Parsonian sociology and the related ascendency of Harvard; McCarthyesque inquiries into the activities of some department members), the department undertook an intensive period of self-reflection aimed at reclaiming its previous glory. These battles between departmental members in the early 1950s defined Park's legacy for the department. In this sense, the first Chicago School was a creation of Fine's (1995) Second Chicago School. These battles underscore the dual nature of the resulting label: the Chicago School exists both as a social structural entity (consisting of particular individuals embedded in a particular social context and producing specific work that had particular consequences) and as a cultural object (with particular meanings that scholars attach to it).

Contemporary scholarship in the Chicago School tradition is not located in Chicago. The connection to Chicago is historic and symbolic. Structurally, the Chicago School tradition has gone through several phases. It began in Chicago and spread, initially through the employment of Chicago graduates, to peripheral centres at other universities (see Abbott [1999, 21] for a discussion of the "descendant departments" literature) or to lone scholars at other universities, such as C. Wright Mills, whose work at Columbia was informed by his "identification with the Midwestern emphasis on symbolic interactionism" (Horowitz 1983, 31). Of notable relevance for Canada, Chicago graduate Carl Dawson was hired in 1922 to head the newly formed sociology department at McGill University. This department also employed Everett Hughes for eleven years between his graduation from and return to Chicago, and, as chronicled by Shore (1987), these individuals and their work significantly affected the direction of social research in Canada. Over time, the Chicago School tradition became a worldwide phenomenon with adherents located around the globe. There are still a number of "semi-centres" of contemporary Chicago School sociology, places where a core group of scholars continue to work within the tradition, such as the Canadian sociology departments at McMaster, Waterloo, and the University of New Brunswick. Even in these centres, however, the Chicago tradition is only one of several approaches represented. Thus, the dominant structural fact of contemporary work in the Chicago School tradition is not its location in Chicago or other "semi-centres" but rather its spatial/geographic dispersal. As processes of departmental interaction have become progressively less important to the maintenance of the tradition over time, the significance of conferences closely tied to the tradition has increased. It is through graduate training with individuals connected to the tradition and meetings like these that new individuals are socialized into the Chicago School tradition.

Our central concern, however, is not with the social structural characteristics of the Chicago tradition or with how the tradition has evolved over time but rather with the Chicago School as a cultural object: the meaning that individual scholars intend to convey when they invoke the label "Chicago School." Some of this work, such as that published in Janowitz's Heritage of Chicago series and Fine's (1995) volume on the Second Chicago School, Abbott (1999, 18) describes as the "manufacturing Chicago" genre, "work deliberately aiming to create a particular vision of Chicago's past." But the vast majority involves the use of substantive ideas attributed to the School in the context of contemporary debates in symbolic interaction, urban studies, race and ethnicity, and so on. Abbott (1999, 22) notes that "most work on the ideas of the Chicago school is openly presentist, explicitly setting those ideas in the immediate context of current debates" and "nearly all this work gives one the feeling that the details of history are less important than its implications for who is 'right.'" These are two sides of the same coin. On the one side, individuals are manufacturing a particular vision of the past that serves their own purposes; on the other side, individuals are invoking a particular vision of Chicago as a means of legitimating their own scholarly work.

In sum, a review of the literature referring to the Chicago School displays one remarkable feature: a singular lack of agreement on the core element of the School. Does the label refer to a theoretical orientation (e.g., symbolic interactionism or concentric zone theory), a methodological approach (e.g., ethnographic fieldwork or participant observation), a particular substantive area (e.g., urban sociology or crime/deviance), or some broad unifying theme (e.g., the importance of context)? All of the above, and more, have been suggested. Succinctly put, there is widespread recognition of the existence and significance of something labelled "the Chicago School of Sociology" but surprisingly little agreement on what an informed sociologist attaches to that label. For us, it is the diversity and plasticity of the content, rather than the substantive nature of the content itself, that defines the distinctive character of the Chicago School.

Gilmore's (1988) distinction between a "school of thought" and a "school of activity" is particularly useful here. According to Gilmore, schools of thought are created from the outside by historians or other interested scholars who look at the situation and decide that certain people share certain ideas, approaches, or other unifying elements and that they thus constitute a school. As detailed above, this is how the cultural object known as the Chicago School came into existence – as a label created by individuals separated in time and space from the activities being examined. Moreover, we agree with Becker's (1999) assessment that the social structural object of Chicago was a "school of activity" rather than a "school of thought." A school of activity is held together through the process of people working together on shared projects – even though their ideas may not be congruent – rather than by shared ideas. This view is consistent with historical descriptions of research at Chicago that emphasize the diversity of approaches and ideas (Platt 1996; Abbott 1999) and with insider accounts like those of Becker (1999) and Hughes, who in a conversation with Blumer said, "I don't like the idea of talking about a

Chicago School or any other kind of school ... go ahead and be a Chicago School if you like" (Lofland 1980, 276, 277).

In sum, our position is that (a) the historical reality at Chicago can better be conceptualized as a school of activity involving a diverse array of theoretical and methodological approaches than as a coherent and cohesive school of thought, but (b) individuals, separated in time or space from the reality on the ground, select those elements of particular scholarly interest or use to them and identify them with the label "Chicago School" in order to capture the clarity and coherence associated with a school of thought, and (c) as a result, when viewed in the aggregate, a number of distinct scholarly communities refer to the Chicago School, but (d) they do not all mean precisely the same thing when using the term.

This constellation of features is not typical of other scholarly communities labelled "school." Think, for example, of the Frankfurt School, of the multiple schools in the social studies of science that proliferated in the late 1970s and early 1980s (e.g., the Edinburgh School, the Bath School, the Paris School), or of the other famous Chicago School: the Chicago School of Economics. In each of these cases, there is a correspondence between the use of the term to define a social structural entity (i.e., to refer to two or more scholars sharing a physical location and working together to develop and disseminate a common mode of thought) and the meaning of the cultural object. The Edinburgh School consisted of Barnes, Bloor, and the strong program in the sociology of knowledge; the Bath School involved Collins, Pinch, and the empirical program of relativism; while the Paris School consisted of Latour, Callon, and actor-network theory and the Frankfurt School of Horkheimer, Adorno, Marcuse, and critical theory. In each of these cases, we find both a clearly defined social structural object (particular individuals who worked together in order to advance particular ideas) and a widely shared cultural understanding of the meaning of that object (a shared cultural object).

The Chicago School varies in several key respects. Most obviously, the Chicago School tradition draws a distinction between the first school (dominated by Park) and the second school (dominated by Blumer). As noted above, the precise nature of the relationship between the two is the subject of significant debate. In other words, the Chicago School tradition consists of two distinct social objects, which may or may not, depending upon the interpretation of a particular individual, be seen as part of a single cultural object. None of the other schools mentioned above has this characteristic. In the one instance where there is a parallel linguistic distinction (between the first and second Frankfurt Schools), both groups are understood as committed to the critical theory project but differ in their specific interpretations of that project. Thus, the two social objects (the early group surrounding Horkheimer and the later group surrounding Habermas) are understood as part of a single cultural object.

Most important, there is little agreement on the exact meaning of the cultural object. We take the position that the cultural object known as the "Chicago School of Sociology" is to other scholarly schools as the Swiss army knife is to the hammer. Most scholarly schools are like hammers; they have a specific, well-defined meaning, purpose, and utility. While there can be some variation – for example, the difference between a claw hammer and a ball-peen hammer – all hammers share a common trait: they are designed to hit something. Similarly, scholarly schools can have variation around a central core element. There is a variety of different strands of Marxism, for example, but they all involve some form of class analysis. The Chicago School, on the other hand, is like a Swiss army knife; it comprises a wide variety of disparate tools, and different people reach for it and make use of it for different purposes. Some scholars see it as a knife, others as scissors, and still others as a leather punch.

As illustrated by this analogy, there is typically a broad scholarly consensus on the fundamental conceptual tool associated with a school. There is no such consensus about the core of the Chicago School. While there may be a variety of local agreements among sets of scholars about the central tool in the Chicago School toolkit, no universal consensus exists on any of them. For some, the central element is the ecological approach to social organization in the urban studies of Park and Burgess; for others, it is the social psychology of Mead; and so on. It is this paradox – that differing groups use the same label to describe what are significantly different emphases within the discipline – that our concept of the Swiss army knife, with its ability to incorporate multiple tools into an object with a single shared label, aims to capture.

The question we pose, therefore, is not the traditional, descriptive one: what is the Chicago School of Sociology? Rather, we pose a comparative, explanatory question: Why is there so much interest in Chicago School sociology? And why do so many people invoke its name for such a wide variety of different purposes? This is a complex question involving multiple factors. Our intention is not to provide an exhaustive account but rather to unpack one particular, largely ignored factor: the symbolic importance of the label. Toward this end, a number of other relevant factors should first be noted. The University of Chicago itself is a first-rate institution, endowed with substantial funds and able to hire topnotch scholars who have produced a wide variety of cutting-edge scholarship. Further, the University of Chicago Press has had a long and well-documented impact on the institutionalization and development of the discipline, most notably through the *American Journal of Sociology* (founded in 1895), the first scholarly journal of sociology published in the United States, and publication of Park and Burgess's (1921) *Introduction to the Science of Sociology*, arguably the first modern sociology textbook and one that defined the structure of introductory texts for decades (Faris 1967, 37–50). Also, because the university boasts one of the oldest and largest graduate programs in sociology, students from Chicago spread out far and wide. Chicago's Department of Sociology is widely portrayed as the first to institutionalize the discipline and as the dominant force in the discipline up to 1935 (Shills 1970). However, while these factors are necessary to understanding the level of interest in sociology done by individuals at Chicago, they do not provide sufficient explanation for the tendency to represent that work as a coherent entity called the "Chicago School."

Moreover, while the Department of Sociology at Chicago has actively promoted itself and its contributions to the discipline and its graduate students have been expected to know the departmental canon, this self-representational process has not uniformly celebrated all Chicago contributions but rather emphasized some contributions while marginalizing others. It was this process of selective retention that, for example, enabled Deegan (1988; this volume) to rescue the work of Jane Addams from obscurity. While it is certainly arguable that the Department of Sociology at Chicago has been particularly successful at branding itself, these efforts alone cannot account for either the degree or the diversity of interest in Chicago School sociology. As this volume documents in detail, a great many scholars who are not and have never been associated with the Department of Sociology at Chicago nonetheless see themselves and their scholarly work as tied to that tradition, however it may be defined. Finally, a substantial number of contemporary references use the label Chicago School non-reflexively.

Without denying the significance of the above factors, we find that they do not sufficiently explain either the extent of attention given to Chicago sociology or the plasticity of the cultural object known as the Chicago School. We argue that the explanation for such a level of attention lies not in the substance of Chicago sociology itself, significant though it may be, but rather in the symbolic significance of the label. Specifically, we argue that Chicago School sociology serves as a symbolic label for the study of the first aspect of American civilization that could legitimate a belief in American exceptionalism and, by extension, since sociology is the study of society, for a distinctly American contribution to sociology. The equation of Chicago School sociology with a distinctly American sociology has frequently been noted (e.g., Matthews 1977; Fine 1995), as has the dynamic openness of the city of Chicago and the lack of fealty to tradition at the upstart University of Chicago (e.g., Faris 1970, 20–36; Bulmer 1984, 12–27). Typically, the city and university are portrayed as fertile ground, as contextual factors that facilitated the germination of the seminal ideas associated with the Chicago School. In contrast, we argue that the symbolic potency of the label lies not in the ideas but rather in the fact that the ideas emerged from empirical research on the city of Chicago. As noted by Chicago graduate and faculty member Gerald Suttles, it was the focus on Chicago, not theory or method, that bound them together:

> What unified the department, if anything ever did, was not method. In the 1930s, 1940s, 1950s, and 1960s, no single method was being preached. Some people were strongly in favor of statistical analysis. Many faculty, including some from the anthropology department, were quite willing to supervise field studies done by other students. What united us was Chicago itself. The overwhelming majority of students and faculty were working on Chicago. They had to look at one another's work. They had to fit their ideas into other people's ideas. This commonality brought students together, not simply to socialize but also to compare what was going on and to argue out the differences among themselves (Jaynes 2009, 388).

Our argument for the central importance of empirical research on Chicago builds on Roderick Nash's (2001) seminal work, *Wilderness in the American Mind*. In that work, Nash traces the evolution of the idea of wilderness. His basic point is that throughout most of Western history, wilderness was a scary place inhabited by Pan, wild men, and other mythical beasts. Civilization was good, wilderness bad. Europeans measured their success by the extent to which they civilized the land and themselves. This attitude both celebrated human accomplishment and subordinated nature. The European preference for civilization over nature can be seen, for example, in the rigidly geometric gardens of Versailles and the trees pruned into box-like shapes that line the Champs-Élysées. It was in America, Nash argues, that wilderness became a positive condition that was appreciated and valued. The reason? Much like Lipset (1988), Nash treats America as a revolutionary society. Having rejected their European ties, Americans needed an identity legitimating that move. But by any traditional measure – in such fields as literature, history, philosophy, architecture, music – the accomplishments of European civilization surpassed those of America. What, then, did America have that Europe did not? A magnificent, awe-inspiring wilderness. Centuries of population growth and development had transformed European wilderness into occupied and civilized land. In contrast, North America was vast, remote, virtually unpopulated, and wild. Wilderness became important not only for its quasi-religious ability to inspire awe but also because of the role of the frontier in forming the individualistic, self-reliant character of Americans (Turner 1921). America came to view wilderness positively, as something to be valued on its own and for its role in forging America's unique and exceptional national character (Nash 2001).

We take two basic points from Nash's account. First, Americans view themselves as exceptional but need some form of ideological justification for that aspect of their collective identity. Second, when America was founded such justification could not be achieved through reference to America's accomplishments as a civilization – thus, the importance ascribed to wilderness. The existence of an ideological justification for American exceptionalism rooted in nature, however, does not preclude the emergence of a parallel justification rooted in civilization. It is our contention that the city of Chicago, the world's first recognizably modern city, provided Americans with the earliest tangible evidence that their civilization had surpassed Europe's.

The most obvious evidence of Chicago's modernity is its architecture. Beginning with the world's first skyscraper, the ten-storey Montauk Building, completed in 1882, Chicago architects developed a series of technologically innovative steel-frame buildings. While buildings in the same style were constructed in New York, Boston, and other cities at roughly at the same time, because of the 1872 fire that levelled four square miles of the central core, little remained of Chicago's traditional architecture and, hence, its innovative style became comparatively prominent. Significantly, contemporary publications referred to the buildings as "commercial style," an explicit linking of the building's form with a kind of economic activity that was every bit as new, modern, and unprecedented as the buildings themselves.

Following Cronon (1991), we view the emergence of this modern form of civilization as contradicting Turner's account. Rather than the development of the frontier leading to the creation of a city, Chicago created its hinterland by serving as a gateway city. It wasn't Chicago's geographical location between two vast watersheds but rather its socially produced location – the result of canals and railroads that moved lumber and retail goods west while grain and cattle moved east – that made Chicago so significant. By portraying Chicago as a capitalist metropolis embedded within a network of commodity flows in which the accumulation of capital led to the progressive control of more and more space and, ultimately, the transformation of that space, Cronon accomplishes two things. First, he explains how Chicago differed from New York, Buffalo, St Louis, and other major urban centres of the time. Second, he documents the emergence of a new form of industrial capitalist empire, one based on the commercial domination of space. Significantly, this was not an empire where all the tribute flowed one way. Chicago's economic ascendancy was paralleled by a rising standard of living on the American farm (Hurt 2002, 221–79) and the emergence of new forms of business (e.g., diversified mail order businesses like Sears Roebuck and Montgomery Ward) that produced goods on an unprecedented scale and sold them by catalogue to rural farmers. Thus, not only was Chicago's commercial capitalism a new form, but, by demonstrably improving the lot of farmers and other groups that had previously been economically marginalized, it laid the foundation for modern consumer capitalism, the belief that a rising economic tide would lift all boats and the expectation of upward mobility associated with the economic strand of the American Dream.

It is important in this light to note the role of Park, Burgess, Addams, and others as sponsors for the studies of Chicago typically associated with early Chicago sociology and, in particular, the way their studies emphasized the social organization of space and provided a liberal critique of this new capitalist form (Smith 1988). But, to reiterate, we are not arguing that the symbolic allure of Chicago School sociology is rooted in specific content. Nor are we arguing cultural Zeitgeist – that the dynamism of Chicago gave rise to a set of unique and important ideas. Our argument is much more prosaic. Early Chicago sociology was empirically focused on the study of cities, and because the sociologists were located in Chicago, the primary city they studied was Chicago. Chicago, for reasons largely independent of the work of sociologists at the University of Chicago, came to be understood as the first modern city, a city that people saw as symbolically encapsulating the emergence of a uniquely American commercial empire in the same way that people see Manchester as symbolic of the British industrial revolution. Hence, Chicago School sociology came to be understood as informing us, in some way, about the ascendance of American civilization.

In short, Chicago School sociology gains its symbolic significance not from what it said but rather from what it was seen to have done – study the emergence of a form of commercial capitalism that was unique in the world, a form of capitalism that seemed to suggest for the first time an ideological justification for American exceptionalism based on the accomplishments of American civilization. Notably, exceptionalism, like its symbolic sibling, the American Dream, is a double-edged sword. On the one hand, there is the promise of something special. On the other, there is the possibility of failure, the recognition that the special promise may not be realized by all. Substantively, both strands are present in the work of the early Chicago sociologists. On the one hand, there is the emphasis on space, time, and social organization so central to understanding the modern form of commercial capitalism pioneered in Chicago (e.g., the concentric zone theory of Park and Burgess). On the other hand, one finds the activist work and concern for social reform of those who recognized that certain groups were not benefitting from the economic boom and that Chicago, as it currently existed, was not delivering its promise to all (e.g., the works of Addams and the Chicago pragmatists).

While the character of the city of Chicago in the late nineteenth and early twentieth centuries may account for the symbolic linkage of Chicago and American sociology early on, it does not fully explain why Chicago School sociology continues to be an evocative representation. Nor does it explain why the Chicago School tradition would appeal, at the symbolic level, to sociologists (like many of those represented in this volume) who have little or no connection with the United States. To understand these matters, we turn to the second strand of our argument: the concept of the Chicago School Diaspora and the process of enactment. We conceptualize a two-stage process. The first stage, described above, emphasizes the symbolic significance of the label of "the Chicago School of Sociology" and, in particular, accounts for both the prominence accorded the concept and the plasticity of its contents. The second stage, described below, explores the process whereby individuals select from and make use of that specified resource. In other words, the first stage explains the global availability of the key figures and ideas of the Chicago School, and the second stage makes sense of how people around the world, including many without direct connection to it, come to select and identify with them.

THE CHICAGO SCHOOL DIASPORA

Whatever is meant when people invoke the Chicago School of Sociology, it is nonetheless a construct that has meaning for them. It is this attachment scholars feel with the School that our concept of the Chicago School Diaspora addresses. By the Chicago School Diaspora we do not mean to invoke an image of the scattering of a people but rather to conceptualize how key ideas and symbolic representations of key figures that people associate with the Chicago School have been dispersed and taken up by scholars, many of whom have no formal relationship with the University of Chicago. Moreover, the Chicago School Diaspora does not refer to a rigid adherence to a standardized set of criteria. Rather, it presupposes the selective incorporation, into their scholarly work and identities, of what people see as Chicago School insights and affiliations with key figures they identify with the Chicago School (Cohen 1985).

Scholars invoking the idea of the Chicago School rarely perceive its diverse manifestations. Instead, they focus on the particular ideas and key figures they find meaningful and see those as representative of the Chicago School. Thus, while the Chicago tradition has multiple symbolic meanings, individuals who locate themselves within the tradition attach it to their work through one or more of those meanings. As a result, individuals mean something specific when they refer to the "Chicago School," but different individuals mean different things when they use the label. Scholars adopt the aspects of the Chicago School they identify with, not unlike what Creedon (1998, 44) calls "pastiche spirituality or religion à la carte." Lofland (1983, 491) makes a related point in noting that "the 'Chicago School' is a kind of projective device; descriptions of it seem to reveal as much about those doing the describing as about the phenomenon itself."

However, the lack of a universally shared meaning concerning the Chicago School does not preclude identification with a "notion" of the Chicago School. In fact, it is the lack of unity of meaning that, we argue, enables the Chicago School Diaspora itself and makes wide-scale identification with the school possible. The very mutability and plasticity of meaning allows one, in Becker's (1999, 8) words, to invent one's "own private Chicago." For some, sociology at Chicago means Blumarian symbolic interactionism and/or Meadian pragmatism, and for others it means Park's human ecology, the emphasis on empiricism championed by Hughes, and/or Goffman's dramaturgy. Some even count the insights of Simmel among influences they associate with the Chicago School, while others contest his inclusion among the key figures of the Chicago tradition (cf. Low 2008).

Two other characteristics of the Swiss army knife metaphor are worth noting. First, the tools housed within the knife shift through time – new tools are added and old tools discarded. Thus, the tradition is dynamic rather than static. In this sense, the Chicago School, like the Swiss army knife, is a brand. There are hundreds of varieties of the Swiss army knife, and the specific tools included in the models offered for sale vary through time. Nonetheless, regardless of what tools are included, even when closed with no tools exposed, it is recognizable as a Swiss army knife. This plasticity and mutability of the Swiss army knife brand is reflected in section V of this volume in which the authors pursue novel methods and theories in extending what they understand as key insights of the Chicago School.

Second, our argument that the boundaries of the Chicago School are more open and diffuse than is often argued should not be interpreted as implying that the content of the Chicago School is arbitrary. While the boundaries of Chicago School sociology are relatively open and diffuse, they still have, at any particular point in time – say, this point in time – some degree of definition or outer limit. Stated another way, the number of tools in the Chicago School Swiss army knife are, in particular times and contexts, limited rather than infinite as people come to agree on a "definition of the situation" concerning what is and what is not the Chicago perspective and method (McHugh 1968, 3). To illustrate, first consider Abbott's (1997) argument that that the Chicago School can best be understood as a "contextualist" alternative to the "variables paradigm" that dominates contemporary American sociology. In other words, the Chicago tradition renders social facts as located in social (and often geographic) space and social time, while mainstream contemporary American sociology treats social facts as abstractions from context whereby a particular variable has the same causal meaning in every context. While not explicit (or even implied) in all the contributions in this volume, the equation of the Chicago School with an emphasis on context is an explicit and substantial element in several chapters (e.g., Nock, Park, Horgan). Now presume that someone offered up Blau and Duncan's (1967) seminal work, *The American Occupational Structure*, as an exemplification of Chicago sociology. This work, produced by two University of Chicago faculty members, is arguably the most influential piece of American sociology produced in the past 60 years. Substantively, it helped to define a distinctly American approach to stratification, while methodologically it demonstrated the theoretical gains associated with shifting the analysis of quantitative data from the then-dominant elaboration approach (Rosenberg 1968) to the current approach based on causal modelling and the general linear model. As such, Blau and Duncan's work represents a major contribution to Abbott's "variables paradigm." Yet Blau and Duncan are not typically associated with the Chicago School, and were someone to argue the relevance of their work to the tradition, the suggestion would be met with resistance by most contributors to this volume (and others who see themselves as the proponents of a contextualist paradigm). In short, while it may not be possible to achieve agreement on the core meaning of the Chicago tradition, it is possible, at any given point in time and among a given group or groups of scholars, to achieve agreement on outer boundaries that establish what the Chicago School tradition *is not*.

Similarly, there is a lack of agreement as to who the central figures of the Chicago School of Sociology are. For example, many scholars identify Herbert Blumer as a primary figure in the school, despite the fact that when he was first developing his version of symbolic interactionism "he was an outsider to the department and became 'famous' … only after he left for Berkeley" (Helmes-Hayes 2008, 2). Similarly, as Helmes-Hayes (2008, 4) points out, "Hughes made no effort to develop 'followers.' Indeed, he emphatically rejected the prospect and disliked the notion that he was seen as a follower – as a member of a Chicago School." Nonetheless, Hughes is identified as a key figure of the Chicago School by non-Chicago scholars from Waterloo, Ontario, to Paris, France (cf. Chapoulie 1987; Helmes-Hayes 2008, 1998). The point is not whether Blumer or Hughes "should" be counted among central members of the Chicago School of Sociology but that people do identify them as members; thus, they are key figures of the Chicago School Diaspora.

On the other hand, the apparent coherence of key figures and key ideas found in the literature on the Chicago School that are embraced by the contributors to this volume (i.e., the prominence of Mead and Goffman and qualitative epistemology) is again explained by their symbolic nature. At the same time that scholars individually select key figures and ideas and give meaning to their personal notion of the Chicago School, they can also come to share meaning, leading, at different times and in varying contexts, to a shared definition of the situation as to what constitutes the Chicago School and Chicago School sociology (Blumer 1969; McHugh 1968). Thus, a context-specific consensus about what the Chicago School is can become crystallized, in Simmel's sense of the term, as interested parties attempt to codify the parameters of what is and what is not the Chicago School in various writings and public pronouncements (cf. Abbott 1999, 4–33). Such writings and pronouncements are among the artifacts of social structure that exist otherwise only as the sum of interaction (Blumer 1969; Simmel in Wolff 1964). This makes the outcomes of the process conceptualized by the Chicago School Diaspora more substantial than merely a matter of whimsy or personal agenda. However, as Simmel points out, there is a temporal gap between those who initially create social structure and those who come after that creation (Wolff 1964, 10). Therefore, the Chicago School Diaspora is an uneven process whereby not all ideas or thinkers will be dispersed, taken up, and/or claimed as key in every instance. Indeed, Becker's (1999) experience as a graduate student at Chicago demonstrates the variability that we argue is fundamental to the Chicago School Diaspora. He writes: "The department did not give us any coherent tradition to receive. We were, instead, confused by the melange of contradictory viewpoints, models, and recommendations the department presented to us. And each of us made what we could of it, emphasizing what we could use, ignoring what we couldn't" (Becker 1999, 8).

The variable nature of the Chicago School Diaspora is further illustrated in Clark's (1975) questioning of why Carl Dawson, a Chicago graduate and first chair of sociology at McGill University, had not been more recognized for his influence on Canadian sociology. In his words, "It may nevertheless appear strange that this native Canadian, teaching almost his whole adult life in a Canadian university, should have had such a limited influence on the development of sociological work in Canada, while a colleague of his, E.C. Hughes, who taught sociology in a Canadian university for no more than eleven years, should have had such a lasting influence" (Clark 1975, 228).

Thus, key figures of the Chicago School Diaspora are important not only as symbolic carriers of ideas but also as sources of symbolic identification themselves. More important, the dispersal of key ideas of the Chicago School via the Chicago School Diaspora does not depend on people, descendants of the school or otherwise, to carry them. Nor does identification with key figures of the Chicago School require contact with descendants of the School. One self-identifies as a Blumerian symbolic interactionist or works in the human ecology tradition of Robert Park. Sometimes this affiliation with the Chicago School is explicit and other times implicit and non-reflexive, as is demonstrated in the various chapters that make up this book. For example, in her contribution, Izabela Wagner explicitly identifies herself as a member of a community of qualitative sociologists who "practise [our] culture treasuring [the] Chicago heritage." Similarly, in asking the question of how "the conceptual framework of symbolic interaction contribute[s] to developing a theory of administrative practice," Scott Grills's identification with the Chicago School is reflected in both his academic writing and in how he carries out his administrative work as a VP Academic. Thus, there are "key ideas" and "key thinkers" of the Chicago School Diaspora because people identify them as such, not because they are objectively identified in that way. The key ideas and key figures of the Chicago School Diaspora appear in this book because they are the ones espoused by scholars identifying themselves and/or their work with the Chicago School. However, this is not to say that because this is a process of subjective identification that the content of the Chicago School Diaspora has no reality. Rather, following Fine's (1999) understanding of "obdurate reality," things can be both subjective in their ontology as well as experientially real. In other words, even if we take the position that reality is socially constructed, what we see as the pragmatic requirements of everyday life means that we experience it as a concrete reality (Fine 1999).

KEY FIGURES OF THE CHICAGO DIASPORA IN CANADA

Canada has been and remains fertile ground for the Chicago School Diaspora. First and foremost, Canadian scholars who did their doctoral training at the University of Chicago had a seminal influence on the development of the discipline of sociology in Canada. Carl Dawson, chair of the first Department of Sociology at McGill University, and Everett C. Hughes, the next full-time faculty member hired for that department, *were* sociology in Canada in the 1920s and 1930s (Clarke 1979; Shore 1987). What is of course significant in the context of the Chicago School Diaspora is that they both did doctoral degrees in sociology at the University of Chicago, working under the supervision of Robert Park. Thus, the role played by Dawson and Hughes in developing the first department of sociology in Canada at McGill University is an important exemplar of the means by which the Chicago School Diaspora was transmitted in Canada.

According to Shore (1987, 95), Robert Park's "human ecology was the framework within which all McGill sociology courses were taught and the frame of reference for all research projects undertaken by Dawson, his colleagues, and his students." Likewise, Hughes "quoted Park all the time" (Becker 1999, 7), and his *French Canada in Transition* is called a classic of fieldwork (Heath 1984) and the "single most well known and highly regarded sociological work on French Canada until recent times" (McGill University 2010). In Clark's (1975, 228) words, "no reading list of a course having to do with Canadian society would be complete if it did not include Hughes's *French Canada in Transition.*" What is important here is not the relative scholarly merit of *French Canada in Transition* but rather the emphasis on fieldwork in sociological research "stemm[ing] directly from the tradition of Park" that was championed by Hughes and became part of the Chicago School Diaspora that was coalescing at McGill (Becker 1999, 7; Clark 1975; Helmes-Hayes 2008). What followed, according to Clark (1975, 231) was "An impressive bibliography" of Canadian fieldwork studies, including "R.A. Lucas, *Minetown, Milltown, Railtown*; Anthony Richmond, *Post War Immigration to Canada*; W.E. Mann, *Sect, Cult and Church in Alberta*; J.R. Burnet, *Next Year Country*; D.G. Clairmont and D. Magill, *Africville: The Life and Death of a Canadian Black Community*" (Clark 1975, 231). It is therefore no accident that William Shaffir (this volume), one of the most significant of contemporary Canadian fieldwork researchers, did his doctoral studies in sociology at McGill. Nor is it surprising that students of his – Scott Grills, Jacqueline Low, Tony Puddephatt (all this volume) – incorporate aspects of the Chicago School Diaspora in their work and their scholarly identities.

More recently, transmission of the Chicago School Diaspora is maintained via the Canadian Qualitative Analysis Conference, currently in its twenty-eighth year. The conference, more affectionately known as The Qualitatives, began in 1984 to provide a supportive environment where sociologists taking a symbolic interactionist perspective and using ethnographic methods in analyses of deviant behaviour could share their research. It was soon broadened to include other substantive areas of research but maintained a commitment to showcasing what participants saw as a Chicago School approach to the ethnographic study of social life. The conference has always included both novice and experienced researchers, making no distinction between them, and thus is a gathering where young scholars can begin their identification with key figures and key ideas of the Chicago School Diaspora. Consider the following anecdote from Scott Grills (this volume): "For me as a graduate student, attending the Canadian-based Qualitative Research Conference (aka the Qualitatives) was the way to meet people like Carl Couch, Jackie Wiseman, Fred Davis, Helena Znaiecki Lopata, Virginia Olsen, Bob Stebbins, Robert Emerson, David Altheide, Jackie Wiseman, Spencer Cahill, and Stan Lyman and by so doing become connected to the narratives that make the history and development of interactionist traditions come alive."

Becker maintains that "the real legacy of Chicago is the mixture of things that characterized the school of activity at every period: open, whether through choice or necessity, to a variety of ways of doing sociology" (Becker 1999, 10). What is significant is that the use of ideas originating from and/or associated with key thinkers of the Chicago School amounts to more than knowledge transfer as, in such cases, the Chicago School is made part of one's scholarly identity and scholarly work. Understanding the Chicago School of Sociology in this way helps to clarify how ideas and symbolic representations of key thinkers associated with the various Chicago Schools have been taken up by scholars who themselves did not train or work at Chicago.

The five sections in this volume illustrate the diversity of both the symbolic representations attached to the cultural object known as the "Chicago School" and the diverse ways contemporary scholars engage with that object. Section I brings together works that (re)visit and (re)interpret key assumptions about and characterizations of the Chicago School. Some of these chapters document the diversity of early Chicago sociology and, in doing so, call into question the proposition that Chicago sociology is (or ever was) a single, coherent, and unified conceptual entity. Others exemplify the view that Chicago School sociology is best understood not as theory or substance but rather as epistemology and method. Section II exemplifies a second way of engaging with the Chicago legacy: through close analysis of the thought of particular key thinkers and the intellectual resources underpinning their ideas. Section III, in contrast, brings together scholars interested in the Chicago School's connection to a specific substantive area: urban sociology. As noted above, one of the key divisions in the meaning attributed to the cultural object labelled the Chicago School revolves around the extent to which the School foregrounded social psychology relative to social organization, particularly urban organization. Taken together, sections II and III highlight this division. Section II focuses on the ideas of Mead and Goffman, two theorists intimately connected with the social-psychological perspective, while section III contains works by authors who place greater emphasis on the importance of social organization and / or understand the work of Robert Park and the study of urban areas as a major component of the Chicago School tradition. Another set of scholars locate the essence of the Chicago School in the post–World War II work that developed into a coherent theoretical perspective, symbolic interactionism. Section IV highlights the notion of process and, in particular, processes of boundary maintenance, construction, and claims-making often associated with the Second Chicago School. Finally, section V illustrates the ongoing malleability of the tradition by bringing together works that expand and extend the tradition in ways not conventionally associated with the first or second Chicago Schools. These organizing ideas and their connection to the individual chapters within each section are developed in greater detail in the five section introductions.

Collectively, these sections illustrate two basic points relevant to the central argument of this introduction: (1) Chicago School sociology does not signify one thing but rather many, and (2) individual authors connect their work to the Chicago School tradition in a way that is meaningful to them but does not encompass the full range of connections evident in the volume as a whole. Hence, individuals mean something specific when they refer to the "Chicago School" as symbolized by the key ideas and figures they espouse, but other individuals mean different things when they refer to the "Chicago School" (because they have identified with different key figures and ideas). Significantly, many of the authors in this volume continue to speak of "schools" or look back to the accomplishments of Chicago School sociology. Thus, they illustrate the ongoing attraction to the rhetorical power invoked by that terminology and how the School itself is perceived as an objective reality.

REFERENCES

Abbott, Andrew. 1999. *Department and Discipline: Chicago Sociology at 100.* Chicago: University of Chicago Press
– 2007. Personal communication, 20 June
– 1997. "Of Time and Space: The Contemporary Relevance of the Chicago School." *Social Forces* 75(4):1,149–82
Becker, Howard S. 1999. "The Chicago School, So-called." *Qualitative Sociology* 22(1):3–12
Blau, Peter, and Otis Dudley Duncan. 1967. *The American Occupational Structure.* New York: Wiley and Sons
Blumer, Herbert. 1969. *Symbolic Interactionism: Perspective and Method.* Englewood Cliffs, NJ: Prentice Hall
Bulmer, Martin. 1984. *The Chicago School of Sociology: Institutionalization, Diversity, and the Rise of Sociological Research.* Chicago: University of Chicago Press
Cavan, R.S. 1983. "The Chicago School of Sociology, 1918–1933." *Urban Life* 11:406–20
Carey, James T. 1975. *Sociology and Public Affairs: The Chicago School.* Volume 16 in Sage Library of Social Research. Beverly Hills, CA: Sage
Chapoulie, Jean-Michel. 1987. "Everett C. Hughes and the Development of Fieldwork in Sociology." *Journal of Contemporary Ethnography* 15:259–98
– 2001. *La tradition sociologique de Chicago, 1892–1961.* Paris: Seuil
Clark, Samuel Delbert. 1975. "Sociology in Canada: An Historical Overview." *Canadian Journal of Sociology* 1(2):225–34
– 1979. "The Changing Image of Sociology in English-Speaking Canada." *Canadian Journal of Sociology* 4(4):393–403
Cohen, Anthony P. 1985. *The Symbolic Construction of Community,* edited by Peter Hamilton. London and New York: Tavistock and Ellis Horwood

Creedon, J. 1998. "God with a Million Faces." In "Designer Gold: In a
  Mix-And-Match World, Why Not Create Your Own Religion?" edited
  by E. Utne. *Utne Reader* 88: July/August
Cronon, William. 1991. *Nature's Metropolis: Chicago and the Great West.*
  New York: Norton
Deegan, Mary Jo. 1988. *Jane Addams and the Men of the Chicago School,
  1892–1918.* New Brunswick, NJ: Transaction
Faris, Robert E.L. 1967. *Chicago Sociology: 1920–1932.* San Francisco:
  Chandler
Fine, Gary Alan. 1999. "Field Labour and Ethnographic Reality." *Journal
  of Contemporary Ethnography* 28(5):532–9
– 1995. *A Second Chicago School? The Development of a Postwar
  American Sociology.* Chicago: University of Chicago Press
Gilmore, Samuel. 1988. "Schools of Activity and Innovation." *Sociological
  Quarterly* 29: 203–19
Harvey, Lee. 1987. *Myths of the Chicago School of Sociology.* Aldershot,
  UK: Avebury
Heath, Christian. 1984. "Review Essay: Everett Cherrington Hughes
  (1897–1983): A Note on His Approach and Influence." *Sociology of
  Health and Illness* 6(2):218–37
Helmes-Hayes, Richard C. 1998. "Everett Hughes: Theorist of the Second
  Chicago School." *International Journal of Politics, Culture, and Society*
  11(4):621–73
– 2008. "Everett Hughes and the Chicago School at McGill University."
  Paper presented at the 25th Qualitative Analysis Conference –
  Qualitatives 2008: The Chicago School and Beyond, University of New
  Brunswick and St Thomas University, Fredericton, NB, 21–4 May
Horowitz, Irving. 1983. *C. Wright Mills: An American Utopia.* New York:
  Free Press
Hurt, Douglas. 2002. *American Agriculture: A Brief History.* West
  Lafayette, IN: Purdue University Press
Jaynes, Gerald. 2009. "The Chicago School and the Roots of Urban
  Ethnography." *Ethnography* 10(4):375–96
Lewis, J.D., and R.L. Smith. 1980. *American Sociology and Pragmatism.*
  Chicago: University of Chicago Press
Lindner, Rolf.1996. *The Reportage of Urban Culture: Robert Park and the
  Chicago School.* Cambridge: Cambridge University Press
Lipset, Seymour Martin. 1988. *Revolution and Counter Revolution: Change
  and Persistence in Social Structures.* New Brunswick, NJ: Transaction
Lofland, Lyn. 1980. "Reminiscences of Classic Chicago: The Blumer–
  Hughes Talk." *Journal of Contemporary Ethnography* 9(3):251–81

– 1983. "Understanding Urban Life: The Chicago Legacy." *Journal of Contemporary Ethnography* 11(4):491–511

Low, Jacqueline. 2008. "Structure, Agency, and Social Reality in Blumerian Symbolic Interactionism: The Influence of Georg Simmel." *Symbolic Interaction* 31(3):325–43

Matthews, Fred. 1977. *Quest for an American Sociology: Robert E. Park and the Chicago School.* Montreal: McGill-Queen's University Press

McGill University. 2010. "McGill Arts Sociology – About Us." http://www. mcgill.ca/sociology/aboutus

McHugh, Peter. 1968. *Defining the Situation: The Organization of Meaning in Social Interaction.* Indianapolis and New York: Bobbs-Merrill

Nash, Roderick. 2001. *Wilderness and the American Mind.* 4th edition. New Haven: Yale University Press

Park, Robert, and Ernest Burgess. 1921. *Introduction to the Science of Sociology.* Chicago: University of Chicago Press

Platt, Jennifer. 1996. *A History of Sociological Research Methods in America.* Cambridge: Cambridge University Press

Rock, Paul. 1979. *The Making of Symbolic Interactionism.* Totowa, NJ: Rowman and Littlefield

Rosenberg, Morris. 1968. *The Logic of Survey Analysis.* New York: Basic Books

Shills, Edward. 1970. "Tradition, Ecology, and Institution in the History of Sociology." *Daedalus* 99:760–85

Shore, Marlene. 1987. *The Science of Social Redemption: McGill, the Chicago School, and the Origins of Social Research in Canada.* Toronto: University of Toronto Press

Smith, Dennis. 1988. *The Chicago School: A Liberal Critique of Capitalism.* New York: St Martin's Press

Turner, Frederick. 1921. *The Frontier in American History.* New York: Holt and Company

Turner, Ralph H. 1988. "The Mixed Legacy of the Chicago School of Sociology." *Sociological Perspectives* 31(3):325–38

Wolff, Kurt H. 1964. *The Sociology of Georg Simmel,* translated by K. Wolff. New York: The Free Press

SECTION I
(Re)Visiting the Chicago School(s)

As editors, we use the label "Chicago School of Sociology" to incorporate both a social structural object (e.g., individuals who interacted together at the University of Chicago) and a cultural object (the meaning attributed to the scholarly work of those individuals). Significantly, scholars continue to work within the tradition of Chicago School sociology and to identify themselves with that tradition, despite the fact that there is no longer an identifiable social structural "school" of Chicago sociology at Chicago. As a result, one aspect of the Chicago School Diaspora involves works that analyze, recover, and reassess the work of the Chicago School.

Section I brings together works that (re)visit and (re)interpret key assumptions about and characterizations of the early Chicago School. Collectively, these chapters contribute to the overall focus of the book in several ways. The first pair of chapters document the diversity of Chicago sociology and, in doing so, call into question the proposition that Chicago School sociology is (or ever was) a single, coherent and unified conceptual entity. In chapter 1, "Hull-House and the Chicago Schools of Sociology: Public and Liberation Sociology on Race, Class, Gender, and Peace, 1892–1920," Mary Jo Deegan describes the predominantly female "Hull-House School" and explores the connections to and differences from the subgroups within the male-dominated first two generations of the early Chicago School: the religious men (Small, Henderson, Zueblin, and Vincent) and the pragmatists (Mead, Dewey, Thomas, Park, and Burgess). In chapter 2, "Was There a Black Chicago School?", Roger Salerno describes the experiences and works of black graduate students during the 1920s and 1930s and argues that their work challenged some of the underlying assumptions of their mentors (Park, Burgess, Wirth). Taken together, these chapters illustrate how previous scholarship has focused disproportionately on the contributions of white, male faculty members and overlooked the contributions of more marginal Chicago sociologists who operated with perspectives different from those traditionally described.

The second pair of chapters explore the question of whether or not qualitative methodology is central to Chicago School epistemology. In chapter 3, "Chicago's Proclivity to Qualitative Sociology: Myth or Reality?", David Nock questions Martin Bulmer's claim that 1970s-era scholarship overemphasized the qualitative nature of Chicago sociology. Specifically, Nock shows that a core group of scholars associated with the Chicago School (Park, Bogardus, Blumer, Eubank, and House), while not uniformly opposed to quantification, were consistent critics of neo-positivism. This theme, that Chicago School sociology is epistemologically antithetical to the characterization of reality associated with the approach that currently dominates American sociology (i.e., statistical modelling based on the general linear model and its assumption that reality consists of fixed entities with variable attributes that operate independent of context) is taken up by Robert Park's grandson in chapter 4, "After the Barren Search for Laws." In it, George Park critiques current sociological practice for preferring indirect inference about social process to the raw observation of human events he associates with the Chicago School.

As a whole, the section illustrates the continuing debate over Robert Park's legacy. Deegan, in particular, sees Park's ideas as a continuation and extension of the work of the Hull-House School and the Chicago pragmatists and, hence, of less significance than they are typically accorded. In contrast, Nock and George Park see the core feature of the Chicago School as a methodological and epistemological orientation they associate with Robert Park.

1

Hull-House and the Chicago Schools of Sociology: Public and Liberation Sociology on Race, Class, Gender, and Peace, 1892–1920

MARY JO DEEGAN

Chicago was a hotbed of social change and reform from 1892 until 1920. Immigration, urbanization, industrialization – these and other great social forces converged and crashed in the city on the edge of Lake Michigan. Sociology and demands for greater human rights – for workers, women, immigrants, people of colour, and children – also emerged at this time. America participated in the Great War in 1917 and 1918, however, which split sociologists along gender fault lines. Before this happened, two great centres for the new study of human behaviour had appeared: Hull-House, a social settlement that was a caldron for social change, and the University of Chicago, a more sober educational experiment pushing for legitimacy in the academy but caught on the cusps of science, progressivism, and the Baptist religion. Both schools of sociology were in the public eye and commenting on the vibrant yet chaotic social changes. Hull-House, associated more with women and innovative social action, and the university, associated more with white men and elite expertise, none-theless often worked side by side between 1892 and the end of World War I in 1918. The women's more radical politics and values were associated with fighting for social justice with the oppressed, what Joe Feagin and Hernan Vera (2008) call "liberation sociology." The men at the university sometimes joined the women in this work, but the male professors usually exhibited more tempered politics and traditional values, which were effective in the public sphere and similar to what Michael Burawoy (2005) calls "public sociology." In this chapter, I briefly review these sociologists' stances on race, class, gender, and peace to document their pattern of public work.

Parenthetically, I should add that even today, despite my best efforts, the intricate links between race, gender, and sociology at Chicago remain opaque to many writers. For example, Roger A. Salerno's discussion of race (this volume) could be significantly recast by consideration of my prior analysis of race and gender at Chicago (Deegan 2002b). The explication undertaken by David A. Nock (this volume) of qualitative work at Chicago would take on a needed corrective feminist face when my prior critiques – especially of Lee Harvey's and Martin Bulmer's accounts of Chicago sociology – are included (Deegan 1988a, 1985, 1990). George Park's otherwise insightful and charming account (this volume) of his grandfather's views on science vs. activism should be re-mediated in terms of my prior analysis of the empirical working relationship between Robert E. and Clara Cahill Park (Deegan 2006). Be this as it may, I begin my chapter by discussing the range of politics and policies underlying liberating and public sociology.

DEFINING PUBLIC AND LIBERATING SOCIOLOGIES

An immediate issue with public and liberating sociologies occurs with the historical treatment of these approaches. Feagin and Vera (2008) embed liberation sociology in more than a century of struggle, placing Hull-House and some Chicago sociologists in a central, founding position, and I share this interpretation. But Burawoy (2006, 14) has a more rootless interpretation that makes it difficult to understand Hull-House and Chicago sociology:

Public sociology must begin back in the university. Its very possibility depends on the recognition of publics, something all too new for sociology. Going back to Durkheim or to Weber we find sociologists suspicious of publics. Durkheim and a long tradition that followed him saw social movements not as the voice of a public but as a sign of social pathology, while Weber spoke of an inarticulate mass given to irrational sentiments, easily manipulated by leaders. It was the idea of a mass society – not a society of publics – that propelled post–World War II sociology in the

United States, justifying on the one side a retreat to professional sociology and on the other side an "applied" or policy sociology designed to regulate politics and consumerism.

I redefine Burawoy's perspective here. Public and liberating sociology must begin back in the university and in social organizations such as social settlements and social movement organizations – for example, the National Association for the Advancement of Colored People (NAACP), a group that Hull-House and Chicago sociologists helped to found, legitimate, and lead. Their sociology recognized publics as central to the discipline. Thus, the history of public and liberating sociology does not logically go back to Durkheim or to Weber but to Jane Addams and George Herbert Mead, sociologists integral to public vitality and empowerment. While Durkheim and Weber defined sociology as distinct from the voice of the public, Hull-House sociologists and Chicago sociologists, especially Chicago pragmatists, trusted publics in a democratic society. These American sociologists encouraged education for citizenship, led and articulated reasons for social movements, and transformed the United States, especially the American welfare state and our understanding of race, class, gender, and nonviolence (Deegan 2008).

HULL-HOUSE, FEMINIST PRAGMATISM, AND LIBERATION SOCIOLOGY, 1892–1920

Addams and her college friend Ellen Gates Starr found a direction for their lives in 1888 after they visited the social settlement Toynbee Hall in London's East End. Here they discovered a group that served the exploited working classes while supporting artisans who harmonized their interests in art, labour, and the community (Deegan and Wahl 2003). Toynbee Hall provided a model for Hull-House, which the women adapted to fit the American creed, with its emphasis on democracy and education, and women's demands to become part of public life while they retained their feminine values of cooperation, emotional connections, and the importance of home and family. Addams, in particular, understood and practised nonviolence as part of her Quaker heritage, her admiration for Abraham Lincoln and the abolitionists, and her support of Leo Tolstoy and Mahatma Gandhi (Addams 1910; 1930). Addams and Starr founded Hull-House in 1889 as a public home within a Chicago neighbourhood undergoing rapid social change and the exploitation and oppression associated with social inequalities. Patriarchs and capitalists, who were white, Anglo-Saxon Protestants, controlled the powers of the state and its violent enforcement of the status quo.

Addams was more charismatic than Starr (Deegan and Wahl 2003) and took the lead, becoming the head of Hull-House. She was known worldwide in the social settlement movement that brought together all classes, social groups, and ages (especially the young and the elderly) as well as the oppressed to form a democratic community able to articulate and enact their ideals and needs. The 1890s were lively, controversial years at Hull-House. Anarchists, Marxists, socialists, unionists, and leading social theorists congregated there. All the early Chicago sociologists, including Albion W. Small, Ernest W. Burgess, Robert E. Park, and George E. Vincent, knew of Hull-House and Addams. But her closest colleagues in sociology at the university were Charles R. Henderson, Charles Zueblin, John Dewey, George Herbert Mead, and W.I. Thomas. These men frequently visited and lectured at the settlement, and "Chicago pragmatism" was born through their collegial contacts and intellectual exchanges. A ground-breaking text, *Hull-House Maps and Papers* (Residents of Hull-House 1895), was published by Hull-House residents in 1895, predating and establishing the interests of the early Chicago male sociologists (Deegan 1988a, 55–69).

Addams surrounded herself with brilliant and dedicated people, particularly women. These women formed a core group who lived at the settlement, wrote together, gathered statistics, investigated factories and industries, conducted health research, examined sanitary conditions, lobbied for legislative and political reform, and organized for social betterment in their congested, immigrant, working-class district. I call this the "the Chicago female world of love and ritual" (Deegan 1996; 2006; 2007; 2008). A large segment of this world created a sociological theory and praxis, "the Hull-House school of sociology" (HHSS). These sociologists wrote hundreds of books and thousands of articles. They founded and led dozens of social movement organizations, such as the NAACP, the National Urban League, the National Consumers' League, the Women's Trade Union League, the Women's International League for Peace and Freedom (WILPF), and the American Civil Liberties Union. They campaigned for the Progressive Party and helped to found numerous government agencies, notably the Children's, Women's, and Immigration Bureaus. Through these groups, the women created a new welfare state, what

I call "the feminist pragmatist welfare state" (see Skocpol [1992] and others on the "maternal" welfare state). Their applied sociology emerged from their conceptual apparatus, feminist pragmatism.

"Feminist pragmatism" is an American theory uniting liberal values and a belief in a rational public with a cooperative, nurturing, and liberating model of the self, the other, and the community. Education and democracy are emphasized as significant mechanisms to organize and improve society. "The community," like the self, is based on the ability to learn, to educate, and to take the role of the other. "Education, art, and play" are social processes that change and structure the mind, self, and society. Feminist pragmatists believe in the essential ability of all people to change; to search for a wider, more-inclusive democracy; to develop a world consciousness and community; and to have the capacity to end major social problems such as war, food shortages, and excessive population growth. This optimistic theory empowers people to confront the horrific inequalities and injustices found throughout the world, in each community, and within each self. Areas of concentration within feminist pragmatism form separate literatures, but I focus here on their ideas and praxis concerning race, class, gender, and peace (Deegan 2002a; 2002b; 2008; see also Seigfried 1991; 1996; 2002; 2006).

THE EARLY CHICAGO SCHOOL OF SOCIOLOGY, CHICAGO PRAGMATISM, AND THE MIXTURE OF LIBERATION AND PUBLIC SOCIOLOGY, 1892–1920

The University of Chicago was founded in 1892, and its Department of Sociology, chaired by Small, was integral to this experiment on the prairie. With Chicago's rapid social change and the exploitation and oppression associated with social inequalities, Chicago sociologists turned to the emerging "city as a sociological laboratory," a phrase Small was using by 1896 in the leading disciplinary outlet, the *American Journal of Sociology* (*AJS*). This journal became the institutionalized nucleus of public sociology as it published the work of both the HHSS and the Chicago school of sociology (CSS).

After the American Sociological Society, now called the American Sociological Association (ASA), was founded in 1905, Small and many of the men of the CSS played important roles in the organization. Many members of the HHSS also immediately joined the group and participated in its meetings, forming another institutional, professional connection.

The religious men of the css – Small, Henderson, Zueblin, and Vincent – combined an interest in religion, social amelioration, and sociology. As Baptist ministers, Small, Henderson, and Zueblin spoke from the pulpit as well as in the classroom. These men, as well as Vincent, were active public speakers in the Baptist adult education program known as Chautauqua. As leading academics, they were interested in social justice, adult education, social movements in public education, libraries, civil activism, and immigrants. Their interests often overlapped with those of the HHSS, although the men were closer to the powerful interests of the elite and public policies supported by them. The University of Chicago institutionalized this social movement through their program of adult and extension education, one of the first university-based programs in the world. The religious men played important roles in this institution, and they were joined by many Hull-House sociologists.

The role of these religious men changed during the first two decades of the twentieth century. In 1908, Zueblin was forced to resign from the University of Chicago after he became increasingly critical of urban politics, parks, art, and corruption. In 1911, Vincent resigned to direct the Laura Spellman Rockefeller Fund. In 1915, Henderson died. When America entered World War I in 1917, Small was the only religious man remaining on the faculty. He had a German wife, and feeling that he needed to defend himself, he adopted a visible pro-American stance in the conflict.

Two other groups also were on the faculty before World War I: the Chicago and the feminist pragmatists.

Chicago Pragmatism

Pragmatism, which started in the nineteenth century at Harvard University, is often slippery to define because of its intentional open-endedness and all-encompassing vision (Deegan 1988a; Rucker 1969). James Campbell (1992, 2) offers an excellent summary of these characteristics: "Pragmatism offered a metaphysics emphasizing process and relations, a naturalistic and evolutionary understanding of intellectual activity as problem-oriented and as benefiting from historically developed methods, and an emphasis upon the democratic reconstruction of society through educational and other institutions." William James, the noted psychologist and pragmatist at Harvard University, announced in 1904 that a "Chicago School of Thought" had emerged. This new, identifiable philosophy was summarized in a series of studies published in 1903 by the Chicago faculty (see Dewey 1903). Five sociologists were Chicago pragmatists prior to 1920: Mead, Dewey, Thomas, Park, and Burgess. The religious men shared many epistemological assumptions with the Chicago pragmatists.

Dewey and Mead came to the University of Chicago in 1894 after they left their jobs at the University of Michigan. Dewey and Mead formed a powerful faculty team and trained W.I. Thomas; Mead trained Burgess, and Dewey trained Park when the latter was an undergraduate at the University of Michigan. Park also worked in philosophy at Harvard from 1903 to 1905, the home of William James. Thus, this group had many commonalities in their work prior to 1920. Dewey, Mead, and Thomas were particularly close to Addams, Hull-House, and feminist pragmatism. Park and Burgess were sometimes close to these colleagues but sometimes more distant because of their more conservative politics, weaker support of women's rights and access to the academy, and pursuit of elite education (Deegan 2007).

I have extensively documented the praxis of Dewey, Mead, Thomas, and Addams elsewhere (see Mead 1999; 2001; Deegan 1999; 2001a; 2008). This group emphasized social change in race, class, and gender relations. They also supported the work of the highly successful Laboratory School, which trained students from the elementary grades through high school, on the campus of the University of Chicago. Their public sociology was called "progressive education" and dramatically changed public and private schools throughout the US from the 1890s until the early 1950s. At the latter date, it came increasingly under criticism, especially in the public school system.

The early men of the Chicago School trained most of the doctoral-level sociologists in the United States and throughout the world. Burgess, one of their students who graduated in 1913, joined the faculty in 1916. Park joined the faculty at the university in 1913 as a part-time instructor. In 1918, when Thomas was dismissed under charges of sexual misconduct with the wife of an American officer serving in the war overseas, Park assumed the vacant position. In addition to these male faculty members, five women were on the faculty in gendered, less prestigious, but long-term positions. One was Annie Marion MacLean, who taught sociology through the Extension Division from 1903 until her death in 1934 (Deegan 1978). The other four women worked in three other, affiliated units in the Department of Sociology, discussed next.

The University of Chicago Social Settlement (UCSS), 1894–1920

In 1894, the University of Chicago Social Settlement (UCSS) was established with the help of Dewey and the religious men. The UCSS was aligned closely with Hull-House through the appointment of its head resident, Mary E. McDowell, a former resident of Hull-House. Mead, Henderson, and McDowell became a new force for public sociology, and they initiated a series of important sociological studies. Edith Abbott and Sophonisba Breckinridge, also Hull-House residents, generated an important group of housing studies that ultimately resulted in several articles published in *AJS* and two books (the culmination of this work is found in Abbott, assisted by Breckinridge and other associates, 1936). In 1928, when the university wished to terminate McDowell as a member of the sociology faculty, Mead successfully defended her position. She remained an officer of instruction in the Department of Sociology until her death in 1936 (see annual *University of Chicago Catalogs*, 1923–34).

The Chicago School of Civics and Philanthropy (CSCP), 1904–1920

Liberating and public sociology are connected fundamentally with citizens' rights and the voice of the community. The development of the Chicago School of Civics and Philanthropy (CSCP) emerged from this same commitment. The primary founders were Graham Taylor, a Baptist minister, sociologist, and the head of the social settlement, Chicago Commons, and Julia Lathrop, a member of the HHSS, with their primary staff members being Abbott and Breckinridge. The female sociologists knew that their "special" interests in women, the home, the family, and housing were not well represented in the male faculty's course offerings. Moreover, although "applied" sociology was integral to the discipline, it increasingly suffered from a second-class status compared to more abstract sociology. Therefore, the "practical" sociologists, primarily females and males later ostracized from the sociological tradition, joined in 1904 to form the CSCP. Addams and the Chicago men frequently gave guest lectures and even taught courses there, weaving their social thought and activism into a coherent praxis (Deegan 1988a, 74–6). It merged in 1920 with other campus divisions to become the School of Social Service Administration (SSA), the professional school of social work at the University of Chicago.

Household Administration

In 1892, Marion Talbot was brought to the University of Chicago to be the assistant dean of women. Her home department was sociology, because she concentrated on the study of the home as an institution and on the social process of creating opportunities for women in higher education. She was trained by Ellen H. Richards at the Massachusetts Institute of Technology in what is now recognized as a foundational approach to the environment or social ecology (Clarke 1973). In 1881, Talbot became a founder of the Association of Collegiate Alumnae, now called the American Association of University Women (AAUW). This organization spearheaded opportunities for educated women in the academy and wider society and was an important organization in Talbot's public sociology (Talbot and Rosenberry 1931). Richards and Talbot were also major figures in the Lake Placid Conferences, which were radical meetings to study the home and its role in society. These conferences became the basis for the later, more conservative discipline of home economics, but the original vision was to redesign the home and its functions in a society where women and men were equals and the home was part of the public sphere (see Clarke 1973). Talbot (1936) was included within the structure, teaching, and practice of sociology at the University of Chicago as the head of "women's work" throughout the institution. In 1895, she became an associate editor of *AJS*, a position she held until her retirement from Chicago in 1925. Here, Talbot critiqued "women's work" in sociology and provided a "woman's perspective" for the most important journal in the discipline.

Talbot and Breckinridge, who became the assistant dean of women, were members of the Department of Sociology at the university for many years. The complex organizational titles and location of the women in a separately administered "woman's department" within sociology called Household Administration fundamentally gendered their work in the discipline (Deegan 1978). In addition to their administrative and teaching responsibilities, Talbot and Breckinridge were intellectual allies. Some themes in their book on *The Modern Household* (1913, rev. 1919), for example, illustrate their ties to Chicago pragmatists, such as Dewey and Tufts, and the feminist pragmatists, Addams and Abbott.

The Department of Household Administration was a major training and teaching area for students, especially female students. Breckinridge trained Abbott there, which ultimately resulted in

Abbott's (1910) classic statement on *Women in Industry*. In 1908, Abbott and Breckinridge moved into Hull-House, beginning an intimate and collegial career pattern unparalleled by any male sociologists. The Department of Household Administration should be considered the first women's studies program in America, if not the world, and firmly based in sociology. It examined women's roles in the economy, politics, government, and the institutions of the home and education.

Institutional Mechanisms Connecting the Hull-House and the Chicago School of Sociology, 1889–1910

Several more institutional structures linked the feminist and Chicago pragmatists. The personal, professional, and public lives of men and women intersected through the family, interpersonal friendships, college training, emerging roles for the new woman, complex voluntary associations (especially women's clubs), and social movements resulting in the feminist pragmatist welfare state. Many wives – including the wives of Henderson, Vincent, Small, Mead, and Thomas – participated in the University of Chicago Social Settlement League (see *University of Chicago Settlement* n.d., a, b; 1901). This work bridged the social settlements, sociology, and women's work in the home.

Many groups outside these institutions created centres of public sociology; the Chicago City Club (1905–20) and the Chicago Women's City Club (1911–20) were two such groups. Founded in 1905, the Chicago City Club (CCC), a male-only group, discussed and debated civic issues. Through an extensive committee structure, they covered virtually every area of urban problems. Mead was a member of the CCC from its founding until the 1920s. He served on the education committee for years and became a well-known civic leader on public education as a result. He was president of the organization from 1918 until 1920 and frequently served on its board of directors. Henderson served on the employment committee, Zueblin was on its municipal parks committee, and Thomas was a member for two years (Deegan 1988a, 74). The Chicago women developed a corollary association in 1911, and the Hull-House women played major roles in its founding and operation. The two clubs comprised a bi-gendered alliance working for the founding of the American welfare state, particularly its foundation in feminist pragmatism (Deegan 1988a). Thus, the early men and women of the CSS, like the HHSS, developed many areas of concentration that form separate literatures, and I study their interest in race, class, gender, and peace next.

STUDYING RACE, CLASS, GENDER, AND PEACE AS LIBERATING AND PUBLIC SOCIOLOGY

The multiple interactions between the HHSS and the CSS resulted in the founding of the NAACP and its Chicago branch, the CAACP. They also founded the National Urban League (NUL) and its Chicago branch, the CUL. These groups are often seen as competing, opposing organiza-, tions, because the NUL was associated with Booker T. Washington and the NAACP was associated with W.E.B. DuBois at a time when each man defined the other as an enemy. The Chicago group, in contrast, developed a "third" perspective – a new conscience against an ancient evil – that involved interracial cooperation, refused to choose between Washington and DuBois, and enacted radical opposition against racism. It emerged from the pragmatist commitment to avoid dichotomies and to practise nonviolence. They favoured the development of an international consciousness and political apparatus, the study of African-American life and culture, and the development of practices to eliminate racial inequality and social injustice, especially in the legal system and the marketplace. They became crucial to changing American race relations (Deegan 2002a; 2002b).

Park served on the executive board of the CUL from 1917 to 1923 and as president in 1917–18, Charles S. Johnson was the director of research from 1918 to 1923, and E. Franklin Frazier was director of research in 1927–28. Members of the HHSS who were also members of the CUL were Edith Abbott, research investigator in 1918, and Addams, a member of the executive board from 1917 to 1935, along with other members of the board, including Sophonisba Breckinridge, 1931–37; Loraine Richardson Green, 1929–37; A. Kenyon Maynard, treasurer, 1916–20; and Mary E. McDowell, who chaired the inter-racial committee from 1919 to 1936 (Deegan 1988b; 2002b).

The HHSS and the CSS encouraged the study of social class and labour relations, analyzing the processes of work, unionization, and worker exploitation. They adapted Fabian socialism to create an American welfare state. During the 1890s, the HHSS successfully worked to enact legislation to end child labour. They were integral to the development of a Federal Children's Bureau, which provided information and collected data to help achieve children's optimal development. The bureau established many public policies, such as initiating the birth and death registry of children; supporting well-baby clinics; and investigating infant, children's, and maternal mortality, juvenile delinquency, child labour, mothers' pensions, and nutrition. They widely distributed this information and advice to thousands of young mothers (Addams 1909; 1910; 1930).

The HHSS and the CSS emphasized urban sociology and the benefits of city life and urban planning, as well as working to solve the problems of poor housing and sanitation. They studied criminology, focusing on juvenile delinquency, the court system, and notions of justice. The HHSS, in conjunction with Chicago clubwomen, faculty wives, and female faculty and students in the CSS, was instrumental in establishing a series of world-class institutions associated with juvenile delinquency and justice. They founded the world's first juvenile court in 1899, developed probation and parole as institutions to reconnect juvenile offenders with the community, and helped to found the family court system, the Juvenile Psychopathic Institute, and the Institute for Juvenile Research (Addams et al. 1927). Mead and Henderson were involved in some of these groups, too (Deegan 2003a; Neeley and Deegan 2005).

They also studied and practised the process of making and enjoying art and aesthetics, connecting art and paid labour and art and the home. The HHSS and the Zueblins played major roles in creating one of the most important arts and crafts societies in the United States: the Chicago Arts and Crafts Society. It was partially based on the British group that emerged from Toynbee Hall, John Ruskin, and Charles Ashbee (Deegan and Wahl 2003).

Women were the focus of study for the HHSS and part of the CSS, especially as mothers, wage-earners, homemakers, and forces for social change. The feminist pragmatists built on traditional and modern ideas of women, which they developed in their writings. Addams and Thomas were particularly important, but Mead, with his views of cooperation and community, also developed a compatible epistemology for understanding women and public social change (Deegan 1988a; 1999). The feminist pragmatist welfare state applied this epistemology and praxis to the state apparatus, creating a system of social welfare with strong support for women and children. Several wives of male Chicago sociologists, most notably Clara Cahill Park, became significant figures in this massive social movement (Deegan 2006; Goodwin 1997; Skocpol 1992).

All of the women and most of the men supported suffrage between 1900 and 1920. Similarly, these two groups supported women's work in sociology as an ideal profession, breaking through traditional barriers to women in the marketplace. But the women were usually far more radical in their view of women's role in the discipline and in public life than the men were. This reflected a general political division between the groups as well as a gendered fault line. This fundamental difference split the largely united schools into two gendered parts, the women practising liberating sociology and the men practising public sociology, over the issue of war and peace.

The work on gender in the HHSS was directly linked to their commitment to world peace. Addams and the HHSS became national and international leaders in pacifism based on their understanding of women as cooperative, nonviolent, and nurturing members of society. Addams held a central position as a pacifist during the Spanish-American War in 1898 and as the author of *Newer Ideals of Peace* in 1907. But it was World War I, starting in Europe in late 1914, that catapulted her to the head of the first international movement of women devoted to peace, the Women's International League of Peace and Freedom (WILPF). Drawing on feminist pragmatism, the HHSS argued that women were the ideal peace-makers (Addams 1907; 1912; 1916; 1976; Dewey 1960 [1922]; Addams, Balch, and Hamilton 2003 [1915]; Deegan 2003b).

This important, worldwide social movement ultimately led to Nobel Peace Prizes for two Hull-House sociologists, Addams in 1931 and Emily Greene Balch in 1946. Helen Castle Mead, her sister-in-law, and her aunt were also active in this group (Deegan 1999). Morris Janowitz (1966) has suggested that the highly visible, national role of Harriet Thomas in WILPF was a major reason for W.I. Thomas being followed and arrested in a sexually compromising position. WILPF connected these wives and other relatives of male sociologists to international pacifism and the Chicago female world of love and ritual.

Prior to America's entry into the Great War, the men were considered "international pacifists." Mead and Dewey, in particular, were local if not national leaders in the analysis of nonviolence, international cooperation, and global change. After 1917, Mead and Dewey became vocally pro-American intervention and participation in World War I. They spoke and wrote as national experts, opposed most critics of the war and, Dewey in particular, opposed the pacifism of Jane Addams. Mead did not support secular opposition to the war, although he allowed for religious-based objections and he placed Addams in this small, acceptable group of protesters (Deegan 2008). Thomas initially shared the positions of his male colleagues, but in 1918 he was fired for moral turpitude, and his sociological career was devastated for the next decade. Thomas's expertise in the study of women and sexuality helped to condemn him in the public eye and stifle his role as a public intellectual for years. Although he was somewhat restored to honour when he was elected president of the ASA in 1928, he never again assumed a prominent public role (Deegan 1988a). Thus, the women became leaders in liberating sociology, and the men became leaders in public sociology during wartime. The women opposed the war: the men dramatically supported it, leading to a division between the HHSS and the CSS that never healed, although individual men regained their alliance with the HHSS after the war (Deegan 2008).

POST–WORLD WAR I SOCIOLOGY

After the war, the men's and women's sociologies became more distinct, with men claiming more science and objectivity and women associating more with the new profession of "social work" and becoming even more politically active as new citizens, critics of American race relations, leaders in women's work for world peace, and advocates of the feminist pragmatist welfare state (Deegan 1988a; 2002a, 2002b; 2007). There were some unsuccessful attempts to force a tie between the departments of household administration and home economics, but Talbot resisted this effort. She saw home economics as evolving into too much emphasis on cooking and cleaning and too little analysis of the home and its connections to politics and society. Immediately after she retired in 1925, the male administrators melded household administration into home economics, a departmental change that she had vehemently opposed.

  After the war, the women saw a bright future ahead. They had won the vote in 1920, and they had already helped to establish the feminist pragmatist welfare state. But the 1920s and 1930s did not see more public power for sociologists, whether male or female. The liberation sociology of Hull-House forged into a more coherent international practice, fighting on the forefront of battles surrounding issues of race, class, and gender and aligned with pacifist goals of disarmament and anti-colonialism and inspired by Gandhi's nonviolent resistance to evil, injustice, and oppression. The men, however, became a new social force and a powerhouse within the discipline. Their approach, also called the CSS, was led by Park and Burgess, who claimed that many of their ideas were new when, in fact, they were continuations or alterations of those of the early men and women of the Chicago School and the HHSS (Deegan 1988a). Park and Burgess trained a remarkable group of students, primarily white men but with some black men and white women, who studied everyday life and developed core ethnographies of different ways to organize the world, especially in the city (Deegan 2001b). The study of class and gender diminished, and the study of African-American life increased, but within the confines of Park's race relations cycle, which emerged from the work of Booker T. Washington and ended in assimilation (Deegan 2002b). The Chicago School had considerable visibility in the wider society and occasionally ventured into public policy, despite the language of the natural sciences. Their public sociology also entered into everyday discourse, especially through their influence on criminology, race relations, and urban studies. Mead's (1932; 1934; 1936; 1938) more conservative postwar ideas were legitimated through a powerful series of posthumous publications, while his more politically active work before the war was generally ignored. But this more familiar story of the Chicago School is beyond my main topic and analysis prior to 1920.

The innovative and critical ideas of the HHSS and the CSS from 1892 to 1920 were accepted by the public. Organic intellectuals in sociology, they developed a sophisticated practice of liberating and public sociology. Their role in shaping American values and actions surrounding the contested terrain of race, class, gender, and peace must be honoured in contemporary public sociology. We should neither turn to Durkheim and Weber to understand public sociology nor act as if the intersection of race, class, and gender are new issues in the profession. We also should note that nonviolence remains integral to obtaining civil rights for the oppressed and disenfranchised. A growing number of sociologists are analyzing this great, alternative heritage and tradition in American sociology. They envision a new and more empowering horizon for action in a more just and liberated society and discipline, and this essay is part of that effort.

REFERENCES

Abbott, Edith. 1910. *Women in Industry*. New York: D. Appleton
– assisted by Sophonisba Breckinridge and other associates. 1936.
   Tenements of Chicago, 1908–35. Chicago: University of Chicago Press
Addams, Jane. 1907. *Newer Ideals of Peace*. New York: Macmillan
– 1909. *The Spirit of Youth and the City Streets*. New York: Macmillan
– 1910. *Twenty Years at Hull-House*. New York: Macmillan
– 1912. *A New Conscience and an Ancient Evil*. New York: Macmillan
– 1916. *The Long Road of Woman's Memory*. New York: Macmillan
– 1930. *The Second Twenty Years at Hull-House*. Illustrated by Norah
   Hamilton. New York: Macmillan
– 1976. *Jane Addams on Peace, War, and International Understanding,
   1899–1932*, edited and with an introduction by Allen F. Davis. New
   York: Garland Publishing
– et al. 1927. *The Child, the Clinic and the Court*. New York: New
   Republic
Addams, Jane, Emily Greene Balch, and Alice Hamilton. 2003 [1915].
   Women at The Hague. Amherst, NY: Humanity Books
Burawoy, Michael. 2005. "For a Public Sociology." *American Sociological
   Review* 70:4–28
– Burawoy, Michael 2006. "A Public Sociology for Human Rights."
   Introduction to *Public Sociologies Reader*, edited by Judith Blau and
   Keri E. Iyall Smith, 1–18. Lanham, MD: Rowman and Littlefield
Clarke, Robert. 1973. *Ellen Swallow*. Chicago: Follett
Campbell, James. 1992. *The Community Reconstructs*. Urbana: University
   of Illinois Press
Deegan, Mary Jo. 1978. "Women in Sociology, 1890–1930." *Journal of the
   History of Sociology* 1:11–34
– 1985. "Institutionalization, Diversity, and the Rise of Sociological
   Research." Review of *The Chicago School of Sociology*, by Martin
   Bulmer. *Contemporary Sociology* 14(May):365–6
– 1988a. *Jane Addams and the Men of the Chicago School, 1892–1920*.
   New Brunswick, NJ: Transaction
– 1988b. "W.E.B. Du Bois and the Women of Hull-House, 1896–1899."
   American Sociologist 19:301–11
– 1990. Reviews of *The Chicago School: A Liberal Critique of Capitalism*,
   by Dennis Smith, and *Myths of the Chicago School of Sociology*, by Lee
   Harvey. *British Journal of Sociology* 41(December):587–90
– 1996. "Dear Love, Dear Love." *Gender & Society* 10:590–607

- 1999. "Play from the Perspective of George Herbert Mead." In *Play, School, and Society*, edited by George Herbert Mead, xix–cxii. New York: Peter Lang
- 2001a. "George Herbert Mead's First Book." Introduction to *Essays on Social Psychology*, edited by Mary Jo Deegan, xi–xliv. New Brunswick, NJ: Transaction
- 2001b. "The Chicago School of Ethnography." In *The Handbook of Ethnography*, edited by Paul Atkinson, Amanda Coffey, Sara Delamont, John Lofland, and Lyn Lofland, 11–25. London: Sage
- 2002a. *A New Woman of Color*. DeKalb: Northeastern Illinois University
- 2002b. *The Sociology of Race Relations at Hull-House and the University of Chicago*. Westport, CT: Greenwood Press
- 2003a. "Katharine Bement Davis." *Women & Criminal Justice* 14(2/3):15–40
- 2003b. Introduction to *Women at The Hague*, by Jane Addams, Emily Greene Balch, and Alice Hamilton, 11–34. Amherst, NY: Humanity Books
- 2006. "The Human Drama behind the Study of People as Potato Bugs." *Journal of Classical Sociology* 6:101–22
- 2007. "Jane Addams." In *Fifty Key Sociologists*, edited by John Scott, 3–8. London: Routledge
- 2008. *Peace, War, and Society*. New Brunswick, NJ: Transaction
- and Ana-Maria Wahl. 2003. Introduction to *On Art, Labor, and Religion*, by Ellen Gates Starr, 1–35. New Brunswick, NJ: Transaction
Dewey, John. 1903. *Studies in Logical Theory*. Chicago: University of Chicago Press
- 1960 [1922]. Introduction to *Peace and Bread in Time of War*, by Jane Addams. Boston: Hall
Feagin, Joe R., and Hernan Vera. 2008. *Liberation Sociology*. Boulder, CO: Paradigm
Goodwin, Joanne L. 1997. *Gender and the Politics of Welfare Reform*. Chicago: University of Chicago Press
Janowitz, Morris. 1966. Introduction to *W. I. Thomas: On Social Organization and Social Personality*, vii–lviii. Chicago: University of Chicago Press
Mead, George H. 1932. *The Philosophy of the Present*, edited by Arthur E. Murphy. Chicago: University of Chicago Press
- 1934. *Mind, Self and Society*, edited by Charles Morris. Chicago: University of Chicago Press

– 1936. *Movements of Thought in the Nineteenth Century*, edited by
Merritt H. Moore. Chicago: University of Chicago Press

– 1938. *The Philosophy of the Act*, edited by Charles W. Morris, John M.
Brewster, Albert M. Dunham, and David L. Miller. Chicago: University
of Chicago Press

– 1999. *Play, School, and Society*, edited by Mary Jo Deegan. New York:
Peter Lang

– 2001. *Essays on Social Psychology*, edited by Mary Jo Deegan. New
Brunswick, NJ: Transaction

Neeley, Elizabeth, and Mary Jo Deegan. 2005. "George Herbert Mead on
Punitive Justice." *Humanity & Society* 29:71–83

Residents of Hull-House. 1895. *Hull-House Maps and Papers*. New York:
Crowell

Rucker, Darnell. 1969. *The Chicago Pragmatists*. Minneapolis: University
of Minnesota Press

Seigfried, Charlene Haddock. 1991. "Where Are All the Feminist
Pragmatists?" *Hypatia* 6:1–19

– 1996. *Pragmatism and Feminism*. Chicago: University of Chicago Press

– ed. 2002. *Feminist Interpretations of John Dewey*. University Park:
Pennsylvania State University Press

– 2006. "The Dangers of Unilateralism." *NWSA Journal* 18:20–32

Skocpol, Theda. 1992. *Protecting Soldiers and Mothers*. Cambridge:
Belknap Press of Harvard University Press

Small, Albion W. 1896. "Scholarship and Social Agitation." *American
Journal of Sociology* 1:581–92

Talbot, Marion. 1936. *More Than Lore*. Chicago: University of Chicago
Press

– and Sophonisba Breckinridge. 1919. *The Modern Household*. Boston:
Whitcomb and Barrows

Talbot, Marion, and Lois Kimball Mathews Rosenberry. 1931. *The
History of the American Association of University Women*. Cambridge,
MA: Houghton Mifflin

University of Chicago Catalogs. 1923–34. Chicago: University of Chicago
Press

University of Chicago Settlement. n.d., a, b; 1901. Pamphlets. Chicago:
Privately printed

2

Was There a Black Chicago School?

ROGER A. SALERNO

Little has been written on the historical importance of black sociology at the University of Chicago. While Chicago had been a scene of segregated dormitories, fraternities, and social clubs early in the twentieth century, the handful of select black students who attended the University of Chicago's graduate program in sociology at that time excelled and became important international figures. At Chicago, many came under the strong influence of teachers such as Robert E. Park, Ernest Burgess, W. Lloyd Warner, and Louis Wirth. African-American students, such as Charles. S. Johnson, E. Franklin Frazier, Allison Davis, Oliver Cox, Hyland Lewis, Horace Cayton, and St Clair Drake, were among those to do ground-breaking work on the black urban experience. Interestingly, only one of the aforementioned ever held a full-time academic post at the university despite that academy's progressive leanings and pioneering ventures into the study of race relations. In a way, all were outsiders. Does the work of this group share common elements? In what way does their work reflect Chicago School sociology? Why has it been critically neglected and excluded from the traditional image of Chicago School scholarship?

The University of Chicago must be critically assessed in terms of its black sociological scholarship and its relationship or lack of relationship to the nearby black community that eventually came to surround the university. I contend that while the University of Chicago's graduate sociology program under the leadership of Robert Park gained international renown, the moderately conservative nature of many of Park's views on race were overlooked, objected to, or modified by his black graduate students who went on to produce important works of their own.

CHICAGO AND THE BLACK EXPERIENCE

The city of Chicago became a social laboratory for urban sociological investigations, in part because of the significant presence of African Americans in that city. Between 1890 and 1915, the black population of Chicago grew from less than 15,000 to more than 50,000 (Spear 1967, 11). By 1920, it had risen to more than 100,000. The University of Chicago played a central role in applying social science to real-world policy issues; chief among these were issues of race relations. One of the bloodiest race riots in the country's history occurred in 1919 shortly after Robert Park's arrival as sociology chair at the university.

Race relations in Chicago were far from quiescent. After 1915, the so-called "great migration" of poor blacks from underdeveloped rural areas in the Deep South to northern cities began. Chicago was a focal point for racial change as unskilled blacks joined the hordes of indigent European immigrants seeking employment in the stockyards, tanneries, foundries, and steel mills of the Midwest. Chicago seemed to offer unprecedented opportunities for the poor during World War I. Between 1916 and 1919, at least 50,000 migrant blacks crowded into Chicago's Black Belt (Spear 1967, 130).

But discrimination against blacks was rampant in Chicago's employment practices. Few if any were allowed entry to white-collar jobs, and most had to compete with newly arriving white immigrants for menial and unskilled positions. Apprentice programs and unions were invariably closed to black employees. It was only when legislative brakes were applied to immigration, and the pool of foreign workers dried up, that African Americans were considered candidates for low-level positions that traditionally went to poor whites. Thus, positions opened up in meat packing companies, manufacturing firms, and corporations like International Harvester. Yet despite these openings, blacks remained at the bottom of the occupational ladder. Often, because of their lack of access to unions, they were used to help break strikes. Blacks moving to Chicago were frequently forced into squalid living conditions in the city's South Side. There, rich and poor alike found housing conditions ranging from "less than desirable" to "festering slums." As thousands migrated from the South, housing rapidly became overcrowded. Most of it was old and in need of repair. Since significantly funded institutions like Hull-House were open to immigrants but closed to black residents migrating from the South, black communities instituted their own settlement houses associated with community churches. As African Americans pushed further into predominantly white ethnic enclaves toward better housing, however, they met violent resistance.

Between 1917 and 1919, locally organized white "athletic clubs" began attacking blacks on the street, and "neighborhood improvement societies" bombed the homes of newly arrived black immigrants from the South. Fuelled by the *Chicago Tribune*, which portrayed newly arriving African Americans as dangerous, shiftless, and lazy, a major race riot broke out in East St Louis, Illinois, in 1917 where fifty people died because of hysteria over the perceived threat of black migrants (Spear 1967, 202). On 10 July 1917, the *Chicago Tribune* called for blacks to return to the South and offered them money to do so. Local schools also became fortresses of white resistance as white principals and parents attempted to prevent their children from having to sit next to black students.

Injunctions were issued against realtors that rented apartments to blacks in so-called "white neighbourhoods." Frequently substandard and separate schools were allocated to newly arriving black children, who were viewed as bringing down the learning standards of white classmates. De facto segregation in city parks and at beaches was maintained and promoted by white public officials, and violent white ethnic gangs terrorized black youth who attempted to use baseball diamonds and recreation centres that had been unofficially declared as "for whites only."

The simmering cauldron of white resentment came to a boil in the spring and summer of 1919. It was then that the bombing of black homes and attacks on black Chicagoans became everyday events. Real estate offices whose agents rented apartments outside of the unofficial Black Belt to people of colour were bombed. White "athletic clubs" attacked blacks who walked beyond the western boundary of their neighbourhood and who entered Washington Park. Two young black men were murdered by a white gang simply because they were in the "wrong neighbourhood." And the police took no action despite a good number of witnesses.

On 27 July 1919, Eugene Williams, a young black man, was stoned by a crowd of white people as he was swimming at Twenty-ninth Street Beach. He drowned, but the police took no action against the perpetrators. Black men on the beach began attacking a group of white men, whom they accused of the crime. Later that evening, whites retaliated by beating, stabbing, and shooting thirty-eight African Americans who had accidentally wandered into white areas. Rioting continued for several days, with enormous property damage; forty-nine houses in the stockyard district were set ablaze and destroyed. Killings and retaliations lasted nearly a full week. The Illinois state militia was called out by the governor to help quell the rioting. A total of twenty-three black people and fifteen white people died, with 348 blacks and 175 whites injured. It was during this very hot summer that Robert E. Park was appointed to a full-time position at the University of Chicago. No longer in only a fall- or summer-quarter position, Park permanently relocated to the university.

ROBERT E. PARK: DEFINING THE BLACK EXPERIENCE FOR THE CHICAGO SCHOOL

Park's long-term interest in race relations had little to do with a passion for social change and more to do with his intellectual curiosity and pragmatic inclinations. Park was influenced by Booker T. Washington in this regard and went on to influence his own students accordingly. He was neither a radical agent of change nor an idealist, and he had little but disdain for those who were. Booker Washington espoused a conservative and accommodationist approach to race relations that had some appeal for him. Before coming to teach at Chicago, he had served as Washington's public relations assistant and ghost writer at Tuskegee. It might be argued that Washington made use of Park as a white middle-class intellectual to sell his conservative program to mistrusting white liberals of his day.

Just prior to Park's employment by Washington, he seriously considered going to South Africa to work for the multi-millionaire Cecil Rhodes, the quintessential Euro-colonialist and founder of de Beers (Matthews 1977, 57). As chance would have it, he was hired by the Congo Reform Association, sponsored by the Baptist Missionary Society. This had little to do with his own interest in Congo reform and more to do with the society's need for a good publicist to help in its campaign to bring to light the bloody abuses of Leopold II of Belgium against Africans in the Congo. It was a way for Park to move out of low-level reporting for $25 per week and onto a more promising career path (Lindner 1990, 32). But as it turned out, Park was essentially contemptuous of the association and its missionaries. In speaking of the campaign against Leopold, he noted, "I didn't take much stock in their atrocity stories" (Matthews 1977, 59). Nevertheless, it was through Park's association with this organization that he was introduced to Washington and eventually was employed by Tuskegee. He saw Washington as a doer and admired him for this.

There can be no doubt of Park's liberal pedigree when it comes to his positions on race relations. While embracing much of Adam Smith's and Herbert Spencer's notions of evolutionary sociology, which helped to buttress industrial capitalism of his day, Park maintained his distance from what he viewed as radical social reformers. Like Max Weber, Park adhered to the notion of value-free research that would unearth an objective truth, an objective reality. He had been warned by William James at Harvard while a student there that he was "not intelligent enough" to make a contribution to the field of philosophy (Matthews 1977, 57).

But what Park did with a part-time teaching post in sociology at the University of Chicago was remarkable. He turned himself into a guru of urban studies, if not the father of American urban sociology. For an aging second-string reporter and publicist with no academic experience other than his own excellent graduate education in Europe and at Harvard, Park became a central figure in sociology at the University of Chicago upon W.I. Thomas's dismissal in 1917. However, if it had not been for the pioneering work of a young associate professor, Ernest Burgess, and the assistance of Chicago graduate students like Louis Wirth, Everett Hughes, and Herbert Blumer, Park's importance at Chicago would likely have been uneven.

It is clear that Park was not fond of men such as W.E.B. DuBois and unconventional thinkers about race. His antipathy even for reformist groups such as the NAACP was well-known. He believed in the evolutionary progress of society guided by natural law and "the invisible hand." His cycle theory of race relations was based upon these concepts. It identified the "inevitability" of an evolutionary chain leading from initial contact and competition to a stage of conflict, then to accommodation, and ultimately to assimilation. For all practical purposes, it was a white liberal perspective. Park was not a believer in radical social change but rather believed that people, through practical circumstance, would eventually see the light. While he was not prejudiced according to the standards of his time, nowhere on record can be found his own opposition to the segregation that existed at the University of Chicago itself. While on one hand he subscribed to the notion of the equal intellectual capacity of white and black men, he asked: "Is the Negro's undoubted interest in music and taste for bright colors, commonly attributed to the race, to be regarded as inherent and racial traits or are they merely the characteristics of primitive peoples?" (Park 1950, 264).

For Robert E. Park, race was never simply biological. This separated him from his reactionary contemporaries. Although he occasionally described Africans as "primitive" and saw black Americans emerging from primitive roots, he rejected the bio-racism inherent in much of the sociology of his day that reduced a person to his genetic essentials; he saw race only as part of this mix. While he purported to assess the importance of black culture, he rarely dipped into the well of biological determinism that characterized the work of William Sumner and William James. When he did, however, his choice of words was often disturbing.

"The Negro is, by natural disposition, neither an intellectual nor an idealist, like the Jew; nor a brooding introspective, like the East African; nor a pioneer and frontiersman, like the Anglo-Saxon. He is primarily an artist, loving life for its own sake. His *métier* is expression rather than action. He is, so to speak, the lady among races" (Park 1950, 280). In commenting on this quote, Ralph Ellison (1964, 308) would later say: "Park's descriptive metaphor is so pregnant with mixed motives as to birth a thousand compromises and indecisions. Imagine the effect such teachings had on Negro students alone!"

Though Park contributed significantly to the field of race relations, he primarily focused on culture, as in the culture of immigrants. In some sense, this was significant among the weaknesses in his thinking on race. On the other hand, as Vernon J. Williams (1996, 88) has noted, "His biracial organization theory was a conservative's mythical formulation of Booker T. Washington's theory of race relations within the historical context of turn-of-the-century sociology." He unflinchingly subscribed to Washington's call for industrial education for the Negro. Biracial social and economic organization was viewed as a means by which racism would eventually be overcome, but in essence it was the existence of races living side-by-side. While such a system would at first maintain "separations" and "distances" between the races, it would encourage personal identification among racial groups living separate and apart from one another. He saw African Americans establishing their own class system that paralleled that of the whites but was culturally distinct from it.

Historian John Stanfield (1985) has made the case that Park's race theory was merely an extension of Washington's. And like

Washington's, the appeal of his ideas on race and the acceptance of segregation and patience with Jim Crow was what endeared him to funding establishments and research foundations throughout the country. How much he influenced Booker T. Washington or was influenced by him is significant. Stanfield makes the point that Park was economically dependent on Washington, and he implies that this had something to do with the conservative hue of his own ideas. However, even after culling a wealth of correspondence between the two men, I see this as simply educated conjecture. There is no solid proof. Park's thoughts on race relations were heavily influenced by his knowledge of blacks in the Deep South. Translating his understanding of rural Southern black culture to what he saw as the African-American urban experience was a challenge.

A central weakness of his work in this regard was his attempt to use some of the same models that W.I. Thomas had been using in examining the turn-of-the-century immigrant experience in adapting to urban America. He understood fully that the black migrant was not a Polish peasant. But on the other hand, it was easy to view race as merely a cultural variable that had some basis in human biology.

There is little in Park's work that recognizes the structural strategy of business and governmental elites to use the flow of immigration to provide cheap labour for industry, nor is there any significant examination of racism as an insidious ideology used to promote the political and economic ends of the most powerful. Park was led by an "invisible hand" assumption of markets and their work. If anything, it is poor communication and uninformed action that constitutes his causal understanding and critique of racial discrimination. He perceived race conflict as a disequilibrium that needed to be addressed. While he did recognize competition for scarce resources as a causal factor leading to white racist practices, he tended to see this as a result of individual and group competition as opposed to racist ideology imposed and institutionally sustained by plutocracy. Mary White Ovington, chair of the NAACP, viewed Park as a "slow going conservative, the astute political kind" who had "never been aggressive" in matters of reform (Matthews 1977, 176).

BLACK STUDENTS OF THE CHICAGO SCHOOL

Beginning with Charles S. Johnson, who studied with the first generation of the Chicago School sociologists, including Albion Small, W.I. Thomas, and George Herbert Mead, and eventually came under the strong influence of Robert Park, African-American students were often welcomed into graduate programs at the University of Chicago. Johnson entered graduate study at Chicago in 1917 and would go on to do outstanding research on the 1919 race riot that rocked the city, becoming research director for the Chicago Urban League, which Park headed, and eventually becoming president of Fisk University in 1947 over the protests of W.E.B. DuBois (Gilpin and Gasman 2003).

When Johnson first came to the University of Chicago, dormitories and dining halls were segregated, as was the university hospital. But this was typical in white American academic institutions. Johnson, who appeared to take it in stride, was the first of Robert Park's black student protégés at Chicago. He worked hard to impress his mentor. His research skills were outstanding – far better than Park's own. While his mind was expansive and sharp, Johnson's published work never critically reached the level of that of E. Franklin Frazier or Oliver Cromwell Cox, who considered him their intellectual inferior (Jones 1974). This has led some of his critics to view him as having held back and moderated his ideas and, as Richard Robbins (1996) notes in his study of Johnson, balanced the pragmatic demands of the society around him with his own ideals.

Johnson recognized in Park a reluctance to associate with activists and what he called "do-gooders." Park trusted Johnson and respected his reserve. A brilliant researcher, he worked tirelessly for the predominantly white commission that studied the 1919 race violence. And while he went along with the commission's conservative recommendations, the investigative work on which they were based was primarily his. Johnson was but the first in a long line of African Americans who would be trained at Chicago and who came under Park's strong influence. Another was E. Franklin Frazier, who would go on to become one of the nation's most respected scholars of the African-American social experience.

Both Park and Frazier were employed by Tuskegee in 1916, but the chief difference here was Frazier's personal embarrassment with this association (Platt 1991, 41–3). After securing a master's degree in sociology from Clark University in Worcester, Massachusetts, in 1920 and a graduate social work degree from Columbia University's social work school, Frazier moved on to direct the social work program at Morehouse, which became Atlanta University.

In 1927, he won a fellowship to the University of Chicago and worked on his dissertation, *The Negro Family in Chicago*, under

Park's mentorship. But he had already developed his ideas on family, which were significantly influenced by W.E.B. DuBois, not Park. Anthony Platt, Frazier's biographer, notes: "Although many young Afro-American intellectuals like Frazier were eager to go to graduate schools so they could equip themselves to become fighters for the 'spiritual and intellectual emancipation of the Negro,' they quickly found themselves in an academic milieu that, though socially liberal compared with black colleges, was extremely paternalistic and demanded a high level of ideological conformity. Dissent was tolerated only within limited parameters. At the turn of the century, academics could not take progressive positions on controversial issues and expect to keep their jobs" (1991, 44).

Frazier's classmates were a *Who's Who* of Chicago sociology, including Herbert Blumer, Robert Redfield, Everett Hughes, and Louis Wirth. But he was into and out of Chicago within a few years. This is not to say that he wasn't influenced by Park. He was, but his disagreements with Park were evident. Frazier was a socialist and a self-professed radical. Although he respected Park's scientific rigor, he viewed his idea that "racial temperament" had a significant role to play in the social life of black people was sheer nonsense (Platt 1991, 90). Frazier went on to publish extensively in the field of race relations, had a long and distinguished academic career at Howard University, and became president of the American Sociological Association in 1948. His work on the African-American family was followed by his 1950 study entitled *The Black Bourgeoisie*. In this controversial work, first published in France, he critically examines what he believed to be a subservient, conservative group of middle-class African Americans who derived their cultural style and religious sentiments from the white middle class. Like W.E.B. DuBois, Frazier would be the target of FBI investigations late in his career (Keen 2004, 88).

Other black intellectuals and scholars also moved through the University of Chicago. Oliver Cromwell Cox, born and raised in Trinidad, began his graduate studies at the University of Chicago in 1930. Prior to this, Cox completed a degree in law at Northwestern and came to the University of Chicago to study economics. He found economics too limiting, however. After completing a master's degree in 1932, he shifted his interest to sociology. At Chicago, Cox had the opportunity to study not only with Robert Park and Ernest Burgess but also with men such as Herbert Blumer, Louis Wirth, W. Lloyd

Warner, and Ellsworth Faris. Although Park retired from Chicago in
1934, his ghost remained there in the form of his students and colleagues as he took up active research and teaching duties at Fisk
University – a predominantly black college in Tennessee where his
former student, Charles S. Johnson, now directed social sciences.

Like Frazier, Cox did not accept many of Park's essential tenets on
race relations, particularly his cycle theory of race relations. Cox, like
Frazier, was rather impatient with the white male Chicago School
crowd. Much further to the political left than his colleagues, he would
go on to write several volumes on class and race and to develop a
fuller critique of global capitalism and its relationship to racism. In
his book, *Race: A Study of Social Dynamics* (2000), he took Park to
task. It was not that Park was insensitive or misguided, he argued:
it was that Park truly lacked historical understanding of the black
condition in America. Cox was highly critical of what he viewed as
Park's tendency to see racism as a product of customs and Southern
folkways as opposed to something more sinister – the need for white
society to dominate and exploit blacks as a means of retaining its
position of privilege. Such a radical view on race was unacceptable to
middle-class white and black society at the time.

A classmate of Cox, Hylan Garnet Lewis, came to the University
of Chicago in 1934 on a Social Science Research Council fellowship
and completed his master's degree in sociology in 1936. Like Cox and
Frazier, Lewis taught at a number of black colleges in the 1940s
and 1950s before settling in to teach at the City University of New
York. In 1952, he was awarded a doctorate in sociology from the
University of Chicago. Known primarily for his ethnographic study,
Blackways of Kent (1955), Lewis left Chicago and never looked back.

H.M. Bond, Bertram Wilber Doyle, and other black graduate students in Park's department in the early and mid-1930s produced
outstanding theses dealing with issues of race. Allison Davis, a young
African-American anthropologist, transferred to Chicago's Anthropology Department from Harvard. There he studied with Robert
Redfield, Park's son-in-law, and later with Lloyd Warner, also from
Harvard, who came to Chicago to teach in 1935. But it wasn't until
St Clair Drake and Horace Cayton arrived on the scene that things
became interesting.

Drake had come to Chicago to study anthropology with Warner,
with whom he had done research at Harvard. He had also worked
in the South with Allison Davis, who was now completing his own

graduate studies. At this time, Drake also settled in to complete his anthropology training and to attend to a major research project with Warner.

Horace Cayton was the grandson of the nation's first black senator and the son of a prominent journalist. While he initially came to the University of Chicago in 1932 to study political science, he was eventually recruited by Louis Wirth to work as his graduate assistant in the Sociology Department, where he worked from 1933 to 1935. It was there that he gained much of his excellent research skills; however, he never completed his dissertation. He went on to work as a community centre director in Chicago and to teach at black colleges in the South. Cayton would cross paths with both Warner and Drake at Chicago and would eventually work with both (Cayton 1963).

Louis Wirth appears to be a pivotal figure here, since he not only introduced a number of these researchers to one another but also, as WPA money rolled into the university, gained control over its direction. Much of it was used to conduct an extensive research project into the so-called "Black Belt" of Chicago. Drake's earlier research for Warner on the black community in Chicago became part of this study's foundation. But Cayton's contributions to the work were significant. Together, Drake and Cayton would edit *Black Metropolis*, which would become a classic study of one of the most dynamic black urban centres in the world.

Despite the wonderful work done by black graduate students at Chicago, only Allison Davis would receive a faculty appointment there. But this didn't occur until the 1960s, and it was in the School of Education, not sociology or anthropology. There were few places in prestigious white institutions for young black scholars. They were expected to go elsewhere – to find positions in black colleges. They were expected to take the word back to the masses of the "lesser educated" in colleges in the South – places that emphasized vocational training, not scholarship. They were expected to carry the message of a cautionary social science – one that emphasized detached scholarship and reserve. Fortunately, many of those trained at Chicago refused to do this.

A BLACK CHICAGO SCHOOL?

It's important to critically examine the term "Chicago School." Howard Becker, a personality often associated with this school of sociology, raises the question of its actual existence. For Becker (1999) and for Jennifer Platt (1996), the Chicago school was never a "school" in its fullest sense. While most students and academics associated with it might have been interested in various aspects of urban living, their research approaches and underlying assumptions were quite diverse. Their foci varied. Ethnographic studies, participant observation, descriptive statistics, and data analysis all had a place there. Ecology, conflict, and functionalism all melded together. And yes, some might call that a school. This said, raising the question of the existence of a Black Chicago School might be begging the question. Of course, there is always a cross-pollination of ideas in any small department, but there are also differences between and among faculty and students. Students who moved through Chicago certainly learned from their teachers. Likewise, their teachers learned from them. We would at least hope so. Students would also reject currents in their teachers' work. We would expect this to be the case here.

Taken as a whole, the work of these particular African-American sociologists provides us with some central features that resonate with the Chicago School sociology touted by Park and Burgess, but much of their work challenged some of its underlying assumptions – particularly the more conservative assumptions of Park such as temperament and innate racial antipathies. Commencing with Johnson, few black sociologists crossed the line between scholarship and activism, however. It was as though being an activist would weaken or bias their findings and offend the social science community upon which research funding was dependent. Most believed, as Park believed, that science needed to be colour-blind. Only in this way would scientific findings have validity. If anything, perhaps Park instilled in his students a notion of caution and pragmatic detachment while finding no difficulty in frequenting the university's Quadrangle Club, which prohibited the admission of women, blacks, and Jews.

Still, the University of Chicago opened its doors to black graduate students at a time when the doors of most white institutions were closed. Rockefeller Foundation monies funnelled through the Laura Spellman Fund and the Social Science Research Council provided financial assistance to African Americans seeking graduate education. The University of Chicago received much of this funding by inviting students of colour to the institution. Furthermore, if the Sociology Department wanted to actually stress studies in race relations, it was natural for it to open its doors to these students – most of whom were mature men with track records in research returning to school for advanced degrees. Mary Jo Deegan (1988; also see Deegan, this volume) gives ample evidence that although women studying sociology at Chicago were also marginalized, they were able to find refuge and support for their more activist inclinations at Hull-House. But even here scholarship was far from radical. Much of it was still influenced by funding, including Rockefeller Foundation money, aimed at programs to Americanize the immigrant, who was seen as posing a danger to social order and stability. Reform organizations promoting racial tolerance, such as the Urban League (headed by Park himself), the Council on Race Relations (headed by Wirth), and the NAACP (presided over by Moorfield Storey, a white attorney) envisaged gradual, orderly change under white direction. Simultaneously, many scholars and reformers hoped that objective scholarship and research (also guided by whites) would not only reveal the inefficiencies of the social system but also guide a natural evolutionary course toward the assimilation of "others" into a new, more stable social order. Whether this "co-optation" was a planned effort to defuse black wrath is interesting conjecture, but it's just that. There indeed was an obvious liberal intention in some funding initiatives to assist the oppressed for the benefit of the system. This ethos still shapes policy today. But the question of whether there was a sinister plot behind all the "do-gooder" work appears to be missing the critical point: all systems work to maintain themselves in the face of a challenge from the perceived "outside." While there was an authentic search for "truth" at Chicago, the legacy of the Chicago School's emphasis on the study of race relations was a call for restraint and reflection.

REFERENCES

Becker, Howard. 1999. "The Chicago School, So-called." *Qualitative Sociology* 22(1):3–12
Cayton, Horace. 1963. *The Long Road: An Autobiography*. New York: Alfred Knopf
Cox, Oliver C. 2000. *Race: A Study in Social Dynamics*. New York: Monthly Review Press
Deegan, Mary Jo. 1988. *Jane Addams and the Men of the Chicago School, 1992–1918*. New Brunswick, NJ: Transaction

Ellison, Ralph. 1964. *Shadow and Act*. New York: Random House
Frazier, E. Franklin. 1950. *Black Bourgeoisie*. New York: Free Press
Gilpin, Patrick, and Marybeth Gasman. 2003. *Charles S. Johnson: Leadership beyond the Veil in the Age of Jim Crow*. Albany: State University of New York Press
Jones, Butler. 1974. "The Tradition of Sociology Teaching in Black Colleges: Unheralded Professionals." In *Black Sociologists: Historical and Contemporary Perspectives*, edited by James Blackwell and Morris Janowitz. Chicago: University of Chicago Press
Keen, Mike Forrest. 2004. *Stalking the Sociological Imagination: J. Edgar Hoover's FBI Surveillance of American Sociology*. New Brunswick, NJ: Transaction
Lewis, Hylan Garnet. 1955. *Blackways of Kent*. Chapel Hill: University of North Carolina Press
Lindner, Rolf. 1990. *The Reportage of Urban Culture: Robert Park and the Chicago School*. Cambridge: Cambridge University Press
Matthews, Fred H. 1977. *Quest for an American Sociology: Robert E. Park and the Chicago School*. Montreal: McGill-Queen's University Press
Park, Robert E. 1950. *Race and Culture*. New York: Free Press
Platt, Anthony. 1991. *E. Franklin Frazier Reconsidered*. New Brunswick, NJ: Rutgers University Press
Platt, Jennifer. 1996. *A History of Sociological Research Methods in America*. Cambridge: Cambridge University Press
Robbins, Richard. 1996. *Sidelines Activist*. Jackson: University of Mississippi Press
Spear, Allan. 1967. *Black Chicago: The Making of a Negro Ghetto*. Chicago: University of Chicago Press
Stanfield, John H. 1985. *Philanthropy and Jim Crow in American Social Science*. Westport, CT: Greenwood Press
Williams, Vernon. 1996. *Rethinking Race: Franz Boaz and His Contemporaries*. Louisville: University of Kentucky Press

3

Chicago's Proclivity to Qualitative Sociology: Myth or Reality?

DAVID A. NOCK

Back in the 1980s, several British sociological historians insisted that seeing the Chicagoans as committed to qualitative sociology was mistaken. The classic early statement of this perspective, Martin Bulmer's (1981) article, "Quantification and Chicago Social Science in the 1920s: A Neglected Tradition," was reprinted in Bulmer's (1984) influential book, *The Chicago School of Sociology: Institutionalization, Diversity, and the Rise of Sociological Research*. Bulmer points out the aphorism taken from Lord Kelvin carved into the Social Science Research Building, "When you cannot measure, your knowledge is meager and unsatisfactory." Bulmer asks, "How does this square with the familiar contrasts which are drawn between the Chicago and Columbia schools of sociology" and with "the predominant identification of Chicago social science with 'soft,' ethnographic methods in the 1920s and 1930s?" (Bulmer 1984, 151). Bulmer's reply is that it does not square very well!

Bulmer (1984, 151–2, 258–9) proceeds to cite a list of well-known sociologists writing in the 1970s as overemphasizing the qualitative nature of Chicago sociology and underemphasizing its quantitative nature. The thrust of Bulmer's argument is that this view of Chicago sociology was a *latter-day construction* of sociological historians in the 1970s, people who were *not* members of the Chicago School in its heyday from 1915 through the end of the 1930s. Bulmer (1984, 152) comments that "[t]his is the legacy that has been left to the discipline when it reconstructs its history *today*" (emphasis added) and that "[t]his image is reinforced by *recent controversies* [emphasis added] over the correct historical interpretation of the origins of symbolic interactionism and sociological social psychology, largely focused on the thought of figures active at Chicago."

Bulmer's (1981, 327) explanation of "the overidentification of Chicago with qualitative research" by sociological historians is rather interesting and ingenuous. Following Jones and Kronus (1976, 3–13), Bulmer argues that there has been a polarization in interests and expertise between *sociological historians*, who have been metrically challenged and tend to overlook the importance of statistics, and *mathematical sociologists* in their histories of the discipline and practitioners of self-consciously scientific or scientistic sub-specialties such as methods, demography, and statistics, who are not much interested in the history of their subjects, because they regard such histories as irrelevant to the state of current research and thus a waste of time. As Bulmer (1984, 188) puts it, they have demonstrated that "interest in quantitative methods and interest in the history of sociology seem to be antithetical." He draws an analogy between "the history of quantitative social science methods [and] the history of physics" in that "those who do physics, and those who write its history, tend to be different people working apart from each other" (Bulmer 1981, 327–8). Similarly, says Bulmer (1981, 328), "practicing quantitative social scientists" have little interest in doing the history of their own specialty, and this leaves the subject open to the more qualitatively minded tribe of sociological historians, who have little aptitude or interest in doing so.

It is not my interest or capacity to debate this analysis; however, Chicago's "overidentification ... with qualitative research" is explained by Bulmer as an artifact of a *later* social construction by sociological historians. He does *not* entertain the possibility that this image of Chicago sociology as consisting of an "overidentification" with qualitative research, a neglect of the quantitative tradition, and a clearly defined epistemological distinctiveness to Chicago and Columbia sociology may actually go back to the heyday of Chicago sociology itself during the 1920s and 1930s. These Chicagoans were *not removed* in time from their contrasts of Chicago and Columbia sociology, and they all fulfilled one or more criteria as Chicagoans, whether as graduate students who achieved permanent positions elsewhere after their Chicago degree (Ellwood, House, Eubank, Bogardus, and Waller), as graduate students who later joined the Chicago faculty (Thomas, Burgess, Blumer, Wirth, and Hughes), or as faculty at

Chicago without a Chicago degree who helped found the Chicago tradition (Small and Park). They maintained personal networks that lasted over lengthy periods of time, and they maintained Chicago sociology and Chicago sociologists as their major scholarly network and reference group.

Bulmer's original depiction has been carried on by Lee Harvey and Martyn Hammersley. Harvey (1987, 74) uses Bulmer's 1981 and 1984 publications in documenting the myths of the Chicago School of Sociology highlighted in the book's title: "The 'Chicago School' is rarely associated with the development or even use of quantitative techniques ... the myth is that Chicago was the home of ethnographic research. Thomas's assertion of the 'perfect' nature of life history as a source of data, Park's apparent opposition to statistics and Blumer's attacks on variable analysis have all been taken as indicative of an antipathy towards quantification by the 'Chicago School.' This ignores the extensive development and use of statistics at Chicago."

Hammersley (1989, 90) suggests that "The idea that the Chicagoans were committed to qualitative sociology is probably even more misleading" – that is, more misleading than the tendency of commentators to attribute Chicago social psychology to the lineage of Blumer–Mead symbolic interactionism. Both Bulmer and Hammersley point to Emory S. Bogardus and even Robert E. Park as maintaining an interest in quantitative sociology. In fact, Bogardus's development of his celebrated social distance scale is credited to Park's encouragement of "students to use quantitative data where available and relevant; and even to develop measurement scales" (Hammersley 1989, 90). This manner of interpreting the work of Park and Bogardus had already been raised by Bulmer (1984, 154), who commented that "[i] t is worth remembering that Park, despite his antiquantitative tendencies, was associated with the inception of one of the earliest attitudes scales."

All this is true to some degree, but it does rather hide and obscure differences and distinctions that were clear enough to contemporary Chicagoans: that there *was* a difference between Chicago sociology and Columbia sociology; that Chicago's strength lay in its qualitative bent and Columbia in its quantitative bent; and the increasing insistence on "the new statistics" that emphasized the production of correlations between variables. In the view of their leaders, anything else was inferior and even non-scientific. Park (this volume) provides a critique of the Columbia approach that resonates with this argument.

CHICAGO'S QUALITATIVE PROCLIVITY AS PROCLAIMED
BY CONTEMPORARY CHICAGOAN FLOYD HOUSE'S
THE DEVELOPMENT OF SOCIOLOGY (1936)

In reasserting the identification of the Chicago School with qualitative
sociology, a lesser identification with quantitative sociology, and a
clear differentiation between Chicago and Columbia sociologies, I
turn to Floyd House's 1936 book, *The Development of Sociology*,
published as the heyday of Chicago sociology was starting to wane. It
is removed by only one year from the appearance of Talcott Parsons's
(1937) *The Structure of Social Action*. However, Parsons only makes
it into the index of *The Development of Sociology* as a translator of
Weber and as a commentator on the now-neglected Pareto. Weber's
substantive sociology, initially popularized by Parsons, is neglected in
favour of the "*verstehen* Weber."

House's own Chicago roots are clear, although he spent most of
his career at the University of Virginia. Born in 1893, he had come
to Chicago in 1922 for the PhD after earlier degrees at the University
of Colorado. After receiving his degree in 1924, he stayed on as an
assistant professor in the department before moving on as head of
the new department at Virginia, where he stayed until his retirement
in 1963. House is a good example of Chicago graduates who
remained loyal to the department, to the university, and to a particular conception of sociology for decades after their physical departure
from the University of Chicago. This resulted from close personal
and intellectual ties, which continued. For example, in his preface,
written a decade after his departure from Chicago, House (1936, vi)
eagerly took "the opportunity to express my lasting indebtedness to
the late Professor Albion Small ... from whom I received my first
formal instruction in the history of sociology and by whom I was
first encouraged to hope that I might write something in that field
worthy of publication." Even more directly, he acknowledged the
influence of Robert E. Park "for the general development and guidance of my own sociological thought" as more important than that
of "any other one person" (House 1936, vi).

House's *The Development of Sociology* was intended as an encyclopedic history of sociology and social thought from ancient times
to the modern era (Plato is cited on thirteen pages, Aristotle on sixteen). As such, one might suppose that the author would be entirely
detached and even-handed, maintaining the objectivity expected of

such encyclopedic authors. To some extent, that is true. F.H. Giddings
is cited in twenty-one pages, Lundberg (an important radical neo-
positivist trained by Giddings's student F. Stuart Chapin) on eighteen, Lichtenberger (Giddings's doctoral student) on fifteen. However,
closer inspection of the citation network makes House's Chicago
bias even clearer. Sixteen individuals were cited on twenty pages or
more. Some of them were acknowledged as early sociologists from
Europe whose star has dimmed *since* 1936, such as Gumplowicz
(33) and Ratzenhofer (21). If one just considers Americans acknowledged as sociologists publishing in the sixty years prior to its publication, one gets a total of nine individuals: Small, Ward, Burgess,
Giddings, Park, Ross, Sumner, Thomas, Znaniecki. Of these, five were
associated with Chicago (Small, Burgess, Park, Thomas, Znaniecki),
one with Columbia (Giddings), and three were early pioneers of
American sociology not directly associated with Chicago or Columbia
(Ward, Ross, Sumner). Giddings had already trained many PhDs who
had obtained positions at prominent universities around America:
Lichtenberger, Ogburn, Chapin, Odum, Hankins, Rice, Gillin, Binder,
Davenport, Todd, Williams, Hall, Sims, and Gehlke (see Bannister
1987, 78, 86). Of these, only James P. Lichtenberger was cited on
more than ten pages (fifteen). Despite being trained in radical neo-
positivism's distrust of social theory and social philosophy as overly speculative, Lichtenberger was a well-known publisher in this
field, and this was what House mainly cited. Perhaps pointedly, the
already prominent Ogburn and Chapin were only cited on seven and
four pages, respectively. If one goes beyond this name citation pattern, a closer textual analysis indicates that a distinct agenda ani-
mates the work. This distinct agenda amounts to a warning about
the over-quantification threatening American sociology, the identification of that threat with Columbia university's department of sociology, and the tendency of such quantitative sociology to ignore or
downplay necessary conceptualization (along with theorizing and
philosophizing).

HOUSE'S DESIGNATED GROUP OF ANTI-NEOPOSITIVIST CHICAGOANS

House goes on to identify the University of Chicago's sociology
department as the major challenger against the trend toward excessive quantification by explicitly highlighting its achievements in

qualitative sociologies. Finally, he identifies a named Group of Five, all with Chicago roots, who stand out against what he considers the threats posed by the radical neo-positivists. Interestingly, two of this group (Robert E. Park and Emory Bogardus) were identified by Bulmer and Hammersley for their sympathies to quantitative sociology, while House identified them as coherent anti-neopositivists. The others include Herbert Blumer, Earle Eubank, and House himself. However, it would be easy to add to this Chicago list of critics of radical neo-positivism, including Herbert Blumer's own mentor at Missouri, Charles Ellwood.

Let me reiterate: the portrayal of Chicago sociology as especially contributing to the development of qualitative sociology is *not simply* a construction of latter-day sociological historians from the 1970s who were historically and geographically separated from Chicago and removed by one or several generations. The critique of radical neo-positivism was part and parcel of Chicago sociology, and it emanated from a number of members of the School in its heyday. Of course, we are not only looking at first-rank or core Chicagoans. In the case of House's Group of Five, Park is the senior faculty member whose name (along with that of Thomas) usually defines the Chicago School. Blumer took his doctoral training at Chicago and received his PhD from there in 1928. He stayed on as a faculty member into the early 1950s and developed the paradigm of symbolic interactionism so clearly identified with Chicago sociology.

Bogardus, House, and Eubank all represent a third type of Chicagoan, sometimes unjustly neglected because they did not stay on as faculty at Chicago but found their permanent careers elsewhere (Bogardus at Southern California, Eubank at the University of Cincinnati, and House at Virginia). Yet as already mentioned, in the case of Bogardus and House, they remained clearly identified with their Chicago mentors and as Chicagoans themselves. These claims about Chicago sociology (with Columbia as the foil) represent a substantial thesis of House's book, even if subtle in its development (Nock 2004). House was always a little understated in his style, perhaps because understatement and scholarly gentility were appreciated at that time. In the final chapter, entitled "Present Sociological Trends and Tendencies," House (1936) abandons his understated style and reaches for his cape!

The chapter begins with a contrast between teaching and research. House (1936, 422) suggests that "the emphasis on research in American sociology" had been so strong within the discipline since about 1925 that the commitment to teaching tended to get lost. Although research might be defined in a variety of ways, House (1936, 422) suggests that it had come to be "preponderantly" defined as "a tendency to the use of statistical and other quantitative methods." Alongside this tendency to the quantitative was a trend toward behaviourism, developed by Bechterev, Pavlov, and Watson outside sociology and adopted by sociologists George A. Lundberg and Read Bain. House (1936, 423) treats behaviourism as the "theoretic justification for the statistical and quantitative tendency of sociological research." A third element of radical neo-positivism, House (1936, 424) argues, is its "tendency to conceive 'research' in such a way as to be depreciatory of all theoretic, and particularly speculative, contributions" and especially in the inclination to disregard "the continual reconsideration of the conceptual terms that form the vocabulary ... of our science [sociology]."

House (1936, 424) emphasizes the need to be "guided by carefully conceived notions about the things to be studied" and points to a gradual development "recently" of thirty or forty items contributing to "the conceptual organon of the science of sociology." However, House clearly regards the radical neo-positivists as deficient in this regard. He willingly grants that "the many accredited sociologists of this country have ... lagged behind the few who have been active in Germany" and acknowledges the superior conceptual and theoretical skills of Tonnies, Simmel, Max Weber, Sombart, and the Pole Florian Znaniecki, adding that "little to the credit of American writers in this special field can be favorably compared" to these European authors (House 1936, 424).

When it comes to American challenges to the radical neo-positivist agenda, House (1936, 422–3) maintains that "[t]he principal exceptions to this trend are constituted by the research undertakings of staff members, students, and former students at the University of Chicago, where under the leadership of several professors of marked ability and influence researches involving primarily the use of case-study and 'natural-history' methods have been executed." Later on, House (1936, 424) specifies his Group of Five "as exponents of the idea that concrete sociological research may be largely futile and even harmful when it is not guided by carefully conceived notions about the things to be studied."

In various places, House justifies his identification of this Group of Five for their critiques of radical neo-positivism. In chapter 33,

"Sociological Theory and Social Research," House (1936, 382) introduces the theme that "since 1920" there had been "a marked increase"
in a form of sociological research "predominantly statistical" that
was antithetical to reviving "interest in the definition of sociological
concepts." In contrast, House (1936, 382) also notes that "a considerable revival" toward greater sophistication in sociological concepts
was underway and that "possibly the most important immediate
causal factor" in this conceptual revival was "the publication of the
Park and Burgess *Introduction to the Science of Society* in 1921 ...
characterized by the vigorous attack it makes upon the problem of
definition of concepts." House (1936) points out that the book was
used as much by graduate students as by undergraduates, its original
target, and credits its appearance with producing "a generation of
University of Chicago graduate students ... strongly impressed by the
idea that the definition of concepts was an important part of the task
of sociological research."

Herbert Blumer, after receiving his Chicago PhD, stayed on as a
faculty member. His article, "Science without Concepts," was clearly
written as a challenge to the radical neo-positivists. In it, Blumer
(1931, 533) commented that "Few things are more irritating than to
read a piece of research conforming most stringently to accredited
techniques and abounding in numbers or units, or elements, only to
discover outstanding sloppiness in conceptual usage." As Bannister
(1987, 176) has written, "Lest the reference be lost, Blumer singled
out the work of the statisticians."

Therefore, it is hardly a naive nomination when House (1936,
385) refers to Blumer's paper as "[p]erhaps the best existing statement of the methodological importance of adequately determined
concepts for the purposes of scientific sociology." House (1936, 385)
comments that Blumer was working on a follow-up paper and that
"it is to be hoped that he will be able eventually to publish other
valuable discussions." This mention of Blumer by House (1936,
384–5) is part of a longer paragraph, which credits Eubank's *The
Concepts of Sociology* (1932) as "a substantial volume" in addressing "the importance of fundamental concepts" as emphasized "by a
committee of the American Sociological Society on the teaching of
sociology in the general introductory college course."

In the chapter on "Statistical Methods and Case Studies," House
justifies his own inclusion in the Group of Five by describing the
"two fairly definite techniques of sociological research" indicated in

the chapter title and noting there is "no little dispute concerning the respective advantages and limitations" of each (House 1936, 367). House (1936, 372) pointedly brings out the association of Columbia University with "statistical sociology" and, although he recognizes the "emphasis on statistical methods which has been so characteristic of Giddings and his students," muses about how much credit should be accorded to Giddings's predecessor, Richmond Mayo-Smith. Whatever the reason or factor, House (1936, 372) acknowledges, "At any rate, from an early date in the history of university instruction in sociology in the United States, Columbia University has been known as the home of statistical sociology."

Given the state of these epistemological wars, then, House's targeting of the problems or shortcomings of statistics in sociology could hardly be described as standing on the sidelines. In fact, House's article on "Measurement in Sociology," with the same themes, appeared in the *American Journal of Sociology* in 1934. The radical neo-positivists F. Stuart Chapin and Read Bain followed with rejoinders in 1935. In his response, House (1936, 376) said, "the two latter papers [Chapin, Bain] are critical discussions of the former [paper by House]." Regarding the contrast between Chicago and Columbia, House found "the impression that Columbia stands for statistical method in sociology, Chicago for case study … widely prevalent among graduate students in sociology at the University of Chicago in 1922."

The one member of House's Group of Five whose nomination is not clearly explained in *The Development of Sociology* is Emory S. Bogardus, who was sufficiently well thought of to be elected president of the American Sociological Society in 1931. Bogardus is mentioned on five pages of *The Development of Sociology*. Two are footnote references; three are on substantive pages. The first is simply a listing of his 1922 volume *A History of Social Thought*. The second, a page reference, comes in a delineation of the division of social psychology into "two different subjects; one … treat[ing] it as a branch of psychology; while the writers of another group, including Bogardus, Williams, Dewey, Znaniecki, and Bernard, treated it mainly as a branch of sociology" (House 1936, 327). Bogardus's famous 1926 work on measuring social distance as perceived among different social groups was cited on page 351 as a footnote. House's last reference to Bogardus is on page 424, designating him as a member of the Group of Five.

Although it is surprising that House does not more clearly justify his identification of Bogardus as a critic of radical neo-positivism, we can fill in this gap by further examining Bogardus's career. He published not one but two books on the history of sociology and social thought. These books were not the sort of publication that the radical neo-positivist W.F. Ogburn anticipated as necessary for the future development of sociology. In his celebrated but controversial 1929 presidential address to the American Sociological Society "Folkways of a Scientific Sociology," Ogburn (1930) suggested that there would be little room in sociology's future for social theory and social philosophy of the traditional, rather speculative sort. Bannister (1987, 178) points out that this address "startled many colleagues at the A.S.S." Because of this "blistering" address, Charles Ellwood, Blumer's mentor at Missouri, added Ogburn to a pre-existing list of sociologists who embraced the discipline as "a dead science" (Bannister 1987, 191, 195). In House's (1936, 422) *The Development of Sociology*, the following passage is undoubtedly a reference to Ogburn's presidential address: "The emphasis on research in American sociology today is so strong that it amounts to a tendency on the part of more than one leading sociologist to assert that sociology is, essentially, a body of research methods and problems, rather than a body of knowledge or a system of concepts."

Bogardus may be known today for his quantitative sociology as evidenced in his social distance scale (Wark and Galliher 2007, 383–95) encouraged by Robert E. Park. However, Thomas E. Lasswell makes clear that he was no narrow radical neo-positivist. He had gone to Chicago after earlier studies at Northwestern University. While working at a boys' club there, he had met the pioneering sociologist Edward A. Ross, been inspired by sociology, and had proceeded to Chicago for the PHD that he attained in 1911. Lasswell emphasizes the impact that Chicago sociology had on him and mentions Small, Park, Mead, Thomas, Henderson, and Angell, noting specific debts he owed Small, Thomas, Mead, and Park. He is careful to point out that Park was "never one of Bogardus' teachers" (Lasswell 1979, 66), since in fact Bogardus had graduated and had left for Southern California years before Park joined the Chicago department. Yet many accounts refer to Bogardus as Park's "student" without further explanation.

Given the importance of such mentors and influences at Chicago, it is understandable that Bogardus showed sympathies for theoretical and conceptual sociology despite his strength in quantitative work. He would have had little sympathy for the "disposition on the part of American sociologists of one school of thought to deny the term 'scientific,' except with marked reservations, to everything in sociology but statistical methods and findings" (Bogardus 1966 [1940], 373). Lasswell (1979, 66) has pointed out that "from Small, he learned sociological theory; from Thomas, the technique and application of the method of gathering life histories by personal interview in order to learn more about the development of attitudes; and from Mead, the sociological aspects of role playing." Lasswell (1979, 67) further mentions that Bogardus encouraged exchanges with non-European sociologists at an early period and that "he had visited personally many European scholars and was a close friend to several of them," specifying Leopold von Wiese, Florian Znaniecki, and Henri Bergson. Given the theoretical and conceptual orientation of European sociology at the time as described by House, Sorokin (1929), and Mannheim (1932), this is another indication that despite his own quantitative prowess, Bogardus's conception of sociology differed from that of the radical neo-positivists.

This overall point can be advanced by a perusal of Bogardus's 1940 text, *The Development of Social Thought*, a work that remained in print for more than a quarter century. It has distinct similarities to and some differences from House's book. The similarities are enough to suggest a general agreement among Chicagoans' view of theory. For example, chapters are devoted to Small, Thomas, Park, Ellwood, and Chicago favourite Simmel. American pioneers Ward and Sumner are given chapters. Gumplowicz is accorded a chapter, and interestingly, he rather than Marx is associated with "conflict social theory." Tarde and Durkheim are each given a chapter, and Tarde's is actually longer than Durkheim's. There is a chapter on Weber's "social understanding." The first Columbia School is not overlooked, with short chapters on Giddings and Odum, although in neither case is the emphasis on their most famous and enduring epistemological work. Chicago's view of Talcott Parsons as late as 1940 is obvious in the absence of any chapter on him, Merton, or other functionalists. If this work is any indication, the theoretical and conceptual view of Chicago sociology thus survived into the middle to late 1960s. With its extensive treatment of the sort of sociology and social thought the radical neo-positivists branded as speculative and non-scientific, the book seems precisely the kind that Ogburn, in his 1929 presidential address (Ogburn 1930, 300–6), consigned to the bonfire as speculative and non-scientific. Much of Bogardus's book covers authors writing before the emergence of sociology: at least 231 pages, documenting social thought in history going back to ancient Egypt, Babylon, India, and Persia and thence to "earliest social thought." In addition, Bogardus's social psychology was evidently more in accord with what House referred to as "American Social Psychology" (chapter 27), one of the longest and best-developed portions of House's book.

WILLARD W. WALLER: ANOTHER CHICAGO CRITIC OF RADICAL NEO-POSITIVISM

At this point, I wish to go beyond the testimony of Chicagoans Floyd House and his designated Group of Five, whose publications emphasized the need to maintain a critical view of statistics (Blumer 1931; House 1934; 1936), the recognition of social philosophy and social thought in its pre-sociological form as a contribution to sociology (House 1936; Bogardus 1966 [1940]), and the recognition that conceptual precision is a key aspect of sociological sophistication that statistical metrics can never replace (Blumer 1931; Park and Burgess 1921; Eubank 1932).

The recognition that Chicago sociology *rejected* identifying statistical and correlative methods as the royal road to knowledge and as granting epistemological privilege and the realization that qualitative methods are often especially useful in developing sociological knowledge was recognized by many other Chicagoans. Robert Prus (1996, 114) suggests that "ethnographic/interactionist research ... became the vital legacy of the Chicago school of sociology," and he proceeds to list the impressive number of Chicagoans who contributed to this qualitative style of research. Richard Evans (1986–87, 119–20) uses the phrase "the case-study-insight method" to identify Chicago's qualitative tradition and points out that when Columbia's Giddings and his graduate students "began to attack the 'case study natural history method,'" this method already "was most closely identified with Chicago." Evans (1986–87, 119) points out that although Chicago sociologists "had long used statistics in their work ... their central methodological apparatus was 'insight' – the ability of the sociologist to empathicly [sic] reconstruct the human situation of which statistics might only be a shadow. Thus, for many Chicago sociologists, qualitative approaches were often much more useful than statistical ones. Sociologists, they believed, needed to see and feel the social situations they were studying – thus Chicago sociologists relied on the case study and the natural history."

Although the emphasis on insight had always been a Chicago insistence, Evans (1986–87, 120) points out that Willard Waller "caught the essence of this position in 1934 when he argued that 'Quantification is not the touchstone of scientific method. Insight is the touchstone.'" Waller's 1934 article, "Insight and Scientific Method," insists that "[t]he essence of scientific method is an attempt to obtain insight." Radical neo-positivists of the Giddings school were not likely to warm to the warning that "[s]tatistics has valid uses but is justified as scientific procedure only to the extent to which it is used to subserve insight," followed by Waller's (1934, 285) observations that the (qualitative) case study was "a most useful" procedure for accessing insight and "[t]he view of scientific method as a struggle to obtain insight forces the admission that all science is half art ... This holds *a fortiori* for sociology." The article itself repeatedly emphasized that statistics were justified only when they could be used to generate insight, that much sociological knowledge depended "as yet [on] generalization from a single case," and that "the belief that what is not quantified is not science" must be rejected (Waller 1934, 285). This was very distant from the radical neo-positivists' position that scientific knowledge advanced from a primitive ideological disposition to observational methods to metrical methods at the apex of scientific achievement. As if adding insult to injury, Waller repeatedly attacked the epistemological position of Karl Pearson, who had provided a philosophical justification for the new correlative statistics in his famous book, *The Grammar of Science*, and whose philosophy of science had been championed by Franklin Giddings as the cornerstone of radical neo-positivism (Hinkle 1994, 35). Waller showed his own Chicago debts by quoting Herbert Blumer at length, from both his "Science without Concepts" and his earlier *American Journal of Sociology* 1930 critique of radical neo-positivist George Lundberg's book *Social Research*.

Waller's somewhat agonistic defence of case study and qualitative sociology against the radical neo-positivists is somewhat ironic, given that his own training as a sociologist had exposed him both to the Chicago School, where he acquired an MA, and later to quantitative sociology when he worked on his PhD at the University of Pennsylvania, where two prominent members were Giddings "men," Stuart A. Rice and James P. Lichtenberger. Prus (1996, 122) points out this interesting situation in his comment that "[w]hile Waller obtained his doctorate from Pennsylvania State University, he received his MA from the University of Chicago and the impact of Waller's earlier education is most apparent."

Waller's life and background have been fully examined by Goode, Furstenberg, and Mitchell (1970). They point out the importance of Waller's "five quarters" spent at Chicago from 1923 to 1926. They emphasize that "Chicago was indeed the only intellectual center of American sociology" and that "[i]f it was possible to receive good training in sociology during the 1920's, only the University of Chicago offered it" (Goode et al. 1970, 20). They mention important figures at Chicago at that time, such as the departmental founder Albion Small, Robert E. Park, Ellsworth Faris, Ernest W. Burgess, and Edward Sapir. They also mention Floyd N. House, "then considered a rising young theoretician of the field" (1970, 20). They mention that Waller was a former secondary school teacher and observe that "[i]n the prestige rankings of graduate students," such secondary school teachers ranked "rather low." Despite belonging "to this low-prestige group, yet the elite of his time did respect [Waller]" (1970, 21). They mention that the emerging elite included one of House's Group of Five, Herbert Blumer. Waller and Blumer met in one of Faris's classes, and they soon "became companions during workouts in the gymnasium and on the track. They talked frequently about athletics. Waller was fascinated by Blumer's stories about his professional football career" (1970, 21).

Waller left for the University of Pennsylvania in 1926 both to enter the PhD program and to teach there as an instructor. Waller came to a department heavily influenced by radical neo-positivism through the influence of Giddings's doctoral students Rice and Lichtenberger. Goode et al. (1970, 28) point out that his exposure to Rice, "a pioneer in the use of quantitative methods," led Waller to collaborate in a quantitative study of stereotypes. This Goode et al. (1970, 28) refer to as Waller's "one foray into quantitative and statistical methods."

Despite his initiation into Columbia-style radical neo-positivism at Pennsylvania, and perhaps because of it, Waller became more epistemologically aware and more committed to the Chicago position. This came about because, as Goode et al. (1970, 26) point out, "Early in his Philadelphia stay, Waller was identified as an exponent of the 'Chicago School,' which was respected but by no means dominant at his new university." In fact, in notes unpublished until 1970, Waller suggested that it was only *after* he arrived at Pennsylvania that he came to consciously identify with "the Chicago system of sociology." This was because Waller (in Goode et al. 1970, 27) met a "Mr. Y. who immediately began to attack the Chicago school of sociology and, as I thought, to ridicule me as a representative of it. He was joking, but he soon got me into a state of mind where I was not joking. I regarded myself as the chosen defender of the Chicago system ... I set out to prove its superiority to all other systems." Goode et al. (1970, 31) point out that Waller "dedicated his [doctoral] thesis to Ellsworth Faris," chairman of Chicago's department, rather than to one of his new connections at Pennsylvania and refer to this as "a sign" of Chicago's continuing influence on him.

Waller's position in "Insight and Scientific Method" did offend the more extreme apostles of radical neo-positivism characterized by Hinkle (1994, 34) as encompassing "A Statistically-Centered, Neo-Empiricist, Neo-positivist Epistemology-Methodology." One of them was George Lundberg. Lundberg had taken his PHD at the University of Minnesota where Stuart Chapin presided as another of the far-flung Giddings "men" and PHDs. He was also influenced by another Minnesota positivist, L.L. Bernard, and eventually by Giddings himself in Lundberg's post-graduate year of 1927 (Evans 1986–87, 120). Goode et al. (1970) point out that Lundberg attacked "Insight and Scientific Method" at the 1935 meetings of the American Sociological Society and that Waller replied to this attack. In the words of Goode et al. (1970, 54), "Waller conceded the importance of operationalism which Lundberg was espousing, but denied that it excluded all other procedures. His response is a thoughtful but severe critique of rigid quantification in social scientific research, in a mechanical imitation of the social sciences." As Richard Evans points out:

By the beginning of the 1930s the two sides of the debate had lined up. On the side of the 'operationalists,' as many quantifiers began calling themselves in the early 1930s, were some of Giddings' more prominent students, Stuart Chapin, Frank Hankins, and others plus a number of sociologists who came from a variety of institutional backgrounds ... On the side of case-study-insight [qualitative] method, the prominent defenders were all Chicago men: Charles Ellsworth [sic; probably a typographical error for Herbert Blumer's Chicago-trained mentor at the University of Missouri, Charles Ellwood], Floyd N. House, Willard Waller, and others (1986–87, 120).

CONCLUSION

To sum up, a trio of British sociological historians writing in the 1980s
have asserted that several features commonly associated with Chicago
sociology were "myths" and misconceptions propagated by latter-day
sociological historians from the 1970s with no direct links to Chicago.
Instead, this trio provide several reasons why these "myths" arose in the
first place. But the features that the British trio have rejected as "myths"
were accepted as valid descriptors and generalizations about Chicago
sociology from as early as 1922 (when House first entered the Chicago
department) and as late as 1936 when he published *The Development
of Sociology* and clearly pointed to "the research undertakings of staff
members, students, and former students at the University of Chicago"
as the "principal exceptions" to the "preponderant ... tendency to the
use of statistical and other quantitative methods" in American sociology. House (1936, 422–33) explicitly points to the Chicagoans' primary
use of case study and natural history methods as examples of these
non-statistical and non-quantitative methods. I believe that behind
these stated differences over methods and other matters there was a
more deep-seated difference, with the Chicagoans rejecting radical neo-
positivism while Giddings and his doctoral students (and eventually
others) championing radical neo-positivism. Given my own experience
with radical neo-positivists from the 1970s, I would warn the British
trio that radical neo-positivists were not tolerant pluralists who just
wanted further recognition of quantitative methods to balance qualitative ones. Radical neo-positivists had a very clear gospel about what
science consisted of, and this led to them to very clear statements over
the years decrying other conceptions of sociology and denying them the
prestige-bearing designation as "science" (see Nettler 1970).

    At any rate, given the choice between the latter-day British "Gang
of Three" of sociological historians from the 1980s and Chicago's
own "Group of Five" from the 1930s writing as contemporary members of Chicago sociology, I have no hesitation in deciding in favour
of the Chicagoans as to what constitutes myth and reality in Chicago
sociology. Bulmer, Harvey, and Hammersley make one good point:
that Chicago sociology should have its quantitative sociology covered in sociological histories. But we do not need to resort to the
language of "myth" and error when we continue to associate the
Chicagoans with an early, special, and enduring proclivity to qualitative methodologies that lasted at least until the end of the 1950s.

REFERENCES

Bain, Read. 1935. "Measurement in Sociology." *American Journal of Sociology* 40:481–8

Bannister, Robert C. 1987. *Sociology and Scientism: The American Quest for Objectivity, 1880–1940*. Chapel Hill and London: University of North Carolina Press

Blumer, Herbert. 1931. "Science without Concepts." *American Journal of Sociology* 36:515–33

Bogardus, Emory S. 1926. "Social Distance in the City." *Proceedings and Publications of the American Sociological Society* 20:40–6

– 1966 [1940]. *The Development of Social Thought*. New York: David McKay

Bulmer, Martin. 1981. "Quantification and Chicago Social Science in the 1920s: A Neglected Tradition." *Journal of the History of the Behavioral Sciences* 17:312–31

– 1984. *The Chicago School of Sociology: Institutionalization, Diversity, and the Rise of Sociological Research*. Chicago: University of Chicago Press

Chapin, F. Stuart. 1935. "Measurement in Sociology." *American Journal of Sociology* 40:476–80

Eubank, Earle E. 1932. *The Concepts of Sociology*. Boston: D.C. Heath

Evans, Richard. 1986–87. "Sociological Journals and the 'Decline' of Chicago Sociology: 1929–1945." *History of Sociology: An International Review* 6–7:109–30

Goode, William J., Frank F. Furstenberg, Jr, and Larry R. Mitchell. 1970. "Introduction." In *Willard W. Waller on the Family, Education and War: Selected Writings*, edited by William J. Goode, Frank F. Furstenberg, and Larry R. Mitchell, 1–110. Chicago and London: University of Chicago Press

Hammersley, Martyn. 1989. *The Dilemma of Qualitative Method: Herbert Blumer and the Chicago Tradition*. London: Routledge

Harvey, Lee. 1987. *Myths of the Chicago School of Sociology*. Aldershot, UK: Gower

Hinkle, Roscoe C. 1994. *Developments in American Sociological Theory, 1915–1950*. Albany: State University of New York Press

House, Floyd Nelson. 1934. "Measurement in Sociology." *American Journal of Sociology* 40:1–11

– 1936. *The Development of Sociology*. New York: McGraw-Hill

Jones, Robert Alun, and Sidney Kronus. 1976. "Professional Sociologists and the History of Sociology: A Survey of Recent Opinion." *Journal of the History of the Behavioral Sciences* 12:3–13

Lasswell, Thomas E. 1979. "Emory S. Bogardus." In *International Encyclopedia of the Social Sciences, Biographical Supplement*, vol. 18, edited by David L. Sills, 65–8. New York: Free Press

Mannheim, Karl. "American Sociology." 1932. *American Journal of Sociology* 38:273–82

Nettler, Gwyn. 1970. *Explanations*. New York: McGraw-Hill

Nock, David A. 2004. "The Myth about 'Myths of the Chicago School': Evidence from Floyd Nelson House." *The American Sociologist* 35:63–79

Ogburn, W.F. 1930. "The Folkways of a Scientific Sociology." *Scientific Monthly* 30:300–6

Park, Robert E. and Ernest W. Burgess 1921. *An Introduction to the Science of Society*. Chicago: University of Chicago Press

Parsons, Talcott. 1937. *The Structure of Social Action*. New York: McGraw-Hill, Free Press. Second edition 1968

Prus, Robert. 1996. *Symbolic Interaction and Ethnographic Research: Intersubjectivity and the Study of Human Lived Experience*. Albany: State University of New York Press

Sorokin, Pitirim. 1929. "Some Contrasts between European and American Sociology." *Social Forces* 8:57–62

Waller, Willard. 1934. "Insight and Scientific Method." *American Journal of Sociology* 40(3):285–97

Wark, Colin, and John F. Galliher. 2007. "Emory Bogardus and the Origins of the Social Distance Scale." *The American Sociologist* 38:383–95

4

After the Barren Search for Laws

GEORGE PARK

This chapter is offered as a step toward bringing scientific rigor into the observation of world-bending mass-belief systems and their political manipulation. I would urge timely attention to the inadequacy of the conventional wisdom on the new turmoil of faith warring and "terror" alerts that have beset the big news of our time since the last century's age of utopian ideology petered out. The premise I propose to explore is this: *Current sociological thought has misdirected our attention by assuming that history can be explained on a storybook cause-and-effect basis.* A reader should accept as a starting point that chaos theory argues sharply against applying chance-free findings to chance-rich event sequences. The reason this caution is regularly ignored in sociological reasoning is that statistical techniques are held to "control" chance. This argument only applies in the actual experimental situation in effect for the time-and-space setting of one's relevant observations. History does not take place in such settings but in a boundless flow of contagious events that, moving at the speed of time, cannot be submitted to observation. The grand uncertainty principle of Heisenberg fades a bit when set beside the vast probability of error in any search for exact observation of human affairs. But I set my stage in this big way only to stake a very small claim. I want my reader to accept the simple premise that observation lies at the heart of all science. It is a premise that Robert E. Park (REP) offered his descendants in sociology not so much through argument as through example. Why has sociology since "the Chicago School" come to prefer indirect inference about social process to the raw observation of human events?

The most relevant answer will surely be found in the structure of action within our sociological professions as such.

My title is "After the Barren Search for Laws," because we are turning away – some of us, at least – from the search for grand theories to a recognition that observable regularities in the human arena need sharpened recognition and contextual understanding, not merely inferential "explanation." In the terms so nicely offered by Abraham Kaplan (1964, 327ff), I like the "pattern" model before the "deductive." In the context of this preference is another: I like actually observing a phenomenon of special interest before I classify it. In the context of this, in turn, is my affinity for the phenomenological way in sociological analysis. I like to say that reasoning from data *is not* reasoning from observation. Simple examples: exact data on your age and work history don't tell me as much about who and what you are as my eyes and ears can tell me; standard measures of "traumatic stress" are not a good basis for taking action unless you are addressing a standard person. I like to say about sociological intercourse that people can talk without a common language but megabytes of data only beep. Depending on bona-fide data for your reckoning of the social reality around you can be simply stupid.

I'll concentrate on what I privately think of as "deep" (insider/ evocative) observation but prefer here just to call "direct observation." Flippant use of direct observation *at second-hand* has often got us lost in the Garden of Wild Rhetoric. I give just one instance. Henry Murray (1938) looked hard for personal "felt needs" that could differentiate individuals in a sample of male students at Harvard. He found a score or more. One example: a "need for achievement" (shortened as "*n*-achievement"). This finding from direct observation was picked up years later and made famous by a crusading follower who thought "we" should train, for example, "Africans" to have more *n*-achievement – this would improve Third-World economies. The evidence from the children's armies and body-hackers around western and central Africa – news about other uses for a blind "achievement" drive – started coming in soon after. Remote sensing can have good uses, but pulling good data out of context can only reveal the one-dimensionality of data as such.

After the barren search for transcendental meaning in human history came sociology. After the barren search for behavioural laws governing every kind of human society came organic/equilibrium models for the structuralist and cultural solitudes for the comparative sociologists or for culture/personality models in anthropology. Out of these worlds of incompatible systems frozen in time came the shrug of relativism. In time, it was answered by an interim flight back to Grand Theory (neo-Marxism for sociology, counter-organic French structuralism for anthropology), as if to say we can find a Theory of Everything if we only knuckle down. When that had had its day, there were the several utterances of a post-modern conviction that, somehow, there were still new things to be said. And somehow, after that was done, the avid reader began discovering that the best sociology had already been written. It was directly concerned with the way things social actually happen. The "applied" fields of social science – politics and economics – have always been happy enough with this situation. I look forward to a time when inductivism will thrive in all our fields and sociologists will find as much to appreciate in human social life as botanists find in their appointed fields. I take it on trust that botanists are driven more by professional curiosity than by n-achievement.

With the Chicago School that bred me, I make a distinction between "direct" and "participant" observation. I use the latter term for getting to know a people by making close friends within it. I use "direct observation" as an opposite to "remote" or "inferential" work relying wholly on archival and survey data. But I like to think that direct observation is inherently a private business. Fieldwork, at least for the ethnologist, is always a little hypnotic, a total immersion in fresh and fascinating sensory experience whose success depends on keeping your head afloat on a stream of novelties you will need to fathom. Progress comes in a broken series of episodes, each belonging to a tale of its own. You will need to brood, or you will never see all the connections. It can involve not so much a bright flash of insight – the sort of flash that does come to you in lively discussions at table or in the lecture hall – but rather, you find yourself drawn by skepsis into meditation and by meditation toward the scattered beginnings of analysis. Never through all of this do you lose yourself to "science." As you come to know where you are in a new culture world, whether far away or just across town, you are drawn in, little by little, by the inherent logic that governs the action of everyday life there. Your proper object now can't be artful construction of a series of learned papers meaningless to your mates there. Your purpose is to know that you know them well: you are at home in the mentality that grows there.

I'm saying that open-air participant observation without this change in your self can't guarantee the insight needed to grasp the ruling elements in this new-to-you social system. Events are a continual distraction. The strain between participating and observing has to drop away. I think this notion will help us later on to understand why REP was sociologist first – always the direct observer he had been as a journalist – then activist, and only third "scientist" in the current meaning. He never dreamt of systematizing history. His "human ecology" called for nothing of that sort, just as Darwin's *Origin* called for a randomizing mechanism to account for the plethora of species, living and extinct. I've always supposed REP saw before he died that Talcott Parsons at Harvard would be prepared to Hegelianize sociology if he could. It is one thing to systematize a garden, another to claim there is only one true way to do it.

I won't ask how important my cast of thought may be for students of Bonóbos. These researchers don't fool themselves that they know how to mingle with their animals – participate in their social lives. They know them and know them well, through the direct observation of social action, understandable in the rainforest in humanist terms but only there presented plain and unvarnished to the eye as among our own kind it never can be. My sceptical remarks are meant for the Humános. We can ask them to do some of our thinking for us, though we had better not let them do it all. Once, long ago, I even supposed in my first field study of a culturally self-contained Humáno community that I might be lucky enough to find and catechize one good informant who would answer all my questions – leaving me only the task of a "write-up." Well, try teaching your child the infinitesimal calculus without the use of graphics. The anthropologist depending on "interviews" must learn to "participate" in the Humáno social life as well, and the sociologist depending on "participant observation" must learn to read minds. This is not what "science" demands – of course, I mean the iconic institution that goes by that name. But the idea of science is something else and would have us read minds as well as we can. For social science, the only reality of deep concern is what REP usually referred to as the "mentality" shared by any self-organized human group. Oddly, students of Bonóbos seem to understand that their subject's mentality is the real object of an observer's game.

You will find in Fred Matthews's thoughtful biography of REP a tone of puzzlement as he asks why it should have taken a Swedish economist (Gunnar Myrdal in *An American Dilemma*, 1944) to properly sound a warning blast on the strategic danger of a continuing racial segregation of black and white in America. Why was the leading American sociologist in the field of race relations not an activist? Perhaps you will agree with me that Myrdal could and would feel privileged as an outsider to blow the horn loud, while an insider – feeling the burden of White Man's Disgrace each time he looked a black friend in the eyes – might see a need to hold fire. Park, of course, crossed over. He wandered the South as a black, "mingling" not just "participating": an observer still but now bearing the stigma of the "coloured man" in public. As far as I know, he never carried a notebook through those months. His object was knowledge. I believe he prized the experience as a needed form of self-improvement. He didn't exploit his experience as a journalist/publicist might but managed to make a living as a free-booting producer for secular leadership on the other side of a daunting colour line.

Direct observation is a prize the sociologist has at hand but which the historian is largely denied. History, as it was when sociology was barely teething, was able through the automatic consensus of hindsight to restrict its scope to matters of agreed significance and known outcome. With the notable facts given, only their rich implications were subject to debate. Since a "science" approach to truth has no relevance in this research, history could be made "perfect enough to convince" when argued skilfully under forensic rules. Sociologists may find the historian suffering from weak evidence exactly about those implications – the very stuff that separates history from chronicle. But the idea of history that R.G. Collingwood (*The Idea of History*, 1944) bequeathed to a fast-growing post-Chicago social science was quite a different idea – historians should devote themselves to the professional recollection of foregone ways of social thought. Notably, sociologists who have since taken up past-time projects are not aiming to explain critical events but to explore historically defined periods in their social settings, open to study under an immersion process closely akin to proper fieldwork. This is a transposition of ethnographic methods to regional cultures in past time, be it the so-called Ancient World or the near-modern ethnos within the sweep of one of our world's yet surviving "great traditions." This kind of sociology brings with it the privilege of "direct observation" in its essentials. There is massive evidence, subjective and physical, to comb – and plenty of brooding time. Participation is ruled out, you may say, but in the four-dimensional studies within a mass society that are still typical of sociology today, the microsociological methods that so well suit the pedestrian community or street gang won't serve. Survey methods can, if there is the will to interpret findings with unhurried care. Participant observers (of the Uncle-always-said type) can only be fifth wheels. Did Talcott Parsons become so wise about what he called "THE family" by butting in on family life in lower middle-class Somerville? I can only picture the quondam master of Grand Theory as a short, stout klutz when it came to fieldwork. Among the many still-readable sociologists who did it right at mid-century last, C. Wright Mills stands out for most of us. Who would say he was not a sharp observer? Direct observation happens face-to-face, mind-to-mind. It is crucial to comprehension, and comprehension is the better part of science. But sharpness in observation is intuitive, personal, a talent born of practice and driven not by duty but by acumen.

The best master of direct observation in our field that I know of was not an accredited sociologist at all but would have belonged instantly in the Chicago circle, at least with Chicagoans of a "qualitative proclivity" in Nock's (this volume) words. I refer to Robert Coles (1997), who practised a methodological approach he called documentary work – a combination of participant observation, unstructured interviews, and narrative techniques, premised on the assumption that the product of documentary work is a social construction emergent from the interaction between the observer and the observed. It is a means of accessing the empirical without falling into the epistemological trap of objectivist posturing. If I were designing a graduate seminar today, I would assign his entire five-volume series, *Children of Crisis* (1964–77), and start by asking why we don't bother with such mundane stuff in sociology. The first answer, I suppose, and perhaps the final one would be along these lines: "Science demands ... because the rules of upper-case Science are humankind's sole means of knowing objective certainty." Well, my riposte is, if the Garden of Eden was evidently quite small (population two), the Garden of Certainty is even smaller. No room for the merely "reasoned" certainties of the hoi polloi there. Very little knowledge has an eternal shelf-life, and none that *is* certain comes close to illuminating social history – which I take to be our subject. Take the methodological positivist seriously, and the scope of your social science must enjoy the approximate dimensions of a downtown garden.

History has known no better scolding than Karl Popper's in *The Open Society and Its Enemies* (1946). His personal crusade against "historicism" was addressed to sociology, though it is hard to find him glossed on that score in either our annals or the historians'. Does history have meaning? None that a bright student would need to download. Certainly, the only laws followed are those of Chaos, though accounts of history are full of cadence, whether for grief or triumph. Life is rich enough in meaning for its greats, their victims, and anyone else who is watching. Like Nature, upper-case History can't be denied instructive power. Any proper social science is open to History's instruction, as (say) Karl Marx was, or his master Georg Wilhelm Friedrich Hegel before him. As Marx rethought Hegel, the rest of us have had to rethink Marx. As he scolded while he pondered, so have we. The proof that we don't just download a pure Marx is that all of us living in relatively open societies know we have to warp Marx to make him relevant – that is to say, the unkindest blow of all would be to style him the Mother of all that Marxism became. Can political ecology reclaim the real KM? Rethinking is the door key to any science that can simply by reason of its nature never be finished.

I'd be liable to blame if, as grandson, I chose to style REP as a father of twentieth-century sociology. He is no guiltier than Marx for the way his ideas have fared in other hands. In particular, he was not responsible for the failure of sociology to become a force in the Westernized world, even in applied fields. What little we have done to sweep the applied science of social work clean of neo-Freudian babble about buried childhood trauma is nicely equalled on the scales of merit to what we have done in the way of keeping third-rate neo-cons out of the White House, mercenary profiteers out of the narcotics industry – or violence out of the streets, the massive prison system, and popular kiddy-crime culture. Why is deregulation any healthier in the case of our quasi-criminal corporate worlds than it is in our crime-breeding ghettos? The world that gave us "Just Say No" also gave us – as a chosen academic elite – the professional savvy to see and demonstrate the absurdities in any "Just-don't-do-it" approach to social control in heterogeneous, stressed-out, neck-high-in-debt, advert-ridden wonder-worlds like ours. As at the opposite pole, the viciously over-armed children's armies and un-uniformed scramblers of central and west and northeast Africa, it is hard to believe that a culture of prudence can be seen to be so totally lacking. On our own continents we surely know, or ought to know, that

our schools should not be designed like factories, that our democracy can't thrive in a laissez-faire moral climate at Political Ground
Zero, that even our society's dearest members (the ones with guaran-
teed free lunch until they "grow up") can only too easily "grow up
absurd" in the routine scramble for self-importance we have relegated them to in their factory schools. All this and so much more.
Some of us rant well and often in the classroom, knowing with a
twinge of bitterness that we won't change the Wisdom prevailing in
the corridors of real life. REP went down to Nashville on his retirement from Chicago, wanting to help some of his former black students to teach a new generation what he supposed sociology ought
to be about. He still thought like a dedicated journalist in one sense.
He thought the written word might make all the difference, just as it
very nearly had in the French Enlightenment. Harangue was not his
instrument. This he would have realized when the plebeian newsletter, which he'd co-conspired with his former instructor in philosophy, John Dewey, met an early end. That was 1892, and the project
was in today's diction a "green" mag to be called *Thought News*.
The founders had a look at the first issue and appear to have conceded it hadn't got either the right title or the right voice. I wish I
could have found the one-time proofs of *Thought News* in our attic
along with the later correspondence between REP and Booker T.
Washington – but the family house was built much later (in Black
Forest style) after the study in Germany, after *The Crowd and the
Public*, on a hill with a clear view far, far from Boston and, inferen-
tially, from Harvard where REP would start (and soon quit) teaching
(German) philosophy.

It would be ten years, much of it spent as a travelling writer and
skilled facilitator in gaining personal acquaintance with race problems in the southern states, before the middle-aged sociologist settled
into academia (at Chicago) as a teacher. He spent that intervening
decade largely as a participant observer, mingler, and brooder on the
unique social structure of the American South. His independent personal style continued at Chicago, reflecting for us a simple fact: having finally found his niche, REP was determined to exploit it to
further the sociological work he had by now planned – not to "make
a good career" and not to take charge and "change the world" but
do whatever he could to make the nation's darker reaches known.
Then as now, the social system was pulling two ways on a social
scientist – toward "relevance" and toward "pure science." But in the

1920s, "relevance" was centred on the tangible "payoff" – "pure science" was effete, a waste of the people's money. Then as now, the loudest *vox* in the populace had a fundamentalist ring.

I am able to say that I think we are more nuanced than that today. One social science (economics) has even become officially "relevant," as confirmed by think tanks, consulting fees, and Nobels. Another branch of sociology (criminology) has facilitated the privatization of a vast prison system, at last making it profitable to keep millions (mainly blacks) indefinitely incarcerated. But I confess I am not very pleased with the way applied science has affected social history in these two cases, though I do feel both cases are indeed "relevant." Poor, dear, flamboyant Grampa would be stomping in his grave, as I'm sure he was when the Black Power movement looked like it was being thrown off-track, when home-grown assassinations came into vogue. Don't we know enough by this time about the vagaries of government and its fatuous complacency to recognize when and where the cleanups are due? I think we do. I have a pretty large library of books that tell all, case by case. I read a dozen journals, mainly but not only on the left, which ferret out and spell out in detail the latest scams funded by funny money. Even television (CNN) records quite a bit of all this, and more "effete" media spell out much more. We are roundly shocked. We discuss it. Then we sit back and wait for the next play, saying why don't "they" do something, just once?

I'll confess some blame. I used to think that my classroom harangues were opening minds. I thought an open mind needs an open society and hell shouldn't bar the way. More recently, I've decided that the problem is a conspiracy to keep good folks in their seats and trust the pilot even when he's diving. I call the recent Taser scandals in evidence. I even think the prescription drug Ritalin really is the opiate of the people just now: is attention deficit a "disorder" when the "order" implied missing is absurd? These are neglectables perhaps, petty complaints. But map them all, and their omnipresence will shake you. I have a suggestion that is slightly new and a bit fragile as big ideas go, but I ask to be taken seriously just for now. There is an idea afloat phrased as "social capital" – an economic term for public goods that could be but normally aren't convertible to currency. My suggestion is to play that game out as a substitute for our quite general concept, social structure. Now start evaluating our "capital" – all our institutions: the values added, the negatives introduced, the needs evoked, needs met.

Every society has "social capital" in the sense that much time and thought and bureaucratic shuffleboard has been invested in its social institutions. Over time, these capital assets may actually appreciate, or they may rot out, possibly leaving the society in crisis. Sometimes we call these institutions "structural" – i.e., we begin to see them as elements of a social structure. But some of the assets are not "structural" in the usual sense we have for the term in sociology. National pride is everywhere valued. It is positive social capital in Quebec – but in Serbia? Some assets, like dance, language, stories and sayings, and (maybe) wisdom, we class as "culture." Now, social capital is shared. As such, it becomes vulnerable to misuse, abuse, intentional innovation, or erosion in the face of invasive events. Individuals either learn to adapt and repair when "things fall apart" – or they may find their old moral strategies becoming "dysfunctional." This is the sociological side of Ritalin's economic success. Another bit would be its success as a teenage now-let's-say-yes drug. Shifting your diction from "social structure" to "social capital" shifts your contextual view of institutions. You can see "social class" or "marriage" or "consolidated high schools" or "endogamy" in both black and red terms – none of that old functionalist insistence that if it survives, it must fit. Don't say good-bye to social Darwinism, then: rather, explore any institution's terms of office in light of its survival value as social capital. A proper sociological study of Ritalin where I live would get into the heart of many matters: youth peer groups, parenthood, medicine, psychiatry, Zeitgeist, regnant mentalities.

Now, finally, look at the institutions of fundamentalism in the several Christian and Muslim denominations. Ask who their institutions belong to. Are they not marginal, back-country populations, powerless to meet the rising expectations of a new and surplus generation? These are the people farthest down, as Booker T. (and REP) would put it. Ask then how power has come into their hands, how they came in possession of this almost invisible social capital. It's not a simple question, but it can be answered in each case, for each region, each immigrant ethnos, each vast expanse of ghetto life in each new city on each continent. But you will not find the answers by supposing that all these threatening signs, the class crimes and suicide bombs, all the bitterly mounting social movements are somehow phony, not truly intentional, not responding to need, not driven by fury, only by the witchery of their self-appointed leaders.

REFERENCES

Coles, R. 1964–77. *Children of Crisis*. Boston: Little Brown
– 1997. "Doing Documentary Work." Oxford: Oxford University Press
Collingwood, R.G. 1944. *The Idea of History*. Oxford: Oxford University
   Press
Darwin, Charles. 1859. *On the Origin of Species*. London: John Murray
   Publisher
Kaplan, Abraham. 1964. *The Conduct of Inquiry: Methodology for
   Behavioral Science*. San Francisco: Chandler
Matthews, Fred H. 1977. "Quest for an American Sociology: Robert E.
   Park and the Chicago School." Montreal: McGill-Queen's University
   Press
Murray, Henry. 1938. *Explorations in Personality*. Oxford: Oxford
   University Press
Myrdal, Gunner. 1944. *An American Dilemma: The Negro Problem and
   Modern Democracy*. New York: Harper Brothers
Park, Robert E. 1972. *The Crowd and the Public and Other Essays*.
   Chicago: University of Chicago Press
Popper, Karl. 1946. *The Open Society and Its Enemies*. London:
   Routledge

SECTION II
Mead and Goffman: Key Thinkers of the Chicago School Diaspora

Another way the Chicago School Diaspora engages with the tradition involves the meaning attached to various key thinkers and the nature and source of their ideas. The Department of Sociology at Chicago has a long and highly prestigious list of former faculty and students. However, not all of them are considered part of the Chicago School tradition: sociology done at the University of Chicago is not the same thing as "Chicago School sociology." Similarly, some individuals associated with the school are accorded more scholarly attention than others, and the amount of emphasis given to a particular individual varies through time.

Three individuals stand out from the rest in terms of the attention they attract from scholars included in this volume: Robert Park, George Herbert Mead, and Erving Goffman. Section II deals with Mead and Goffman, and section III contains chapters based on Park's work. Thus, the chapters in sections II and III illustrate the ongoing significance of particular theorists and provide concrete examples of the differing ways scholars engage with these key theorists of the Chicago School Diaspora. Moreover, these two sections document the ongoing debate within the Chicago School tradition over the relative importance of social psychology (section II) and social organization (section III).

The first pair of chapters in section II focus on the ideas of George Herbert Mead (1863–1931). Mead, who taught at Chicago from 1894 until his death in 1931, was an important early contributor to the social psychology strand of Chicago School sociology. In chapter 5, "Finding G.H. Mead's Social Ontology in his Engagement with Key Intellectual Influences," Anthony Puddephatt reconceptualizes Mead's social ontology by contextualizing his thought in relation to a diverse set of intellectual influences: Kant, Hegel, and the romantic idealists; Darwin and evolutionary thought; Peirce, James, and the American pragmatists; and the orientation to time, perspective, and emergence evident in the works of Whitehead and Bergson. In chapter 6, "Mending Mead's 'I' and 'Me' Distinction," Gary Cook, through a close reading of Mead, identifies a number of inconsistencies in Mead's use of the terms "I" and "me" and suggests five modifications in how the terms are conceptualized and applied in order to retain their analytic power while removing the inconsistencies.

Erving Goffman (1922–1982) is the subject of the second pair of chapters. The juxtapositioning of Mead and Goffman is informative in several ways. In comparison to Mead, Goffman's formal association with Chicago was very short. Goffman was a graduate student at Chicago, completing his MA and PHD in 1949 and 1953, respectively, and then left for a faculty position at Berkeley. Moreover, whereas the interest in Mead represents a desire to examine and unpack ideas at the centre of much Chicago School sociology, much of the interest in Goffman focuses on understanding boundaries: Is he or is he not a symbolic interactionist? How is it that he is so heavily cited yet not incorporated into mainstream sociology? In chapter 7, "Working the Chicago Interstices: Warner and Goffman's Intellectual Formation," Greg Smith and Yves Winkin explore the connection between Goffman and William Lloyd Warner, a Chicago faculty member rarely associated with the Chicago School but one whom they see as a key figure for understanding Goffman's ideas. In chapter 8, "Reading Goffman: On the Creation of an Enigmatic Founder," Isher-Paul Sahni articulates the complex set of factors responsible for Goffman's enigmatic status within the discipline of sociology: someone who is recognized as an influential figure but resists absorption into mainstream sociology.

5

Finding G.H. Mead's Social Ontology in His Engagement with Key Intellectual Influences

ANTONY J. PUDDEPHATT

George Herbert Mead is a central figure in the Chicago School tradition, leaving a lasting influence on generations of sociologists. His teachings on social psychology have formed the basis for how sociologists conceive of the self, social action, and the interplay of the individual and society. Mead's (1934) classic book *Mind, Self, and Society* is standard reading for any course on social psychology or sociological theory. As a result of the wide dissemination of Mead's basic ideas, sociologists have been influenced by Mead in a variety of ways, but it is the symbolic interactionists who have been most central in expositing Mead's thought and defining his significance as an important sociological thinker (e.g., Blumer 1966; 1969; 2004; Manis and Meltzer 1978; Prus 1996). As a result of this collective definition, Mead has been deemed most important for his contributions to the study of symbolic interaction, while his pragmatist contributions and his thoughts about the importance of materialist, temporal, organic, and non-symbolic processes in social conduct are often neglected (for discussions of this, see Joas 1985; Cook 1993; Puddephatt 2009). This often leaves a distorted view of Mead's social ontology on the part of the sociological community; that is, his bedrock assumptions about the nature of social life are often simplified or misunderstood.

In this chapter, I illustrate how Mead's neglected emphasis on the material, organic, and non-symbolic foundations of social life is vital to a more complete understanding of Mead's thought about the social. I accomplish this by providing a brief intellectual history of Mead, showing his connection to other prominent thinkers. I then discuss the growth of his ideas by considering how he engaged with several important intellectual precursors, drawing contrasts with them in an effort to articulate his own position. The development of Mead's thought is difficult to map accurately, because it is complex and spans a number of diverse influences. Still, it is possible to achieve a reasonable context of his intellectual development through Mead's own admissions of his intellectual debts (e.g., Mead 1909; 1930; 1936a; 1936b), his biographical history (Joas 1985; Cook 1993; Deegan 2001), and various secondary accounts (Doan 1956; Lowy 1993) that compare Mead's thought to his contemporaries, glean his major influences, and attempt to distill his more original contributions.

From this, I discuss implications for a more complete understanding of his assumptions about meaning, knowledge, and social action. I demonstrate the importance of social action as a material practice in Mead's thought as a way to overcome the problems germane to the various idealist approaches he would be influenced by but inevitably strive to move beyond. At the same time, I show that Mead was no naive realist either and also distanced himself from this by arguing for the relativity of perspectives and the processual way in which we generate intersubjective meanings in the world around us. What remains is a pragmatist and naturalistic conception of the social as a building up of meaningful perspectives that are nevertheless richly grounded in the concrete material environments of actors through time.

KANT AND THE ROMANTIC IDEALISTS

Mead was heavily influenced by Kant early on when he began his studies at Oberlin College in the 1880s (Joas 1985, 16–18). Mead valued Kant's recognition that knowledge is not a passive product of bare perception or a result of atomistic inputs from the sensate phenomena of the so-called empirical world (Mead 1936a, 66–84). As such, Kant rejected the assumptions of the empiricists who presupposed the status and form of the object to be conceived. Instead, he stressed that bare perception is meaningless without the hidden categorical framework of the mind that organizes perceptions into recognizable forms. Kant believed that we all share the same universalizing criteria for the organization of phenomena; thus, there is a mutually agreeable foundation on which to build abstract law, reason, and ethics.

Mead celebrated Kant's stress on the importance of the active, perceiving subject in experience, as well as the importance of universalizing schemes of perception that allow the social collective common ground to build shared agreements on truth, justice, and so on. The position of the subject and, moreover, the relation between the subject and environment in determining the forms we experience is a vital contribution of Kant and deeply influenced Mead (Cook 1993, 9). However, Mead's view of the subject and of how the categories of perception that guide experience are formed in the individual differs substantially from Kant. While Kant viewed these schemas as universal, given to the individual at birth, Mead saw the subject as a social creation, an emergent product of social and perceptual experience.

Instead of Kant's pre-given universal noumenal structure, the individual draws up schemes of perception organically from prior social and perceptive experiences in the world. For this reason, Mead was drawn to the post-Kantian German idealists (Mead 1936a, 85–126), such as Fichte, Schelling, and Hegel, and the American Josiah Royce, who all saw the perceiving self, and the organizational categories by which judgments are made, as emergent with ongoing experience. Rather than being static, argued these post-Kantian idealists, the perceiving self is not fixed but a product of ongoing experience. For Fichte, Hegel, and Schelling, objects and forms arise processually through the dialectic of experience and communication. For Hegel, this dialectic involves the introduction and adaptation to problems and conflicts as they arise. Mead was enamoured by Hegel's insistence on the dialectic, and this formed an organizing principle that weaves throughout all of Mead's thought.

This Hegelian picture of the self as emerging from the community through the conflicts that arise between social universals and individual experience can be seen in the philosophy of Mead's teacher at Harvard, Josiah Royce. Royce's commitment to idealism was strong and ever-present in his assumptions about culture (Smith 1966). Royce was steadfast that locating philosophy purely within the bounds of the practical was narrow and argued that this approach missed the much deeper and rewarding importance of the spiritual and transcendent truths to be found in idealism. For this reason, Royce was somewhat in conflict with the pragmatists, and his ideas were therefore against the grain of what was to become a distinctly American philosophical tradition. Mead (1930, 223) writes: "[N]o American, in his philosophical moments ... would have felt himself at home in the spiritual landscape of Royce's Blessed Community ... I can remember very vividly the fascinations of the idealisms in Royce's luminous presentations ... It was part of the escape from the crudity of American life, not an interpretation of it."

Despite Mead's dislike for Royce's idealism, he was greatly influenced by him and the Hegelian tradition he embodied, in at least three ways. First, Royce followed Hegel in arguing that individual consciousness is not pre-given or static but is a community product; individual self-consciousness requires the awareness of other selves who help to define and shape one's own self. It is only here that one can perceive oneself as a thinking subject. Second, despite this emphasis on community, Royce was still a proponent of voluntarism and agency and emphasized the importance of understanding the self-directed role of the individual within the community (Royce 1920). Thus, the notion of liberty and freedom to act as one chooses was important to Royce, and we can see this running through Mead's later conceptions of voluntaristic action, albeit in more secular ways. For Mead, explanations for self-directed and spontaneous behaviour were rooted much more in the biologically based dialectic of the "I" and "me" distinction (see Cook, this volume) rather than in a divine conception of the soul. Third, Royce's largely Hegelian epistemology in which knowledge is rooted first and foremost in the social community, over and above the individual, was another influence on Mead's social conception of science, politics, and the development of meaning and knowledge (Silva 2008).

Mead's criticism of Hegelian thought and romantic idealism lies first in the fact that the dialectic of human progress was assumed to be teleological, toward an already established goal of divine reason. Mead staunchly rejected this view and instead applied the dialectic of progress in a contingent way (see Mead 1930). Like Dewey, Mead believed that goals are not absolute or predetermined and do not accord with the grand logic of a higher spiritual order. Rather, goals themselves arise for people in the process of experience, determined by emergent events and lines of adaptation and problem-solving engaged in by the social community. While Mead was optimistic about progressive change, he also felt that concepts like truth, justice, and morality are unfinalizable products, which change and adapt to the flux of specific problem-situations and human needs as they arise. Progress is a contingent march in which the ends are determined largely by the means as they are organized in conduct.

CHARLES DARWIN AND EVOLUTIONIST THOUGHT

Clearly, Mead saw much value in the contributions of the Hegelian idealists but disdained many of their spiritual assumptions. This led him to look for a notion of creative progress rooted in the biological and material struggles of the natural world. Mead rejected Hegelian thought in part because of its dualist tendency to consider the spirit separately from the material plane and looked for a system that would treat spirit, body, and nature as a unity. For Mead, idealism did not take adequate account of the biological and psychological knowledge of human action that, he believed, could do wonders to inform a more naturalistic conception of philosophy (Mead 1909). Instead of thinking about evolutionism merely as a spiritual inter-play of ideas, Mead preferred the Darwinian doctrine of science that implied that forms are born out of physical and material processes. Rather than keeping the spheres of the rational and the material separate, Mead spent his life trying to show their intimate connec-tion through a non-dualistic approach to process philosophy whereby self-consciousness and intelligence were emergent products of adap-tive processes in the natural world. Mead preferred the non-teleolog-ical and contingent structure of Darwin's system of thought as a way to understand process and change at the organic level and the seam-less transfer of this to cultural and psychical adaptation within the human group. Mead (1909) was prescient in his observation that Darwinian thought had and would retain a profound effect on the content of philosophy at large. Mead provided examples of this, showing that philosophical realism, as well as the pragmatist philos-ophy he himself embraced, largely arose within the intellectual cli-mate of modern research science (Mead 1932, 113–33). Mead (1909, 4) credits the philosophical turn of evolutionist philosophy to Thomas Malthus's influential warnings about population expansion and the geological discoveries of Sir Charles Lyell, who "saw indica-tion neither of a beginning nor an end ... he and those who immedi-ately preceded him were at work upon a history of the earth's surface and led men to see in the forms that they found about them the results of operations which persisted while the forms changed."

Darwin's explanation of natural selection showed that the forms of animals and plants emerge through a larger process of adjustment to ongoing forces and conditions. Mead preferred Darwinist notions of evolution because of his naturalistic preference to ground so-called ideal processes of the mind appropriately within their material root in physical life processes, which Mead saw as the root of creativity. Mead (1909, 13–14) wrote: "The decisive character of Darwin's work lay in the fact that he proved that there are causes in nature which could lead to such a fashioning of the form in this process of adjustment. The statement of Hegel is from within from the analysis of the process of reason. The statement of Darwin is from without from the study of animal and vegetable nature and the struggle for existence that he saw so dominant but so creative." Indeed, Mead's preference for materialist and environmental accounts of the rise of forms and eventually, and through the same fundamental process, culture and the life-world, almost echoes Marx's (1978 [1845], 155) argument that "life is not determined by consciousness, but consciousness by life." Mead also preferred a philosophy built on an analysis of the needs of life within material forces and conditions, not on an ideal plane of pure linguistic thought and spiritual development alone.

For Mead, problematic situations in harsh environments of action are where the root of creativity, and the evolution of human culture, progresses. For Mead (1936a, 383), intelligent responses to problems of food supply, water, digestion, and energy form the basis of many of our modern institutions. Human intelligence and its higher institutional form of modern research science is an adaptation to the conditions imposed by the external material world. Mead provides other examples of societal evolutionism in the development of law and science, both institutions that result through problem-solving adaptations to the changing needs of society. Manning (2005) has suggested that Mead was also influenced by the American social Darwinist William Sumner, and one can see similar sorts of statements about social organization in the work of Cooley (Archibald 1978). Mead (1936a, 373) directly credits Comte, but more definitively Spencer, as coming up with the organic conception of society as the evolution of a set of "social habits." Mead saw institutions as forming emergently in response to the particular needs of people who then come together to solve problems in the physical and social environment through collective action. It is through the repetition of these collective problem-solving acts that habits and institutional structures form and sediment.

AMERICAN PRAGMATISM

Mead obviously gathered major intellectual support from the pragmatist tradition of which he was a part. Charles Sanders Peirce (1935) is often credited as the founder of pragmatism and considered by many to be the greatest of American philosophers because of his ability to move seamlessly between philosophy, logic, mathematics, and science (Smith 1966). Fundamentally, he argued that knowledge is not a product of the ideal forms carried in our heads, nor the reality of the presumed percept of experience. Rather, Peirce founded reality in the practical effects we imagine of objects, which are generated in the process of experience. Peirce (1935, 402) writes, "consider what effects ... we conceive the object of our conception to have. Then, the conception of these effects is the whole of our conception of the object." For Peirce, we can never know more than the external performances of objects allow us. As Mead would later argue, the inner meaning of an object is only ever understood through its outer exhibitions.

The definition of intelligence as the successful execution of previously blocked action was a major inspiration for Mead and allowed him to bridge the social-psychological components of organismic action with pragmatic accounts of truth. This strand of thought located intelligence within action and the imagination and realization of practical effects in the formation of meaning (Mead 1929; 1930; 1936a; 1936b). For the pragmatists, the major difference separating organic life from the inorganic is that the former is able to direct its own actions. As such, we share with plants and animals the inner power to be active in the world, rather than simply reacting, like billiard balls, to environmental conditions. Mead (1936a, 345) credits both James and Dewey with the pragmatic notion of intelligence as synonymous with the capability for action that had been previously blocked: "[I]ntelligence in its simplest phase, and also in a later phase, really lies inside of a process of conduct ... A plant shows its intelligence by driving down its roots, in its adjustment to the climate. When you get into the animal kingdom, you find much more adjustment ... the intelligence of the human form is one which has arisen through its ability to analyze the world by discrimination, and, through significant symbols, to indicate to other forms with which it works and to the form itself what the elements are that are of importance to it ... the test of intelligence is found in action."

While Mead never studied directly under William James, he certainly had access to his ideas at Harvard and used much of his work throughout his career. James's interests in psychology provided the starting point for his exploration of the subject as an organic, cognate, and self-directed inquirer. This led to an epistemology that differs remarkably from most traditional metaphysical systems of thought (Mead 1930). Like Peirce, James sought the meanings for things in their practical effects and truth in the realization of action. Mead became deeply influenced by this naturalistic, physiological, and psychological starting point of inquiry into studies of knowledge: "[F]or James the act is a living physiological affair, and must be placed in the struggle for existence ... efficacy can be determined not by its agreement with a pre-existent reality but by its solution of the difficulty within which the act finds itself. Here we have the soil from which pragmatism sprung" (Mead 1930, 223–4).

By locating knowledge and truth within the physiological "struggle for existence," Mead found continuity between the pragmatists' assumptions of knowledge as a naturalistic product and the scientific findings of Darwin and Lyell. Beyond locating intelligent thought within organic processes of problem-solving adaptations to harsh environments, there was a psychological grounding for James's test of truth, which shaped Mead's analysis of the act. James equated truth with the psychological satisfaction of enabling an action that was previously blocked. Mead is critical of this purely psychological account of truth, since it is left wanting epistemologically. Nevertheless, the satisfaction actors experience in the final, "consummatory" phase of Mead's (1938, 23) theory of perceptive action forms an important part of his own brand of pragmatism. Still, Mead preferred to consider action and the generation of meaning as a thoroughly social process, rooting knowledge and truth beyond the psychology of the individual and into the shared symbols of the social community.

In this sense, Dewey's version of pragmatism is probably the closest to Mead. Dewey's (1896) article, "The Reflex Arc Concept in Psychology," stressed that stimulus alone is not enough to understand organismic responses, because the organism itself selects and interprets stimuli before acting on them. Mead's (1938) work in *Philosophy of the Act* explained that impulses are only the beginning of the four phases of the perceptive act, which ultimately forms conduct and helps with the selection of new stimuli. This process was clearly influenced by the active, processual, and instrumental emphasis Dewey placed on the organism in its relation to nature. Mead (1934, 10–11) echoed this in his critique of the pure behavioural assessments of human action seen in the work of John Watson. Mead argued that individuals not only select and change their environmental stimuli, they also interpret impulses and allow conduct to play out through the internal conversation of the mind. Thus, it is not enough to study only external behaviour, since much of human conduct plays out symbolically in the internal psyche through self-communication, which plays a major hand in determining the social action that results.

Dewey also influenced Mead's overall epistemological stance, which connected pragmatic action with symbolic universals that are built up within the social world. We can see the impact of Dewey's conception of meaning and the necessity of the social in the development of Mead's own thought: "The title that Dewey gives to these objects of thought is 'meanings'; and by this title and his account of the origin and function of meanings he brings them within the field of conduct, and in so doing this adds another category to reality – the category of the social" (Mead 1936b, 77–8). Dewey was a major influence on Mead's conception of social psychology, education (e.g., Deegan 2001), and how knowledge is arrived at within the functional parameters of the human group. However, Mead was critical of Dewey in at least one way. While Dewey recognized the possibility that different socialization experiences could lead different individuals to develop different sets of meanings for the same things, he neglected to explore this possibility in full. Mead (1932) realized the importance of the multiplicity of divergent perspectives that might emerge in the social world and the centrality of this problem for the content of individual and social experience. He gathered much of his inspiration in this regard from the realist philosophy of Alfred North Whitehead.

WHITEHEAD AND BERGSON: TIME, PERSPECTIVES, AND EMERGENCE

Mead (1932) takes up Whitehead's thought explicitly in his paper on the "objective reality of perspectives." Mead argued that organisms acquire their perspectives through experiences gained at different phases of their life process. It makes no sense to think of a being in isolation from its past social and perceptual experiences. If we move beyond one individual to consider the experiential reality of a social community (not to mention a large metropolitan city), we have a whole host of overlapping and intersecting life processes, each with its own objectively forming, yet unique and personally experienced, perspectives. This gets yet more complicated when one considers that each actor's perspectives and attitudes are being shaped in large part by their intersection with others. For Mead, understanding how these life processes overlap is vital to understanding how they interrelate and affect each other. Mead (1938, 541) wrote: "The organization of different time systems ... is involved in the organism itself. The organism in its own perspective could not be what it is if it were not for the other time systems and their organisms ... the preservation of the organisms is dependent upon the favorableness of the adjustment of each organism to an environment which consists of other organisms in their perspectives." Mead thus grounds the ontological reality of social life naturalistically, in the real world of "physico-chemical properties" of organismic interactions that overlap in time.

According to Cook (1993), Mead discovered and began writing about the philosophy of Whitehead sometime after 1925. Since Mead died in 1931, it is safe to assume that any writings to do with Whitehead represent Mead's more mature thought. Mead was captivated by Whitehead's consideration of Newtonian relativity as a philosophical problem (see Mead 1932, chapter 4). Perspectives, while different, are objective constructions emanating naturalistically from organisms physically acting in environments of space and time. The problem for Whitehead was that if all perspectives are real, yet different from one another, how can they be reconciled? Mead's answer to Whitehead's dilemma was social-psychological – by placing oneself in the role of the other (both spatially and psychically), one imagines the objective reality of the other's viewpoint. If both actors do this, and are able to communicate, they can mutually generate a translatable universal by mutual role-taking. Thus, through communicative dialogue, actors convert unique perspectival experiences into shared symbolic universals. While Whitehead saw this agreement as a sign of the transcendent nature of certain aspects of empirical reality, Mead considered it nothing more than a localized construction with universal significance at the social level. While Mead rejected Whitehead's realism here, the convergence of perspectives under shared symbolic universals (language) is not a completely arbitrary social construction, fiction, or flight of fancy. Mead's assumptions about the social genesis of knowledge go beyond a simple consensus notion of truth. It also goes a long way in overcoming dualism by recognizing that perspectives are not generated in an ideal plane of disembodied language games but are genuine "slabs of reality," or material products of the process of nature (Mead 1932, 171–82; Burke 1962).

More can be learned by considering Mead's interest in the philosophy of Henri Bergson. Bergson argued that scientific rationality and symbolization are fundamental failures in that these forms of intelligence are mere instruments of action in the world and cannot deliver truth. Rather, the very process of abstracting reality in rationalistic formulas of knowledge serves to distort reality in order to enable action (Mead 1936a, xiv). This is connected to Bergson's consideration of time, since the scientific conception of a "knife-edge" present is a distortion of how temporality is actually experienced. Mead (1936a, 300) wrote of Bergson's view: "[O]ur experience, our feelings, our sensations, are extended over our present; and one present extends over another so that there is a flow in which the past is really reflected into the future, and the future back into the past. That, Bergson says, is the nature of reality. It is not that which can be expressed in points and instants; it must be expressed in duration." Yet in order for a scientist, or the everyday person, to make sound predictions and judgments, the distorted "spatial" perspective that assumes discrete time slices must be utilized. Nevertheless, this is contrary to the subjective interpretation of duration in experience, which would so capture Mead's (1932; 1936a; 1938) attention in his later years as he would consider the social-psychological implications of subjective time durations and the organization of the past from the perspective of the present (Maines, Sugrue, and Katovich 1983; Maines 2001).

Further, Bergson offered Mead a source from which to develop a theory of novelty by providing an account of unpredictability in emergent experience. Bergson argued that the failure of rationalism can be seen in the fact that there is no way to accurately predict all of the permutations of the future. There is always, in the flowing present, the tang of novelty and surprise in even the most seemingly predictable events. This emergent character of nature became a cornerstone assumption in his theory of the human capacity for creativity. If future experiences can never be fully anticipated, one has an endless source of emergent experiences to provide for creative and intelligent thought. Again, it is the uncompromising complexity found in the concrete reality of the material world that guarantees a constant source of novelty and impetus for emergent change, at the level of knowledge, yes, but, at a more fundamental level, culture as well.

MEAD'S ONTOLOGY: ACTION AND SOCIALITY

I have considered Mead's engagement with a variety of thinkers in an effort to show that his unique philosophical and sociological accomplishment can be seen in the successful merger of a number of schools of thought, including Hegelian idealism, Darwinist evolutionism, physiological social psychology, pragmatism, Whitehead's concern with relativity and the intersection of multiple perspectives, and Bergson's view of temporal emergence. This allowed Mead to root perception, social experience, and knowledge all within the field of human action. It is in action that Mead finds the genesis of reality, knowledge, meaning, mind, self, institutions, intersubjectivity, morality, and all of social life. In linking these schools of thought to analyze action within the full matrix of life processes, he would consider the ability of actors to move from one frame of experience to another within social action as his theory of sociality (Doan 1956; Lowy 1993; Mead 1932). According to Cook (1993), Mead never finished this synthesis to his own satisfaction. Nevertheless, we can gain at least a rough picture of Mead's social ontology by taking stock of his major ideas that culminated in the intellectual dialogues just reviewed. This shows that for Mead, human meaning develops through processes that are not reducible to the linguistic realm of human interaction alone. Thus, a sole focus on the symbolic and language-based aspects of Mead's thought in regard to the generation of meaning, common to many progenitors of symbolic interactionism, is inadequate (see also Joas 1985; Cook 1993). By drawing together the key aspects of Mead's social ontology here, I hope to provide a more expansive account of Mead's thought that links his social psychology to questions of physical perception, space, temporality, and the construction of knowledge in concrete environments of action.

The accounting for Mead's social ontology begins by recognizing the importance of *Mind, Self and Society* (1934). Here, Mead considers the thought experiment of how symbolic meaning evolves from gesture–response patterns formed within the social act between two or more actors. The idea is simple in that the first actor gestures toward another in some fashion and judges the meaning of the gesture by the response of the second actor to it. Then, subsequent acts are crafted as adjustments to the first action in an effort to bring about intentions that are based on the imagined perspective of the other. It is through this adjustive process that shared belief systems and abstract universals can be constructed and adopted into social communities. What is perhaps most important to this process of social action is that over time, the first actor must "take the role" of the other, imagining the desired or expected actions from the perspective of the second person through previous patterns of gestural and later symbolic interaction.

Second, Mead placed a great deal of emphasis on perception and the formative function of the act in experience. Reality, for Mead, is not found within the internal state of the mind, nor in the object that lies outside of awareness. Rather, for Mead (1938, 16), "[t]he 'what' of the object is, then, the expression of the whole of which both environment and organism are essential parts." Thus, the "what" of objects in experience are relationally determined, defined through the actions and interactions of organisms with these objects. Mead conceived of these perceptual acts that give rise to meaning in four stages: impulse, perception, manipulation, and consummation. An intelligent organism has an impulse toward action, perceives the world in order to act toward the thing, engages in physical manipulation with the target object, and finally satisfies the unfolding act by consummating, or satisfying the intentions of the act that was begun. By engaging in these various phases of gestural exchange, the meaning of the object is generated in relation to the organism. This meaning can then be symbolically represented, later utilized, and shared with others with the use of language.

What links the previous ideas together is that Mead considered perception as a fundamentally social act in itself. As Joas (1985) and Habermas (1987) have noted, the perceptive act itself became a social enterprise for Mead, since he would explicitly cite the need to "take the role" of objects in order to best plan their manipulation through action. For Mead, physical manipulation of objects in the environment is fundamentally the same as social negotiation with other selves. Mead (1932, 137) wrote: "[T]he organism in grasping and pushing things is identifying its own effort with the contact experience of the thing. It increases that experience by its own efforts ... the organism ... becomes endowed with that inner nature of pressure which constitutes the inside of the physical thing. It is only so far as the organism takes the attitude of the thing that the thing acquires such an inside." Thus, the fundamental process of understanding is the same in social life as in physical perception. We only come to understand other people by taking on their role. It is similarly only possible to understand the so-called "inner qualities" of things by assuming their role, by pre-visioning their conduct in action, and by feeling their physical resistance within our own bodies What is perhaps equally important is that while the self as a subject can, for Mead, only come into being by encountering attributions from other selves (Mead 1934), the self as a physical thing can only arise through interaction with other objects: "[T]he individual's organism comes into experience only as other objects define and orient it ... We see the object not simply as offering passive resistance, but as actively resisting us ... the attitude of the thing's response to pressure is identical with that of the organism, though opposite in direction. This opposition reveals itself in the appearance of the organism as a physical object" (Mead 1932, 148–50).

In sum, the self as an object is just as dependent on the physical environment as it is on the social world. Symbolization and the judging of future conduct in the physical world (see Mead 1938, 357–442) represents the fitting of one's own frame of reference to another that lies in a projection into the future. We have a unified theory of meaning that is reducible to action through subjectively experienced temporal durations and the ability to role-take into other objects, as well as other temporal and spatial frames and other organismic (and even inorganic) imagined perspectives. I hope this discussion provides insight into Mead's social ontology and his conception of how knowledge emerges from our overlapping webs of action and experience. By fostering a stronger awareness of Mead's view of sociality in all of its complexity, interactionists will not only have a richer understanding of an important intellectual predecessor but will also have more ammunition with which to contribute in meaningful ways to other emerging fields of study.

For example, Mead's close analysis of the generic aspects of perceptive action might fruitfully contribute insights to the "practice turn" in social theory (Schatzki, Knorr-Cetina, and Savigny 2001). More specifically, by generating parallels between human and non-human gestural exchanges and showing how non-symbolic processes of physical action get routed into codified knowledge, Mead's framework may help in studies that try to understand the translation of tacit understandings into more explicit forms of knowledge (Collins 2010). Further, for Mead, physical perception and reality construction does not happen only through the "filter" of linguistically acquired meaning frames but rather is a constitutive part of developing those meaning frames. In the words of Bruno Latour (2005), Mead's staunch rejection of dualism results in a broad "reassembly of the social," since physical experience can shape our language, consciousness, and meaning frames just as much as the latter can affect the former. By treating scientific objects, technological artifacts, and natural environments as taking an active role in the construction of meaning through inter-corporeal and gesture–response processes, Mead had a view of the social fabric that extends far beyond the human world alone (Puddephatt 2005). Finally, Mead's theory of the social is thoroughly embodied. His view of perception and all of social action is concrete in its emphasis on space, time, and physicality but also on the biological body (Rosenthal and Bourgeois 1991). Perception is seen as an irreducible connection between the embodied self and the environment, and this connection, operating within a framework of ongoing action and adjustment, is the root of meaning. If symbolic interactionists were to follow Mead's lead here and embrace these aspects of his social ontology, they would be in much better shape to contribute meaningfully to these rapidly expanding fields of practice theory, science and technology studies, and embodied theories of knowledge and action.

REFERENCES

Archibald, W. Peter. 1978. *Social Psychology as Political Economy.*
Toronto: McGraw Hill
Blumer, Herbert. 1966. "Sociological Implications of the Thought of
George Herbert Mead." *American Journal of Sociology* 71(5):535–44
– 1969 *Symbolic Interactionism: Perspective and Method.* Berkeley:
University of California Press
– 2004. *George Herbert Mead and Human Conduct,* edited by Thomas J.
Morrione. Walnut Creek, CA: Altamira
Burke, Richard. 1962. "G.H. Mead and the Problem of Metaphysics."
Philosophy and Phenomenological Research 23(1):81–8
Collins, Harry. 2010. *Tacit and Explicit Knowledge.* Chicago: University
of Chicago Press
Cook, Gary A. 1993. *George Herbert Mead: The Making of a Social
Pragmatist.* Chicago: University of Chicago Press
Deegan, Mary Jo. 2001. "Introduction: George Herbert Mead's First
Book." In George Herbert Mead, *Essays in Social Psychology: George*

Herbert Mead's First Book, edited by Mary Jo Deegan, xi–xliv. New
Brunswick, NJ: Transaction

Dewey, John. 1896. "The Reflex Arc Concept in Psychology."
Psychological Review 3:35–70

Doan, Frank M. 1956. "Notations on G.H. Mead's Principle of Sociality
with Special Reference to Transformation." *Journal of Philosophy*
53(20):607–15

Habermas, Jurgen. 1987. *The Theory of Communicative Action: Lifeworld
and System: A Critique of Functionalist Reason.* Boston: Beacon Press

Joas, Hans. 1985. *G.H. Mead: A Contemporary Re-examination of His
Thought.* Cambridge, MA: MIT Press

Latour, Bruno. 2005. *Reassembling the Social: An Introduction to Actor-
Network Theory.* Oxford: Oxford University Press

Lowy, Richard F. 1993. "Mental Sociality as Ultimate Reality and
Meaning in the Thought of George Herbert Mead. *Ultimate Reality and
Meaning* 16(1–2):56–72

Maines, David. 2001. *The Faultline of Consciousness.* New York: Aldine
de Gruyter

– Noreen Sugrue, and Michael Katovich. 1983. "The Sociological Import
of G.H. Mead's Theory of the Past." *American Sociological Review* 48:
161–73

Manis, Jerome, and Bernard Meltzer. 1978. *Symbolic Interaction: A
Reader in Social Psychology.* Boston: Allyn and Bacon

Manning, Philip. 2005. *Freud and American Sociology.* Cambridge, MA:
Polity Press

Marx, Karl. 1978 [1845]. "The German Ideology." In *The Marx-Engels
Reader*, edited by R. Tucker, 146–200. New York: W.W. Norton

Mead, George Herbert. 1909. *On the Influence of Darwin's Origin of
Species.* Unpublished manuscript

– 1929. "A Pragmatic Theory of Truth." *Studies in the Nature of Truth:
University of California Publications in Philosophy* 11:65–88

– 1930. "The Philosophies of Royce, James, and Dewey in Their American
Setting." *International Journal of Ethics* 40:211–31

– 1932. *The Philosophy of the Present.* Chicago: Open Court Publishing

– 1934. *Mind, Self and Society from the Standpoint of a Social
Behaviorist.* Chicago: University of Chicago Press

– 1936a. *Movements of Thought in the Nineteenth Century.* Chicago:
University of Chicago Press

– 1936b. "The Philosophy of John Dewey." *International Journal of
Ethics* 46:64–81

- 1938. *The Philosophy of the Act.* Chicago: University of Chicago Press
- 2001. *Essays in Social Psychology,* edited by Mary Jo Deegan. New Brunswick, NJ: Transaction
Peirce, Charles Sanders. 1935. *Collected Papers of Charles Sanders Peirce,* edited by Charles Hartshorne and Paul Weiss. Cambridge: Harvard University Press
Prus, Robert. 1996. *Symbolic Interaction and Ethnographic Research.* Albany: State University of New York Press
Puddephatt, Antony J. 2005. "Mead Has Never Been Modern: Using Meadian Theory to Extend the Constructionist Study of Technology." *Social Epistemology* 19(4):357–80
- 2009. "The Search for Meaning: Revisiting Herbert Blumer's Interpretation of G.H. Mead." *The American Sociologist* 40(1–2): 89–105
Rosenthal, Sandra, and Patrick Bourgeois. 1991. *Mead and Merleau-Ponty: Toward a Common Vision.* New York: State University of New York Press
Royce, Josiah. 1920. *The World and the Individual.* London: MacMillan
Schatzki, Theodore R., Karin D. Knorr-Cetina, and Eike Von Savigny, eds. 2001. *The Practice Turn in Contemporary Theory.* London and New York: Routledge
Silva, Filipe Carreira da. 2008. *Mead and Modernity: Science, Selfhood, and Democratic Politics.* London: Lexington Books
Smith, John E. 1966. *The Spirit of American Philosophy.* New York: Oxford University Press

6

Mending Mead's "I" and "Me" Distinction

GARY A. COOK

No aspect of George Herbert Mead's social-psychological theorizing is more in need of clarification and repair than his attempt to distinguish between the two dimensions of the self he calls the "I" and the "me." (For other aspects of Mead's social theorizing, see Puddephatt, this volume). Charles Morris tries to clarify this distinction in his editor's introduction to Mead's most widely read work, *Mind, Self and Society* (Mead 1934), but his effort leaves much to be desired. The "me," Morris says, consists of "the attitudes [or response-tendencies] of others organized and taken over into one's self," while the "I" is the "impulsive" or "biologic" individual underlying this acquired social structure and continuing to react back upon it (Mead 1934, xxiv–xxv). One need only pay careful attention to the variety of ways in which Mead at one time or another characterizes the "I" and the "me," however, to arrive at serious doubts concerning the adequacy of Morris's interpretation. It certainly has a basis in much of what Mead says about this distinction in *Mind, Self and Society* (e.g., Mead 1934, 175, 178, 194, 196–200, 209–10, 213); moreover, it can perhaps be made to square with Mead's assertions that the "I" is inherently uncertain or unpredictable (Mead 1934, 176–9) and that it is a source of novelty in our conduct (Mead 1934, 178, 197–8, 202–4, 209). But how can it be made to fit with his repeated claims in his earlier essays that the "I" is a subject (while the "me" is an object) of experience (Mead 1964, 55, 140–1, 142–5) or his claims there and in *Mind, Self and Society* that we do not directly experience the "I" but encounter it only when it has passed into memory and become a part of the "me" (Mead 1934, 174, 178, 203)? And how can it encompass Mead's occasional suggestions that the "I" is a definite and singular personality that mirrors the structure of his or her society from a unique perspective (Mead 1934, 200–1) or that the "I" is an immediately present and ongoing "response" (Mead 1934, 175–6, 182, 196, 277) or a "living act" (Mead 1934, 203, 279)?

Just these sorts of questions led William L. Kolb, one of the earliest critics of this distinction, to argue that the presentation of the "I" and "me" contrast in *Mind, Self and Society* is fundamentally flawed: Mead, he says, there uses the "I" concept as a "residual category" for a group of "heterogeneous phenomena" having little in common beyond the fact that they cannot be explained in terms of the social structure he attributes to the "me." The best way to overcome the confusion created by this distinction, Kolb concludes, is to throw out the concept of the "I" while at the same time re-examining the several different sorts of phenomena that Mead "cloaked" with this concept (Kolb 1944, 292, 295).

At least two subsequent commentators, J. David Lewis (Lewis 1979) and the present author (Cook 1972; reprinted in Cook 1993), have made attempts to rescue Mead's distinction from Kolb's criticisms, but each has done so only by overlooking some of the things Mead says about the "I" and the "me" in his lectures or writings. Lewis admits that there are unfortunate ambiguities in Mead's various explanations of the "I" and the "me," but he holds that most of the confusion surrounding this distinction is due to misunderstandings on the part of Mead's critics. Such confusion, he maintains, can be overcome by what he calls a "strict social behaviorist interpretation" of Mead's concepts. The interpretation he offers agrees with that of Morris in regarding the "me" as an acquired social attitude or set of such attitudes present in the conduct of a human individual; it identifies the "I," however, not with an impulsive or biological individual but with an immediately present response on the part of that individual to his or her "me" (Lewis 1979, 265–71). This approach to Mead's concepts, like that of Morris, does justice to some of the things said about the "I" and "me" in *Mind, Self and Society*, but it ignores what Mead has in mind when he speaks of the "I" as a subject and the "me" as an object of experience, and it fails to explain adequately why the "I" would be any less predictable or exhibit any less of an acquired social structure than the "me." My own earlier essay, on the other hand, explains how Mead worked out the distinction between the self as subject and the self as object in some of his early published writings, but it fails to acknowledge the important respects in which Mead at many points in *Mind, Self and Society* departs radically from this version of the "I" and "me."

Recently, two additional authors have laid the groundwork for a new and more probing critique of Mead's distinction. Jurgen Habermas has suggested that the meanings Mead assigns to the terms "I" and "me" are "surreptitiously altered" as his thought develops. Mead, he says, initially uses them to draw an epistemic or knowledge-related distinction in several of his early essays: here the "I" is construed as the subject and the "me" as the object of experience in an attempt to explain how the self can become an object of knowledge to itself. But later, Habermas claims, the terms "I" and "me" take on new meanings as Mead attempts to explain how the individual comes to exercise responsible self-control or self-determination. The "me" is now the agency of self-control provided by the internalized attitudes or expectations of others; the "I" is the source of impulses that are at least partially subjected to the control of the "me" and that sometimes bring renewal to the established forms of social control (Habermas 1992, 178–80).

Habermas goes on to use the latter (Morris-like) version of these terms for his own purposes without pausing to engage in a thorough critical examination of the problems and inconsistencies involved in Mead's "I" and "me" distinction. Patchen Markell, on the other hand, offers just such a critique in the course of an essay on the use made of this distinction by Axel Honneth – another writer in the tradition of critical social theory. Markell argues that the meanings of the "I" and the "me" undergo a number of transformations in Mead's various discussions of these concepts and that the version of this distinction that Honneth borrows from Mead "actually represents Mead's own partial slide away from a different, more promising way of using these terms" (Markell 2007, 101). The version of the "I" and "me" distinction that Markell finds Honneth borrowing from Mead is a variation on the interpretation offered by Morris and used also by Habermas: the "me" is here seen as an internalized set of social attitudes representing the individual's community, and the "I" is regarded as a reservoir of psychical energies or inner impulses that interact with the "me" (Markell 2007, 109–10). The version of the distinction that Markell finds "more promising" is one initially worked out by Mead in the early essays in which he contrasts the self as subject with the self as object (Markell 2007, 119–21). Both of these versions of the "I" and "me" distinction, Markell contends, are present in *Mind, Self and Society*, where they are mixed together in a kind of unresolved tension. Mead's tendency to slide back and forth between these two versions is "the central ambiguity" that afflicts Mead's use of the terms "I" and "me" in *Mind, Self and Society* (Markell 2007, 121–4).

The view for which I want to argue in what follows agrees in many respects with that of Markell; it could, in fact, be regarded as an affirmation and extension of Markell's interpretation of the relevant Meadian texts. It arose, however, not from a reading of his excellent analysis (which I did not discover until the body of the present paper had already been written) but from an attempt to rethink and then correct a claim I had made in my own earlier essay mentioned above. In that essay, I incorrectly suggested that Mead's uses of the terms "I" and "me" in *Mind, Self and Society* were "a consistent outgrowth" of the analysis of these dimensions of the self presented in the early published essays in which he had first introduced these concepts (Cook 1972, 184–5; Cook 1993, 64–6). I continue to think that the more clear and less problematic account of the "I" and "me" distinction found in Mead's earlier published essays provides the best basis for an understanding of Mead's remarks about these concepts in *Mind, Self and Society*, but I now see that the latter are in many cases not at all a consistent extension of the former. I shall therefore begin here with a brief review of Mead's earlier account in order to show that this distinction becomes confused and confusing only when it is subsequently reformulated in *Mind, Self and Society*. This confusion, I shall claim, stems from the fact that the meaning of the term "me" undergoes a significant shift during the course of that volume. This shift results in a series of discussions in which the contrasting terms "I" and "me" are unknowingly used to designate two quite different and incompatible versions of Mead's "I" and "me" distinction. The problems that begin to afflict this distinction in *Mind, Self and Society*, I shall suggest, can best be mended by returning to the version found in Mead's earlier essays. This first version of the distinction should then be further elaborated in ways that allow for more adequate expression of various Meadian insights regarding the social nature of the self.

MEAD'S EARLY USE OF THE TERMS "I" AND "ME"

Mead's earliest published use of the distinction between the "I" and the "me" appears in his 1903 essay entitled "The Definition of the

Psychical" (Mead 1964, 25–59), an essay in which he sought to explain the part played by subjective or "psychical" consciousness in the creative process through which human individuals revise the meanings they attribute to the objects of their experience. Mead here embraces a pragmatic or functionalist theory of experienced objects and reflective thought based upon views set forth by John Dewey in his 1896 essay on "The Reflex Arc Concept in Psychology" (Dewey 1972). We will need to look briefly at this theory in order to obtain the background needed to make Mead's initial use of the "I" and "me" distinction intelligible.

Experienced or empirical objects, Mead holds in this and other early essays, derive their characters from the functional roles they play in our conduct; our responses to these objects, the uses we make of them, are what give them their experienced meanings. Objects as they exist in our experience, in other words, are not simply given but are in part constructed or "constituted" by our actions with respect to them. Once we become familiar with such objects and acquire habitual ways of responding to them, they take on meanings that are funded with the lessons of past experience – meanings that guide our subsequent dealings with them (Mead 1964, 8).

As long as our conduct involving these experienced objects proceeds in an unproblematic manner, Mead contends, their meanings are for us unquestioned features of our objective empirical world. But when an object surprises us, when our actions with respect to it lead to unexpected results, then it begins to call forth conflicting reactions; its meanings for our conduct become uncertain. In situations of this kind, our habitual behaviour typically gives way to a phase of reflective thought whose task is to bring about a revision of the meanings that have broken down. It is just here, Mead suggests, that subjective or psychical consciousness comes to the fore and plays a functional role in the economy of our conduct. The free play of ideas in the flow of such subjective consciousness is what makes possible the rise of novel combinations of ideas and new meanings. In this reconstructive phase of conduct, the individual attends to fragmentary meanings that have lost their objective status and are for the time being regarded as states of his or her own personal and private consciousness. This subjective or psychical phase of experience occupies a functional position midway between the old objective meanings that have broken down and the new objective meanings that have yet to be established. When a solution to the problem is found, when new meanings are discovered that resolve the conflict so that conduct can once again proceed, the psychical phase of conduct will have done its job, and the new meanings it has discovered will take their place as objective components of a reconstructed world of objects (Mead 1964, 8, 12–16, 40–2).

This, in brief, is Mead's understanding of how the psychical consciousness of the human individual functions as a means of cognitive reconstruction. But what is the relationship between the introduction of creative novelty involved here and the individual human self? It is to answer this question that Mead first employs the terms "I" and "me" in his 1903 essay. In doing so, he draws upon a distinction that had already been given wide currency through the psychological writings of William James. Consider, for instance, the succinct summary contained in the following passages quoted from the chapter on "The Self" in James's *Psychology: The Briefer Course* (James 1892, chapter xii, 176–216):

> The Me and the I. – Whatever I may be thinking of, I am always at the same time more or less aware of myself, of my personal existence. At the same time it is I who am aware; so that the total self of me, being as it were duplex, partly known and partly knower, partly object and partly subject, must have two aspects discriminated in it, of which for shortness we may call one the Me and the other the I. I call these "discriminated aspects," and not separate things, because the identity of I with me, even in the very act of their discrimination, is perhaps the most ineradicable dictum of common-sense (James 1892, 176).

> The I, or "pure ego," is a very much more difficult subject of inquiry than the Me. It is that which at any given moment is conscious, whereas the Me is only one of the things which it is conscious of. In other words, it [the I] is the Thinker; and the question immediately comes up, what is the thinker? Is it the passing state of consciousness itself, or is it something deeper and less mutable (James 1892, 195–6)?

Mead uses this Jamesian distinction in his early essays to make the simple point that we can think of the relationship between our self and our self-conscious experience in two distinguishable ways. On the one hand, we can regard the self of self-consciousness as a meaningful experiential object that plays an important role in guiding much of our conduct. This is the aspect of the self that Mead here intends to indicate by the term "me"; it corresponds to what James, following the lead of Immanuel Kant, sometimes calls the "empirical self" or the "empirical ego." On the other hand, we may think of the self also as the subject to which the "me" of self-consciousness appears. This subject self is what Mead has in mind when he speaks of the "I." It corresponds to what James, again following Kant and various post-Kantian authors, sometimes calls the "pure ego" or the "transcendental ego" (Mead 1964, 53–5, 140–3; James 1892, 176, 196).

Mead has this Jamesian version of the "I" and "me" distinction in mind when he asks in his 1903 essay which of these two aspects of the self we should regard as the locus of the novel meanings and reconstructive processes involved in the functional work of psychical consciousness. It is evident, he claims, that it cannot be the "me," for the "me" is itself an experienced object; as such, it "belongs to the world which it is the function of this [psychical] phase of consciousness to reconstruct" (Mead 1964, 53). The psychical phase of experience and its reconstructive activity must therefore be identified with the subject "I" rather than with the object "me." We do, of course, tend to refer the fragmentary ideas present in the flow of psychical consciousness to the "me" of introspective self-consciousness insofar as we regard these ideas as items in our personal and private consciousness. But on Mead's view, this reference is only a convenient way of organizing in consciousness some of the conditions for the solution of the problem we are confronting. In fact, the active process of reconstruction going on in psychical consciousness must have its source in something more than an object self that is a presentation of consciousness. The "something more" involved here is the "I." It is "the self functioning, the point of immediacy that must exist within a mediate process. It is the act that makes use of all the data that reflection can present, but uses them merely as the conditions of a new world that cannot possibly be foretold from them. It is the self of unnecessitated choice, of undreamt hypotheses, of inventions that change the whole face of nature" (Mead 1964, 53–4).

This use of the "I" and "me" distinction, we should note, predates any published version of Mead's social-psychological account of the self. He did not begin to present his key social-psychological doctrines in print until a series of essays that appeared between 1909 and 1913. And he did not offer any extended remarks concerning the relation between these doctrines and his "I" and "me" distinction until the publication of his essays entitled "The Mechanism of Social Consciousness" (1912) and "The Social Self" (1913). Moreover, the new social-psychological ideas he introduced in these essays do not essentially alter the distinction between the "I" and the "me" he had introduced in "The Definition of the Psychical."

In "The Mechanism of Social Consciousness" (Mead 1964, 134–41), for instance, Mead offers a genetic and social account of the "me" of self-consciousness. Among the experiential objects that acquire functional meaning for us in the course of our conduct, he holds, are empirical selves. First we learn to recognize the empirical selves of others, which we accomplish by acquiring habitual ways of responding to these others in the course of our social conduct. Other selves are, in this sense, social objects, objects constituted by the roles they come to play in our social behaviour. Then, gradually, we begin to respond to our own actions, especially our own vocal gestures, as others respond to them. By thus "taking the roles or attitudes of others," we become meaningful empirical objects to ourselves. In this manner, we move from consciousness of other selves to personal self-consciousness: we acquire a "me," an object self of our own, in contrast to the selves of others (Mead 1964, 139–40).

The key to making sense of what Mead is saying here is to bear in mind once again his pragmatic or functionalist theory of experiential objects. An experienced object, according to this view, is a presentation that arises as a phase of ongoing conduct. And this presentation always consists of some stimulus content plus some response or responses interpreting that content, infusing it with meanings or imagery drawn from past experience. Some ongoing pattern of response is thus always required for the occurrence of an experienced object. And when the experienced object involved is the "me" of self-conscious experience, this ongoing pattern of response is what functions as the "I" with respect to which the "me" makes its appearance.

The Meadian "I," in other words, is here regarded not merely as a Jamesian subject but as the behavioural equivalent of the Jamesian "thinker" or "passing state of consciousness" referred to in the passage from James cited above: it is an ongoing process of response that is interpreting or giving meaning to some stimulus content in the present in order to yield an experienced object. If the stimulus content is provided by the individual's own gestures or talk, and if this content is interpreted by the individual's own acquired social responses, then the resulting object will be the empirical object self or "me" of that individual's self-consciousness. Meanwhile, the ongoing process of response, the "I," is always behind the scenes; it is never a player on the stage of presented objects (Mead 1964, 140–1).

These, then, are some of the chief points Mead makes about the "I" and the "me" in his publications predating the 1928 course lectures upon which *Mind, Self and Society* is mainly based. We might well wish that he had gone on to elaborate and enrich his discussion of both the subject and the object sides of the self in these early essays, but at least his remarks here provide a clear, suggestive, and logically consistent framework for further development. We shall now see, however, that once he takes up these terms again in *Mind, Self and Society*, their use becomes a good deal more problematic.

MEAD'S USE OF THE TERMS "I" AND "ME" IN *MIND, SELF AND SOCIETY*

Some of the passages in which the terms "I" and "me" appear in *Mind, Self and Society* are obviously intended to reiterate the Jamesian distinction we have just examined. Mead tells us once again, for instance, that the self is distinguished by its capacity to be both a subject and an object to itself (Mead 1934, 136–8, 172–3) and that the object self in this relationship is what he means by the term "me" (Mead 1934, 173–5). Moreover, he continues to say in various places that the "me" is a social object – i.e., an object of experience made possible by the fact that human individuals "take the attitude or role of the other" and thereby import into their own conduct those attitudes or response-tendencies that their actions typically call forth in the behaviour of others (Mead 1934, 171–5). Similarly, there are passages here in which the "I" continues to be regarded as a presupposition, but never a presentation, of immediate experience. The "I," as Mead puts it, "does not get into the lime-light"; we only become aware of it as a historical figure, as a part of a present "me" that was the "I" of an earlier time (Mead 1934, 174). And, finally, the "I" is again held to be a source of novelty in our conduct: "It is because of the 'I' that we say that we are never fully aware of what we are, that we surprise ourselves by our own action" (Mead 1934, 174).

So far we are on familiar ground. But as Mead proceeds to flesh out his views in *Mind, Self and Society*, we begin to notice a significant shift in the way he speaks of the "me" phase of the self. In his early essays, he had emphasized the manner in which the organized sets of social attitudes that individuals import into their conduct subsequently take the form of responses to their own gestures, thus giving rise to the empirical object self or "me" of their self-consciousness; now, however, we find many passages in which he speaks of these sets of attitudes as if they themselves were the "me" or "me's" of our experience. Mead tells us, for instance, that "[t]he 'I' is the response of the organism to the attitudes of others; the 'me' is the organized set of attitudes of others which one himself assumes" (Mead 1934, 175). Or, again, he says that the self is essentially a social process involving these two distinguishable phases: the "me" consists of a group of attitudes that represent the others in one's community; the "I" is the response of the individual to these attitudes, a response that is never altogether socially determined and that may bring about change in these attitudes and the community from which they have been imported (Mead 1934, 178–9, 194–9, 209–11, 214–15). One might claim, of course, that Mead is drawing attention to the same aspect of human social conduct whether he speaks of a set of internalized social attitudes as playing a key role in constructing the "me" or as themselves being the "me." This may well be the case, but when one is trying to understand Mead's "I" and "me" distinction, this change from the former to the latter way of speaking makes a very big difference.

Let me unpack this last point. If we simply identify or equate the "me" with a set of acquired social attitudes, as Mead appears to do at numerous points in *Mind, Self and Society*, then the term "me" no longer designates the object self of self-consciousness. (It is rather an example of what Mead calls a "generalized other.") And if the term "me" no longer designates the object self of self-consciousness, then it no longer makes sense to think of the corresponding "I" as the subject of such self-consciousness. We have, in short, abandoned the underlying logical framework of Mead's earlier Jamesian (or subject-object) version of the "I" and "me" distinction. Furthermore, if the "I" is no longer the subject of self-consciousness, what is it? How are we to think of it in a way that meshes with the new conception of the "me"? *Mind, Self and Society*, as most readers know, is notoriously vague when it comes to providing an answer to this question. The "I," we are here told, carries on a kind of conversation or reciprocal interaction with the "me," and in this interaction the "I" typically plays the role of the less conventional, less predictable, and more innovative partner (Mead 1934, 197–200, 214). But the closest Mead comes to giving a more definite answer to the question about the identity of the "I" that is said to interact with the newly conceived "me" is when he equates it with the response of the individual human organism or biological individual to the set of social attitudes that constitute the "me" (Mead 1934, 175–7, 196–9). This, of course, is the definition of the "I" that Lewis seizes upon, and it is a variation on the definition to which Charles Morris gives his endorsement in his introduction to the volume. But it is not the only version of the newly conceived "I" found in *Mind, Self and Society*: sometimes the innovative and unconventional "I" is regarded as being more fully socialized than the "me" – as in those passages where Mead suggests that the "I" may criticize and reject certain conventional attitudes of its current community by appealing to its vision of a possible alternative society in which certain ideals (e.g., ideals of justice, benevolence, or democracy) are more fully realized (Mead 1934, 199, 216–18).

Thus we arrive at a new (albeit somewhat vague) non-Jamesian version of the "I" and "me" distinction in *Mind, Self and Society*, one that at times stands alongside, and at other times seems to replace, Mead's earlier Jamesian version of this distinction. That these two versions of the "I" and "me" distinction are not only different but logically incompatible can be seen by considering those passages in which Mead continues to speak of the "I" as acting behind the scenes and as becoming an item of conscious experience only after it has passed out of the present moment, at which time it may appear as part of a new "me" (Mead 1934, 174–6). This whole way of speaking presupposes a Jamesian "I" that exists only in the immediate present and a Jamesian "me" that is an object self. If we embrace the new non-Jamesian version of the interacting "me" and "I," there is no reason at all why one of these two participants in the interaction should be any more "behind the scenes" than the other. Nor would it any longer make sense to speak of one of these participants (the "I") as becoming a part of the other (the "me") at some later moment.

We should note, further, that if one interprets Mead's revised version of the "I" and "me" distinction along the lines suggested by Charles Morris and most other commentators, it is logically inconsistent with the pragmatic or functionalist view of experiential objects upon which Mead bases his attempt to explain how the human individual becomes an object to himself or herself. Let us recall how this view of experiential objects enters into Mead's earlier way of drawing the "I" and "me" distinction: he there treats the "I" not only as a Jamesian subject but as an ongoing process of response that in part constructs the "me" or object self. Now add to this Mead's view that the "me" is a social object, an object whose meaningful properties derive from social responses or attitudes imported into our conduct through the behavioural mechanism of "taking the attitude of the other." These two claims reveal that Mead's theory concerning the construction of the self as a social object requires us to locate in the "I" all those acquired social responses and attitudes involved in the construction of the social "me" of self-conscious experience. In short, if we accept Mead's functionalist view of experiential objects, then we cannot attribute social structure only or primarily to the "me," and we cannot regard the "I" as some kind of merely biological, impulsive, or non-social response to this social structure.

Furthermore, Mead's new way of making the "I" and "me" distinction in *Mind, Self and Society* is untenable even if it is considered in isolation from the assumptions of its predecessor, for this distinction does violence to many of Mead's most important social-psychological insights – namely, those concerning the extent to which the structures taken over from our social experience come to permeate and shape human conduct, thought, and awareness. What Mead should say, given the basic thrust of his social-psychological theorizing, and what his second way of making the "I" and "me" distinction prevents him from saying consistently and well, is this: Our personalities have their foundation in an original set of biological and social tendencies. But these tendencies come to fruition in our personalities only through a process of expression in which they acquire complex social structures. Our personalities may not be completely harmonious or coherent; they may and usually do contain tensions between different social structures or patterns of social response. This is only to be expected, since our selves or personalities reflect the social processes within which they arise. But social structures go all the way down in our personalities. When we respond to others or to ourselves, our responses almost always exhibit some kind of social structure. It is just this way of thinking to which Mead's second way of formulating the "I" and "me" distinction does violence. The distinction between a socially structured "me" and an "I" that seems to have no inherent or acquired social structure forces Mead into an unduly dualistic way of thinking about the relation between social structure and the conduct of the human individual.

RECONSTRUCTING MEAD'S DISCUSSION OF THE "I" AND "ME"

Where then should we go from here with Mead's "I" and "me" distinction if we wish to preserve and build upon what is valuable in Mead's view of the self? I want to conclude this paper by outlining five suggestions having to do specifically with the revision and application of this distinction as it relates to other key elements in his social theory of the self.

1. The second version of the "I" and "me" distinction as it is presented in *Mind, Self and Society* should be expunged from Mead's theory of the self for the reasons outlined above. The terms "I" and "me" should not be employed to stand for, respectively, socially unstructured and socially structured aspects of the self. Any points Mead wanted to make when he spoke of these matters can be made equally well by means of other terms in his theoretical vocabulary – terms such as "impulses," "individual human organism," and "generalized other." The terms "I" and "me" should be used only in ways consistent with Mead's use of them in his earlier essays. This means that we should think of the "I" and "me" as the subject and object poles of a cognitive structure arising within the conduct of the human biological individual once that conduct acquires a particular level and kind of social complexity.

2. The content and function of the "me" or empirical self should be discussed in a much more thoroughgoing manner than we find in Mead's writings. One would like to see, for instance, further elaboration of the different dimensions of the "me" and the different roles that these play in guiding our self-conscious conduct. Mead has little to say about this matter, but his theory could easily be developed along lines suggested by William James when he discusses "The Material Me," "The Social Me," and "The Spiritual Me" in his chapter on "The Consciousness of Self" in *The Principles of Psychology* (James 1890, chapter x).

3. More should also be said about the "I" and the way in which we can best think of this aspect of human conduct. Mead is on the right track, I believe, in those passages of *Mind, Self and Society* where he speaks of the "I" as the "living act" (Mead 1934, 203) or the "unitary life-process" of the organism (Mead 1934, n175) within which the "me" arises as a meaningful social object. But we need to elaborate upon this suggestion by saying more about the role of social

habits or attitudes in giving shape to such living acts. In particular, attention should be paid to the importance of those habits that shape our ongoing conduct but never become a part of the "me" of self-consciousness (see Mead 1934, 163). Since Mead's discussion of the self is heavily cognitive in nature, it might help in this regard to adopt the term "personality" as a more general term encompassing not only those cognitive structures related to self-consciousness but also habits and various non-cognitive factors that play a part in shaping the conduct of the human individual.

4. The relationship between the individual self and his or her society should be discussed in terms that do not echo the kind of dualistic thinking encouraged by the second version of the "I" and "me" distinction employed throughout much of *Mind, Self and Society*. Mead is surely correct to emphasize the fact that while individual human personalities are shaped by the social structure of their communities, they may also react to these structures in ways that bring about social change. But in this connection it is important to note that these reactions are themselves almost always an expression not simply of biological impulses but of various social patterns within the socialized personalities involved. "Conflicts among individuals in a highly developed and organized human society," Mead notes at one point in *Mind, Self and Society*, "are not mere conflicts among their respective primitive impulses but are conflicts among their respective selves or personalities, each with its definite social structure ... and each with a number of different social facets or aspects, a number of different sets of social attitudes constituting it" (Mead 1934, 307). Similarly, critical reactions of individuals to aspects of their own communities typically involve conflicts between the particular sets of social attitudes that shape these selves and some other set of attitudes in the larger society with which they are not in harmony.

5. Finally, a Meadian treatment of the "I" and "me" within the context of a genetic and social account of the human personality clearly needs a more fully developed theory of socialization than any Mead offers in his writings or lectures. Mead tells us that each human personality acquires a social structure that reflects the structure of its community in its own distinctive and individual manner (Mead 1934, 201–2), and he tells us repeatedly that the mechanism of socialization through which this occurs is primarily the human tendency to "take the attitude or role of the other." But beyond this he offers us no way of explaining why the "I's" and "me's" of particular

individuals take on just those social structures that they do in the course of their social experience.

One of the great ironies of G.H. Mead's intellectual legacy is that his considerable influence upon the sociological approach to human personality is due almost entirely to the publication of *Mind, Self and Society* – a book that he did not himself write and that presents some of his key social-psychological ideas in an overly truncated and misleading fashion. Many readers of this book do not realize, for instance, that the terms "behaviorism" or "social behaviorism" he there uses to characterize his orientation amount to little more than new names for an old way of thinking – i.e., for an approach to human social behaviour that borrows its concept of action from John Dewey and the early Chicago School of psychological function-alism. Similarly, there is little in this book that adequately indicates the extent to which Mead's genetic and social account of self-con-sciousness is grounded in his pragmatic view of experienced objects as entities whose meaningful characters are in part constructed by the conduct within which they play a functional role. Nowhere is the inadequacy of *Mind, Self and Society* more evident, however, than in its distinction between the two aspects of personality Mead calls the "I" and the "me." I have tried to show in the present essay that the discussion of the "I" and the "me" in *Mind, Self and Society* contains an incoherent mixture of two different versions of this distinction – only one of which is tenable within the context of Mead's overall social-psychological project. Those who want to build upon Mead's ideas about the human self should therefore give up both the attempt to salvage everything that Mead says about the "I" and "me" in this volume and the attempt to construe this distinction along the lines proposed by Mead's editor, Charles Morris. They should instead seek to elaborate upon the Jamesian version of this distinction set forth by Mead in his earlier published essays.

REFERENCES

Cook, Gary. 1972. "The Development of G.H. Mead's Social Psychology." *Transactions of the Charles S. Peirce Society: A Quarterly Journal in American Philosophy* 8:167–86
– 1993. *George Herbert Mead: The Making of a Social Pragmatist.* Urbana and Chicago: University of Illinois Press

Dewey, John. 1972. "The Reflex Arc Concept in Psychology." In *John Dewey: The Early Works*, vol. 5, 1882–98, edited by Jo Ann Boydston, 96–109. Carbondale: Southern Illinois University Press

Habermas, Jurgen. 1992. *Postmetaphysical Thinking: Philosophical Essays*. Cambridge, MA: MIT Press

James, William. 1890. *The Principles of Psychology*. New York: Henry Holt and Co.

– 1892. *Psychology: The Briefer Course*. New York: Henry Holt and Co.

Kolb, William L. 1944. "A Critical Evaluation of Mead's 'I' and 'Me' Concepts." *Social Forces* 22:291–6

Lewis, J. David 1979. "A Social Behaviorist Interpretation of the Meadian 'I.'" *American Journal of Sociology* 85:261–87

Mead, G.H. 1932. *The Philosophy of the Present*. La Salle, IL: The Open Court Publishing Company

– 1934. *Mind, Self and Society: From the Standpoint of a Social Behaviorist*. Chicago: University of Chicago Press

– 1938. *The Philosophy of the Act*. Chicago: University of Chicago Press

– 1964. *Selected Writings*, edited by Andrew J. Reck. Indianapolis: Bobbs-Merrill

Markell, Patchen. 2007. "The Potential and the Actual: Mead, Honneth, and the 'I.'" In *Recognition and Power: Axel Honneth and the Tradition of Critical Social Theory*, edited by Bert van den Brink and David Owen, 100–32. Cambridge: Cambridge University Press

7

Working the Chicago Interstices: Warner and Goffman's Intellectual Formation

GREG SMITH AND YVES WINKIN

It is easy to overlook the important role played by William Lloyd Warner (1898–1970) in the development of sociology at the University of Chicago. Perhaps it is because Warner never quite fitted the standard profile of the "Chicago School" sociologist. Warner was not an urbanist, not an ecologist, not an interactionist, in any of the senses that these terms are usually understood. Appointed associate professor at Chicago in 1935, he brought a range of intellectual preoccupations of clear relevance to Chicago sociology in the post-Park 1930s. His accumulating expertise as a research manager and practitioner made him a significant player in the Second Chicago School (Fine 1995) of the 1940s and 1950s. Warner was a hybrid figure, holding a joint appointment in anthropology and sociology at Chicago from 1935 to 1959. Apparently, Warner was seen as a "marginal man" by no less than Robert Park, who coined the concept (Lindner 1996, 163–4).

Warner chose to occupy the space between the differing academic cultures of anthropology and sociology, productively exploiting that space to develop new programs of research and to draw in psychologists and others sympathetic to his interdisciplinary endeavours. He helped to found the Committee on Human Relations in Industry at Chicago in 1943 and acted as its first chairman (Gardner and Whyte 1946, 506n1). Warner also became heavily involved in the work of the Committee on Human Development (Abbott and Graziano 1995, 225). Thus, Warner's research activities were never simply located in Chicago's famed Department of Sociology. From the mid-1940s,

Warner looked beyond the academy: with Burleigh Gardner, he founded Social Research, Inc. (SRI) in 1946, which was based initially in an office in the prestigious Hyde Park Bank Building on East 53rd Street. SRI was a market research agency that broke new ground by using qualitative methods to reach beyond the narrow understandings of consumer behaviour previously obtained by market researchers through telephone surveys and opinion polls.

Commentators on Goffman's writings (e.g., Collins 1980; Spillius 1993; Becker 2003) as well as Erving Goffman himself (Verhoeven 1993, 321) have acknowledged Warner's influence on the development of Goffman's sociological perspective. Warner lent continuity to Goffman's graduate studies as the only member of the Chicago faculty serving on the committees of both Goffman's master's thesis (1949) and his doctoral dissertation (1953). The title of Goffman's first paper, "Symbols of Class Status" (Goffman 1951), clearly bears the imprint of some of Warner's Yankee City preoccupations with class and symbolism. In 1949, Warner was instrumental in securing the opportunity for Goffman to carry out his Shetland Isle research (Winkin 1988). When Goffman returned from Europe to Chicago in the early 1950s, Warner helped him to obtain paid employment on a commercial project for Social Research, Inc. (SRI 1953). Warner appears as a generous patron who provided continuous intellectual and professional support for Goffman during his sometimes difficult times as a graduate student at the University of Chicago between 1945 and 1953.

However, unlike Everett C. Hughes, Goffman's other significant Chicago teacher (Jaworski 2000), Warner is fast becoming a forgotten figure, someone who is little noticed and under-studied in many accounts of the Second Chicago School. Our chapter seeks to remedy this oversight by documenting the Warner aspect of Goffman's Chicago story. We shall show that Goffman exposed some of the difficulties of working within a Warner frame and used the gaps and problems he identified as an opportunity to test out and develop his own emergent sociological framework. This process of critically reworking a strict Warnerian approach we characterize as "working the Chicago interstices" and suggest that it assists a closer understanding of how Goffman's singular (see Sahni, this volume) sociological approach arose.

Efforts to investigate the Goffman–Warner relationship are doubly compromised by some significant archival absences. Goffman, a very private person, was reluctant to respond to biographical inquiries.

Thus, there is no official Goffman archive: no depository of notes, drafts, correspondence, and photographs made public for scholars to ponder. The situation for the would-be archival researcher is no better in Warner's case. Warner's papers were trashed without proper authorization. Mildred Warner reports that following her husband's death in May 1970, it took her a couple of months to get around to visiting Warner's office at Michigan State University, where he had worked since 1959 as professor of social research. When she did, she found that the "banks of files" her husband had "accumulated through forty years" (M.H. Warner 1988, vii) had disappeared. Thus, scholars lack the key documents to directly investigate the relationship between Warner and one of his most gifted students, and more indirect methods must suffice. Information was gathered by two principal means: the recollections of colleagues who studied or worked with them and records recovered from public archival sources. "Salvage biography" seems an apt term to describe our investigation.

READINGS OF THE GOFFMAN–WARNER RELATIONSHIP

Two approaches to the relationship of Goffman to Warner are prominent in the critical literature. The first is that Warner was an early but not persisting influence that Goffman put behind him as he developed his own distinctive form of sociological thinking. Tom Burns expresses this view pungently: "His first paper, 'Symbols of Class Status,' is best seen as a departure point, a 'goodbye to all that' – to Lloyd Warner in particular" (Burns 1992, 11–12). Burns adds that while Goffman was still at Edinburgh (i.e., no later than mid-1951), he was already talking about the themes of the papers he would later write in the 1950s. Burns's view implies that Goffman reached a turning point during the research sponsored by Edinburgh's anthropology department between 1949 and 1951. On this view, Warner was associated with old ways of doing sociology at a time when Goffman was seeking to forge something new. For the turning-point thesis, Warner was an early but insignificant influence largely irrelevant to the shape of Goffman's mature sociology.

In contrast to this view, there is the interpretation of the Goffman–Warner relationship advanced by Randall Collins (1980; 2000 [1986]; 1988). It might be termed the abiding influence thesis. Collins's general thesis is that "the deepest layer in Goffman's works, his core intellectual vision, is a continuation of the Durkheimian tradition" (Collins 1988, 43). Collins sees Warner as the principal Chicagoan source of the Durkheimian elements that would exercise a continuing influence on the broad development of Goffman's thought. Collins's account proposes that Warner made analytical, methodological, and substantive impacts on Goffman. Analytically, Collins treats Warner as the key Chicago figure to advance Goffman's schooling in Durkheimian symbolic analysis, reaffirming and consolidating the introduction to Durkheim's sociology that Goffman obtained as an undergraduate from C.W.M. Hart at the University of Toronto. Methodologically, Collins suggests that Goffman follows Warner's pioneering trail at a more micro level. Like Warner, Goffman appreciated the value of applying anthropological methods to aspects of contemporary society – in Goffman's case, to the minutiae of face-to-face interaction. But there was also a substantive debt: the focus on stratification. Although class figured explicitly in the "Symbols" paper (Goffman 1951), its presence was also evident in Goffman's first book, *The Presentation of Self in Everyday Life*, in the class differences inflected through the many studies of occupations and professions that serve as illustrative material (Boltanski 1973). More specifically, Goffman's interactional analyses, such as the front/back region distinction, developed the project that Warner's class analyses began by showing how class barriers were manifested in interaction rituals. For Collins, Warner "was extremely important for what Goffman achieved in his early works" (Collins 2000 [1986], 78).

Tracking influence through publications also proves difficult. As far as we have been able to ascertain, Warner does not cite Goffman, let alone quote him, anywhere in his published work. Perhaps we should not be surprised. Partly, it is a matter of timing. A substantial part of Goffman's famed work did not appear until the last decade of Warner's own life, by which time Warner's interests and ways of working were firmly established. Goffman's published citations of Warner (Goffman 1952a, 457n.; Goffman 1953, 64n1; Goffman 1961, 70n35; Goffman 1963, 63n35; Goffman 1983, 10) are few in number yet convey a close familiarity with the detail of Warner's work.

Our approach to the Warner–Goffman relationship concentrates on Goffman's graduate studies at the University of Chicago. Drawing upon published sources, unpublished documents, and interview materials gathered as part of an intellectual biography, we trace some of the paths followed by graduate student Goffman. Close study of these materials sheds important light on Goffman's response to Warner's teaching. In this chapter, we show how Goffman began his graduate training at Chicago allied to the Warner camp but soon developed critical distance from it. His first work, his master's thesis, took up openly Warnerian concerns and approaches. We suggest it marked a pivotal point in Goffman's intellectual development, providing an opportunity for critical engagement with Warner's sociology. In the course of his graduate studies at Chicago (1945–53), Goffman's intellectual allegiances shifted toward the approach of Everett Hughes, whom Goffman would later identify as his most important teacher at Chicago. However, the process was not straightforward and unilinear. In staking out the interaction order as a new domain of analysis for sociology, Goffman capitalized on the intellectual and practical resources provided by both Warner and Hughes.

1945: WHEN ERVING MET LLOYD

Erving Goffman first registered as a graduate student at Chicago in the fall quarter of 1945. Many of his fellow students were US war veterans returning to university under the provisions of the GI Bill. The sudden influx of large numbers of graduate students – there were so many that temporary housing had to be built on the Midway Plaisance (the mile-long park to the immediate south of the University of Chicago campus) – meant that the few professors were much in demand and that books were hard to find in the library. In these special circumstances, a vibrant student culture emerged (Fine 1995).

Goffman was in among that crowd, but his personal trajectory differed from many others. He was not an American citizen and had not served in the military during the war. Born in Canada in 1922 of Ukrainian Jewish parents, he went to St John's Technical High School, Winnipeg, which provided many pupils with an educational culture that encouraged questioning and debate (Winkin 2010). Graduating from St John's in 1939, Goffman then enrolled at the University of Manitoba in the same city. At this stage, he intended to major in natural sciences. By Goffman's third year at Manitoba, however, his interests had turned toward the social sciences (Smith 2003). He left in 1942, but it is not clear what he did next. He was rejected for military service (Winkin 1991) and is thought to have worked for Canada's National Film Board in Toronto in the summer of 1943. Dennis Wrong later claimed that he encouraged Goffman to return to Toronto to complete his undergraduate studies (Winkin

1988). He obtained a bachelor's degree in the November 1945 convocation of the University of Toronto.

At Toronto, he was influenced by the teaching of C.W.M. Hart, a Durkheimian who took students through the then untranslated *Suicide*, and by Ray Birdwhistell, a young instructor who was just beginning to formulate the detailed studies of body motion that he would later name kinesics (Winkin 1988). Linking Hart and Birdwhistell was the figure of W. Lloyd Warner. Both Hart and Warner had conducted anthropological fieldwork in Australia and were part of the same circle around Radcliffe-Brown in Australia during the 1920s. Birdwhistell was a student of Warner's who was intrigued by the possibility of connecting the detailed analysis of body motion to Warner's class categories – a connection about which Goffman would later express some scepticism (see Winkin 1984). At Toronto, Goffman began his relationship with Elizabeth Bott (Spillius), daughter of Edward A. Bott, head of Toronto's Department of Psychology. The two of them moved together to Chicago that fall, she to register in the anthropology department, he in sociology.

Where was Lloyd Warner in his academic career in 1945? The short answer would be: pretty much at the top of his game. In many respects, the 1940s represent the most successful decade of Warner's career. He was full professor at a prestigious university, he had won wide recognition for his pioneering research, he was successful at attracting research funding, there was a continuous flow of publications – he was even satirized in John P. Marquand's 1949 novel, *Point of No Return* (Ingersoll 1997). By the mid-1940s, Warner had entered a period of high productivity that he was to sustain to the end of his life. His work was taking new directions, notably toward the areas of symbolic analysis and audience research.

Indeed, since returning from Australia in the late 1920s, Warner's career had been on a roll. Resuming his studies at Harvard, Warner soon found himself in demand to conduct, direct, and advise on a series of major research projects. Much of this work involved teams of researchers. Collaborative working soon became second nature to him. In the early 1930s, Warner worked with Elton Mayo on his research at the Western Electric Company's Hawthorne plant in Cicero, Chicago. He then obtained funding from the prime minister of Ireland, Eamonn de Valera, to help underwrite the costs of the multidisciplinary Harvard Irish Survey, products of which included Arensberg and Kimball's famed monograph *Family and Community in Ireland* (1940). In the 1930s and 1940s, he directed research into ethnicity and politics in Georgia, Chicago, and Illinois. But Warner is probably best remembered for his substantial investigation in the "Yankee City" series of books that did so much to stimulate debate about class and community. In 1945, when Goffman arrived in Chicago, the third volume of his Yankee City series had just appeared (Warner and Srole 1945). In the following year, Warner co-founded Social Research Inc. with Burleigh Gardner, the innovative market research agency that applied qualitative and anthropological techniques to consumer behaviour. Warner's developing connections with the business world also helped to fund a pioneering study of the audience for a popular radio series in 1945 (Warner and Henry 1948). This was the study to which Goffman would link his master's thesis research.

Warner took very seriously the task of mentoring and encouraging students and colleagues (Levy 2008). Indeed, it could be said that Warner's role at Chicago bears comparison with Park's role a generation earlier. Like Park, Warner did much to encourage students' own research, often by finding work for them on one of his big research projects. In addition, Warner regularly taught core graduate research training courses offered to sociology and anthropology students. The research for his Yankee City series was an early example of what has come to be known as "anthropology at home." While planning and conducting this research, Warner consulted with Park. He also acknowledged how key 1920s Chicago studies, such as *The Gold Coast and the Slum, The Ghetto*, and *The Gang*, inspired his research work in Newburyport (Lindner 1996, 102).

When Goffman arrived at Chicago in 1945, he had already read Warner's work (Spillius 1993) and, perhaps informed by Birdwhistell, was aware of Warner's significant reputation. Spillius has noted Goffman's great respect for Lloyd Warner around this time. It certainly influenced his initial choice of courses on the MA sociology, and in the fall 1945 quarter, he took two courses with Warner. At 3 p.m. each Monday, Wednesday, and Friday, he would attend Warner's class on Comparative Institutions, then in the following hour would take Warner's and Robert Havighurst's class, The Individual and Society. Warner was also a key teacher on the compulsory course, Advanced Field Studies: The Community (Sociology 301A), taught by members of the department (University of Chicago 1945).

Goffman took Sociology 301A in the fall of 1945 and by the beginning of 1946 had started to work on his master's thesis under

Warner's supervision. Sociology 301A was a mix of social stratification theory, British social anthropology, and "community studies." Warner arranged the class into "committees," which were to report on different "communities" in Chicago (Italian, Ukrainian, black American, Anglo-Saxon, for example). For Warner, communities in all societies were organized in "social structures" or institutions, like the family, the church, the social class, the caste. The "committees" of students had to report on one of the social structures of their community. Social classes were seen as the fundamental structure that stratified American society, but they were not presented as antagonistic – there certainly were no class struggles in Warner's vision of the social world. For him, members actually assigned social class positions to each other, so he saw the six classes he dealt with not as "categories invented by social scientists to help explain what they have to say" (Warner et al. 1949, xii) – rather, they existed in people's minds. Fieldworkers just had to ask, and people would tell them where they and their neighbours socially belonged. It was all a matter of "interconnectedness," as he put it while clasping his hands and cracking his fingers in front of his students. Warner cut a worldly and somewhat flamboyant figure in the classroom. He could be even more impressive in direct dealings with students. Ray Birdwhistell (n.d., 2) recalled: "In the one-to-one he was unbeatable. He abandoned his entrepreneurial and managerial presence and became himself, a deeply concerned human being."

WORKING WITH THE WARNER TEAM

In the 1940s, the MA degree in sociology at the University of Chicago was a demanding course of study and research training that normally took three years to complete (University of Chicago 1945, 241). Goffman may have been aiming to complete the degree in two years and by the fall of 1946 had met all the divisional, minor, and elective requirements and had completed nine of the fifteen required courses in sociology. It was not without difficulty: in some courses he had to obtain extensions to complete the work. Goffman began his graduate studies at a determined pace that showed he was serious about finishing the MA in two years, yet in the end it took him four. What happened? He does not seem to have taken any courses from the end of the summer quarter of 1946 until the beginning of the fall quarter of 1948. This was perhaps a difficult time in his personal life. Elizabeth Bott broke up with him, and he was working as a night watchman so that he could pay his bills. The break from classes may also have been due to the very real problems that Goffman ran up against in completing his MA thesis research, the data collection stage of which began in autumn 1946.

The MA regulations recommend that students make an early start on their thesis preparations. Goffman followed this advice and began his MA thesis work by the spring of 1946 (Goffman 1948b). He became interested in the Thematic Apperception Test (TAT), a projective test that Warner was using in the "Big Sister" study (Warner and Henry 1948). It seems likely that Goffman was one of the "field staff" who collected data for the "Big Sister" project (see Warner and Henry 1948, 12n6). In addition, Goffman piloted his own use of the TAT on a collection of six fellow graduate students in a paper that served as a course requirement for work for Sociology 301A (Goffman 1948b). Goffman (1946) presented a thesis state-ment outlining his research proposal to the Department of Sociology on 2 August 1946. It was approved by Ernest Burgess as chairman of the Department of Sociology later that same day.

Goffman's planned MA thesis is set squarely within a Warner frame. At this time, Warner and his colleague William E. Henry were work-ing on the "Big Sister" study, a project commissioned by the Columbia Broadcasting System (CBS) to investigate how a sample of mainly upper-lower- and lower-middle-class housewives (the "Common Man level" in Warner's homely conceptualization) used a popular daytime radio serial entitled "Big Sister." The TAT was the major instrument Warner and Henry used to establish characteristics of the housewives' personalities and the nature of their family and interper-sonal relations. They wanted to establish the effect of the "Big Sister" program on its predominantly female audience, and their report offered an early contribution to what is now known as the uses and gratifications approach to media effects. It showed how "Big Sister" served an educational function, helping women to resolve their own emotional and interpersonal dilemmas while at the same time subtly endorsing the housewife role over career-woman alternatives.

By the summer of 1946, with the Warner–Henry study in progress, Goffman saw how he could use its methods and data to address his own research question. Goffman's (1946) thesis statement sets out his thinking at this time. The document is a model of clarity and pre-cision. In six points, the whole thesis is delineated: 1. Introduction;

2. Status of the Field; 3. Leading Ideas (and the hypothesis); 4. Data; 5. Tools and Techniques; 6. Approximate Outline of Thesis.

Goffman's 1946 thesis statement and the opening pages of the 1949 master's thesis show how he conceived his work as development out of Warner and Henry's (1948) "Big Sister" study. However, its aim was much more specific. While Warner and Henry addressed a range of research questions about the social characteristics of the audience and the meaning of the radio program to women listeners (see Warner and Henry, 1948, 8–9), Goffman focused on a single general relationship – between personality and socio-economic status. Goffman wanted to use the TAT to find features of the women's personalities that were shaped by their socio-economic status. Warner and Henry's study concentrated on working-class women. Goffman would select a more middle-class sample of wives of professional and managerial workers using Warner's criteria of occupation, source of income, education, house type, and area lived in (Warner and Henry 1948; Warner et al. 1949). In the fall of 1946, Goffman began interviewing in the Hyde Park (HP) district adjacent to the university. He undertook fifty interviews. Three women were excluded because their socio-economic status fell outside Goffman's sampling frame, leaving a sample of forty-seven.

The hand of Warner and his associates is also evident in how Goffman framed his hypothesis:

Housewives who live in residential districts and whose husbands are of the white-collar or skilled-labor occupational groups tend to organize their life experience differently from university trained housewives who live in the better residential districts of Chicago and whose husbands are of the professional or high-income groups. The following covert behavior characteristics are more manifest in the lower socio-economic stratum than in the higher: stereotyped and strained interpersonal relations, apprehension of the unknown, conception of the outer world as a source of disappointment and frustration, lack of personal control and personal resources, fear of overt expression of impulses, and distrust of heterosexual relations (Goffman 1946, 3).

The terms by which the "covert behavior characteristics" are described are taken, as Goffman acknowledges, from Warner (see Warner and Henry 1948, 20–1; Warner 1952, 196). Goffman also planned to use the same ten TAT cards in the same sequence that the Warner–Henry study did. In 1946, Goffman's aim was to compare two samples: the Common Man–level TAT responses gathered in the "Big Sister" study and those generated by his own HP interviews. That way, he could investigate differences in personality due to socio-economic status. In any event, it was not to be.

RESEARCH AS A LEARNING EXPERIENCE

The first part of the thesis defined projective techniques (chapter i), traced the history of H.A. Murray's Thematic Apperception Test (chapter ii), sharply explained its limitations (chapter iii), and suggested alternative approaches (chapter iv). Although written in stern academese, the twenty-three pages made clear that Goffman thought little of Murray's technique. He would have gladly avoided it (he seemed to say implicitly) if he had been free to do so: "The six aforementioned limitations of Murray's approach are sufficiently severe to have discouraged the use of it in this thesis" (Goffman 1949, 19) – yet he did, but in a twisted way.

The second part of the study gave details on the sampling procedures. Goffman was introduced to his first Hyde Park high-income housewife through Burgess; she was the past-president of the Illinois chapter of the League of Women Voters. She gave the name of seventeen members who lived in Hyde Park and so started to roll the snowball. Goffman also incorporated TAT data from nineteen American Nisei women, who were interviewed by William Caudill for another study. Sure enough, Goffman described his data collection as pretty faulty – a strategy used by every student in the world (exhibit your mistakes before you can be criticized for them). But Goffman also hinted at problems that were Warner and Henry's responsibility – a rather daring move for a MA student.

First, Goffman flatly stated that the CBS data was collected by students of Warner and Henry in the context of a classroom exercise. Henry "briefly trained" them in the technique of administering the TAT, and Warner sent them to the field. Second, he noticed that the subjects of the CBS sample were not chosen randomly but "from a list of women who had written fan letters to a radio program" (Goffman 1949, 34–5), a mode of selection that introduced a severe bias. Third, he devoted two pages to show that when Warner's objective indicators of socio-economic status were scrutinized, they turned out to agglomerate people who had little in common socially. The criticism ultimately became quite explicit: "Nor does it make much sense to match or control the samples for age, marital status and number of children (as was done in this study) when it is not known whether the strata are the same in these respects" (Goffman 1949, 37). In other words, Goffman again let the reader understand that he was led to conduct what would have been a meaningless study if he had not tried to rescue whatever could be rescued.

The third part of the thesis proved to be much more than a simple patch-up. Rebuking Murray's loose psychological definition of "projection," Goffman referred to a broad array of disciplines (from linguistics to philosophy of science), names (from Whorf to Cassirer), and rather esoteric titles (from "The Punctual and Segmentative Aspects of Verbs in Hopi" to *The Metaphysical Foundation of Modern Physical Science*) in order to suggest that the notion was crucial in several sciences to address the issue of symbolic construction of the world:

> Presumably the plethora of possible worlds is reduced to an order that is consistent with the social life of the group. The possibility of creating this order is presumably based on the process of abstraction, whereby an aspect of an event is used as a screening device for sorting out the whole event. By emphasizing some differences and neglecting others, a large number of different events can be handled by a relatively small number of concepts ... It is assumed, then, that meaning is injected into the world in accordance with rules observed by members of a group for selecting, classifying and organizing aspects of events. It is also assumed that these rules are somewhat arbitrary from the point of view of the hypothetical external world. Therefore these rules constitute a form of projection, and it is in this sense that the term is used in this study (Goffman 1949, 42).

Although quite familiar to philosophers, such a "constructivist" perspective was not very familiar to sociologists and anthropologists at the time, even among those with "Culture and Personality" proclivities. Thanks to his wide reading, especially in linguistics, Goffman formulated all by himself a bold, if not original, framework for a sociologically relevant interpretation of TAT responses. They could be seen, he argued, as products of the "constituent premises or modes of thought" (Goffman 1949, 43–4) of specific social groups. The characteristics of the responses given by members of the group under scrutiny needed be isolated and classified, and it was these features of the response, not the personalities of the sampled individuals, to which he now turned. Goffman thus devoted the last thirty-five pages of his study to organizing the kinds of responses he got in the two samples. In so doing, he exhibited three features of his future writings: arborescent taxonomies, ephemeral conceptualizations, and oxymoronic expressions.

First, he opposed responses that only addressed the "task of constructing a reply" to those that assumed that "the task of making believe has already been accepted as the background of the situation" (Goffman 1949, 46–7). The second kind of response was split into two kinds – note the growth of the tree. On the one hand, there were "direct" responses: the subjects treated the images as though they depicted real events; on the other, there were "indirect" responses: the subjects avoided "the obligation of assuming the momentary 'reality' of the representations" (Goffman 1949, 47). Such distinction was certainly familiar to aesthetics scholars but not to clinical psychologists dealing with TATs. Goffman was quietly subversive, and subversive he surely was when he denounced the traditional psychological assessment of short responses. When subjects only offered an "identification" such as "This is a young boy and a violin" or simply enumerated the items in the picture instead of inserting them into a coherent story, they were said, argued Goffman, "to have a low grade of intelligence." Actually, they could just be "bored with the test and impatient with its failure to provide a worthy mental challenge" (Goffman 1949, 48), as his HP subjects demonstrated. Although Goffman's main objective was not to constantly lambast Murray et al., he apparently could not refrain from doing so as he went along. Meanwhile, however, he sketched a fresh interpretation of (direct) responses that were formulated through stories. Noting how stereotyped such stories were, he suggested the notion of "turning-point" to refer to the narrative power of dramatic events such as love or death to explain the past and shape the future of the characters. Turning-points are crises that abruptly redirect lives and simplify the narrator's task: "The formulation of a turning-point makes it easy to fit the items of a picture into a single plot. The past and future of a scene need not be reconstructed imaginatively. This effort is unnecessary because a turning-point takes precedent over any past event, and at the same time contains a complete future for each of the picture characters" (Goffman 1949, 54).

Goffman's conceptual strategy was at work for the first time. The expression was first framed by quotations marks and defined functionally. In later uses, quotation marks were dropped, and the newly elevated, former common-sense expression had to fly analytically on its own. It maintained some visibility until the end of the chapter on appearance and then crashed. Goffman would offer such a tragic life course to hundreds of "low-range" notions, carving for his work a position between full-fledged ethnography and full-fledged theory. The best of the MA thesis was still to come.

When Goffman came to discuss "indirect responses," his craving for neat categorization showed up again. There were three ways to avoid direct responses, and one of the ways was split into four alleys. Subjects could first refuse to show sympathy for the dramatic plight of the characters depicted in the TAT plates. Goffman noticed they would speak in a "sing-song voice, or in a flat empty tone, or in a tempo sufficiently fast to signify impatience and irritation" (Goffman 1949, 59). Then, subjects could address the content of the pictures but in such a way that they avoided a straightforward response. They would individualize the character ("I think of young Menuhin when I look at this"), they would refer to magazines or movies ("This looks like a picture out of *Cosmopolitan*"), they would interpret the scene in eerie terms ("Well, looks like a picture in a fairy tale"), or they would see the scenes as "symbolic" ("Woman on right represents earthy part of life"). And finally, subjects could comment on the very mode of representation used in the TAT rather than deciphering the content ("Comes to mind it's a kind of sloppy sentimental painting without an interesting composition").

Indirect responses were more frequent in the HP sample (high-income housewives) than in the CBS sample (low-income housewives). At that point, Goffman made a jump. In describing the ways his HP subjects responded, he had already demonstrated a keen interest in the paralinguistic and nonverbal features of their talk. Now he was going to relate their avoidance of direct responses to the ways they arranged their ... living rooms. Nothing to do with a "habitus" à la Bourdieu, but still, the move was bold: "This avoidance corresponds to the refusal of HP subjects to be completely bound by the norms that govern conventional treatment of the living-room" (Goffman 1949, 64).

As Goffman interviewed the "bourgeoisie" (our term) of Hyde Park in their living rooms, he had an opportunity to take a close look at the furnishings and other objects. In his report in the final chapter of the thesis, he became more the astute ethnographic observer and ironic writer that readers would get to know ten years later than he was in the previous chapters. After noting that the American living room was a place "to exhibit the crucial social values of respectability and wealth," he offered a very Goffmanesque listing of persona non grata in such a sanctuary: "Except under special conditions, it is taboo for children, servants, tradesmen, dogs and dirt to enter this room" (Goffman 1949, 66). But his point was precisely that his HP subjects went beyond such values and made their living room simply livable, comfortable, and practical, no matter how stylish the furniture was (Goffman mentioned three recurring styles of eighteenth-century furniture with a connoisseur's pen: Chippendale, Hepplewhite, Sheraton). They were not bound by the conventional definition of the living room, and such "disinclination" was reflexive of their relaxed relation to norms in general. Goffman seems to have taken much pleasure in spotting objects that showed their owners' desecrated attitude toward their living rooms. He used the books, the typewriters, or the Mexican pottery to suggest that such living rooms were multifunctional. And he indulged another use of Burke's "perspective by incongruity" to make his point: "In many livingrooms the ritual of order and cleanliness was nicely violated by the permitted presence of a dog, a child, a huge toy, or a fireplace-basket of coal or wood."

He also enjoyed the very demeanour of his interviewees. Some wore men's shirts and slacks; some made direct reference to sex in their conversation; some sat across their seats. But Goffman was not fooled: it was all "conspicuous" (he used the term twice in the same paragraph). Their "polite use of impolite profanities" showed they did not transgress norms; they were just relaxed about them – "cool." Or as he put it, in vintage Goffman style: "These movements seemed to be a sign that the subject was in control of her inhibitions, rather than a sign that impulses were in control of the subject" (Goffman 1949, 70).

Finally, he tabulated the magazines HP subjects regularly received. Sure enough, the *New Yorker* came first, showing up twenty-seven times (in a sample now reduced to thirty-nine subjects). With its ironic tone, self-reflexive cartoons, and careful distance from everyday news, the *New Yorker* was the perfect reading for his "disengaged" subjects.

When Goffman came to his conclusions, he had an easy win. He was careful not to say that lower socio-economic status led to "conservative" attitudes toward norms, as reflected in the higher proportion of direct responses to TAT pictures, or that higher socio-economic status led to "liberal" attitudes. In fact, he was careful enough to end chapter xi on a cautionary note: "It is beyond the scope of this thesis to suggest the ways in which this pattern of disengagement appears in the conjugal, domestic, social and political life of HP subjects" (Goffman 1949, 70). But he had managed to show that TAT could be used to generate interpretations on socially bound behaviour, away from clinical readings or "Culture and Personality" framing. He probably suffered during his four-year attempt to rescue shoddy data and turn it into an original thesis. But he may have had a good time observing the urban bourgeoisie of Hyde Park, and in his final sentence he allowed his admiration to show through in a very Goffmanesque oxymoronic way: "It appears, then, that HP subjects have a sophisticated approach to certain norms of thought and conduct. Perhaps this is caused by their extensive education and by the opportunities they enjoy to engage in artistic or representational forms of recreation. Or perhaps education and art are merely the leading expressions of a general trend towards the corruption of single-mindedness" (Goffman 1949, 77).

Goffman's handling of his MA thesis was bold and imaginative: he abandoned an apparently well-constructed research plan in the face of reasoned objections and located an alternative topic, offering a kind of ethnography of the research interview. Yet the broad form of the critique was in some ways anticipated by Warner. In the first volume of the Yankee City series, Warner (Warner and Lunt 1941, 5–6) suggested that research was "fundamentally a learning process for the scientist who does it." In language that anticipates contemporary concerns about researcher reflexivity, Warner maintained that the researcher should "communicate" the "process" through which the results of any investigation are obtained. That recommendation of the importance of attending to processes of knowledge construction is evident throughout Goffman's thesis. In effect, Goffman starts to develop his own distinctive perspective by working in the interstices of the problems and methods suggested by Warner. The outcome is not the kind of wholesale critique of which Warner would soon become an easy target. Rather, it is subtler, a genuinely productive critique that opens the way to those now famous studies of the interaction order.

THE ATTENUATION OF AN INFLUENCE

When Goffman returned to classes in the fall quarter of 1948, a paper prepared for Ernest Burgess's Seminar on Personal and Social Disorganization would become his first publication, "Symbols of Class Status" (Goffman 1951). The 1948 paper, "The Role of Status Symbols in Social Organization," showed that Goffman was continuing to take seriously Warner's interests in markers of social difference. However, Goffman introduced a disjunctive element absent in Warner. He observed that there is "the constant possibility that symbols may come to be employed in a fraudulent way, to signify a status which the signifier does not in fact possess" (Goffman 1948a, 4). Misrepresentation could be curtailed by six very general "restrictive devices." The same problematic – "a symbol of status is not always a very good test of status" (Goffman 1951, 295) – drives the published version. While the labelling of the six devices differs, the broad structure of the published version can be seen in the 1948 draft. Goffman (1951, 294) expressed his gratitude "to W. Lloyd Warner for direction."

Somehow, in 1948 Goffman emerged from his self-imposed exile as the figure his fellow students all looked up to – the one they regarded as most likely to succeed. The 1948 paper was presented at the 1949 meeting of the University of Chicago's student organization, the Society for Social Research. By late summer, Goffman had completed his thesis and the remaining taught course credits he needed for the master's degree, which was awarded in December 1949. By then he was on the other side of the Atlantic, just settling into Britain's most northerly hotel, on Unst, Shetland.

The Unst fieldwork provided the crucible that formed Goffman's distinctive contribution to sociology, the notion of the interaction order. Goffman spent as much time as he could on the island but had to return to Edinburgh to fulfill some of the obligations of his assistantship. It was probably on one of these occasions that Goffman (1971, v) "almost met" A.R. Radcliffe-Brown, the leading advocate of Durkheimian perspectives in the anglophone world. Warner gave the Munro lectures at Edinburgh in 1950 (Warner 1952), and Radcliffe-Brown may have been in the audience.

On Unst, Goffman conducted his research self like a Warner-trained community studies investigator – studying the local history, participating in local rituals, conducting interviews, taking photographs, collecting biographies, even using the TAT on occasion (Winkin 2000). To what extent did these activities represent genuine research activities of the kind a community study demanded – or were they just a "cover story" (Goffman 1989) to disguise his real interests in the interaction order? It is difficult to know when Goffman actually hit upon the idea of the interaction order, but the idea was in place by the time Goffman wrote his PhD thesis statement in May 1952 (Goffman 1952b).

Returning to Chicago, Goffman gave a talk about his research experience in Shetland at Warner's seminar, The Web of Life (Levy 2003). Warner hired Goffman on a SRI project examining the occupational dilemmas of service station dealers. As a consultancy report, the SRI study (SRI 1953) does not have Goffman's name on the cover, although Goffman (1959, 115) later makes his close involvement in it evident. Based on interviews with 204 service station dealers, the report gives a deeply Hughesian analysis of the dilemmas and contradictions facing dealers (see Smith 2006, 21–3). In all likelihood, Goffman would only have carried out a small portion of the 204 dealer interviews (Levy 2008). SRI pioneered the use of group interviews (now known as focus groups) and projective tests (Karesh 1995). While some of the analysis and writing bears the imprint of Goffman's increasingly distinctive sociological outlook, the final report would have been written and edited by SRI's Earl Kahn (Levy 2008).

By 1952, Goffman's intellectual allegiances were shifting toward Everett Hughes, whose influence was becoming conspicuous, notably in "On Cooling the Mark Out," published that year (Goffman 1952a). Hughes was originally nominated as part of Goffman's dissertation committee, along with Warner and the newly recruited Donald Horton. However, Hughes's place was taken by Anselm Strauss, possibly in recognition of Hughes's increased administrative responsibilities as chairman of the Department of Sociology (Abbott 1999). Hughes may have seemed to offer Goffman a more congenial sociological outlook than Warner, one more attuned to the ambiguities and ironies of social life.

Goffman has been described as a "reluctant apprentice" (Jaworski 2000; see also Vienne 2010) of Hughes – as someone who publicly concealed his indebtedness to Hughes in the early stages of his career while privately acknowledging the debt. For his part, Hughes found Goffman's admiration disingenuous at times (Collins 2000 [1986]). Hughes here appears as the reluctant master. The picture is complicated by a misleading comment of Goffman's, who introduced himself at a Macy Conference as follows: "I was trained at the University of Chicago by Lloyd Warner, who was a student of Everett Hughes" (Goffman 1957, 12).

Goffman's claim does not square with the history. Warner and Hughes considered each other as equals, were sympathetic to each other's work, and were long on friendly terms with each other. Abbott and Gaziano (1995) also note that Warner and Hughes were allies in Department of Sociology infighting in the early 1950s. The eulogy Hughes wrote after Warner's death in 1970 begins: "Lloyd Warner and I were not boys together. We met when we were in our late thirties, and sparred a bit until we discovered we were both much more interested in how people and their cultures and societies work than in the names of departments or disciplines" (Hughes 1970). At the time Goffman landed in Chicago in 1945, there can be little doubt that Warner enjoyed a more prominent academic profile than did Hughes. Hughes's star did not begin to rise until the 1950s.

Still, it is harder to find traces of Warner's thinking in the mature Goffman than it is to detect Hughes's influence. One overlooked potential influence is Warner's notion of the individual's "social personality" as: "the total social participation of that organic item in its particular part of the society" (Warner 1937, 278). Participation was introduced in Goffman's (1953, 217–41) dissertation and was later developed in the notions of participation units and participation status (Goffman 1971; 1981). Goffman's ideas about the person ground Warner's concept of the "social personality" in the interaction order. At Chicago, Goffman's single completed course in the social psychology area of specialization was Warner and Havighurst's The Individual in Society. He audited but did not complete Blumer's symbolic interactionist course (Winkin 1985).

Burns is right to say that from the early 1950s on, Goffman largely turned his back on what Warner stood for. We have shown that Goffman was never a straightforward student of Warner's. He absorbed some of Warner's approach and ideas in order to adapt them to his emergent sociological perspective. Goffman was less in the business of intellectual rupture and more interested in working in, through, and beyond the ideas he received from his teacher Warner. So while there is a turning away on Goffman's part, it was not a complete "goodbye to all that." Rather, it shows the creative development of ideas on Goffman's part, steps toward a sociology of the interaction order.

Collins's argument about the significance of Warner as the conduit of anthropological thinking in Goffman's sociology deserves strong reaffirmation. For more than two decades, Goffman was a member of both the American Sociological Association and the American Anthropological Association, and his academic post at Pennsylvania, the Benjamin Franklin Chair in Anthropology and Sociology, was a joint appointment identical in disciplinary title to Warner's at Chicago. Goffman's only published dedication as a frontispiece to one of his books was to Radcliffe-Brown in *Relations in Public*. From Radcliffe-Brown's work, Goffman learned the centrality of the comparative method and extracted "a model for writing papers" (Verhoeven 1993, 321). The tradition of the laying on of hands still persists in anthropology. As a student of Warner's, Goffman could trace his lineage through him to Radcliffe-Brown and beyond Radcliffe-Brown to Durkheim.

While personally, temperamentally, and professionally Warner and Goffman were very different, it is not unreasonable to suppose that some aspects of Warner's modus operandi rubbed off on Goffman. Warner built up teams and was seriously committed to collaborative work. On the other hand, Goffman was a great individualist who never collaborated (to the point of publication) with anyone in his life. Both enjoyed profiles as public sociologists without compromising the academic basis of their work. For better or worse, Warner was an exemplar of the academic entrepreneur, constantly curious, seeking out opportunities, possessed of the energy and people skills to organize and inspire colleagues and students. Goffman was caught up in Warner's net at the outset of his graduate career before he began to critically distance himself from those sociological positions of Warner's that Goffman felt were untenable. Notwithstanding the many flaws Goffman and other critics discerned in Warner's assumptions and procedures, Warner may well have offered Goffman *a general model of how to be a sociologist* that Goffman could adapt and make his own. Goffman could have learned about ways of being a successful academic from Warner: of the overwhelming importance of sustaining a persistent research orientation in the face of many competing academic and extra-curricular demands; of the utility of directing that orientation to research publication by constantly securing the space for research and writing to be done; and of the value of pursuing your ideas wherever they lead. And all this is best done by disregarding published commentary critical of your ideas. Warner remained unresponsive to his critics, believing that it would deflect him from producing the original research work he felt he must produce (Warner 1969). Perhaps the most abiding practical lesson Goffman learned from Warner was the value of ignoring your critics.

REFERENCES

Abbott, Andrew. 1999. *Department and Discipline: Chicago Sociology at One Hundred*. Chicago: University of Chicago Press
– and Emanuel Gaziano. 1995. "Transition and Tradition: Departmental Faculty in the Era of the Second Chicago School." In *A Second Chicago School? The Development of a Postwar American Sociology*, edited by Gary Alan Fine, 221–72. Chicago: University of Chicago Press
Arensberg, Conrad M., and Solon T. Kimball. 1940. *Family and Community in Ireland*. Cambridge, MA: Harvard University Press
Becker, Howard S. 2003. "The Politics of Presentation: Goffman and Total Institutions." *Symbolic Interaction* 26(4):659–69
Birdwhistell, Ray L. n.d. Interview – memoir of W. Lloyd Warner
Boltanski, Luc. 1973. "Erving Goffman et le temps du soupçon." *Social Science Information* 12(3):127–47
Burns, Tom. 1992. *Erving Goffman*. London: Routledge
Collins, Randall. 1980. "Erving Goffman and the Development of Modern Social Theory." In *The View from Goffman*, edited by Jason Ditton, 170–209. London: Macmillan
– 1988. "Theoretical Continuities in Goffman's Work." In *Erving Goffman: Exploring the Interaction Order*, edited by Paul Drew and Anthony Wootton, 41–63. Oxford: Polity Press
– 2000 [1986]. "The Passing of Intellectual Generations: Reflections on the Death of Erving Goffman." In *Erving Goffman*, vol. I, edited by Gary Alan Fine and Gregory W.H. Smith, 71–83
Fine, Gary Alan, ed. 1995. *A Second Chicago School? The Development of a Postwar American Sociology*. Chicago: University of Chicago Press
Gardner, Burleigh B., and William F. Whyte. 1946. "Methods for the Study of Human Relations in Industry." *American Sociological Review* 11(5):506–12
Goffman, Erving. 1946. Thesis Statement for the Master's Degree in Sociology, University of Chicago, 2 August

- 1948a. "The Role of Status Symbols in Social Organization." Paper for Seminar on Personal and Social Disorganization, Soc 475. Ernest Watson Burgess papers, Box 131, Special Collections Research Center, The University of Chicago Library
- 1948b. "Field Report for Soc 301A." Paper for Advanced Field Studies: The Community, Soc 301A. Ernest Watson Burgess papers, Box 131, Special Collections Research Center, The University of Chicago Library
- 1949. *Some Characteristics of Response to Depicted Experience.* MA thesis, Department of Sociology, University of Chicago
- 1951. "Symbols of Class Status." *British Journal of Sociology* 2(4):294–304
- 1952a. "On Cooling the Mark Out: Some Aspects of Adaptation to Failure." *Psychiatry* 15:451–63
- 1952b. Draft of PhD Thesis Statement. In *Bios Sociologicus: The Erving Goffman Archives,* edited by Dmitri N. Shalin. http://cdclv.unlv.edu/ega/documents/eg_thesis_statement_52.pdf
- 1953. *Communication Conduct in an Island Community.* PhD dissertation, Department of Sociology, University of Chicago
- 1957. "Interpersonal Persuasion." In *Group Processes: Transactions of the Third 1956 Conference,* edited by Bertram Schaffner, 117–93. New York: Josiah Macy, Jr, Foundation
- 1959. *The Presentation of Self in Everyday Life.* New York: Doubleday, Anchor Books
- 1961. *Encounters: Two Studies in the Sociology of Interaction.* Indianapolis: BobbsMerrill
- 1963. *Stigma: Notes on the Management of Spoiled Identity.* Englewood Cliffs, NJ: PrenticeHall
- 1971. *Relations in Public: Microstudies of the Public Order.* New York: Basic Books
- 1981. *Forms of Talk.* Oxford: Basil Blackwell
- 1983. "The Interaction Order." *American Sociological Review* 48:1–17
- 1989. "On Fieldwork, Transcribed by L.H. Lofland." *Journal of Contemporary Ethnography* 18:123–32

Hughes, Everett C. 1970. Eulogy for Lloyd Warner, 2 June. Everett Cherrington Hughes Papers 1922–1982, Box 70. Special Collections Research Center, University of Chicago Library

Ingersoll, Daniel W., Jr. 1997. "A Tale of Two Cities: Warner and Marquand in Newburyport." *Anthropology and Humanism* 22(2):137–49

Jaworski, Gary D. 2000. "Erving Goffman: The Reluctant Apprentice."
  Symbolic Interaction 23:299–308
Karesh, Michael. 1995. "The Interstitial Origins of Symbolic Consumer
  Research: Social Research, Inc., the Bureau of Applied Social Research
  and the Social Scientific Study of Consumption." MA research paper,
  Department of Sociology, University of Chicago
Levy, Sidney. 2003. "Roots of Marketing and Consumer Research at the
  University of Chicago." *Consumption, Markets and Culture* 6:99–110
– 2008. Personal communication to Greg Smith
Lindner, Rolf. 1996. *The Reportage of Urban Culture: Robert Park and
  the Chicago School*. Cambridge: Cambridge University Press
Smith, Greg. 2003. "Chrysalid Goffman: A Note on 'Some Characteristics of
  Response to Depicted Experience.'" *Symbolic Interaction* 26(4):645–58
– 2006. *Erving Goffman*. London: Routledge
Spillius, Elizabeth Bott. 1993. Letter to Greg Smith, 9 December
SRI (Social Research, Incorporated). 1953. *The Service Station Dealer:
  The Man and His Work*. Mimeographed report prepared for the
  American Petroleum Institute. Chicago: SRI
University of Chicago. 1945. *University of Chicago Calendar 1945. The
  University of Chicago Official Publications*, vol. xlv, 1945–46
Verhoeven, Jef. 1993. "An Interview with Erving Goffman, 1980."
  Research on Language and Social Interaction 26(3):317–48
Vienne, Philippe. 2010. "The Enigma of the Total Institution: Rethinking
  the Hughes–Goffman Intellectual Relationship." *Sociologica* 2.
  http://www.sociologica.mulino.it/journal/article/index/Article/
  Journal:ARTICLE:419/Item/Journal:ARTICLE:419
Warner, Mildred Hall. 1988. *W. Lloyd Warner, Social Anthropologist*.
  New York: Publishing Center for Cultural Resources
Warner, William Lloyd. 1937. "The Society, the Individual, and His Mental
  Disorder." *American Journal of Psychiatry* 94:275–84
– 1952. *Structure of American life*. Edinburgh: University of Edinburgh
  Press
– 1969. Letter to Michael Banton, 14 February
– and William E. Henry. 1948. "The Radio Daytime Serial: A Symbolic
  Analysis." *Genetic Psychology Monographs* 37:3–71
Warner, William Lloyd, and Paul S. Lunt. 1941. *The Social Life of a
  Modern Community*. New Haven, CT: Yale University Press
Warner, William Lloyd, Marchia Meeker, and Kenneth Eells. 1949. *Social
  Class in America: A Manual of Procedure for the Measurement of
  Social Status*. Chicago: Science Research Associates

Warner, William Lloyd, and Leo Srole. 1945. *The Social Systems of American Ethnic Groups*. New Haven, CT: Yale University Press

Winkin, Yves. 1984. "Éléments pour une histoire sociale des sciences sociales américaines: une chronique: entretien avec Erving Goffman." *Actes de la recherche en sciences-sociales* 54:85–7

– 1985. Interview with Herbert G. Blumer

– 1988. *Portrait du sociologue Erving Goffman: les moments et leurs hommes*. Paris: Seuil/Minuit

– 1991. Interview with Thomas Goffman

– 2000. "Baltasound as the Symbolic Capital of Social Interaction." In *Erving Goffman*, vol. 1, edited by G.A. Fine and G.W.H. Smith. London: Sage

– 2010. "Goffman's Greenings." In *The Goffman Companion*, edited by Michael Hviid Jacobsen. Routledge

8

Reading Goffman: On the Creation of an Enigmatic Founder

ISHER-PAUL SAHNI

Erving Goffman is arguably the most read and influential sociologist of the twentieth century (Fine, Manning, and Smith 2000, ix; Oromaner 1980; Scheff 2006, 2). Yet despite his standing as a major figure (Branaman 1997; Fine, Manning, and Smith 2000; Lemert 1997) and a "contemporary classic" (Jacobsen 2010, 4), he clearly resists absorption into mainstream sociology, leading many to label him enigmatic (Lemert 2003; Posner 1978, 67; Scheff 2006, 2–3; Smith 2006, 126) and underscore the fact that he "is generally regarded in a pejorative way by rank and file sociologists" (Posner 1980, 293). Consequently, even the most cursory perusal of the literature reveals that disagreement regarding the import of his approach, as well as the nature and bearing of his contribution to the discipline, still glaringly outweighs consensus. Hence, this chapter draws on the hermeneutics of reading so as to explain the enduring nature of the controversy. Focusing on the substance and content of the debates themselves, it elucidates the interrelated impact of the immanent (textual) and contextual (cultural and institutional) factors that shaped the reception of his work and his standing as an enigmatic founder.

SITUATING AN ENIGMA: APORIAS OF THEORY AND THEORETICAL – PEDIGREE IN GOFFMAN'S WRITINGS

Among the more ubiquitous criticisms of Goffman is the assertion that he cannot unequivocally be placed in a particular theoretical tradition (Fine, Manning, and Smith 2000, ix; Williams 1983, 99). Unravelling the claims made in this connection requires dispelling,

first and foremost, the notion taken for granted in nearly all introductory and social psychology textbooks that he clearly belongs in
the symbolic interactionist camp. Hence, it must be noted that even
though he begrudgingly accepted the label, he was notoriously reti-
cent about his pedigree and actually pronounced his preference for
the structural functionalist moniker and even that of Hughesian
urban ethnographer (Verhoeven 1993, 318–19). That conjecture
persists despite Goffman's own declaration vindicates the reign of
interpretation over authorial intention. But this explanation of
Goffman's outsider status is insufficient in itself. The reasons for
Derrida's immense success as a philosopher prove in this respect to
be extremely instructive: he gained prestige by, among other things,
referencing high-status cultural works and engaging wholeheartedly
in intellectual debates (Lamont 1987, 592–3, 599). Turning to
Goffman, we find that many have remarked upon his idiosyncratic
style of referencing (Williams 1983, 99) and the sparse cross-refer-
ences to his own work (Ditton 1980, 2; Smith 2006, 5) and that he
seldom cites symbolic interactionists (Collins 1988, 42; 2000 [1986],
73). Of greater significance, though, is his complete disinterest in
connecting his work with that of others (Posner 1978, 67; Psathas
1996, 391) and steadfast unwillingness to debate his position or
situate himself within a theoretical tradition (Goffman 1981, 61). It
is, therefore, mendacious to fit him into a school of thought; he did
his best to avoid aligning himself, "even to the point of declaring a
belief in conceptual eclecticism" (Burns 1992, 6).

Intellectual legitimation occurs when a theory is recognized as
part of a field. And this results if the theory is defined as important
by its producer and its institutionalization, which depends on meeting certain academic requirements, contributing to a cognitive field,
and creating research teams, institutes, and journals. In addition, the
ancillary validation of peers and the intellectual public is required
(Lamont 1987, 586). Goffman's resolute refusal to engage in debate
and thereby clarify and align his theoretical position exasperated his
colleagues but also accounts, in part, for his popularity in other
fields and, conversely, his standing as a maverick within his own
discipline (Atkinson 1989, 59–61; Edmondson 1984, 147; Fine,
Manning, and Smith 2000, ix; Posner 1978, 70; Strong 2000
[1983], 40). On the one hand, this supports the contention that
major figures attempt to surmount their master's legacy (Alexander
1982, 7) and "reverse the flow of influence" (Travers 1999, 171).
And, as Smith (this volume) notes, Goffman had an admirable talent

for extending received ideas in imaginative and innovative ways. On the other hand, it also seems to certify that the reader's inability to clearly situate Goffman within an intellectual tradition underlies his anomalous relation to mainstream sociology inasmuch as "all writing is performed under the constraint of being a recognizable genre of writing within some cultural array" (Green 1988, 59). Taken together, these undermined the cognitive marker afforded his readers by a familiar pre-interpretive frame of reference from which to start.

Closely linked to the preceding criticism is the censure of Goffman for failing to develop an overarching theory (Fine, Manning, and Smith 2000, ix), leading a host of interpreters to conclude that he is too microscopic and, in the end, unsystematic (Mote 2001, 229; Scheff 2006, 2–3). This claim foregrounds the cumulative quality his writings ostensibly lack. Insofar as there is no overall study where Goffman brings together all his core ideas, many reviewers have condemned his work as no more than a compilation of commonplace notes and observations (Burns 1992, 2; Giddens 1988, 251–5). So it would appear that generality is really the issue at hand, leading Hall to anoint Goffman as the most accurate sociologist while conceding that his texts are hard to read not because of an abundance of detail but a dearth of generalizations (Hall 1977, 535). And here a strong case can be made for his having adopted the essay – a thoroughly personal enterprise rooted in everyday experience that champions an exploratory form – as his genre (Strong 2000 [1983], 40–1). In this vein, Collins draws attention to Goffman's distinctive way of writing: he always finished with "a literary flourish rather than by driving home a theoretical point" (Collins 2000 [1986], 75). And it is precisely for this reason some argue that although there is a systematic social theory to be found, considerable effort is needed to uncover it (Giddens 1988, 250; Rawls 1987, 136), while others contend that the coherence of his work is more easily sensed than articulated (Hymes 1984, 621; Smith 1999, 6; Strong 1988, 228). What is important to note here, however, is the commentators' widespread awareness of, and focus on, the decisive impact of his style. It is to this that I now turn.

IT CUTS BOTH WAYS: GOFFMAN'S STYLISTICS

Goffman once declared: "the French are totally locked up in a world that consists of persons who have written things. An entirely literary world" (Verhoeven 1993, 344). It is interesting, therefore, that in an age that tried its best to avoid style, he embraced it (Fine 1999, 182) and striking how, more than any other sociologist, it is said that "Goffman was a *stylist*" (Atkinson 1989, 59). Hence, remarks abound about his "talent" for writing in layers (Collins 2000 [1986], 75), his "wit and grace" (Smith 2006, 2) and "intense" (Freidson 1983, 359), "dart-like style" (Watson 1999, 153), all of which "regales" (Winkin 1983, 111) the reader. More than anything else, then, the literature underscores the fact that his "verbal and writing styles were very powerful" (Marx 1984, 655). When viewed as a performance, effective writing prompts the reader's participation by "relying on signs, symptoms, analogies, conventions and assumptions ... despite the risks of misunderstanding which this involves" (Edmondson 1984, 151). Using a range of rhetorical devices, Goffman's writings engender both; he embodies the "aesthetic ability to condense and articulate 'ideological reality' through appropriate rhetorical tropes" (Alexander 1987, 30–1).

In their seminal exegesis of *Asylums* (1961), Fine and Martin (1990) meticulously cull Goffman's alternating use of sarcasm, satire, and irony. While humour allows him to effectively break the mirror of illusion (Winkin 1999, 34–5), they also highlight his converse proclivity for presenting remarkable events in an unremarkable way (Fine and Martin 1990, 105). In this respect, he can been seen as emulating Brecht's estrangement effect so that his narrative talent also lies in "a facility to point out things about social life *at once* completely new *and* instantly recognizable" (Giddens, quoted in Grimshaw 2000 [1983], 6). In this way, his words "invite and challenge the reader's sympathetic involvement with the text" (Atkinson 1989, 74). In order to accomplish this particular effect, Goffman relies on parataxis – that is, "the construction of arguments by means of repetition, [ironic] juxtaposition, antithesis and elaborations on those methods" (Atkinson 1989, 63). Another analogous device he deploys, following Burke, is the art of incongruity (Lofland 1980), which lends his work a "sparkling" quality by sprinkling "his texts with incongruous phrases" and "creating an ideal-typical model and applying it to various areas of social life not usually connected to each other" (Treviño 2003, 21). Goffman in effect breaks the consistency rule according to which things make conventional sense, which "allows him to make the next move of finding and showing an apparently powerful unity in this diversity" (Watson 1999, 147).

Tropes notwithstanding, the perspective by incongruity is fully reliant on ordinary knowledge (Watson 1999, 149), which does not negate Goffman's use of an extensive and inventive metaphorical vocabulary (Berger 1986, xiv). He was indeed "a master coiner of exactly the apt concept," many of which have become taken-for-granted terms in our lexicon (Lofland 2000 [1981], 158). This appeal to lingua franca is, of course, not haphazard; "he resorts to the conventions of ordinary language for a release from the corrosion of self-doubt and the reader's mistrust" (O'Neill, quoted in Cohen and Rogers 1994, 311). And what is more, his "linguistic populism adds democratic spice to academic prose with mock egalitarianism capable of cutting highfalutin scholarship down to size" (Cohen and Rogers 1994, 311). In other words, a key element of his "persuasive power" lies in the ability to reach an extraordinarily wide audience because his style does not rest on "conventional canons of scholarly self-presentation" (Atkinson 1989, 60). In sharp contrast to the "ponderously theoretical abstract writings" of some of his colleagues, "Goffman's books were immediately seen as vital and contemporary and they filled a gap that was opening between everyday experience and sociological theory" (MacCannell 2000 [1983], 13). He thus described "people in a non-theoreticised manner which is in keeping with the everyday perceptions which we evolve during social interaction with one another" (Edmondson 1984, 151). By the same token, though, he also wants to dispute the common-sense views that are so "deeply embedded in people's social consciousness, and unlikely to be abandoned without considerable persuasion" (Edmondson 1984, 148). His works are classical, because "one must return to them in order to experience and to understand just what the nature of interactional motivation really is" (Alexander 1987, 29–30). Goffman, therefore, aligns himself with perennial ethnographers who convince us "not merely that they themselves have truly 'been there,' but (as they also do, if rather less obviously) that had we been there we should have seen what they saw, felt what they felt, concluded what they concluded" (Geertz 1988, 16). Persuading "us that this off stage miracle has occurred, is where the writing comes in" (Geertz 1988, 5).

Because Goffman in so many respects wrote "like an angel" (Burns 1992, 2), several reviewers have been moved to proclaim him one with novelists, essayists, and literary authors (Burns 1992, 3). Thus Berman's (1972) "glowing tribute" to Relations in Public (1972) draws a parallel to Kafka and brands Goffman as one of the greatest writers of our times (Fine and Martin 1990, 95). This affinity, however, is also the source of some of the most trenchant criticisms levelled against him. Sociology's dependence on "lay linguistic usage" is hard to overstate (Watson 1999, 142–3). But if, as Watson (1999) appreciates, it goes unrecognized, it is because the discipline was forged via a confrontation with, and ultimate rejection of, literary genres (Lepenies 1988, 3–7). Consensus holds that the opposite of fiction is fact (Wellek and Warren 1977, 34). So style, it follows, is seen as peripheral and secondary (Green 1988, 14); interlocking reading conventions hold that "the content of sociological writing is separable from its style" (Green 1988, 17). Consequently, "the scientific value of sociological writing (its truth value) is to be found in content, not style. Style can obscure truth value through bias and 'noise,' but cannot positively possess it" (Green 1988, 17). As a result, "attention to such matters as imagery, metaphor, phraseology, or voice is supposed to lead to a corrosive relativism in which everything is but a more or less clever expression of opinion" (Geertz 1988, 2). The self-presentation and sensitization that are integral parts of Goffman's rhetorical reasoning (Edmondson 1984, 157) have thus occasioned the perceived detrimental fusion of style and substantive analysis in his sociology (Fine, Manning, and Smith 2000, xxii). In its harshest tone, critics argue that his "narrative self-indulgence" prevents him from fashioning a coherent and/or new theoretical framework (Cohen and Rogers 1994, 304, 315–16).

Here again the case of Derrida is informative. His distinct and sophisticated rhetoric seemed to be a prerequisite for intellectual legitimation and success (Lamont 1987, 592). However, his style and unconventional approach also account for his eventual decline in popularity, as does the move from a limited to general public, which saw his work increasingly at odds with traditional disciplinary norms (Lamont 1987, 607–8). There was, likewise, a wide audience for Goffman's writings, insofar as academic treatises began to be published as pocket books (Winkin 1999, 40). The staggering sales of *The Presentation of Self in Everyday Life* (1959) and *Stigma* (1963) bear witness to this and his reputation as a layman's sociologist (Burns 1992, 1; Posner 1978, 68; Scheff 2006, 2). Conversely, reviews of his work in academic journals were scarce (Posner 1978, 68). So Goffman's signature style, all told, is held responsible for his having "always buried his theoretical message" (Collins 2000 [1986],

75), a situation aggravated by the fact that it was by and large not valued by his discipline (Abbott 1997). The preceding, it goes without saying, points to the crucial interaction between the immanent features of his work and the context in which it surfaced. This is the subject of the following section.

ON THE MARGINS OF THE MAINSTREAM: GOFFMAN, CULTURE, AND THE ACADEMIC COMMUNITY

When examining the contextual setting, two things must be considered: the American cultural Zeitgeist and the academic community's self-understanding. Those (Gouldner 1970; Manning 1976; Sennett 1973; Young 1971) who have read Goffman as symptomatic of broader historical changes treat his "sociology as the theoretical embodiment of the experiences and values of the appearance-conscious, other-directed new middle class" (Smith 1999, 5) – of American society "following the decline of the moral discipline provided by the Protestant ethic" (Giddens 1988, 253). But this view, prescient as it is, runs the risk of ignoring his Victorian sensibilities (Manning 1976) as well as the fact that "he actually worked out his own, admittedly perverse and muted, social critique of American society in the 1950s" (Lemert 1997, xxiv). The other side of this coin is the cultural capital gained by providing the public with the image of a charismatic avant-garde intellectual (Lamont 1987, 594). It is precisely for this reason that "he appealed to rebellious students in transition from protective and secure middle-class environments, to the life styles and cultural and political themes that were to characterize the mid-sixties to the mid-seventies" (Marx 1984, 654). Put another way, "Goffman was an individualist in an era when individualism was the ideal, when the avant-garde went to all sorts of extremes to set themselves off from others" (Collins 2000 [1986], 75). Ironically, though, critics contend that "the pursuit of a sociological decimation of conventional Western liberal notions of the individual is an analytic impulse animating much of Goffman's sociology" (Smith 1999, 10). Hall, however, convincingly argues that most of these detractors are existential in the sense that "they believe that human beings are possessors of an irreducible 'real-self' which is judged of great moral worth; all stress the potential of men as free and creative actors" (Hall 1977, 536). So, in point of fact, they call for authenticity – authenticity "in the sense of being true to one's self at all costs; their argument is essentially an anti-social one which could be summed up as 'Put yourself above social practices'" (Hall 1977, 540–1). But Goffman, to the contrary, encourages us to be suspicious of pseudo authenticity (Hall 1977, 548) and underlines the minimum disruption to our personal self that we strive for and, therefore, the kindness, tact, and circumspection demanded of the self in a social world.

Reproaches of his putative anti-individualism are ancillary to a much more common rebuke: cynicism. "Both sociologists and laymen alike tend to focus on the hideous side of Goffman's work" (Posner 1978, 71). It has been said that his approach is "cold-eyed and sour" (Karl Scheibe, quoted in Scheff 2006, 2), that his socialized self is an unreservedly manipulative one (Hepworth 1980, 87; see also Cuzzort 1969; Messinger, Sampson, and Towne 1962). This portrayal ultimately "misinterprets the analytic spirit of his dramaturgy," for it "confuses his analysis of what people do with claims about what they are" and assumes "that social life depends on the use of dramatic techniques to do things together ... It does not claim that people are manipulative or deceptive by nature" (Schwalbe 1993, 341). For Goffman, "all interaction is a moral enterprise involving the attribution of human character" (Hepworth 1980, 85). It demands moral obligation (Rawls 1987) and the allied virtues of trust and reciprocity (Giddens 1984, 70). When seen in this light, he is a cynic only on the surface (Collins 1988, 42); moral obligations, he maintains, arise simply "because of the way we encounter pressures from each other in specific situations to help each other construct a consistent definition of reality. In order to live up to this *external* morality, one is forced to have a non-moral, manipulative self as well" (Collins 1980, 182).

In opposition to the Machiavellian characterization, then, two readings have emerged. One crafts a prosaic Goffman whose universe is "neither intrinsically moral nor immoral" (Tseëlon 1992, 125). For this Goffman, the truths of human interaction "were more often than not cold ones" (Berger 1986, xviii). The emphasis is accordingly placed on the fact that his "brilliant excursions often end with a shrug, a twisting of the corners of the mouth through closed lips, an upturned palm of powerlessness: almost as if saying, in effect, I don't particularly like it, but that's the way it is" (Berger 1986, xvii). The other depicts him as a moralist (Atkinson 1989, 61; Burns 1992, 15) who attempts "to illuminate aspects of human life that most of us overlook and to show us more of humanity there than we could otherwise see" (Freidson 1983, 362). This Goffman exhibits a deep concern for the self in an oppressive world and mounts a passionate defence of its dignity and value.

The host of interpretations covered thus far and those that follow below speak to the fact that Goffman "lived across several intellectual generations, and was adept at creating a leading position for himself in each one" (Collins 2000 [1986], 73). Arguably, the chief factor working against him was that he came on the scene at a time when sociology was dominated by naturalistic and functionalist paradigms and quantitative models (Alexander 1987, 40; Fine, Manning, and Smith 2000, xvii; Giddens 1988, 251; Marx 1984, 650). Goffman, however, was a true product of the Chicago School – that is, of its deep seated scepticism of functionalism, governing interest in sudden dramatic change, totalitarian control, and conformity, and role in spearheading the development of interpretive methods and substantive analysis (Fine, Manning, and Smith 2000, xvii). More important, at the time "the discipline of sociology was self-confident and optimistic about its ability to advance knowledge and solve social problems ... Nor was there the slightest doubt that sociologists were uniformly good, serving just and humane ends" (Marx 1984, 650). And here the University of Chicago stood out; there was "always an ironic twist in the Chicago way of looking at the world" (Winkin 1999, 34). They were no "'do-gooders' ... Their stance was 'cool'" (Winkin 1999, 35). Exposing the dark side of institutions, the fragility and underlying chaos of the social bond (Manning 1976, 18), the prevalent anxiety about shame and embarrassment (Scheff 2006, 35, 40), and the less than self-possessed nature of human beings rubbed many the wrong way. In relation to the prevailing school of thought, then, he was "a rule-breaker, and rule-breakers invite the vultures to gather" (Berger 2000 [1973], 286). But he would again find an equally fertile and hospitable home in the radical and intellectually pluralist environment of Berkeley in 1958 (Marx 1984, 650). However, as the tide turned in the early 1960s and into the next decade, he resisted the pull of Marxism (Burns 1992, 12) and was thus subjected to a new barrage of condemnations. These quite simply challenged his detachment from strong political implications (Berger 1986, xvi). Indeed, his work was "judged politically suspect, if not downright conservative, since he treats the ground rules of 'public order' on which impression management lies as if they were natural rather than the product of social pathology" (Hall 1977, 535). The conservative view (see Dawe 1973), however, ignores his assertion that "mutual dealings … could probably be sustained with fewer rules or different ones" (quoted in Hall 1977, 544). It also underestimates his "capacity to view the world on a slant and this perspective has potentially subversive implications" (Posner 1978, 72). So Goffman, as it were, is "accused of guilt by association" (Hall 1977, 544). He found a highly congenial home in Chicago but was shunned by the then reigning cultural ideology and intellectual current. For the same reason, though, he was readily embraced by others – they being mostly students with counter-cultural leanings and critical sociologists. It would take a little more than decade following the publication of *The Presentation of Self* before Goffman's approach began to be ardently contested but also vindicated – an unabated project that continues to this day.

CONCLUDING REFLECTIONS: TENTATIVE THOUGHTS ON THE BEARING OF PERSONALITY

MacCannell notes that "it would be difficult to find a more confused, hostile, and *ad hominem* set of reviews than those written by his [Goffman's] colleagues over the years" (MacCannell 2000 [1983], 9). It is not my intention to contribute to the latter, not only because its heuristic value can be as misleading as it can be fecund but also because Goffman was an intensely private person, making any such endeavour particularly difficult. Hence, Smith (this volume) explains: "There is no official Goffman archive: no depository of notes, drafts, correspondence, and photographs made public for scholars to ponder." Nevertheless, I would like to tentatively assess to what extent his own world view is embodied in his work and what effect his peculiar personality conceivably had on his standing at the margins of mainstream sociology's networks – both personal and institutional.

The first point worth noting is that Goffman was an outsider to mainstream American culture, ethnically, geographically, and socially (Fine 1999, 179–81; Lofland 2000 [1981], 165; Winkin 1999, 39), leading Berger (2000 [1973]) to remark: "he will never lose the outsider's lurking knowledge that it is all some grisly game" (quoted in Lofland 2000 [1981], 165) and Winkin to stress his interest in "denouncing fabrication, illusion, and false pretences of natural 'distinction'" (Winkin 2000 [1992], 208). It is thus reasonable to assume this is why he adopted an ironic style, inasmuch as "irony is the foot-man/handmaiden of detachment. Irony belongs to the outsider's dialectic between the incongruous *is* and *ought*" (Fine 1999, 182). Clearly, Goffman "was drawn to disjunctive scenes. He had a voyeur's interest in the intimate details of other's lives, and a strong eye for the ironic and poignant" (Marx 1984, 653). In this vein, the second point when it comes to Goffman is that it is undoubtedly "a matter of some controversy to ascertain the intellectual and moral identity of the man behind the mask" (Posner 1978, 68).

The fact that he notoriously showed little interest in forging connections with the academic community deserves consideration, because the ineluctably collaborative nature of innovation hinges on personal contact with a "shadow group" (Baehr 2002, 66; Collins 2004, 192; Gouldner 1980; Lamont 1987, 600). It is significant, therefore, that more stories are told about Goffman by people who encountered him than about any other sociologist (Berger 1986, xi). His mysterious and mercurial character was tremendously appealing (Marx 1984, 655). Yet with it came a propensity to test and haze those he met (Lofland 1980, 21), to be cruel, wounding, and hostile (Scheff 2006, 7), sour and sardonic and downright eerie, to learn more about interaction by observing than by engaging in it (Erwin 2000 [1992], 94n1). In addition to the undeniably off-putting nature of these traits, his "painful shyness" made him reject strangers' attempts to establish a relationship (Grimshaw 2000 [1983], 6). Conversely, Berger recalls that people could suddenly become self-conscious of their own behaviour when Goffman entered the room, fearful of revealing something embarrassing that he might later comment on (Berger 1986, xii). And his lack of conventional personal manners, it would seem, was matched by a lack of professional manners (Strong 2000 [1983], 41). It is not unthinkable, then, that these foibles vitiated the development of enduring personal, institutional, and intellectual affiliations. This conjecture can also be extended to Goffman's graduate students, for despite his reputation as a generous and helpful albeit abrupt teacher (Scheff 2006, 8, 11), these qualities would have negatively affected the establishment of his own independent school of thought (Mullins 1973); he conspicuously did not cultivate a following (Marx 1984, 652) or "produce a close-knit school of younger scholars who saw themselves as following his agenda" (Fine, Manning, and Smith 2000, ix–x).

This chapter was galvanized by Goffman's enigmatic and still contested standing as a founding figure. His idiosyncratic footing, I proffer, provides the case in point for understanding the mechanisms by which a discipline's founder is created. I have substantiated this claim by first demonstrating the ample and detrimental confusion that results from the fact that he is not easily pigeonholed. This problematic, I further argued, stems largely from his distinct writing style; it is the most important factor responsible for Goffman's popular appeal as well as the one that significantly hindered many from taking his sociology seriously as conventional sociology. Finally, understanding these immanent determinants requires embedding them in the context in which his work was received: the dominant American intellectual and academic culture at the time further relegated Goffman's theory to the margins of the discipline.

The above reveals the crucial question of Goffman's narrative style and, accordingly, raises two issues: the distinction between fact and fiction is not a fruitful one, because texts are constructed to be read in a particular way (Eagleton 1983, 1, 8–10). If we adhere to a reductive positivist definition that limits truth to methodically verifiable data, then literature cannot be treated in earnest as a form of experimental truth (Wellek and Warren 1977, 34). Indeed, it is for this reason that novelists – and Goffman – have the unique ability to make "us perceive what we see, imagine what we already, conceptually or practically, know" (Wellek and Warren 1977, 33). Most recently, scholars aver that post-modernism promotes an open-ended standpoint and thus applaud the fact that Goffman's "texts have a relatively open structure, many possibilities of reading and interpretation are available to the reader" (Vester 1989, 191; see also Edmondson 1984, 155; Tseëlon 1992, 125). This foregrounds an issue that remains unexamined by the numerous perspicacious studies of his style: what makes a (his) text open-ended? And this, in turn, raises the question of what makes his narrative sociological? The answers to these questions have broad implications; they will bring us closer to an understanding of the enduring quality of classic texts and the rhetorical techniques of sociological discourse.

REFERENCES

Abbott, Andrew. 1997. "Of Time and Space: The Contemporary Relevance of the Chicago School." *Social Forces* 75(4):1,149–82

Alexander, Jeffrey C. 1982. *The Antinomies of Classical Thought: Marx and Durkheim*. Berkeley: University of California Press

– 1987. "The Centrality of the Classics." In *Sociological Theory Today*, edited by Anthony Giddens and Jonathan Turner, 11–57. Stanford: Stanford University Press

Atkinson, P. 1989. "Goffman's Poetics." *Human Studies* 12:59–76

Baehr, Peter. 2002. *Founders, Classics, Canons: Modern Disputes over the Origins and Appraisal of Sociology's Heritage*. New Brunswick, NJ: Transaction

Berger, Bennett M. 1986. Foreword to *Frame Analysis: An Essay on the Organization of Experience*, by Erving Goffman, xi–xviii. Boston: Northeastern University Press

– 2000 [1973]. "A Fan Letter on Erving Goffman." In *Erving Goffman*, vol. I, edited by Gary Alan Fine and Gregory W.H. Smith, 278–89. London: Sage. *Dissent* 20 (1973):353–61

Berman, M. 1972. Review of *Relations in Public*, by Erving Goffman. *New York Times Book Review* 27 February

Branaman, Ann. 1997. "Goffman's Social Theory." In *The Goffman Reader*, edited by Charles Lemert and Ann Branaman, xiv–ixxxii. Malden, MA: Blackwell

Burns, Tom. 1992. *Erving Goffman*. London: Routledge

Cohen, Ira J., and Mary F. Rogers. 1994. "Autonomy and Credibility: Voice as Method." *Sociological Theory* 12:304–18

Collins, Randall. 1980. "Erving Goffman and the Development of Modern Social Theory." In *The View from Erving Goffman*, edited by Jason Ditton, 170–209. London: Macmillan

– 1988. "Theoretical Continuities in Goffman's Work." In *Erving Goffman: Exploring the Interaction Order*, edited by Paul Drew and Anthony Wootton, 41–63. Oxford: Polity Press

– 2000 [1986]. "The Passing of Intellectual Generations: Reflections on the Death of Erving Goffman." In *Erving Goffman*, vol. I, edited by Gary Alan Fine and Gregory W.H. Smith, 71–83. London: Sage

– 2004. *Interaction Ritual Chains*. Princeton, NJ: Princeton University Press

Cuzzort, R.P. 1969. *Humanity and Sociological Theory*. New York: Holt, Rinehart and Winston

Dawe, Alan. 1973. "The Underworld of Erving Goffman." *British Journal of Sociology* 24:246–53

Ditton, Jason. 1980. "Editors' Introduction: A Bibliographic Exegesis of Goffman's Sociology." In *The View from Erving Goffman*, edited by Jason Ditton, 1–23. London: Macmillan

Eagleton, Terry. 1983. *Literary Theory: An Introduction*. Oxford: Basil Blackwell

Edmondson, Ricca. 1984. *Rhetoric in Sociology*. London: Macmillan
Erwin, Robert. 2000 [1992]. "The Nature of Goffman." In *Erving Goffman*, vol. I, edited by Gary Alan Fine and Gregory W.H. Smith, 84–96. London: Sage. *The Centennial Review* 36(2) (1992): 327–42
Fine, Gary Alan. 1999. "Claiming the Text: Parsing the Sardonic Visions of Erving Goffman and Thorstein Veblen." In *Goffman and Social Organization: Studies in a Sociological Legacy*, edited by Greg Smith, 177–97. London: Routledge
– Philip Manning, and Gregory W.H. Smith. 2000. Introduction. In *Erving Goffman*, vol. I, edited by Gary Alan Fine and Gregory W.H. Smith, ix–xliv. London: Sage
Fine, Gary Alan, and Daniel D. Martin. 1990. "A Partisan View: Sarcasm, Satire and Irony as Voices in Erving Goffman's *Asylums*." *Journal of Contemporary Ethnography* 19:89–115
Freidson, Eliot. 1983. "Celebrating Erving Goffman." *Contemporary Sociology* 12:359–62
Geertz, Clifford. 1988. *Works and Lives: The Anthropologist as Author*. Stanford, CA: Stanford University Press
Giddens, Anthony. 1984. *The Constitution of Society*. Cambridge: Polity Press
– 1988. "Goffman as a Systematic Social Theorist." In *Erving Goffman: Exploring the Interaction Order*, edited by Paul Drew and Anthony Wootton, 250–79. Oxford: Polity Press
Goffman, Erving. 1959. *The Presentation of Self in Everyday Life*. Garden City, NY: Doubleday Anchor
– 1961. *Asylums: Essays on the Situation of Mental Patients and Other Inmates*. New York: Doubleday Anchor
– 1963. *Stigma*. Englewood Cliffs, NJ: Prentice-Hall
– 1967. "The Nature of Deference and Demeanor." In *Interaction Ritual: Essays on Face-to-Face Behavior*, 47–95. Garden City, NY: Doubleday
– 1972. *Relations in Public*. Harmondsworth, UK: Penguin
– 1981. "A Reply to Denzin and Keller." *Contemporary Sociology* 10:60–8
Gouldner, Alvin W. 1970. *The Coming Crisis of Western Sociology*. New York: Basic Books
– 1980. *Two Marxisms: Contradictions and Anomalies in the Development of Theory*. London: Macmillan
Green, Bryan S. 1988. *Literary Methods and Sociological Theory, Case Studies of Simmel and Weber*. Chicago: University of Chicago Press
Grimshaw, Alan D. 2000 [1983]. "Erving Goffman: A Personal Appreciation." In *Erving Goffman*, vol. I, edited by Gary Alan Fine and Gregory W.H. Smith, 5–7. London: Sage

Hall, John A. 1977. "Sincerity and Politics: 'Existentialists' vs. Goffman and Proust." *Sociological Review* 25:535–50

Hepworth, Mike. 1980. "Deviance and Control in Everyday Life: The Contribution of Goffman. In *The View from Erving Goffman*, edited by Jason Ditton, 80–99. London: Macmillan

Hymes, D. 1984. "On Erving Goffman." *Theory and Society* 13:621–31

Jacobsen, Michael Hviid. 2010. "Goffman through the Looking Glass: From 'Classical' to Contemporary Goffman." Introduction to *The Contemporary Goffman*, edited by Michael Hviid Jacobsen, 1–47. New York: Routledge

Lamont, Michèle. 1987. "How to Become a Dominant French Philosopher?" *American Journal of Sociology* 93:584–622

Lemert, Charles. 1997. "Goffman." In *The Goffman Reader*, edited by Charles Lemert and Ann Branaman, ix–xliii. Malden, MA: Blackwell

– 2003. "Goffman's Enigma." Series editor's foreword to *Goffman's Legacy*, edited by A. Javier Treviño, xi–xvii. New York: Rowman and Littlefield

Lepenies, Wolf. 1988. *Between Literature and Science: The Rise of Sociology*. Translated by R.J. Hollingdale. Cambridge: Cambridge University Press

Lofland, John. 1980. "Early Goffman: Style, Structure, Substance, Soul." In *The View from Erving Goffman*, edited by Jason Ditton, 24–51. London: Macmillan

– 2000 [1981]. "Erving Goffman's Sociological Legacies." In *Erving Goffman*, vol. I, edited by Gary Alan Fine and Gregory W.H. Smith, 156–78. London: Sage. *Urban Life* 13(1): (1981):7–34

MacCannell, Dean. 2000 [1983]. "Erving Goffman 1922–1982." In *Erving Goffman*, vol. I, edited by Gary Alan Fine and Gregory W.H. Smith, 8–37. London: Sage

Manning, Peter K. 1976. "The Decline of Civility: A Comment on Erving Goffman's Sociology." *Canadian Review of Sociology and Anthropology* 13:13–25

Marx, Gary T. 1984. "Role Models and Role Distance: A Remembrance of Erving Goffman." *Theory and Society* 13:649–62

Messinger, S.L., with H. Sampson and R.D. Towne. 1962. "Life as Theater: Some Notes on the Dramaturgic Approach to Social Reality." *Sociometry* 25:147–60

Mote, Jonathon E. 2001. "From Schütz to Goffman: The Search for Social Order." *The Review of Austrian Economics* 14:219–31

Mullins, N.C. 1973. *Theories and Theory Groups in Contemporary American Sociology*. New York: Harper and Row

O'Neill, John. 1981. "A Preface to Frame Analysis." *Human Studies* 4:359–64

Oromaner, Mark. 1980. "Erving Goffman and the Academic Community." *Philosophy of the Social Sciences* 10:287–91

Posner, Judith. 1978. "Erving Goffman: His Presentation of Self." *Philosophy of the Social Sciences* 8:67–78

– 1980. "Rebuttal: Oromaner Paper." *Philosophy of the Social Sciences* 10:293–4

Psathas, George. 1996. "Theoretical Perspectives on Goffman: Critique and Commentary." *Sociological Perspectives* 39:383–91

Rawls, Anne Warfield. 1987. "The Interaction Order Sui Generis: Goffman's Contribution to Social Theory." *Sociological Theory* 5:136–49

Scheff, Thomas J. 2006. *Goffman Unbound! A New Paradigm for Social Science*. London: Paradigm

Schwalbe, Michael L. 1993. "Goffman against Postmodernism: Emotion and the Reality of the Self." *Symbolic Interaction* 16:333–50

Sennett, Richard. 1973. "Two in the Aisle." *New York Review of Books*, 1 November

Smith, Greg. 1999. "Interpreting Goffman's Sociological Legacy." Introduction to *Goffman and Social Organization: Studies in a Sociological Legacy*, edited by Greg Smith, 1–18. London: Routledge

– 2006. *Erving Goffman*. London: Routledge

Strong, P.M. 1988. "Minor Courtesies and Macro Structures." In *Erving Goffman: Exploring the Interaction Order*, edited by Paul Drew and Anthony Wootton, 228–49. Oxford: Polity Press

– 2000 [1983]. "The Importance of Being Erving: Erving Goffman, 1922–1982." In *Erving Goffman*, vol. I, edited by Gary Alan Fine and Gregory W.H. Smith, 38–47. London: Sage

Travers, Andrew. 1999. "Non-Person and Goffman: Sociology under the Influence of Literature." In *Goffman and Social Organization: Studies in a Sociological Legacy*, edited by Greg Smith, 156–76. London: Routledge

Treviño, A. Javier. 2003. "Erving Goffman and the Interaction Order." Introduction to *Goffman's Legacy*, edited by A. Javier Treviño, 1–49. New York: Rowman and Littlefield

Tseëlon, Efrat. 1992. "Is the Presented Self Sincere? Goffman, Impression Management and the Postmodern Self." *Theory, Culture and Society* 9:115–28

Verhoeven J. 1993. "An Interview with Erving Goffman, 1980." *Research on Language and Social Interaction* 26:317–48

Vester, Heinz-Günter. 1989. "Erving Goffman's Sociology as a Semiotics of Postmodern Culture." *Semiotica* 76:191–203

Watson, Rod. 1999. "Reading Goffman on Interaction." In *Goffman and Social Organization: Studies in a Sociological Legacy*, edited by Greg Smith, 138–55. London: Routledge

Wellek, René, and Austin Warren. 1977. *Theory of Literature*. 3rd edition. New York: Harcourt Brace Jovanovich

Williams, Robin. 1983. "An Appreciation of Sociological Tropes: A Tribute to Erving Goffman." *Theory, Culture and Society* 2:99–102

Winkin, Yves. 1983. "The French (Re)presentation of Goffman's *Presentation* and Other Books." *Theory, Culture and Society* 2:109–13

– 1999. "Erving Goffman: What Is a Life? The Uneasy Making of an Intellectual Biography." In *Goffman and Social Organization: Studies in a Sociological Legacy*, edited by Greg Smith, 19–41. London: Routledge

– 2000 [1992]. "Baltasound as the Symbolic Capital of Social Interaction." In *Erving Goffman*, vol. I, edited by Gary Alan Fine and Gregory W.H. Smith, 193–212. London: Sage

Young, T.R. 1971. "The Politics of Sociology: Gouldner, Goffman and Garfinkel." *American Sociologist* 6:271–81

SECTION III
The Chicago School Diaspora: Urban Ecology

Robert E. Park (1864–1944) taught at Chicago from 1914 until his retirement in 1936. Park's legacy is multi-dimensional and, among other things, is associated with a particular epistemological orientation (see section I), a general emphasis on social organization (and, more specifically, understanding organization in terms of human ecology), and a particular substantive area (urban sociology). Moreover, Park played a significant role in facilitating the use of Chicago as a research laboratory. The chapters in this section, crudely organized in terms of the historical emergence of the ideas used to discuss urban settings, illustrate the myriad of ways Park's focus on the urban setting has been taken up. They also illustrate a third way in which the Chicago School Diaspora engages with the tradition. Whereas section I focused on conceptualizing the School and section II on the theoretical ideas of selected key individuals, section III is tied together by a substantive topic: the city.

In chapter 9, "Nels Anderson and the Chicago School of Urban Sociology," Rolf Lindner uses the example of Park's student Nels Anderson to document the connection between German romanticism and Park's urban sociology in a manner that resonates with George Park's observations on the importance of contextual understanding (chapter 4). In chapter 10, "Flop Houses, Fancy Hotels, and 'Second-Rate Bohemia': Zorbaugh's *The Gold Coast and the Slum* and the Gentrification Debate," Mervyn Horgan reinterprets the work of one of Park's graduate students (Zorbaugh) in order to shed new light on the processes whereby the physical proximity of radically different types of urban locations generate new and locally distinct cultural forms. In so doing, Horgan shows the insufficiency of analyses associated with the spatial turn in geography and re-establishes the importance of context and meaning for understanding social organization. In chapter 11, "Urban Sociology in Poor Cities of Africa and the Middle East: A New Methodology Inspired by Robert E. Park's Urban Ecological Approach," Thomas K. Park, Luis Cisneros, Edward Nell, and Mourad Mjahed describe a method for using diachronic remote sensing via satellite to reconstruct change in urban housing, a method they argue is consistent with Park's urban ecology approach to understanding cities. In chapter 12, "Tourist Zones, Emotional Buttons, and the Ubiquitous Beggar," Gary Bowden builds on Park's notion of particular zones of urban activity to explore the dynamics of cross-cultural contact in developing countries. In chapter 13, "Constructions of Public and Private Spheres in the Soviet Communal Apartment: Erving Goffman's Notion of Territories of Self," Defne Över links together Goffman's concern with regions (manifest in his notion of territories of self) with a particular form of urban construction (the communal apartment) in order to critique a universalist understanding of the distinction between public and private. In chapter 14, "Urban Imagery, Tourism, and the Future of New Orleans," Mark Hutter and DeMond S. Miller link Park's claim that a city is a "state of mind" with later theoretical strands to explore the urban rebuilding, rebranding, and re-identification of New Orleans after Katrina.

As noted in the introduction, one of the key fault lines dividing interpretations of the meaning of Chicago School sociology turns on the relative emphasis given to social organization versus that given to social psychology. The chapters in this section, in general, place greater emphasis on social organization than those in the other sections. But even within this section, tension remains between chapters placing heavier emphasis on the organizational roles of time and space (e.g., Park et al.) and those predominantly emphasizing meaning (e.g., Hutter and Miller). Despite the differences, there is a shared emphasis on the importance of context – that meaning is not universal but, rather, embedded in spatial-temporal organization.

9

Nels Anderson and the Chicago School of Urban Sociology

ROLF LINDNER

In his seminal essay on "Deep Structures in Social Science," Alvin Gouldner (1973) differentiates between classical and romantic thinking in the social sciences. Whereas classical thought stresses the universal applicability of standards, norms, and values, romantic thinking emphasizes their relativity. Seen thus, romantic thinking inherently possesses a tendency to shatter norms. Looking at American anthropology and sociology, not only as theoretical and research activities but as modally differentiated occupational subcultures, Gouldner suggests that anthropology still remains the more romantic, and sociology the more classical, discipline. Gouldner gives several reasons for his suggestion. First of all, the anthropologist's method is far more personal, requiring the involvement of the anthropologist's person, whereas the sociologist is commonly seeking to extricate his or her person from the research. Second, the very activities of the anthropologist require him or her to go to more exotic and romantic locales, whereas sociology remains, for the most part, a study of the familiar and the commonplace. Third, the anthropologist is more concerned with presenting concrete ethnographic details than the sociologist who, instead, is more inclined to elaborate on his or her abstractions. The anthropologist writes about extraordinary locales that have colour and vividness, persuading and convincing the reader through the presentation of an interlocking set of mosaic details, which establish the anthropologist's intellectual authority because they imply his or her personal presence in the locale under discussion. To the anthropologist, the concrete details are often regarded as valuable in their own right, whereas to the sociologist the details are often stage props subordinated to the development of generalizations.

Although, in Gouldner's view, romantic thinking is chiefly found in the discipline of cultural anthropology while classical thinking manifests itself as a discipline in sociology, he nevertheless is aware that certain schools of thought within American sociology are relatively more romantic. The purest vein of romanticism in American sociology is, in his opinion, to be found in the Chicago School of Urban Sociology. This Chicago standpoint embodies a species of naturalistic Romanticism; it prefers the offbeat, for instance, the extreme case, to the familiar average case; the evocative ethnographic detail to the dispassionate and dull taxonomy; the sensuously expressive to dry, formal analysis; informal, naturalistic observation to formal questionnaires and rigorous laboratory experiments; the standpoint of the hip outsider to that of the square insider. In short, as the nineteenth-century Romantics might have said, they prefer the standpoint of bohemians to that of philistines (Gouldner 1973, 346).

Gouldner attributes this state of affairs to the fact that the founders of the Chicago School were most closely linked to the German tradition. But there are actually important factors arising out of their own cultural tradition that helped to promote the formation of a romantic attitude as a motivation. In this context, it is of particular significance that, in the romantic view, variety is in itself of value; the romantic attitude is in essence pluralistic. It directs attention toward hitherto neglected areas of social life, thereby producing to some extent a "democratization" of the concept of the data. Furthermore, within this attitude, there is an implicit critique of the conventional world view: "To the Romanticists, every object was a world in itself, every grain of sand a cosmos. Each object being uniquely individual was therefore worthy of attention in itself; it was valuable in itself not simply as a paradigm to be emulated or decried. It was seen as worth knowing quite apart from its moral implications, and not because it needed to be reformed and improved. Romanticism thus contributed to a concern with the lowly or deviant parts of the social world" (Gouldner 1973, 351).

Walt Whitman is generally considered the spiritual founding father of the romantic interest in human diversity, which was at the same time based on an underlying democratic impetus. For the younger generation at the end of the nineteenth century, who were rebelling against moral and cultural confinement, Whitman was the guiding light of cultural dissent. At the turn of the century, coming out in support of Whitman meant declaring oneself a cultural dissi- dent. Robert Park also came out in support of Whitman during this period. In a speech entitled "Walt Whitman," which he gave in 1930 to the Chicago branch of the Walt Whitman Fellowship, he revealed his enthusiasm for Whitman:

> As a young man I was thrilled by the note of insurgency in the "Song of Myself" and in the "Children of Adam." I looked for- ward with confidence to when thought and literature in America should be free, untrammeled by the traditional forms and the inherited conventions ... When I first encountered Whitman I was, as I have said, disturbed and unsettled, but I had my moments of ecstasy also. I was a newspaper man then, as Whitman had been. A newspaper man, more than most people, I suspect, knows, and feels, and is thrilled by the vast, anonymous and impersonal life of the city. Walking on upper Broadway or down to the Battery on a bright afternoon, or watching the oncoming and outgoing human tide as it poured morning and evening over Brooklyn Bridge, was always for me an enthralling spectacle. I remember writing, not a poem, but an article for the Sunday paper, on that theme. It was for that reason, no doubt, that I began to read with a certain amount of enthusiasm Whitman's musings on the city's surging life. Crossing Brooklyn Ferry, you remember, inspired Whitman to reflections upon life and death and I felt, as he did, that there was something inspiring, majestic – in the spectacle of the manifold and multitudinous life of the city (Freedman 1970, 103).

Park's enthusiasm for Whitman is characteristic of many of the young intellectuals of his generation, who, seeking what Whitman termed "something yet unfound," broke with tradition. For them, the metropolis becomes a domain of experience, which leaves behind all that is provincial and narrow; it is a place characterized by heteroge- neity of opinions, lifestyles, and cultures, which permits subjectivity and an experience of one's self.

If Chicago sociologists prefer the standpoint of the bohemian to that of the philistine, this preference is probably best shown by their interest in the hobo. Robert Park supposedly suggested the term "Hobohemia" to Nels Anderson instead of the more usual – and more accurate – "Main Stem" to describe Chicago's West Madison districts. As Albert Parry (1960) tells us in his history of the bohemian in the United States, the word emerged in the bohemian circles of Greenwich Village. In Chicago, Ben Reitman was a representative of this cultural hybrid of hobo and bohemian, "a curiously exotic figure, outrageously Byronesque," as Roger Bruns (1987) wrote in his hobo history *Knights of the Road*. And it was Reitman who suggested to Nels Anderson that he carry out an investigation of homeless men in Chicago, a study that became *The Hobo*. In his essay "The Mind of the Rover: Reflections upon the Relation between Mobility and Locomotion," Robert Park provides a remarkable example of the romantic attitude ascribed to Chicago sociology. In this essay, later reissued as "The Mind of the Hobo," Park characterizes the hobo as "the bohemian in the ranks of common labor. He has the artistic temperament" (Park 1923, 270). It is not by chance that in this context he mentions Walt Whitman as "the most eminent of all hobo poets."

With this emphasis on the bohemian side of the hobo's lifestyle, Park accentuates an aspect of the latter's existence that was somewhat neglected, even avoided, by Anderson. For Anderson, the hobo was first of all an itinerant worker, not a rover, an emphasis with biographical roots. In an autobiographical sketch with the Phoenix edition of *The Hobo* (1961), Nels Anderson notes that his father, Nels Anderson, Sr, after immigrating to the United States in 1882, had lived five years as a hobo and had worked as a coalminer, lumberjack, and bricklayer. Nels Anderson, Jr, like most of his brothers and sisters, followed the example set by his father. Only two of the nine children became farmers, as their father had wished them to. Rather: "Four of the boys became migratory workers before settling on other careers. My three sisters also left home and did some moving about before settling. But none of my family became a drunkard, gambler, or loafer. All became self-supporting in some occupation above common labor. In that solid sense my parents did not fail" (Anderson 1967, vii).

It is very clear from this passage that Anderson was upset, even insulted, by the contemporary insinuation that the career of a migratory worker necessarily ended in his becoming a drunkard or a loafer (see Brown, this volume). This explains Anderson's repeated emphasis on the hobo as above all else a special category of worker, someone who was historically indispensable when it came to tapping natural resources. It is the worker's pride that comes to the fore in passages like these. In his autobiography, the need to justify himself leads to a portrayal of the hobo life that makes it appear joyless: "One often hears or reads bits on these jungles (summer camps of the hobos), about the 'merry hobo' singing and such stuff. There or elsewhere, I never heard singing" (Anderson 1975, 95). The emphasis is on looking for work, contracting for work, and itinerant journeys from one workplace to the next. In this way, the stress is placed on the prime importance of the domain of work, and there remains no place for romanticism of any kind. At the same time, the fascination associated with this form of migratory work gets almost completely lost: the allure of an unfettered form of work, which drove Anderson's father and brothers "out on the road" again and again. Instead, in his autobiography Anderson paints the picture of a puritanical existence, one he led for six long years, from 1906 to 1912, working as, among other things, a navvy, casual crop-picker, and carpenter. The *Milk and Honey Route*, a handbook for hobos, is written in a completely different mood. Anderson published it in 1930 under the pseudonym "Dean Stiff." Reitman (1930, 59) reviewed the book as one written by "a sociologist gone poetic."

But Nels Anderson (1967 [1923], xxi) did his research at a time when most of the old-timers were already figures of the past: "It is clear now, although it was not recognized fully at the time, that the hobo was on his way out" and, as he wrote later, "his kind of labor was going out of demand at the time *The Hobo* was written." The itinerant worker as a social type was, first and foremost, the product of the economic and social conditions that Anderson recorded and which were disappearing along with the frontier. It is not by chance that the hobo had been called the belated frontiersman. To the extent that the migratory worker comes up against the limits of the economic basis of his way of life as a result of the closing of the frontier, it is not incorrect to characterize the hobo as a kind of bohemian, someone who always manages to muddle through. When removed from their social base, the cultural elements of hobo life – their vernacular, songs, and legends – take on a life of their own. The social type of the hobo as a migratory worker is joined by the cultural figure of the hobo as bohemian, who swears "that when work becomes an art and a joy, he will take off his coat and go to work." The person who says this, the "Hobo King" Dan O'Brien, is himself a symptom of the new age. Choosing a king of the hobos – a title that was hotly disputed in the 1920s and 1930s – only makes sense if it is a prize for the pureness of lifestyle. Only by placing the emphasis on voluntary exile do we arrive at the division into "genuine" – that is, "freely chosen" – and "forced" vagrancy, into authentic and faked identities, a division that can be found as a formal principle in subcultures to the present time. At this stage, what remains of primary importance is the non-conformist lifestyle and not the itinerant way of life. A way of life bound to economic conditions evolves into a condition of quasi-professional outsiders, which stresses the bohemian features of the hobo existence – "love of individual freedom," "deviations from conventions," "absent time budgets" – above and beyond their real significance and then condenses them into a lifestyle. In their search for authenticity, the marginal intelligentsia of the 1910s and 1920s "discover" a new cultural hero, the hobo, who goes to work when it becomes an art – an "American Cultural Hero" (Feied 1964), still lingering on as a bohemian in Kerouac's *On the Road*.

The neologism "Hobohemia" was a term that defined the consequent merging of these new lifestyle hobos. It is this bohemianization of the hobo existence that gives it its romantic flavour. Robert Park's characterization of the hobo as "the bohemian in the ranks of common labor" resonates with this contemporary view. "To many of the Chicagoans," Gouldner (1973, S.346) argues, "the demi-monde is not only a fact of life, to be treated like any other, but also provides a standpoint for pronouncing a judgement upon respectable society." And, I would add, this applies to a considerable extent to the second generation. "Indeed," Gouldner (1973, S.346) continues, "they seem to speak on behalf of the demi-monde, and to affirm the authenticity of 'disreputable' life-styles." It is in this vein that Park comes to praise "the most eminent of the hobo poets," Walt Whitman, who "reflected the restlessness and rebelliousness and individualism of the hobo mind not only in the content but in the very formlessness of his verse: 'What do you suppose will satisfy the soul, except to walk free and own no superior?'" (Park 1923, 270). It is the aesthetic relation to the object that distinguishes Romanticism in social science. Abbott (2007) has recently followed in Park's footsteps with an impressive plea for a lyrical sociology.

The Hobo was the most romantic tale of all Chicago monographs – at least the book had been advertised as such. "I am curious about The Hobo," said the order-form, and the ad promised that the reader could peer behind the scenes, be surprised at the hobo's philosophy and diverted by the poetry in his songs of the road. Though we have to consider the text as copy, it nevertheless demonstrates the changed attitude toward an outsider who represented a romantic bohemian lifestyle rather than a way of life that merely meant filling a gap in the labour market (cf. Brown, this volume). Can we assume that this change of attitude toward the hobo – from a societal menace to a cultural symbol of freedom – has something in common with the shift of the sociological viewpoint – from prevention to understanding – that characterizes the Chicago school (Lindner 2006)? Anderson may have been the first and only freshman to arrive at Chicago by freight train – "riding the rods," as the hobo jargon has it – but he did so not to express a romantic temper but rather simply because he was penniless. It seems quite reasonable to say that Anderson was not a romantic at all, at least not in the sense elaborated here. His critical stance toward his fellow students gives us a sense of a person who was not only "a stranger at the gate" of the university but also an outsider among his middle-class fellows. As he writes in his autobiography (Anderson 1975, 165): "if I spoke of the hobo or other men in my sector of Chicago, their ways of life and work, it was all remote from their understanding. They would respond with some sort of Weary Willie [a hobo caricature] humor, which reminded me over and over of a sort of cultural gap between my colleagues and me ... their values and outlook were so different from mine." In a personal interview with Roger Salerno in 1981, Anderson states: "There were a lot who wouldn't mix with me because they belonged to a different social strata" (Salerno 2006, 94). This experience is very similar to that of the first generation of British scholarship boys, all marginal men in academia, like Richard Hoggart, Raymond Williams, and Stuart Hall, who were given a grant to study at Oxford. "I 'hear' that Oxford now principally as a particular pitch of the voice ... The upper-middle-class English male commanding attention to confidently expressed banalities as a sort of seigneurial right," remembers Hall in his memoirs (Hall 1989, 19). Anderson would have spoken of "hokum" – that is, the nonsense spouted by the sophisticated who know not whereof they speak. Down to earth and earnest, Nels Anderson felt that a craftsman knew and obeyed the rules of his trade, and he expected the same would hold for students and professors (Anderson 1983, 397). His time as a migratory worker evidently shaped Anderson's attitude (habitus) in which work ethic was packed along with pride in craft skill. He applied this ethic to sociology; to him, the sociologist was above all a craftsman, who must fully master the trade – the complete opposite of a romantic conception. Noel Iverson (1978, 183) described Anderson in his homage as "a man at once practical and fanciful, [he] combines the engineer's solid grasp of materials with the inventor's playful search for new solutions." Such a combination, however, also marked out the good, versatile migratory worker, who worked in such diverse areas of employment as mining, railroad construction, farming, or forestry. His concern was for the ordinary man, as Iverson emphasizes, "for the unproclaimed accomplishment, especially by those who have added something of value to our lives: the workman, the inventor, the engineer, the craftsman" (Iverson 1978, 183). Nels Anderson played a key role in developing the fields of labour and welfare in the United States. In Germany he is known for his work with the Office of Labor Affairs, which reorganized the free labour unions, and as the director of the UNESCO Institute of Social Research in Cologne. He was in charge of the major Darmstadt-Study, published in nine volumes between 1952 and 1954. This study too is evidence of Anderson's lifelong involvement in labour issues. As he (1956, 144) himself noted in retrospect, the study was originally "supposed to investigate social problems of the working class in a number of cities, so as to familiarise the young labor union officials with the concerns of the workers." In the end, however, it proved the first and the most extensive community study ever to be carried out in the Federal Republic of Germany. Anderson understood sociology as a service to society. The last volume of the "Darmstadt-Study" dealt with how workers see trade unions and works committees, demonstrating that Nels Anderson was a man for whom labour issues were of crucial importance and that he himself was also a craftsman.

REFERENCES

Abbott, Andrew. 2007. "Against Narrative: A Preface to Lyrical Sociology." *Sociological Theory* 25:67–99

Anderson, Nels. 1956. "Die Darmstadt-Studie – Ein Informeller Rückblick. In *Soziologie der Gemeinde*, edited by René König, 144–151. Sonderheft 1 der Kölner Zeitschrift für Soziologie und Sozialpsychologie. Opladen: Westdeutscher Verlag

– 1961 [1923]. *The Hobo: The Sociology of the Homeless Men.* Chicago: University of Chicago Press
– 1975. *The American Hobo: An Autobiography.* Leiden: E.J. Brill
– 1983. "A Stranger at the Gate: Reflections on the Chicago School of Sociology." *Urban Life* 11:396–406
Bruns, Roger A. 1987. *The Damndest Radical: The Life and World of Dr. Ben Reitman.* Chicago: University of Chicago Press
Feied, Frederick. 1964. *No Pie in the Sky: The Hobo as American Cultural Hero in the Works of Jack London, John Dos Passos and Jack Kerouac.* New York: Citadel Press
Freedman, Florence B. 1970. "A Sociologist Views a Poet: Robert Ezra Park on Walt Whitman." *Walt Whitman Review* 16:99–104
Gouldner, Alvin W. 1973. "Romanticism and Classicism: Deep Structures in Social Sciences." In *For Sociology: Renewal and Critique in Sociology Today,* edited by Alvin Gouldner, 323–66. London: Basic Books
Hall, Stuart. 1989. "The 'First' New Left." In *Out of Apathy: Voices of the New Left,* edited by Robin Archer, Diemut Bubeck, and Hanjo Glock, 13–38. London: Verso
Iverson, Noel. 1978. "Homage to a Pioneer." *International Journal of Comparative Sociology* 19:3–4
Lindner, Rolf. 2006. *The Reportage of Urban Culture: Robert Park and the Chicago School.* Cambridge: Cambridge University Press
Park, Robert Ezra. 1923. "The Mind of the Rover: Reflections upon the Relations between Mentality and Locomotion." *The World Tomorrow* September
Parry, Albert. 1960. *Garrets and Pretenders: A History of Bohemianism in America.* New York: Covici Friede
Reitman, Ben L. 1930. Review of *The Milk and Honey Route: A Handbook for Hobos,* by Dean Stiff. *American Journal of Sociology* 37:158–9
Salerno, Roger A. 2006. *Sociology Noir: Studies at the University of Chicago in Loneliness, Marginality and Deviance, 1915–1935.* Jefferson: University of North Carolina Press
Stiff, Dean. 1930. *The Milk and Honey Route: A Handbook for Hobos.* New York: Random House

10

Flop Houses, Fancy Hotels, and "Second-Rate Bohemia": Zorbaugh's *The Gold Coast and the Slum* and the Gentrification Debate

MERVYN HORGAN

1929 – Chicago's cultural hotspot is a place called The Drake Hotel. The Drake was a residential hotel for the elite, part of the Gold Coast, the greatest concentration of wealth in Chicago. The Gold Coast was cheek by jowl with a slum, Little Hell, the greatest concentration of poverty in Chicago. 2009 – Toronto's cultural hotspot is a place called The Drake Hotel. It is located in a former rooming house in the heart of Queen West, a neighbourhood at the centre of Toronto's recent cultural "renaissance." Toronto's Drake borders an area with one of the highest concentrations of poverty in urban Canada.

From the moment it opened its doors in its newest incarnation, Toronto's Drake has been at the centre – both physical and symbolic – of a battle around the cultural and economic life of Toronto's west end. The opening of The Drake has been interpreted variously as: a signal of the rapid demise of a large stock of privately held affordable housing in the form of rooming houses; a booster of real estate prices; a part of Toronto's much celebrated (in Toronto at least) cultural renaissance; the triumph of commerce over art; and the emergence of something akin to what Zorbaugh calls a "second-rate bohemia" (1976 [1929], 88). Despite these differences in interpretation, most agree that The Drake symbolizes gentrification in the west end. In this chapter, I draw on a much-cited, little-read classic of the Chicago School to analyze the socio-spatial context of The Drake's emergence in Toronto. Throughout, I seek to highlight the ways that close spatial proximity of radical social differences generates material worthy of close sociological scrutiny.

Needless to say, Toronto of the 2000s differs from Chicago of the 1920s. But, in the spirit of recovering the Chicago School's experimental moment, I will highlight points where each time and place resonates with the other. That these two hotels from different times and different places share the same name is a happy coincidence that provides a springboard for investigating the contemporary relevance of a neglected classic of Chicago School sociology.

Harvey Warren Zorbaugh's *The Gold Coast and the Slum* (hereafter *The Gold Coast*), an oft-cited but little-read study of an area close to Chicago's Drake Hotel, is notable as an exemplar of Chicago School work (Hunter 1983), given its use of multiple methods (Bulmer 1984) and its lyrical prose (Abbott 2007). Zorbaugh's account described the ways that the close proximity of wealth and poverty formed the "nondescript community" (Park 1976, xvii) of Chicago's Near North Side in the 1920s. In particular, Zorbaugh's short chapter on the bohemian village of Towertown – an area that lay between the Gold Coast and Little Hell – signals an important early effort to understand the interplay between demographic, economic, and cultural transformation at the level of the neighbourhood.

This chapter has two central and interrelated aims: first, to recover *The Gold Coast* from the scrap heap of the history of sociology; and, second, to take the serendipitous naming of The Drake Hotel in Toronto as a springboard for a reinvigorated reading of Zorbaugh. I begin by looking at the initial reception and subsequent citations of *The Gold Coast*. Here, I demonstrate how engagement with *The Gold Coast* has waned over time and outline a number of reasons for the relative neglect of this particular work. This leads into a discussion of the sidelining of Chicago School–style work in urban studies more generally in which I argue that the particularly scathing criticisms of the Chicago School from our cousins in geography have continued to go largely unanswered. In order to remedy this, informed by Chicago School–style work, I offer a critique of the largely meaning-blind orthodoxy that prevails among many geographers. From *The Gold Coast*, I tease out Zorbaugh's nascent under-formulated understanding of the processes by which cultural change happens at the neighbourhood level. Today, this process is familiar to us as "gentrification," a word coined much later (Glass 1964). While not arguing for a wholesale revival, I argue that close attention to the descriptions offered by Zorbaugh provides us with a lens through which to uncover the paradoxes of what I term the interactional landscape of contemporary Western cities and the conceptual landscape of contemporary urban studies. In response to criticism from geographers, I offer a robust defence of Chicago School–style work that places the methodological promiscuity and descriptive thickness of *The Gold Coast* at its centre. This leads to a call for conceptual expansion in contemporary urban investigations by refocusing attention on the city as a site where the physical proximity of radically different subject and group positions generates particular and locally specifiable cultural forms. Framed as an intervention in the gentrification debate in contemporary urban studies, I draw on Zorbaugh's description and analysis to unpack the dynamics of local-level change in the neighbourhood where Toronto's Drake Hotel is located. In so doing, I show how Zorbaugh's work can form part of a meaning-centred sociospatial-sensitive approach to counter the more linear economically determined orthodoxy dominant in contemporary urban studies.

For Faris, the Chicago School was characterized by an "atmosphere of adventure, exploration and responsibility for opening up new directions of sociological research" (1967, 88). My intent in this chapter is to open new directions for both Chicago-inspired work and sociology more generally. First, let us recover Zorbaugh's study from the "enormous condescension of posterity" (Thompson 1980, 12) by looking at early reviews of *The Gold Coast* and subsequent citations of the book in sociology and beyond.

RECEPTION: REVIEWS, CITATIONS, CRITIQUES

Though regularly cited as a Chicago School classic, *The Gold Coast and the Slum* has been increasingly neglected by urban sociologists. When first published in 1929, the book received positive reviews, with several reviewers commenting on Zorbaugh's richly descriptive writing. Rupert Vance noted that Zorbaugh continued in the vein of the Chicago studies of the time, combining "the verve of journalism with the restraint of science ... a book of vivid scholarship, written by a real personality who has not hesitated to peep into the crannies of urban life ... The whole study is illuminated by a literary style, vivid, crisp, and alert" (Vance 1929, 320–1). Other reviews also pointed to the richness of Zorbaugh's description but saw literary flair as indicative of a lack of scientific rigor in the scholarship. For example, while Howard Becker's review of the same year commented on Zorbaugh's prowess as a writer, he also noted that anyone familiar with University of Chicago work, and Park and Burgess's introductory text *The City* in particular, "will not find much that is new in the way of theoretical background." Becker goes on to call Zorbaugh "a colorist rather than a draftsman" (1929, 203), an incisive claim given the subsequent waning of theoretical engagement with *The Gold Coast*.

In the decade following its initial publication, the book was regularly cited. By the 1940s, William Foote Whyte had developed a critique (1943a) of the model of social disorganization favoured by Zorbaugh. Indeed, Whyte's celebrated *Street Corner Society* (1943b) can be read as a response to Zorbaugh's failure to distinguish between different kinds of slums in *The Gold Coast*. For Whyte, Zorbaugh focused too much on social disorganization and not enough on reorganization. Indeed, most references to Zorbaugh in the 1940s and 1950s continue along these lines, critiquing the social disorganization thesis.

Although one might expect citations of a text to vary radically over time, with occasional peaks and troughs following the ebbs and flows of theoretical controversies and the vagaries of intellectual fashions, citations of *The Gold Coast* show a rather remarkable evenness over the past fifty years. Books may well receive attention on publication, only to quickly fade from memory. On the surface at least, this does not seem to be the case with *The Gold Coast*.

A citation analysis using the ISI Web of Knowledge through the Social Sciences Citation Index reveals relative consistency in the number of journal articles referencing *The Gold Coast*. While citations of *The Gold Coast* for the 1960s number only twenty-four, somewhat surprisingly, citations of *The Gold Coast* have been notable in their steadiness since that time, with fifty-five citations in the 1970s, fifty-nine in the 1980s, fifty-five in the 1990s, and fifty-five in the 2000s. As any Chicago School–informed sociologist worth their salt will tell you, numbers furnish us with partial truths and sometimes obscure a more nuanced story: the quantity of citations tells us little of their content. Indeed, careful scrutiny of the content of articles citing *The Gold Coast* reveals an altogether different picture.

While the numbers remain quite consistent, the relative importance of *The Gold Coast* to any specific article's argument or content has waned considerably over the past half century. For example, in the early 1970s one sociologist invoked something he called "the Zorbaugh tradition," focused on emphasizing the "disorganizing aspects of urbanization" (Feagin 1973, 132). While the moniker does not seem to have stuck, on occasion flurries of citations arise that are primarily concerned with highly critical (and brief) discussions of the disorganization thesis. In fact, one has to look quite closely to find any article that engages Zorbaugh's text as anything other than a representative of this more or less entirely discredited thesis, with very few taking up any other aspect of *The Gold Coast* in a substantive way.

As far as I can determine, Albert Hunter is the only person to have published a journal article that explicitly deals with *The Gold Coast* as its point of focus. Drawing on his own field research conducted in Chicago in the 1970s, Hunter turns to Zorbaugh's book in an attempt to use "replication research as a method of historical analysis" (1983, 462). Hunter returns to areas studied by Zorbaugh and enters a reflexive "dialogue with Zorbaugh's original work, asking where he had gone, what he had observed, and how he thought about it" (Hunter 1983, 462). Since Hunter's piece was published, surprisingly little has been written about *The Gold Coast*, even though, as indicated above, numbers of citations remain consistently high.

What then accounts for the relative stability in numbers of citations of *The Gold Coast* in the recent past? In addition to those rare articles that take up some element of Zorbaugh's argument (however briefly), we find *The Gold Coast* cited in a remarkable array of fields and subdisciplines: local history, ethnic history (Italian, in particular), criminology, neighbourhood studies, housing studies – even in an article on football hooliganism! That said, none of these types of citations dominate. Recently, there has been a renaissance of interest in the chapter on Towertown in particular. At the time Zorbaugh was writing, Towertown was "a thriving gay ghetto" (Bergquist and McDonald 2006, 3), leading recent scholars to draw on Zorbaugh's account of Towertown to flesh out gay and lesbian urban histories (Heap 2003; Churchill 2009). In another vein, Rosemont's (2003) elaborate collection of accounts and descriptions of Towertown's most celebrated institution, The Dil Pickle Club (sic), includes an excerpt from *The Gold Coast*. Here we find Zorbaugh's "dour, puritanical, hard-hearted maunderings" included as part of the "Critics" section, since they reflect a "dominant or 'official'" (Rosemont 2004,

38) view that betrays a class-based prejudice against the sorts of rad-
icalism to be found in The Dil Pickle Club and Towertown more
broadly. Here, *The Gold Coast* appears less as a sociological study in
its own right and more as a historical document useful in uncovering
Towertown's history as a site of queer life and political activism.

The only journal article published in the past 25 years that actually discusses *The Gold Coast* in detail is Andrew Abbott's (2007)
call for a "lyrical sociology." Abbott's focus is Zorbaugh's ability to
construct a compelling narrative by way of his literary flair rather
than the specificities of his argument. Beyond this lone example, the
overwhelming majority of the remainder of citations of *The Gold
Coast* tend to offer a surface-level critique of the work or, more
likely, merely mention Zorbaugh's name as part of the list of Chicago
School usual suspects: Park, Burgess, Cressey, Wirth, Zorbaugh, and
so on. This relegation to an interchangeable element of a rote list of
Chicago sociologists seems to indicate that few scholars in the recent
past have taken *The Gold Coast* seriously as anything other than a
work of historic interest.

While difficult to assert with certainty, we might speculate that there
are several reasons for the relative neglect of this book: Zorbaugh's
descriptive and largely journalistic writing; the time- and space-bound
nature of the study; its explicitly moralistic overtones; the fading from
view that happens with time; and, perhaps, the study's apparent irrel-
evance to the trajectory of neighbourhood-level research over the past
four decades. Moreover, neither Zorbaugh's disinclination to outline a
theoretical or methodological program nor the normative underpinning of *The Gold Coast* – which tends heavily towards reformism –
have served the book well in the long term.

While any or all of the above may be sufficient grounds for the
waning of attention to this specific study, an examination of the
investigative landscape of urban studies more generally yields what
I think are the most salient reasons. Above, I pointed to criticism of
Zorbaugh's reliance on the social disorganization thesis from within
the discipline of sociology (Feagin's "Zorbaugh tradition"). If we
situate Zorbaugh within the more general sidelining of Chicago
School–style work, which occurred with the advent of the double
whammy of Parsonian grand theory and purely quantitative variable analysis that forcefully took hold of US sociology in the immediate aftermath of the School's ascendancy, then we find further
cause for the decline in engagement with *The Gold Coast*.

While these intra-disciplinary sources of explanation for the decline are powerful ones, they are perhaps a little too inward-looking. An appreciation of the overall sidelining of Chicago School–style studies of the city, particularly since the 1970s, requires awareness of changes outside of the discipline, especially among scholars in geography who brought very different theoretical and methodological orientations to bear on the city. Here, I want to turn to criticisms of the Chicago School from critical geography, outline their bases, and sift through some of these critiques to assess their validity, legitimating some critiques and undermining others where appropriate.

Inspired in part by the early work of Manuel Castells (1977; 1978), geographers were at the centre of the 1970s "spatial turn" in urban studies and social science more generally that is now fully threaded through the social sciences. According to Castells (1978, 8), studies of the city prior to the spatial turn concentrated only on the collection of data to formulate "a few *ad hoc* hypotheses or descriptions of particular situations which are always impossible to generalize from." Chicago-style empiricism – what he calls "poetical" or "anthropological" – failed to generate adequate theories of urbanity, since context-specific data could only be useful if it was used to generate theories rather than as an end in itself. However, Castells is a sociologist, and it is with geographers, particularly David Harvey, the most vocal and consistent critic of Chicago-style work, that I locate the transformation of urban studies connected to the decline of Chicago-inspired work. Though antagonistic to the Chicago School more generally, Harvey's criticisms bear little or no resemblance to those inside the discipline (Nock, this volume). Instead, Harvey proceeds to wage an ideological battle with the Chicago perspective by way of critique of the latter's conceptualization of space.

In an article first published in 1978, Harvey (2001) pits his work, as a "marxist challenger," in direct opposition to what he calls the "bourgeois social science" of the Chicago School. Here, I want to briefly address this (rhetorical) challenge to Chicago-style sociology. Harvey (2001, 68) begins innocently enough, asking what happens when "scientists from radically different traditions seek to understand the same material phenomena." This leads to the forceful claim that Chicago School work is from the perspective of capital, while his work is "drawn up in terms of the opposition of *labour*" (Harvey 2001, 70, italics in the original) – hence, "bourgeois social science" versus its "marxist challengers." This basic distinction guides much of his argument; Chicago work is posited as some sort of handmaiden of capital to be resisted by work that can see and analyze the "social totality." A number of further claims are built on top of this rhetorical distinction.

Harvey claims that the Chicago School "attempts to construct a view of the world from outside ... [and] leaves the world by way of abstraction in order to understand it" (2001, 88–9). As I read this, I couldn't help but scratch my head and wonder whether Harvey and I were talking about the same work, the same decidedly non-Aristotelian sociologists who conducted door-to-door surveys and in-depth interviews and engaged in various forms of participant observation – sociologists who were very much involved in primary research and suspicious of groundless abstraction. Close examination of Harvey's criticism of Chicago work reveals his consistent failure to be explicit about the texts generally agreed to be representative of Chicago School work. Harvey's pointed critique includes not a single reference to anything produced during the highlight years of the Chicago School: Harvey neither names nor quotes a single purveyor of "bourgeois social science," Chicago School or otherwise. Indeed, much of his argument seems to fundamentally misunderstand Chicago work and, more than this, betrays little familiarity with the actual studies themselves.

Harvey goes on to criticize the time- and space-bound nature of Chicago work, with the claim that Chicago-style work involves endless description of specific places and so is incapable of generating general theories. He points pejoratively to studies of things like "kinship in Dar-es–Salaam in the postcolonial era" (2001, 72) as an example of a study that is just too focused, just too particular, too taken by fragments. While such a study would be fragmentary, social reality is comprised of fragments that we, as social scientists, whether thrown under one label or another, seek to bring together and understand the extent to which they are discrete, interconnected, and/or influenced by larger, more comprehensive structures.

Straw men, particularly when constructed independent of real engagement with texts and resources, are easily destroyed. Armed with a crudely caricatured representation of Chicago School work, Harvey first claims that the Chicago School is too concerned with specificity, with local detail, and then claims that it abstracts too far from reality. One wonders which criticism we are to take, since we cannot take both. To say that the Chicago School was characterized by a purely objective approach or that it was too concerned with detail undermines the richness of the idiographic insights it produced.

While he does not name it outright, we can assume that part of Harvey's disdain for Chicago-style work derives from discomfort with the ecological approach favoured by many early scholars. Stating it more clearly, Soja (1989, 178) refers to the "obfuscating ideology of naturalism," which veils the "powerful instrumentality" (i.e., capital) shaping the spatial form of the city.

As the flawed theoretical hook on which much Chicago work hung, urban ecology looks only to ecological sources for any given city's spatial form. Most urban geographers only encounter the Chicago School through Burgess's zonal hypothesis. It is important to point out that any work using a concept or principle from ecology is not necessarily flawed in its entirety simply by virtue of drawing on a theoretical framework worthy of critique. Unfortunately, the explanatory weakness of Chicago School ecology has led critics to reject Chicago School work wholesale. I too am critical of ecology, particularly since it tends to naturalize given social and spatial arrangements. As such, it is worthy of critique, especially if one is engaged in a social science that seeks to be both critical and in some way transformative. The task then is to examine what remains of Chicago School work, *The Gold Coast* in particular, when we remove the veneer that ecology provides. In so doing, we find that the Chicago School can only be taken as a desire to naturalize any particular social order or economic context when it is viewed monolithically and myopically.

Soja's reference to Chicago School "naturalism" provides us with an opportunity to make an important distinction between two kinds of naturalism often conflated but certainly distinct: one that takes existing conditions as the natural order of things and goes about describing this order as a reflection and/or extension of nature (as in urban ecology), and another that seeks to examine the world as it appears, taking this as raw material to be analyzed and understood. This latter form of naturalism does not rest on the claim that how the world is, is how it ought to be; rather, it resists such a normative claim and involves itself in studying the given, recognizing the space- and time-bound character of that given without seeking to universalize from it. My reading of Chicago School work reformulates it as an iteration of this second form of naturalism.

BEYOND THEORETICAL ORTHODOXIES

The shift in urban research outlined above contextualizes how and why *The Gold Coast* has been sidelined. Moving from urban studies in general to gentrification research in particular, the pattern of waning engagement with Chicago School–style research is replicated on a different scale. Critical geography provides the primary theoretical lens for understanding gentrification. With a theoretical starting point aimed at understanding a social totality, critical geographers typically locate causality for local-level processes extra-locally. Through this lens, gentrification can be analyzed as anything from a coping strategy of London's middle class in the face of globalization (Butler and Robson 2003) to middle-class revanchism against poorer residents in New York (Smith 1996): less a bourgeois social science than a social science of bourgeois life. Other gentrification works look at policy documents (Slater 2004), thus telling us little about lived experience, while studies of advertising, store fronts, and architecture (Mills 1993) tell us little of usage. Without slighting the arguments of these writers, their acceptance of an overarching theoretical frame places severe limitations on local-level research. Social relations, face-to-face interactions, and group culture are treated as dependent variables in a linear and direct chain of causality – mere effects. The space-forming capacities of capital are taken as primary. In turn, spatial relations largely determine social relations. Ironically, such studies occasionally mimic the spatial determinism of urban ecology that critical geographers so readily critique. Gentrification appears here as a generalizable spatial process that unfolds according to the vagaries of capitalism's global–local configurations. Consequently, much gentrification research offers limited understanding of social interactions and the lived experience of the rapid transformation that defines the process.

What, for example, of the relative autonomy of interactional processes or of the cultural processes bolstering, facilitating, and justifying spatial reorganization? To elaborate these dimensions of transformation of urban locales, we need the wide-angle lens of Chicago School–style work. First, this work needs to be excavated of the form of naturalism privileged by ecology.

The Ecological Veil

Critiques of Chicago School ecology from critical geographers must be taken seriously. Specifically, Zorbaugh's focus on ecology as a naturally unfolding process must be taken for the significant shortcoming that it is (thus, my view of ecology differs markedly from Park et al., this volume). This, though, does not mean we cast aside Chicago

School work as mere "bourgeois social science." While ecology offers crude tools for creating cursory descriptions of demographic changes and unfolding patterns of development, it is important that we not confuse the limited accounts it offers with an explanatory model or a capacity to predict. Ecology does not in itself give us access to an understanding of how and why the city's spatial form changes. Ecology's explanatory force is thin and its outlook blinkered.

Chicago School work in general (and *The Gold Coast* in particular) tends to take ecological terms as statements of fact. Succession, for example, is viewed as a natural process, and so, taking the process as a given, many Chicago School studies merely described areas where succession was occurring. How and why succession happened is unsatisfactorily theorized; it is simply a natural and inescapable fact of urban life. This is a weak way to think about an imminently social process, the unfolding of which is no more inescapable than the displacement that comes with eviction from a rooming house to make way for a hotel. Succession then serves to veil rather than to explain. Instead of accepting succession as a natural – and, therefore, inevitable – process, if we reframe it as displacement we are led to pose questions of a different order than those asked by one beholden to an ecological view of urban transformation. What chains of decision-making lead to displacement? How do particular subject positions come to be privileged or degraded, as worthy of displacing or being displaced? Who is displaced, by what means, and to where? Revisiting *The Gold Coast* with the gentrification process rather than ecological succession in mind, we can begin to think differently about neighbourhood-level change and its broader structural contexts.

As a result of the ascendancy of critical geography, there is a dearth of Chicago School–style work explicitly focused on gentrification and a glut of research emphasizing political economy. By the same token, works in the Chicago tradition have largely ignored criticism from critical geographers, preferring to see the differences as ideological and therefore insurmountable rather than as possibly complementary and mutually reinforcing. Work that traverses both perspectives could open up new veins of research into the symbolic dimensions of economic changes, the situational dynamics of slumming, and the significance of cultural codes for accelerating and justifying gentrification.

By decoupling Chicago School work from ecology, we can jettison the conceptual deadweight attached to succession and think instead about displacement. This allows us to refocus our attention on the kinds of displacement Zorbaugh describes in the chapter on Tower-town. Taking critiques of ecology as legitimate, we can return to Zorbaugh's text, set aside those elements explicitly focused on ecology, and ask: what remains of value? What we find is that Zorbaugh's text approached cultural and economic transformation in ways that have been sidelined, if not entirely lost, in social science. His rich – and occasionally "thick" – description of each of six adjacent areas and the people who populate them signals a new way of thinking about urban research and gentrification. Actively doing primary research based on firsthand ethnographic investigation quickly brings the researcher to the limits of a purely critical geographic approach. If theory comes first, then methods are sought that are appropriate to that theory, rather than insights produced out of engagement with the place or phenomena under investigation. The spirit of Chicago work demands attention to people, places, and phenomena above felicity to any one theoretical perspective. If we draw out the non-ecological elements of Chicago School work and treat ecology as a metaphor for social and spatial change rather than an accurate description of social reality, then we can return to *The Gold Coast* in search of fresh insights.

Interactional Landscapes

Before turning to the substantive content of Zorbaugh's book and its resonances with contemporary Toronto, I want to briefly sketch the contours of a sensitizing concept – interactional landscape – that draws together the disparate modes of urban analysis outlined above. With this concept I bring together the sensitivity to meaning and interactions from Chicago-style ethnography with the focus on the economic and spatial processes organizing urban spaces from critical geography. The concept plays off Abbott's (1999, 202–5) discussion of the "interactional field" that he identifies with Zorbaugh's work, though with interactional landscape I seek to more explicitly bring critical geography into dialogue with the Chicago School (see also Dear 2002).

Interactional landscapes involve two dimensions. Interaction refers to the face-to-face scene of interaction, to social situations and the dialogical contingencies of a social encounter. Landscape here refers both to space and to its representation, treated together, mutually

forming and mutually reinforcing. To understand landscape, constructed as it is here, we cannot think of it independently of the interactions that occur within it, interactions that it not only houses but
that are also shaped by it. The relationship between the two elements
is not a unidirectional causal relation: as landscapes shape interactions, so too do interactions shape landscapes. I propose interactional
landscape as a conceptual tool that oscillates freely between scales of
analysis as it traverses the differing spatial and analytic contexts thus
far treated as distinct. I use this concept to train our analytic vision
on both the structural production of inequality and the generation of
exclusion through interactions in particular social settings.

Thus, the interactional landscape of any given neighbourhood can
be altered or shifted in the process of gentrification: the changing
characteristics of interactants and patterns of interaction modify the
landscape of the locality, and simultaneously the landscape shapes
the kinds of interactions that occur there, potentiating some, offset-
ting others, making particular kinds of encounters more or less
likely. My intention with this juxtaposition is to overcome any
straightforward opposition between the terms and offset any suggestion that an analysis trained on one is automatically in opposition to
or incompatible with consideration of the other.

Undoubtedly, the descriptive content of *The Gold Coast* is specific
to its place and time. Nonetheless, the characteristics of its study
area, its descriptive mode, and its multi-methods approach offer
valuable if somewhat crude theoretical and methodological tools for
neighbourhood-level research. Such an approach is capable of thick-
ening structural analyses, giving flesh to their bare bones, animating
staid unpeopled analyses with characters and types, with real interactions and personal experiences. The textures of such a densely
woven study could do justice to the complexity of the gentrification
process and the neighbourhoods where it occurs.

GENTRIFICATION AND "SECOND-RATE" BOHEMIA: TOWERTOWN TO QUEEN STREET WEST

The term "gentrification" was coined in 1964 by Ruth Glass, took on
a negative connotation among academics in the late 1970s and mid-
1980s, and entered popular vocabulary in the late 1980s/early 1990s.
Despite the recent vintage of the term, the Chicago School fascination
with the transient and the marginal suggests that gentrification is

something that would have interested them. Veiled behind Zorbaugh's faithfulness to the ecological idea of "succession" is an account of the basic characteristics of gentrification: the rich encroaching on the poor, the increased popularity of "slumming," the seeming inevitability of displacement, heightened community conflict, artistic bohemias as intermediaries and buffers. Surprisingly, Zorbaugh largely resists the tendency toward romantic narrative that often coheres to such areas and ways of life (see Brown, this volume). Instead, the "frontier" – a description of gentrifying areas favoured by researchers and the popular media alike – is rendered evocatively by Zorbaugh (1976 [1929], 105) as a "half-world" of transient housing lying "on the frontier of the slum," mixing the slum's "shabbiness ... with the march of the city."

The ethnographic work carried out in 1920s Chicago cannot claim to be more than a snapshot of that particular place at that particular time, just as a map of a city cannot claim to be that city. Partly a big-picture thinker, but not in the systematized and abstract theoretical mode that would come to dominate American sociology by the mid-twentieth century, Zorbaugh sought with *The Gold Coast* to paint a comprehensive and detailed picture of the various lives lived cheek by jowl. Unlike most of the output of the Chicago School, this is not a focused study of one group, one place, or one institution. His big idea was to undertake a necessarily provisional and impressionistic account of the variety of experiences contained within a relatively small area of the city.

The six chapters that make up the core of the data in the book are organized in a gradual descent in both spatial and social location. We begin with the heavenly riches of the Gold Coast and five chapters later have descended into Little Hell. In the middle of this descent lies the world of rooming houses, what Zorbaugh calls the Rialto of the Half-world and Towertown. Towertown is dealt with quickly – and, it must be said, quite cynically – in one of the shortest chapters in a book of twelve short chapters.

The area of Chicago known as the Gold Coast is home to The Drake Hotel, whose opening in 1920 Zorbaugh recounts through newspaper coverage. It was "a social event in the better sense, a landmark in the life of the community. Its location fixes a new focus, around which will grow a small new city of theatre, clubs and fashionable shops. It will be, in fact, the centre of a new age of fashion ... Celebrities of all high varieties will pass in and out its doors ... In a word, the Drake should be a mirror of the time as great hostelries have been in every age and land and clime" (*Chicago Daily Tribune*, 30 November 1920, quoted in Zorbaugh 1976 [1929], 40).

While the spatially segregated zones that Zorbaugh describes do not map precisely onto the landscape of contemporary Toronto, it is certainly possible to discern the copresence of these distinctive worlds in the same space as one walks west on Queen Street. The Drake's owner, Jeff Stober – a former dotcom businessman with no prior hotel experience – describes his first encounter with the building: "When I first walked into the Drake in the summer of 2001, it was part flophouse and part crackhouse. I fell in love with the historic spiral staircase – the centrepiece of the main lobby. I was struck by this touch of glamour in an otherwise seedy establishment. A perfect starting point, I thought, to create a democratic hub and cultural pathfinder, in the midst of a re-energized indie art gallery district" (The Drake Hotel).

As with its Chicago namesake, the opening of Toronto's Drake Hotel was greeted with much fanfare in the local media. Soon international travel magazines and hip city guides followed with glowing reports on what was apparently an entirely new way of thinking about hotels. Event organizers at the hotel are called "cultural curators," and they refer to The Drake as a "cultural community centre." The hotel's website heightens these ideas: "think Berlin art salon of the 1920s infused with a modern twist," while the menu is described as "free-spirited," with everything half-price for something called the "starving artists buffet" on weekday afternoons.

Again, like Chicago's Drake of the 1920s, Toronto's Drake is adjacent to a neighbourhood with a high concentration of single-room-occupancy accommodation. This area, known as Parkdale, is a relatively dense settlement of older-stock housing: a mix of Victorian mansions chopped up into ten-plus-unit crumbling rooming houses and several mid-twentieth century high-rise buildings providing privately owned rental accommodation, most of it still relatively affordable. Parkdale is not quite a "slum" in the contemporary sense (Davis 2006), but the area is characterized by poverty. The median income for 2006 was $23,000, slightly more than 55 per cent of the national figure, with one-third of the residents living on less than $20,000 a year. In Parkdale, 92.5 per cent of residents are tenants, compared to a city-wide average of 51 per cent.

Parkdale is certainly a poor area, but most interesting are the changes that have occurred since Stober bought a "flophouse" and converted it into a fancy hotel. Between 2001 and 2006, the median income in South Parkdale rose by 27.8 per cent, largely attributable to a 50 per cent increase in those earning over $100,000. Consequently, property prices have soared, and the remaining rooming houses that have not been converted to single-family homes now sit beside young, rich families, many drawn from the creative class. One inter- viewee, a successful commercial photographer with two young chil- dren, laughs as he tells me, "I don't have to go far for my work, I just take pictures of crackheads in Parkdale."

As it appears in *The Gold Coast*, Towertown is an area that a pres- ent-day observer would recognize as ripe for gentrification. More important, what Zorbaugh says about Towertown resonates with areas undergoing rapid transformation in Toronto. "[B]izarre and eccentric divergencies of behaviour ... are the color of bohemia" (1976 [1929], 87) where gather "rebellious but sterile souls whose radical- ism runs to long hair, eccentric dress, lilies, obscenity, or a Freudian interpretation of dreams" (1976 [1929], 91). He quotes Genevieve Forbes at length, and she notes "these amateur intelligentsia began to splash a bit of red paint over a rickety stair and call it a studio. To sprawl scraggy letters of a flip phrase across a shingle and make a tea shop ... The old days of rigorous apprenticeship were going. Anybody could be an artist or a poet. And pretty nearly everybody was" (quoted in Zorbaugh 1976 [1929], 92). Commentators like Forbes reserved a cynicism bordering on vitriol for those still about the place in the mid- 1920s when rising property values, driven by the luxury shopping district on nearby Michigan Avenue, were pricing out many of the artists. Towertown became a tourist attraction, further alienating its bohemian denizens.

By the Great Depression, the colony of artists had disappeared (Rosemont 2004). We know that at the time Zorbaugh (1976 [1976], 88) was studying it, Towertown's time was passing, and he was aware of this, stating "Towertown has degenerated, so far as art is concerned, into a second-rate bohemia." This phrase, "second-rate bohemia," is so wonderfully evocative that it needs little explana- tion. The bohemia of Towertown was, as Zorbaugh seems to imply, a buffer where the rich could slum it for a while (Heap 2009). Zorbaugh was cognizant that this rising popularity would quickly lead to displacement. The more general principle appears to be that the proximity of wealth drives processes of displacement, but rather than focusing on the political economy of this process, *The Gold Coast* looks at the sorts of groups and interactions characteristic of the transition. Gentrifying areas are those places where social distances come most sharply into focus by virtue of the physical proximity of marked social distance. To this end, *The Gold Coast* is focused on the coexistence of vast social differences, sketching out the ways that the peculiar mix of social distance and physical proximity make the city both an intriguing social form and an obstinate object of social scientific inquiry.

CONCLUSION

For Park, the "new social order" instituted by the city "is neither absolute nor sacred, but pragmatic and experimental" (1967, 5). The Chicago School offers a rich heritage, but it should not be treated as something sacred to be left untouched and revered. If the city is pragmatic and experimental, then so too should be the approaches of those who wish to study it. In this chapter, I have taken one emblematic text from the Chicago School's most productive period and worked with it, treating it pragmatically – as a resource that can be used to understand a pressing contemporary urban issue (gentrification) – and experimentally, as a springboard for generating new research questions, illuminating murky corners, and highlighting blind spots in contemporary gentrification research.

With work from the Chicago School, "the heart of the matter was not the ideas and techniques, but the attitude and emotion" (Abbott and Graziano 1995, 255), and this is perhaps the part of the legacy we ought to retain. *The Gold Coast* is an exemplar of the orientation of Chicago School–style work, governed less by theoretical orthodoxy than by a spirit of discovery, a going out into the world and taking whatever that world presents. This perspective yields an implicit critique of contemporary work focused first on explaining social totality.

What then does work that marries the best of critical geography and Chicago-style ethnography look like? Are there any practitioners we can point to as exemplars? Mitchell Duneier's (1999) *Sidewalk* is a contemporary Chicago-style ethnography that, though much lauded, still retains something of the ecological orientation that I seek to excise. As with his Chicago School forebears, he pays much attention to the everyday life-worlds of a marginal urban population but does so with little reference to the struggles around Tompkins Square Park or the gentrification of the Lower East Side that have been instrumental in shaping the interactional landscape of the sidewalk that he studies. Thus, his analysis fails to incorporate the myriad insights on urban space that have come to us by way of critical geography.

Loïc Wacquant's (2002) scathing and much-discussed critique of *Sidewalk* is based in part on what he calls the "neo-romantic" outlook of the book and on Duneier's failure to take spatial processes seriously. His critique tells us something of the shifting tectonics of scholarly discourse around the contemporary city. Wacquant, who is today one of the best-known urban ethnographers, focuses primarily on coercion and control, both physical and symbolic, in the contemporary city. While this focus runs the risk of reducing marginalized populations to their determination by socio-spatial forces (2001), he is careful to resist the impulse toward reductionism that sometimes adheres to a spatial sensibility and tempers this with a strong understanding of the tactics used by the marginal to survive and the meanings that they attach to their interactions (1999). This latter strand requires Chicago-style attention to everyday life, and so his work moves relatively seamlessly between observations informed by critical geography, analyses of specific policy proscriptions, ideological shifts writ large, and ordinary life as lived in marginal neighbourhoods. While the areas studied by Wacquant are not explicitly gentrifying, many of his insights resonate with the socio-spatial processes that we find in gentrifying areas.

Richard Lloyd's *Neo-Bohemia* (2006) most closely approximates the kind of work I call for here. In this study, Lloyd uses a narrative of personal involvement in the music scene of Chicago's Wicker Park area in the 1990s to weave together an analysis of the dynamics of displacement through the intertwining and mutually supporting processes of economic and cultural transformation characteristic of gentrification. His ethnography is peopled (Fine 2003) in the best Chicagoan sense: it neither exoticizes nor romanticizes those it engages, and, significantly, it is spatially attuned without resorting to the naturalizing inevitability of an ecological model.

Lloyd examines the dynamics of socio-spatial change in ways more alive to and fully engaged with the complex nexus of social relationships that animate the process than one finds in the spatio-centric, non-ethnographic accounts offered by critical geographers (Smith 1996; Slater 2004). Lloyd fleshes out these dynamics more thickly, seeing them not only descriptively or critically but also as meaning-filled and intersubjectively negotiated and enacted. The richness of his description echoes Zorbaugh's, albeit in a contemporary idiom, and so models for us the continuing value of evocative writing as a tool for enlivening our sense of a place and a time and for transmitting research findings across diverse times, places, and audiences.

> Great office buildings and towering apartment hotels cast their shadows over the old stone fronts that harbor studios. Rising land values and rents make Towertown too expensive a place for young artists and students, for bohemians and itinerant radicals, to live. Studios and tearooms are replaced by offices and shops. The tides of the city rush along the streets. The life of the "village" begins to disintegrate ... A decade more, and Towertown may be little more than a memory (Zorbaugh 1976 [1929], 103).

Perhaps it is the case that all bohemias become second-rate the moment they are publicly identified as bohemian, or, as Lloyd claims, bohemias are "always already over" (2006, 237), inevitably evoking nostalgia for pasts that are affectively missed but that never quite existed. Though this may sometimes be the case, we cannot be certain that it is a generalizable principle, save to say that in Toronto the conversion of a flophouse to fancy hotel signalled the sort of social and cultural transformation hinted at in *The Gold Coast*'s discussion of Towertown. Thinking with Zorbaugh, then, I call not for a nostalgic return to a romanticized past. Instead, I treat *The Gold Coast* as a resource to be reread and recast in light of contemporary concerns. The city of 1929 is gone save for its representations; the city of today demands specialized tools, some entirely new – and a few that can perhaps be recast from older ones.

REFERENCES

Abbott, Andrew. 1999. *Department and Discipline: Chicago Sociology at 100*. Chicago: University of Chicago Press

– 2007. "Against Narrative: A Preface to a Lyrical Sociology." *Sociological Theory* 25:67–99

– and Emanuel Gaziano. 1995. "Transition and Tradition: Departmental Faculty in the Era of the Second Chicago School." In *A Second Chicago School: The Development of a Postwar American Sociology*, edited by Gary Alan Fine, 221–72. Chicago: University of Chicago Press

Becker, Howard P. 1929. Review of *The Gold Coast and the Slum: A Sociological Study of Chicago's Near North Side*, by H.W. Zorbaugh. *Annals of the American Academy of Political and Social Science* 145:202–3

Bergquist, Kathie, and Robert McDonald. 2006. *A Field Guide to Gay and Lesbian Chicago*. Chicago: Lake Claremont Press

Bulmer, Martin. 1984. *The Chicago School of Sociology: Institutionalization, Diversity and the Rise of Sociological Research*. Chicago: University of Chicago Press

Butler, Tom, and Garry Robson. 2003. *London Calling: The Middle Class and the Re-making of Inner London*. Oxford and New York: Berg

Castells, Manuel. 1977. *The Urban Question: A Marxist Approach*. London: Edward Arnold

– 1978. *City, Class and Power*. London: Macmillan

Churchill, David S. 2009. "The Queer Histories of a Crime: Representations and Narratives of Leopold and Loeb." *Journal of the History of Sexuality* 18:287–324

Davis, Mike. 2006. *Planet of Slums*. London: Verso

Dear, Michael. 2002. "Los Angeles and the Chicago School: Invitation to a Debate." *City and Community* 1:5–32

Duneier, Mitchell. 1999. *Sidewalks*. New York: Farrar, Straus and Giroux

Faris, Robert E.L. 1967. *Chicago Sociology: 1920–1932*. San Francisco: Chandler

Feagin, Joe R. 1973. "Community Disorganization: Some Critical Notes." *Sociological Inquiry* 43:123–46

Fine, Gary Alan. 2003. "Towards a Peopled Ethnography: Developing Theory from Group Life." *Ethnography* 4:41–60

Glass, Ruth. 1964. Introduction to *London: Aspects of Change*. Centre for Urban Studies. London: MacKibbon and Kee

Harvey, David. 2001. *Spaces of Capital: Towards a Critical Geography*. New York: Routledge

Heap, Chad. 2003. "The City as a Sexual Laboratory: The Queer Heritage of the Chicago School." *Qualitative Sociology* 26:457–87

– 2009. *Slumming: Sexual and Racial Encounters in American Nightlife, 1885–1940*. Chicago: University of Chicago Press

Hunter, Albert. 1983. "The Gold Coast and the Slum Revisited: Paradoxes in Replication Research and the Study of Social Change." *Urban Life* 11:461–76

Lloyd, Richard D. 2006. *Neo-Bohemia: Art and Commerce in the Postindustrial City*. London and New York: Routledge

Mills, Jennifer. 1993. Myths and Meanings of Gentrification. In *Place/Culture/Representation*, edited by James Duncan and David Ley, 149–69. London: Routledge

Park, Robert E. 1967. *On Social Control and Collective Behavior*. Chicago: University of Chicago Press

– 1976. Introduction to *The Gold Coast and the Slum: A Sociological Study of Chicago's Near North Side*, by Harvey Warren Zorbaugh, xvii–xxii. Chicago: University of Chicago Press

Rosemont, Franklin. 2003. *The Rise and Fall of The Dil Pickle: Jazz-Age Chicago's Wildest and Most Outrageously Creative Hobohemian Nightspot*. Chicago: Charles H. Kerr

Slater, Tom. 2004. "Municipally Managed Gentrification in South Parkdale, Toronto." *The Canadian Geographer* 48:303–25

Smith, Neil. 1996. *The New Urban Frontier: Gentrification and the Revanchist City*. New York: Routledge

Soja, Edward W. 1989. *Postmodern Geographies: The Reassertion of Space in Critical Social Theory*. London and New York: Verso

The Drake Hotel. www.thedrakehotel.ca

Thompson, E.P. 1980. *The Making of the English Working Class*. London: Penguin

Vance, Rupert. 1929. Review of *The Gold Coast and the Slum: A Sociological Study of Chicago's Near North Side*, by H.W. Zorbaugh. *Social Forces* 8:320–1

Wacquant, Loïc. 1999. "Inside 'the Zone': The Social Art of the Hustler in the American Ghetto." In *The Weight of the World: Social Suffering in Contemporary Society*, by Pierre Bourdieu et al. Stanford: Stanford University Press

– 2001. "Deadly Symbiosis." *Punishment and Society* 3:95–133

– 2002. "Scrutinizing the Street: Poverty, Morality, and the Pitfalls of Urban Ethnography." *American Journal of Sociology* 107:1,468–532

Whyte, William Foote. 1943a. "Social Organization in the Slums." *American Sociological Review* 8:34–9

– 1943b. *Street Corner Society*. Chicago: University of Chicago Press

Zorbaugh, Harvey Warren. 1976 [1929]. *The Gold Coast and the Slum: A Sociological Study of Chicago's Near North Side*. Chicago: University of Chicago Press

11

Urban Sociology in Poor Cities of Africa and the Middle East: A New Methodology Inspired by Robert E. Park's Urban Ecological Approach

THOMAS K. PARK, LUIS CISNEROS, EDWARD NELL, AND MOURAD MJAHED

The sociology department at the University of Chicago in the first half of the twentieth century was inspirational in many ways, but two ideas, traceable to Robert E. Park (Abbott 1997; Chapoulie 1996; Fine 1995; Goist 1971; Park 1936a; 1936b) need to be addressed early on in this chapter. The first is the fundamentally Hegelian notion that ethnicities should be allowed to fully develop their originality before being induced to assimilate into the larger culture with its well-known implication that progressive, interventionist do-gooders would most likely do more harm than good (Lindner 1996, 204). The second, derivative, idea was that variables should be seen as contextual (or relative: see Lindner, this volume) and not universal: this included the fundamental ethnographic idea that judgment required prior understanding and a faith in pluralism or lack of conviction in the perfection of societies' current norms. These two basic starting points were turned into a general methodological rule that social causality had a local context and that communities had their own logic as well as place in a larger sphere (Goist 1971).

The idea that communities should develop their own genius before being expected to assimilate is an American form of democracy, with obvious roots both in Hegel and Simmel (Park's thesis advisor), that differs dramatically from Rousseau's idea of establishing a system based on the general will (in practice, the majority) and appointing a government to implement this system (Mjahed 2009). In the American system, pluralism and cultural transformation (see Horgan, this volume) are basic, and their repression less natural than in the French system.

If we expect different groups in society to develop their own potential in order to optimally contribute later to a rich and pluralistic society, it also makes little sense to evaluate their progress using universal measures / variables. Foucault's (1972) inspired critiques of the social construction of norms and deviance are obviously relevant, though they rely on a master narrative of governance more natural to the French idea of democracy, even if the US in the immediate postwar years was also heavily into repressing deviance. The Chicago School under R.E. Park's guidance not only refrained from advocating clumsy interventionist fixes for minority communities, it positively advocated evaluation and study based on a thorough contextual analysis as an explicit alternative to holding up local ways of doing things to some national norm (Breslau 1990). This intrinsically anthropological and relativistic approach implied that variables themselves needed to be contextual. The causality implied by contextual variables has since been both advocated and well defended by Karl Popper (1990).

A contextual variable in this sense would be one whose significance was derived from the local matrix in which it was embedded. An educational variable such as years of schooling for women might, in one context, be highly related to child health and the educational success of children yet, in a second context, be highly connected to the educational success of children but show no positive relationship to child health. The two contexts might differ in the general level to which modern hygiene is institutionalized. Obviously, normal behaviour in one context can be quite abnormal in another, but the same behaviour (e.g., machismo) can also be progressive or socially problematic in different contexts (e.g., peasants resisting landlords or males in an urban situation ending up in jail).

While these differences can be assimilated into the "universal" variable approach originally pushed at Harvard and Columbia (Chapoulie 1996, 10–11), the advantages of viewing variables such as "years of schooling of women" or "deviance" as contextual variables are many. The contextual approach does not assume that variables have some Platonic existence and causal efficacy derived from that existential status; rather, it assumes that things that might appear superficially to be the same are anything but the same, and it implies that there is value to viewing variables as embedded in a local matrix. The proper assessment of their significance and causal roles, then, requires qualitative research (disembedding).

The alternative, derived from the Harvard and Columbia survey traditions, gave rise to the sorts of statistics collected by the World Bank and the United Nations. While these numbers are not useless, their inadequacy has been evident for decades and on show in particular since the 1980s when efforts to push a global perspective failed so miserably in Latin America, eastern Europe, sub-Saharan Africa, and many parts of the Islamic world. Some efforts have been made to address the simple-mindedness of universal variables but only in the most egregious cases such as per capita GDP. Simple comparisons of per capita GDP are so meaningless that purchasing power parity (PPP) alternatives have been substituted (though even this alternative neglects within-country variation in the basket of commodities it presumes are consumed).

The urge to have simple universal variables is understandable, but it needs to be resisted for both practical and philosophical reasons. To claim that per capita GDP or even its PPP alternative has some automatic social causality, in the way mass or speed are always significant variables in particle physics, is to commit Whitehead's fallacy of misplaced concreteness: imagining that an abstraction has real-world existence and, consequently, causality. This does not preclude that many simple demographic variables have statistically similar impacts across cities (Bettencourt et al. 2007); it is merely to note that the abstraction (statistic) itself has no real world existence.

Comparable but implausible claims about education, socialization, or normality are only partially concealed by appeals to statistical causality. In contrast, a claim, such as that in a particular context (e.g., health, logistics, environment, cultural beliefs, or economic structure), PPP per capita GDP might correlate well with significant bases for decision-making and empowerment, is not obviously wrong as long as it is seen as a proxy for causality rather than a real-world cause. Ignoring the context causes problems in physics itself (apples do not fall in an orbiting spacecraft), but problems arising from ignoring context in socio-economic studies lead both to significant misunderstandings and to a reification of abstractions.

The reliance on universal variables has been driven in large part by the difficulty of collecting convincing qualitative data on a large scale. The so-called Penn tables (maintained at the University of

Pennsylvania) used to calculate purchasing power parity versions of per capita GDP require a major data collection effort that remains woefully inadequate. To do something comparable for adolescent socialization or education would be unimaginable. Unfortunately, qualitative research tends to be small-scale and has had difficulty anchoring an argument on a broader scale. In consequence, qualitative research has often abdicated the field to quantitative research based on obviously shaky epistemological foundations.

SCALING UP: QUALITATIVE VARIABLES
FOR LARGE CITIES

This chapter builds on a National Science Foundation–funded project (1998–2003 NSF #9817743 and #0138217) designed to develop a methodology to study large and poor urban areas using diachronic remote sensing to reconstruct change in urban housing (Park and Baro 2003; Park et al. 2003). This reconstruction of urban change was then used to develop a sampling methodology to facilitate the low-cost study of large cities. By using spatial distribution, historical change, environmental assessments, and qualitative assessments of housing, a sampling frame could be created to study a variety of socio-economic and health issues.

Some linkages between the new methodology and the early twentieth-century approaches developed by the Chicago School, such as its ecological framework (Berry and Rees1969; Entrikin 1980; Faught 1986; Helmes-Hayes 1987; Maines, Bridger, and Ulmer 1996), are obvious. Our current research and its new sampling methodology allow us to bridge the gap between local qualitative analysis in the humanistic tradition (Hughes 1954; Lindner 1996; Smith 1984) and broad comparative analysis in a promising way. While modern rapidly growing cities in poor countries do not show the same spatial patterns as early twentieth-century Chicago, many of the key concerns of the Chicago School are still important components of urban research.

We argue for a methodologically new approach that remains compatible with the Chicago School emphasis on contextual variables, its pragmatist focus on communication, and consensus-building as transformative (Smith 1984, 355), as well as its critical stance toward patriarchal notions of development and its core neo-Kantian perspective on the value of qualitative analysis given the inevitable role of culture in shaping perspectives on reality. Thus, this chapter focuses on the value of modern sampling methodology and computer modelling in designing qualitative research in one place that can be rigorously compared to similar work in other places (Park, Mjahed, and Cisneros 2005).

On a philosophical level, our approach to modelling urban areas allows us to blend ideas from complexity theory with the neo-Kantian framework of the Chicago School. Positivism of whatever strain supposes a relationship between reality and science that has been mortally wounded only by modern epistemological thought, though it ought to have been largely precluded by Kant's *Critique of Pure Reason*. Such a non-tentative (e.g., positive) relationship is now thought to be implausible and unnecessary for science. Even Popperian conjecture and refutation arguments precluded positivist positions, and more recent constructivist and sceptical ideas have made positivism seem naive.

Models inspired by complexity studies have many non-positivistic characteristics. Typically, the modellers' vocabulary includes notions such as feedback, sensitivity to initial conditions (growth paths), equilibria, transitions, scaling (e.g., dendritic transport system), hierarchy, and self-organization to represent within the model a reality outside the model that does not lend itself to a coherent positivistic interpretation. If we assume a model is (at best) a simulacrum or a model of a model, a usage suggested by Per Bek following Baudrillard (Batty 2005, 515), and that it need only approximate reality in some significant ways but does not rely on reality's causes, the model can illuminate potential relationships but need not have actual intelligent or creative agents (e.g., guided trial and error in the model can substitute for inspiration in the real world). Computer models can use deterministic statistical or chaotic causality to simulate a range of different non-deterministic behaviour in the real world. If this parallel result captures the options available to people and the probable scale of influence of real-world variables, it will be able to raise key questions that different policies may bring to the fore in a far less objectionable way than trying those policies out in the real world. The model as an explicit Kantian mental structure thus emphasizes the indirect character of human efforts to understand the world.

Table 1
Sample transformational growth matrix

Indexical variables row value = x, column = y	HH Y	HH H	HH Ed	HH Emp	L Env	L Sch	L Econ
HH Income		x:y	x:y	x:y	x:y	x:y	x:y
HH Health	x:y		x:y	x:y	x:y	x:y	x:y
HH Education	x:y	x:y		x:y	x:y	x:y	x:y
HH Employment	x:y	x:y	x:y		x:y	x:y	x:y
Local Environmental	x:y	x:y	x:y	x:y		x:y	x:y
Local Schools	x:y	x:y	x:y	x:y	x:y		x:y
Local Economy	x:y	x:y	x:y	x:y	x:y	x:y	

N.B. Normalizing x and y to between –1 and 1 will allow estimates of the influence (value) between indexical variables in each direction to be comparable between matrices.

In the real world, agents may have free will, intelligence, memory, and obstinacy as well as encounter structural constraints created deliberately by other agents or due to the unforeseen consequences of others' activities. Braudel's short- and long-term dynamics may operate in the real world, but a substitute for them can be inserted into a model (viewed as a simulacrum) without direct implications for the existence of free will or agency. Thus, demographic growth can easily be simulated in a model along with its consequences for rent, income, or health. Similarly, extreme environmental impacts on health from a range of pollution sources are far better simulated than tried out in the real world.

At the core of our proposal to model cities in order to critique urban and development policies is a transformational growth matrix (TGM) of interactive indexical variables (Nell 2009) that captures the local variable context and does not assume, for example, that education or health expenditures have the same implications everywhere.

Table 1 illustrates a sample TGM with a few indexical variables for both household (HH) and local infrastructure estimates. The matrix measures reciprocal influences of each variable on the other to capture the local context in a way that can be compared with other locations in the city. It is important to realize that influences are two-way and need not be the same. Thus, if HH health and HH education are positively influenced by environmental quality, only HH education may have a reciprocal positive influence on environmental quality. Similarly, it may be that the local economic infrastructure implemented by an NGO may positively influence HH income, but viewed more broadly, HH income on average may have a negative influence on how much infrastructure an NGO installs. We cannot assume, therefore, that influences between two indexical variables are equal in each direction, but it is easy mathematically to estimate each direction independently.

Transformation growth matrices (TGMs) are measures of qualitative relationships between indexical variables (such as for education, health, income, demography, political awareness, or capital availability) that are normalized on a scale of negative one to positive one. This scaling facilitates later comparisons. Variables are assumed to be contextual: e.g., three years of Quranic school can mean something quite different in different parts of a city. Given their qualitative focus, it is easy to incorporate such variables as Bourdieu's cultural, economic, and social capital into indexical variables of household capital along with variables that capture local non-household infrastructure.

The TGMs are created from a range of qualitative and quantitative research in each case and so to some significant degree capture some abstract aspects of the local context, including what have been termed development traps. In our model, they can also be influenced by policy and the evolution of the agents, much as policy and human behaviour affect local opportunities in the real world. The greater realism of our contextual local matrices, even if they reveal the enormous range of possible impacts and opportunities, does not in any way guarantee that the model correctly predicts long- or short-term impacts. We are not in the business of prediction. We would argue that the model raises many relevant questions, does not obscure intra-urban variability as much as current approaches, and recognizes that universal variables are likely to conceal as much as they reveal.

The methodology allows the blending of formal (scientific) sampling with ethnographic-based qualitative analysis. Multiple TGMs allow one to both synthesize relationships and discern external (geopolitical or political) influences. Despite the qualitative nature of the assessments, TGMs can be compared at many scales of analysis: within subunits of a city, between cities, or even between countries. Because a TGM captures key elements of the real-world context, they also have great potential for modelling. We propose to incorporate them into an ABM (agent-based model) through incorporation into a GIS linked to the ABM (using the Simphony environment developed at Argonne National Labs by Michael North and colleagues).

This will allow us to have agents with common characteristics achieve different results based on the socio-economic context in which they are located (within the model). It also allows us to transform that context using structural adjustment policies (SAP) (e.g., the implications of less local funding for education or health can be translated into contextual changes affecting agent behaviour via transformation of the TGM). The model, at its most general, will attempt to produce a parallel simulated city in which key processes play out much as they would in the real world but without real-world consequences for human suffering or prosperity.

If the model is well done, it can suggest thresholds and conjunctures that may have critical implications in the real world over the short or long term. The human mind is poorly equipped to appraise the development paths of complex systems without computer assistance, while computer models are quite good at playing out the consequences of complex behaviours and can do so in a modest amount of time. Viewed as a simulacrum only, the model cannot predict outcomes in the real world, but it can certainly raise many potential issues that will have escaped the attention of planners who base their efforts on simple statistics or general economic or psychological models.

In our preliminary research in six cities in Africa (Marrakech, Dakar, Bamako, Niamey, Dodoma, and Gaborone), we collected empirical data that supported the value of contextual variables. It indicated, for example, that household size had quite different connections to education, income, and social mobility in different sectors of the same city as well as between cities (Park and Baro 2003; Park et al. 2003; Park, Mjahed, and Cisneros 2005). Our preliminary agent-based model, randomly distributing among its "agents" the values for variables for education, social mobility, and generosity toward kin (larger households in Africa include non-nuclear family kin), suggested that even in a simple model, a small number of household sizes (a selection of narrow ranges between five and forty) evolved to be viable long-term in particular contexts (the model had five socio-economic contexts defined in terms of income opportunities and cost of living), while most household sizes were transitory. The model thus reproduced easily the general form of the empirical data without us introducing any specific city data. While this research can be seen as suggestive, it is no substitute for the more rigorous research project we propose in this chapter.

CONCLUSION

In this chapter, we argue for a new urban methodology for the twenty-first century but one that is also anchored in a classic socio-logical approach developed at the University of Chicago. We can summarize the approach in the following way: (1) Process diachronic urban imagery. (2) Create urban classes as a sampling frame using the history of urban forms (e.g., a slum with twenty years of conti-nuity would be an urban class different from either a new slum or a former chic neighbourhood that had descended into poverty). (3) Drop sampling points in each urban class. (4) Do qualitative ethno-graphic and survey research in the neighbourhood of each point on a broad range of socio-economic topics. (5) Create a TGM for each point by analyzing both the qualitative and quantitative data in each class, and normalize through comparison with data from other classes. (6) Model ethnographically informed agents within a spa-tially informed digital environment (using, for example, Simphony from Argonne National laboratory, Michael North), creating a "sim-ulacrum" or model of a model of reality that parallels but does not duplicate real-world causality or creativity. (7) Synthesize develop-ment and SAP policies, and introduce them into the digital model. (8) Run variations of said policies within the model. (9) Extract rel-evant possible consequences of said policies across the urban land-scape from the model, and look for traces of past policies and possible continuities of past and current policies embedded in the TGM matrices. (10) Finally, use the model and its implications to critique current development policy. At a minimum, any number of new questions and possible relationships may appear worth discus-sion, and the heterogeneity of potential policy impacts can become an obvious issue for discussion.

In brief, we argue that in addition to a diachronic remote sensing–based sampling methodology developed earlier, three other new methodologies – transformational growth matrices, agent-based models, and Simphony (a software allowing the full linkage of an ABM with a geographical information system appropriate to urban research) – can be combined into a coherent urban approach. Such a methodology depends very much on the quality of the data collected in the first place. Because the TGM is perfectly compatible with qual-itative data, we can hope for excellent data. Thus, observations of the quality of education rather than the number of years can easily

be incorporated into the construction of different indexical education variables for different places. Similarly, intra-urban comparative assessments of socialization or health practices would be just as
easily incorporated.

This will also allow us to identify development traps and critique
development approaches, including structural adjustment policies,
as they have been and are being applied in the poor countries of the
globe in a far more comparable and detailed way than has hitherto
been done. Just as important, we feel that our approach will allow
us to foreground qualitative research in a way that allows it to claim
broad significance and escape the charge that it produces idiosyncratic data with little claim to generality.

REFERENCES

Abbott, Andrew. 1997. "Of Time and Space: The Contemporary Relevance
    of the Chicago School." *Social Forces* 75(4):1,149–82
Batty, Michael. 2005. *Cities and Complexity: Understanding Cities with
    Cellular Automata, Agent-Based Models, and Fractals*. Cambridge, MA:
    MIT Press
Bettencourt, Luis, Jose Lobo, Dirk Helbing, Christian Kühnert, and
    Geoffrey West. 2007. "Growth, Innovation, Scaling, and the Pace of Life
    in Cities." *Proceedings of the National Academy of Science*
    104(17):7,301–6
Berry, Brian J.L., and Philip H. Rees. 1969. "The Factorial Ecology of
    Calcutta." *American Journal of Sociology* 74(5):445–91
Breslau, Daniel. 1990. "The Scientific Appropriation of Social Research:
    Robert Park's Human Ecology and American Sociology." *Theory and
    Society* 19(4):417–46
Chapoulie, Jean-Michel. 1996. "Everett Hughes and the Chicago
    Tradition." *Sociological Theory* 1:3–29
Entrikin, J. Nicholas. 1980. "Robert Park's Human Ecology and Human
    Geography." *Annals of the Association of American Geographers*
    70:43–58
Faught, Jim. 1986. "The Concept of Competition in Robert Park's
    Sociology." *Sociological Quarterly* 27:359–71
Fine, Gary Alan. 1995. *A Second Chicago School? The Development of a
    Postwar American Sociology*. Chicago: University of Chicago Press
Foucault, Michel. 1972. *The Archaeology of Knowledge and the Discourse
    on Language*. New York: Pantheon Books

Goist, Park Dixon. 1971. "City and 'Community': The Urban Theory of
Robert Park." *American Quarterly* 23:46–59

Helmes-Hayes, Richard C. 1987. "A Dualistic Vision: Robert Ezra Park
and the Classical Ecological Theory of Social Inequality." *Sociological
Quarterly* 28(3):387–409

Hughes, Everett C. 1954. "Robert E. Park's Views on Urban Society: A
comment on William L. Kolb's Paper." *Economic Development and
Cultural Change* 3(1):47–9

Lindner, Rolf. 1996. *The Reportage of Urban Culture: Robert Park and
the Chicago School*. Cambridge: Cambridge University Press

Maines, David R., Jeffrey C. Bridger, and Jeffery T. Ulmer. 1996. "Mythic
Facts and Park's Pragmatism: On Predecessor-Selection and Theorizing
in Human Ecology." *Sociological Quarterly* 37(3):521–49

Mjahed, Mourad. 2009. "Neighborly Governance: Neighborhood
Associations and Participative Democracy in Tucson." PhD dissertation,
University of Arizona

Nell, Edward J. 2009. "Interaction between Economic and Social
Variables: The Transformational Growth Matrix." In *Institutional and
Social Dynamics of Growth and Distribution*, edited by Neri Salvadori,
288–322. Cheltenham, UK: Edward Elgar Publishing

Park, Robert Ezra. 1936a. "Human Ecology." *American Journal of
Sociology* 42(1):1–15

– 1936b. "Succession, an Ecological Concept." *American Sociological
Review* 1(2):171–9

Park, Thomas, and Mamadou Baro. 2003. "The Six Cities Project:
Developing a Methodology of Surveying Densely Populated Areas Using
Social Science Assisted And Diachronic Remote Sensing Based
Classification of Habitation." *Journal of Political Ecology* 10:1–23

Park, Thomas, J.B. Greenberg, E.J. Nell, S.E. Marsh, and M. Mjahed.
2003. "Research on Urbanization in the Developing World: New
Directions." *Journal of Political Ecology* 10:69–94

Park, Thomas, M. Mjahed, and L. Cisneros. 2005. "Modeling Complexity
in Urban Spaces of the Developing World: An Ecological Approach to
Socio-economic Strategies." Paper presented at the Next Generation
Simulations of Human–Environmental Interactions Working Group
Conference, Santa Fe Institute, University of Arizona and Arizona State
University, Tucson, Arizona, 12–14 December

Popper, Karl. 1990. *A World of Propensities*. Bristol: Thoemmes

Smith, Susan J. 1984. "Practicing Humanistic Geography." *Annals of the
Association of American Geographers* 74(3):353–74

12

Tourist Zones, Emotional Buttons, and the Ubiquitous Beggar

GARY BOWDEN

Scene 1: Siem Reap, Cambodia: Pity. I am standing on the sidewalk contemplating a restaurant menu when a forty-ish local stops beside me. My attention is drawn to him by motion in my peripheral vision. His left hand removes his hat and swoops down in a single motion, presenting it like an offering dish. At the same time, his right leg rises until the upper leg is parallel to the ground – displaying the amputation below the knee. Without saying a word, he looks directly and deeply into my eyes, then at the hat, and back at me.

Scene 2: Mumbai, India: Guilt. Two youths, approximately eleven years old, carrying plastic bags, are walking down the street. They offer to shine my shoes for about one-twentieth the rate that others want for a shine. As I remove my shoes, each of them takes various shoe polishes, cloths, and other relevant materials from his bag. While they shine my shoes, they explain that they would be able to work at the train station charging "the standard rate" if only they had a $7 shine box – a wooden box designed to hold their materials, with a place for the client to rest his/her foot during the shine. For only $7 – nothing to me, the price of a single meal – I could change their lives forever by providing them with the tools that would enable them to earn a respectable living.

These are just two examples of the myriad begging stories any Western tourist will bring back from travels in the developing world. They are, however, examples chosen with a purpose. Note the identification of distinct emotions associated with each of the above stories. The Cambodian beggar trades in pity. He hopes I will feel sorry for him because of his amputation. In contrast, the Indian kids trade in guilt, pointing to the massive disparities in our living standards and the ease with which I could transform their lives.

In this chapter, I argue that beggars in different countries disproportionately select certain styles of pitch from the universe of potentially existing begging pitches. As a result, there is an underlying similarity in the emotional appeal of typical begging pitches in each country, but the nature of that emotional appeal differs from country to country – in the above examples, pitches based on pity in Cambodia vs. pitches based on guilt in India. However, this chapter isn't about begging per se. Rather, it uses begging as a strategic site to illustrate one element of the process of tourist–local interaction: the selection of the emotional button used in appeals to tourists. To explicate this phenomenon, the chapter is divided into four sections. The first describes the method employed in this study. The second discusses begging as an occupation. The third outlines the concept of a tourist zone. The final section discusses the process by which particular emotional buttons become attached with the typical begging pitches found within a country.

METHOD

This study mixes autoethnography (Ellis and Bochner 2000) with traditional ethnographic observation (Spradley 1980) and retrospective interpretation. I spent the first six months of 2005 on my first visit to Southeast Asia, spending approximately one month per country in Thailand, Laos, Vietnam, Cambodia, Nepal, and India. I did not go there with the intention of studying begging. The interest arose in my attempt to come to grips with an observation about myself: each time I entered a new country, I became tired. Reflecting on the feeling, it was apparent to me that it wasn't physically based. My health status, level of physical activity, sleep, quality of diet, and other such factors remained largely constant throughout the period.

While I have travelled a fair amount, this was my first trip to Asia. Midway through the trip – as I crossed the border from the laid-back, idyllic 4,000 Island region of southern Laos to the rugged (and significantly more disconcerting) Wild West–like vibe of Stung Teng, Cambodia – I realized that the exhaustion seemed emotionally based, linked to the stress of entering and adapting to a new culture. Further reflection, however, led to the realization that the emotional exhaustion wasn't tied to general culture shock but, rather, to a more specific experience: the emotional demands of dealing with the requests to help others, particularly beggars. But such requests were ubiquitous throughout the region. Thus, my autoethnographic reflections uncovered an apparent paradox: why, when confronted with a seemingly constant stimulus (the request for money or other goods), did my reaction heighten (as if presented with a novel stimulus) when entering a new country and then decrease (as if becoming habituated to that stimulus) after a period of time in that country?

In sum, it wasn't until midway through my travels in Southeast Asia that begging and the interaction of beggars with tourists moved from something I experienced to something I saw as a strategic research site for unpacking key elements of the process of tourist–local interaction. At this point, I began more traditional and systematic observation of beggars, reconstructing previous encounters, making notes on new encounters, and unobtrusively observing the activities of particular beggars for periods of twenty minutes to one hour (e.g., while having a drink in a street cafe). My aim in doing this was not to undertake a traditional ethnography of the beggaring subculture but, rather, to more fully understand the origins of my own emotional reactions. That analysis, however, benefits from an appreciation of begging as an occupation.

BEGGING AS OCCUPATION

Tourists typically encounter the beggar as a lone individual personally asking them for something and, as a result, tend to construct them as isolated, marginal individuals. This construction does not accord with either my own observations or those of the surprisingly small number of academics who have systematically studied begging in the developing world. Beggars are typically embedded in social, ethnic, or cultural networks in which begging is an occupation (Chaudhuri 1987; Igbinovia 1991; Swanson 2007).

Two examples from my own observations illustrate this point. Kathmandu, Nepal, had a variety of bakeries that put their baking on sale at half price at the end of the day. In addition to the Western tourists drawn to the bargain prices, the streets would fill with children begging for food. A substantial proportion of the tourists would give food to the children, often inquiring what they wanted before entering the bakery to make their purchase. However, the children had an economic relationship with the shop owners. They would tuck away a portion of the food they were given and later return it to the store-owner to be sold again.

While walking down a central street in Siem Reap, Cambodia, I passed a young mother with a child who followed me for fifteen or twenty metres, repeatedly asking for money. As I continued down the street, something seemed amiss and awkward in the way she, mid-pitch, abandoned me and started walking back in the opposite direction. Over the next several days, I observed that she always appeared at the same late-afternoon time and stood in the same location. Several other beggars repeatedly occupied other locations along this central street. They each had a specific territory that they remained within. The abruptness with which she abandoned me was an artifact of those territorial divisions and her desire not to infringe on the territory of the neighbouring beggar. My presumption, though I have no direct evidence of this, was that the territories were assigned by some controlling individual for whom they worked rather than by an emergent cooperative relationship.

In sum, my own rather cursory observations were consistent with scholarly writing and NGO reports suggesting that begging is often an organized occupational activity. This fact is important for two reasons. First, it suggests that beggars are embedded in a multi-layered network, both social and occupational, that provides a variety of channels for exchange of information about tourists and their reactions. Second, it explains certain aspects of begging behaviour and location. Beggars are not encountered everywhere in a particular city; as described below, they are found almost exclusively in tourist zones.

TOURIST ZONES

Park, Burgess, and McKenzie's (1925) concentric zone theory, as noted by both Horgan (this volume) and Park et al. (this volume), argues that social processes result in the creation of distinctive zones within a city. I use the concept "tourist zone" in a similar way – to describe an area that is both spatially identifiable and socially distinct. Broadly speaking, tourist zones are those locations that draw large numbers of tourists and typically fall into one of two categories: (1) tourist attractions such as Angkor Wat or the Great Wall of China and (2) portions of cities where there are clusters of tourist amenities (hotels, restaurants, travel agencies, and so on). These areas are publicly known and commercially reinforced (e.g., identified with detailed maps in guidebooks).

Tourist zones in Southeast Asia have a distinctive social dynamic that distinguishes them from other areas of the city or region. This dynamic has two major features. First, in contrast to other areas of the country, tourist zones are characterized by a comparatively balanced representation of tourists and locals. Kanter (1977) classified groups based on the relative proportion of members from the two social categories: (a) uniform groups (composed entirely of one social group); (b) skewed groups (a few token members of one group mixed with an overwhelmingly dominant proportion of the second group); (c) tilted groups (a substantial majority from one group mixed with a sizable minority from the second); and (d) balanced groups (in which the representation of each group is roughly equal). Throughout most parts of Southeast Asia, Western tourists are tokens. Inside tourist zones, however, the same tourists make up substantial minorities and in some cases, such as inside Angkor Wat, substantially outnumber the locals. This point is significant, because, as Kanter (1977) notes, it affects social processes. For example, Kanter describes how the experiences of women who are tokens (make up less than 5 per cent of the upper management) in a corporation have an experience different from that of women who work in more balanced organizations. Tokens face special situations: they attract attention because they are unusual, differences between the majority and minority types (males/females) are exaggerated, and characteristics of the token are distorted to fit stereotypes of their general type.

Tourist zones are where individuals from both groups interact with and come to understand one other. The majority of tourists come from Western nations, and, hence, tourist zones are places where oriental and occidental cultures meet. This is not to suggest that they are the only locus of culture contact but rather that the social dynamics of these areas differ from those of less-visited areas. In contrast to other areas of these countries, cross-cultural contact is a routine and expected occurrence. As a result, it takes on a regularized, routinized, and distinctive form. More important, it means that information about Westerners is more readily accessible in these areas and, since many of the locals have businesses catering to the tourists, the end result is an area with a more equitable construction of cultural norms. Or, more simply stated, tourist zones are less like Southeast Asia and relatively more like the West. Through ongoing interaction with a large number of tourists, the locals who frequent these zones come to understand how foreigners act and think and take account of this knowledge in order to more effectively provide the services that the tourists desire.

Further, the manner in which tourists and locals engage the tourist zone is different. Locals who frequent tourist zones (e.g., hotel or attraction staff, vendors, beggars, tour operators) visit the zones daily over a prolonged period of time. In contrast, a typical tourist visits the zone for a few days and then moves on. Thus, unlike the situation in Kanter's study of organizations, where both the men and the women of the corporation interacted with the same individuals over a prolonged period of time, the interaction structure in a tourist zone is both shorter in duration and asymmetric. Because they have such limited contact with individual tourists but encounter an ongoing stream of tourists, locals come to understand tourists primarily as exemplars of particular social types rather than as individuals. Their observations are frequently extremely acute, as the following description of backpackers (taken from a T-shirt titled Khao San Road Syndrome and sold in Bangkok) indicates:

I shall wear as big a backpack as possible to bear proud witness of my creed.
I shall not leave Khao San Road without a Lonely Planet Guide.
I shall wear the traditional international backpacker's uniform and don at least one piece of clothing (e.g., conical hat in Vietnam, a Krama in Cambodia, etc.) to show my oneness with Asian people.
I shall eat banana pancakes and Phad Thai on a regular basis.
I shall stay in the cheapest guest house. More money for beer.
I shall drink the local beer, for I shall always endeavour to be in tune with local culture and because it is cheapest.
I shall make pilgrimage to a Full Moon Party on Hat Rin at least once in my life.
I shall bargain without mercy and hone my skill to a sharp edge so that I can proudly proclaim our sacred motto "I get it for less than the locals."
I shall not leave Khao San Road without having my hair coloured, dreadlocked, corn-rolled or shaved off.

Ironically, I was standing beside a male American in his early twenties when I first encountered this T-shirt in a vendor's stall on Khao

San Road. As we read the list together, he said with a hint of surprise in his voice: "I've done all those things except number nine!" It was through reading the T-shirt that this non-reflexive youth came to recognize himself as a representative of a particular social type and realize that others viewed him in that light and not in terms of his own self-conception of himself as a unique individual. Because tourists flow through the zones, locals construct them almost entirely as representatives of social categories, typically either by social type (backpacker, sex tourist) or by nationality.

From the perspective of the tourist, tourist zones not only make travel easier, they also play a major role in the tourist's understanding of the host country and its culture. Each country's tourist zones contain unique and symbolically powerful tourist attractions – the Great Wall in China, the Tuol Sleng Genocide Museum in Cambodia, the Taj Mahal in India – that are so well known that they become part of the tourist's understanding of the country even if they don't visit them. Tourists know about these sights from guidebooks, conversations with others, and direct experience. In general, Westerners know relatively little about Southeast Asian countries, and hence, their construction of the country and its people is disproportionately affected by a small number of iconic (and stereotyped) elements. The following quote, taken from a travel blog, exemplifies the experience of many tourists:

> We did not know that much about places to visit in Cambodia, except what we had read in our travel books the week before in Bangkok. Because we only had time to see the "must see" spots, we were happy to arrange a package tour for our time there. We quickly realized (and remembered) that Cambodia is a war-torn country, with millions of landmines waiting for victims, but is seemingly recovered from its most recent disaster of the Khmer Rouge genocide in the 1970s. Even with this terrible history the people of Cambodia were friendly, and the country welcomed tourists (Dan and Kristen 2001).

This basic and stereotyped understanding is often expanded and reinforced through aspects of direct experience. Thus, for example, contracting a driver to take you to the Tuol Sleng Genocide Museum outside Phnom Penh typically results in a stop at a firing range located about a kilometre from the museum where you are presented with a menu of firing options, ranging from a few dollars to shoot a pistol to several hundred to shoot a rocket-propelled grenade (even more if you wish to shoot at a particular target, such as a cow or the remnants of a tank). The drivers bring you there because they receive a cut from any sales they deliver. And they bring you to the range before the museum, knowing individuals are less likely to be in a trigger-happy mood after visiting the museum. Such experiences act to expand and enhance the rather shallow tourist knowledge, in this case by underscoring the rough and tumble spirit of a culture that could turn against itself, as happened in Cambodia during the period of the Khmer Rouge.

Tourist zones are also where beggars are found. Two main reasons account for this fact. First, tourists, not locals, are the primary objects of begging. Thus, from a purely practical point of view, it makes sense for beggars to go to locations where tourists are present. Second, begging is, for many, an occupation and as a result displays many of the characteristics of work. Specifically, many beggars "go to work" in the sense that they devote a particular part of their day to the activity and go to a particular location to carry it out. As a result, a beggar who asks a passing tourist for money in the tourist zone will frequently ignore the same tourist if they encounter each other outside the tourist zone or at a time when the beggar is not "at work." Finally, it should be noted that begging pitches trade almost exclusively in emotion. Because of communication difficulties (inability to speak the tourist's language) and the short time frame of the typical beggar–tourist interaction, beggars have little opportunity to make purely rational arguments regarding why the tourists should give them money. Emotional pitches benefit from both their relative power and the fact that they are not constrained by the time or language that limits rational appeals.

LOOKING-GLASS LOCALS AND THE SELECTION OF EMOTIONAL BUTTONS

It is through the process of repeatedly interacting with tourists, primarily in tourist zones, that beggars within each country come to disproportionately select the particular emotional appeal that characterizes their country. The process involves what I term the looking-glass local, a variant on Cooley's (1902, 183–4) concept of the looking-glass self (see Grills, this volume, for a more detailed discussion of the symbolic

interactionist conception of self). Yeung and Martin (2003) characterize the looking-glass self in terms of three main components: (1) we
imagine how we appear to others; (2) we imagine the judgment of that
appearance; and (3) we develop our self through reference to the judgments of others. Thus, in the case of beggars, they (1) imagine how
they appear to tourists; (2) they imagine the tourist's judgment of that
appearance; and then (3) they develop their begging pitch through
reference to their sense of the tourist's judgment. However, in contrast
to Cooley's process in which individuals imagine appearances and
judgments based on a shared understanding of a common culture,
beggars construct their understanding of the looking-glass local in
terms of the stereotypical and conventionalized understanding of their
country and its citizens that tourists possess from reading guidebooks,
discussions with other tourists, direct experience, and so on. Thus,
Cooley's self-image is replaced by a vision of a collective self: how the
beggar perceives the tourist's perception of the dominant characteristics of his or her culture (collective self). Thus, since the evaluation of
their begging pitch is based as much as or more on a collective self
than on an individual self, beggars within a particular country tend to
select begging pitches that play off the same collective representation
and, hence, display an underlying similarity in emotional tone.

Stated another way, beggars are faced with a marketing dilemma.
It is hard to pitch to the individual needs of the tourist (i.e., to tailor
one pitch to the yuppie and another to the backpacker). On the
other hand, most tourists, irrespective of their social type, share the
same simplified and conventionalized understanding of the local culture. This is a single shared resource that the beggar can exploit for
use with all tourists, whatever their social type. As a result, pitches
within a particular country focus on specific emotional buttons.

In conventional language, the term "pushing an emotional button" is used to refer to the process of triggering a particularly strong
emotional reaction in someone else. Marketers frequently talk about
the need to "push the customers' emotional button" (Feig 2006).
Marketing research shows that most customers buy on the basis of
emotion but justify the buying using logic. For present purposes, the
phrase refers to the particular emotion targeted by a specific beggar's
pitch. Like traditional advertising, the beggar's pitch selects one
emotional response from the variety of possible ones and targets it.

To exemplify this process, I return to the cases described at the
beginning of this chapter. The beggar in Cambodia uses the display

of his amputated limb to trade on the tourist's knowledge of the country's recent tragic past (e.g., genocide, landmines, killing fields) and the tourist's understanding of this legacy on the Cambodian population. Most tourists to Cambodia, for example, learn that Cambodia has one of the highest levels of amputation in the world, largely a result of the number of unexploded landmines that still litter much of the country. These factoids, coupled with stereotyped historical knowledge about Cambodia's recent past, lead most tourists to have feelings of sympathy and pity for the Cambodian population and what they have been through. In the preceding example, the beggar uses his embodied condition to particularize this emotional appeal. His presence confronts the tourist with a specific manifestation of a nationally specific form of suffering and, as such, both reinforces and personalizes the tourists' stereotyped understanding of the country's history. Most important, however, the beggar's appeal evokes an emotional response – pity – that corresponds with the tourist's pre-existing attitude toward the locals based on his or her stereotyped understanding of the country's history.

Similarly, most tourists to India have a stereotyped idea of a country in the process of transforming itself, where pockets of economic growth and the emergence of a middle class are providing increasing opportunity for a rising standard of living. Thus, in contrast to Cambodia where the tourist observes poverty and hardship as the legacy of a harsh history with little evidence the future will be much brighter, in India these same conditions are constructed in terms of a narrative that emphasizes opportunity and hope. The pitch of the Indian beggars plays on this knowledge. Rather than simply asking for money, the pitch is contextualized in terms of work (shining shoes) and opportunity (the need for the box to enable them to earn a real living). Note, however, that the pitch is fundamentally emotional rather than rational. A key element in the pitch involves the comparison between Western and Indian standards of living – "for the cost of a meal you can transform our lives" – and the sense of guilt that failing to help the children produces. As with the Cambodian example, the Indian illustration reflects convergence between a key aspect of the tourist's truncated understanding of the country and its culture and the emotional button pushed by the beggar's pitch.

Since the above examples were chosen for their ability to clearly exemplify the main point of this chapter, I conclude with a number of subtleties. First, the argument that there is an underlying emotional similarity in the begging pitches of a particular country – that is, that they push the same emotional button – does not imply that the pitches themselves are similar. The same underlying scaffolding can be used to construct a wide variety of distinct pitches. A typical tourist visit to Angkor Wat, for example, is not complete without watching the sun set from the top of one of the monuments. The hundreds of tourists waiting for the sunset are met by a small army of children who spend their time alternately running up and down the monument, bringing tourists beer or other items from the concessions at the bottom or begging. These children are exceptionally adept at displaying their knowledge, whether by identifying coins from around the world or, as I saw one small boy do, walking up to individuals and saying hello to them in their native language prior to engaging them in conversation and asking for money. After watching him flawlessly identify the native tongue of individuals from several countries without hearing them speak (not just generic North Americans but Italians, Czechs, and Koreans as well), I asked how he knew. He said that he knew which languages the various guides spoke and, hence, spoke to the tourists in the language spoken by their guide. Here the beggar is, in essence, performing a magic trick: using private knowledge to conjure up a reaction of amazement among the tourists he engages. In each of these cases, the identification of coins or of languages, the beggars are displaying abilities that exceed what the tourists expect to encounter. Note, however, that such portrayals of individual ability fit the Cambodian narrative. Despite the tragedies of the country's past, these individuals have triumphed and persevered, but without the aid of the tourist, their efforts and abilities will go unrecognized. The emotional punch in these narratives of triumph against all odds comes from the contrast between their displays of individual achievement and the expectations the tourist holds as a result of the country's troubled past. In this case, the tourist doesn't feel pity for the beggar but rather pity for the fact that such a remarkable person resides in a nation where their abilities will remain unrecognized. In short, while there is little similarity in the details of the begging pitches of the amputee and the linguist, both pitches trade on a feeling of pity in the tourist.

Second, the nature of the emotional button involved can place significant constraints on the beggar's performance. Goffman's ideas of dramaturgical performance (1959) and stigma management (1963) help to explicate the process. The amputee, for example, runs the risk of making the tourist uncomfortable with his stigma, something that would decrease the likelihood of getting money. As I observed him over the period of several days, it became clear that he had developed a performative strategy designed to minimize this possibility. When approaching individuals who hadn't already noticed him, he would stand close to them before drawing their attention by doffing his hat and using it as an offering dish. This motion served the dual purpose of drawing the tourist's gaze downward where they could not help but notice the amputation and, equally significant, preventing the tourist from focusing on the amputation. In this way, he made sure that the tourist was aware of the amputation while, at the same time, minimizing any potential discomfort in the tourist by focusing attention on the movement of the hat rather than his leg.

Finally, I am not arguing that all begging pitches within a particular country revolve around a particular emotional appeal. I am arguing that there exists a spectrum of emotional appeals and that while one can find examples of virtually every type of appeal in a given country, the begging pitches within a particular country disproportionately emphasize one particular emotional button. In particular, it was argued that begging pitches in Cambodia emphasize pity while those in India emphasize guilt. The selection of the particular emotional button is not a random process. It emerges through a process of tourist–local interaction in tourist zones where beggars come to construct pitches that resonate in deep ways with the stereotyped images of the country that are held by the majority of tourists. Stated another way, the tourist's conventional understanding of the country serves as a resource that beggars creatively exploit in the process of developing their pitches. And since this resource is both specific to the country and fairly stable, through time beggars in a particular country develop a variety of different ways of effectively playing off that resource that differ from the pitches developed in other countries.

REFERENCES

Chaudhuri, Sumita. 1987. *Beggars of Kalighat Calcutta*. Calcutta: Anthropological Survey of India
Cooley, Charles H. 1902. *Human Nature and the Social Order*. New York: Scribner's

Dan and Kristen. 2001. Dan and Kristen's Web. http://www.danciprari. com/worldtrip/cambodia.htm

Ellis, Carolyn, and Arthur P. Bochner. 2000. "Autoethnography, Personal Narrative, Reflexivity: Researcher as Subject." In *The Handbook of Qualitative Research*, edited by Norman Denzin and Yvonne Lincoln, 733–68. Thousand Oaks, CA: Sage

Feig, Barry. 2006. *Hot Button Marketing: Push the Emotional Buttons That Get People to Buy*. Cincinnati: Adams Media

Goffman, Erving. 1959. *The Presentation of Self in Everyday Life*. New York: Anchor

– 1963. *Stigma: Notes on the Management of Spoiled Identity*. New York: Prentice-Hall

Igbinovia, Patrick Edobor. 1991. "Begging in Nigeria." *International Journal of Offender Therapy and Comparative Criminology* 35(1):21–33

Kanter, Rosabeth Moss. 1977. *Men and Women of the Corporation*. New York: Basic Books

Park, Robert, Ernest W. Burgess, and Roderick D. McKenzie. 1925. *The City*. Chicago: University of Chicago Press

Spradley, J.P. 1980. *Participant Observation*. New York: Holt, Rinehart and Winston

Swanson, Kate. 2007. "'Bad Mothers' and 'Delinquent Children': Unravelling Anti-begging Rhetoric in the Ecuadorian Andes." *Gender, Place and Culture* 14(6):703–20

Yeung, King-To, and John Levi Martin. 2003. "The Looking Glass Self: An Empirical Test and Elaboration." *Social Forces* 8(3):843–79

13

Constructions of Public and Private Spheres in the Soviet Communal Apartment: Erving Goffman's Notion of Territories of Self

DEFNE ÖVER

The conceptual categories public and private are constantly contested in our everyday lives. Even the simplest debates – about our rights to private property; the occupation of a shared space of living; the form of our relations with family members, neighbours, and strangers; our styles of dressing; and a state's right to intervene our ways of living – involve the distinction between public and private spheres. In all our relations to people, objects, and spaces, we demarcate boundaries between public and private. These unconsciously drawn boundaries often correspond to the boundaries drawn by other members of our society. However, they may vary across cultures.

Debates over cultural variation in the boundaries between public and private and on a normative definition of the two concepts are prominent themes in academic discussions that cover "a variety of subjects that are analytically distinct and at the same time overlapping and intertwined" (Weintraub 1997, 3). In this chapter, in a way similar to Horgan's (this volume) culture-sensitive approach to contemporary urban studies, I critique the universalist Enlightenment understanding of public and private. As noted by Park et al. (this volume), the Chicago School treats concepts as contextual rather than universal. In line with this thinking, I use Gerasimova's (2002) work on Russian communal apartments to argue that Erving

Goffman's notion of "territories of self" provides a culture-sensitive approach to the public and private division. Indeed, following Park et al.'s assertion (this volume) that the emphasis put on contextuality led to adoption of ethnography as the major methodology in the studies of the Chicago School, throughout this paper I support my argument with ethnographic data.

The communal apartments that emerged after the October Revolution as part of utopian government policies offer an opportunity to contest universalist Enlightenment understandings of privacy and allow for the development of a normative definition of the two categories without ignoring the cultural specificity of their forms. The particularity of communal apartments as a form of dwelling, where privacy could be examined in depth, lies in the discrepancy between the utopian state ideologies and the results of their implementation as policies – that is, the dream of the abolishment of private property and the actual result of abolishing it.

The relationship between public and private has overlapping economic, social, cultural, and political dimensions, and, as manifest in the domain of housing, it has a clearly visible physical appearance (Madanipour 2003, 3). The Soviet communal apartment, which resulted from economic policies aimed at abolishing private property, was a means of state control over citizens and an illustration of alternative routines of everyday life (Boym 1994). It thus provides an opportunity to question the universalist public and private dichotomy in its economic, social, and political dimensions.

In this framework, I combine Erving Goffman's theoretical understanding of privacy with second-hand ethnographic data collected in communal apartments by Ilia Uthekin. Thereby, following Gerasimova (1999), I first show how the very public spaces of the Enlightenment understanding suddenly become private in other contexts, and vice versa. Second, I argue that the government housing policies aimed at abolishing the bourgeois notion of privacy through abolishment of private property led to the emergence of different spheres of public and private in the everyday lives of communal apartment dwellers. I conclude by focusing on the discrepancy between state utopias and the outcomes of implemented policies and argue that a normative definition of privacy based on self-control allows us to understand the boundaries between public and private as always subject to change.

COMMUNAL APARTMENTS

Following the 1917 Revolution, Bolsheviks strove to revolutionize every aspect of domestic life (Spagnolo 2006). Communal apartments emerged in the context of the post-revolutionary expropriation of private property and resettlement of private apartments in urban centres where most residential buildings had become the property of the state (Fitzpatrick 1999). Communal apartments were defined as "an apartment in a house which belongs to the state housing fund or to the municipal housing fund ... and in which some tenants live" in the law on "the allocation of vacant dwelling space in communal apartments in St. Petersburg." However, they were actually more than a judicial notion. They connoted "a form of living together with strangers" (Gerasimova 1999, 109). They mainly consisted of all-purpose rooms integrated with places of communal use such as shared bathrooms, corridors, and kitchens. Life in the communal apartments was marked by posted schedules of communal duties and endless complaints among neighbours (Utekhin 2003). Residents were mostly people from different classes who were complete strangers to each other and were brought together by the local Housing Committees. Housing Committees had the right to evacuate existing residents if they thought they were class enemies and move new residents into already occupied apartments (Fitzpatrick 1999). Thus, a bourgeois family apartment could suddenly become a multi-family or communal apartment whose new inhabitants were usually from classes lower than the original ones. In the Stalin era, apartments with one room per family were typical forms of housing in Russian cities, where "only a highly privileged group had separate apartments" (Fitzpatrick 1999, 47). Control of these apartments was in the hands of the municipal soviets (Boym 1994; Gerasimova 1999).

Communal apartments were a revolutionary experiment flowing from the utopian ideologies of Russia in the 1920s. Utopias of the time were guides to life and blueprints for social change (Fitzpatrick 1999). They were intended to alter the commonplaces of culture and the division between public and private spaces. Accordingly, soviet house-communes, palaces and parks of culture, workers' clubs and artists' labour collectives, and, later, collective farms were intended to replace old forms of sociability in apartments and barracks or cafes and pubs (Boym 1994). As Walter Benjamin stated: "Bolshevism has abolished private life ... Apartments that earlier accommodated single families in their five to eight rooms now often lodge eight. Through the hall door one steps into a little town ... even in the lobby one can encounter beds ... there is no 'homeyness.' But neither are there any cafes ... the tensions of public life are so great that they block off private life to an unimaginable degree" (Benjamin and Jennings 1999, 30).

The "house-commune" was the dominant utopian dwelling form, a model of socialism in one building (Stites 1999, 263). House-communes aimed to break apart the structure of the bourgeois family and institute relations of proletarian comradeship among the inhabitants – that is to say, "Palaces to the workers" (Gerasimova 1999, 110)! Maintenance of the kitchen and the rearing of children were to be shared in order to avoid the burdens of the bourgeois family, as reflected in one of the slogans of the time: "Down with the dictatorship of the kitchen!" (Boym 1994, 128).

House-communes were established in the 1920s both in the country and in the city. However, despite the immense growth of the Soviet urban population during the 1930s, they were abolished. Instead, as the government strove for realization of state utopias, it focused its attention entirely on reconstruction of already existing quarters (Fitzpatrick 1999). The turn toward reconstruction and partitioning of already existing bourgeois quarters did not mean abandoning the idea of subverting the structure of the bourgeois family and instituting relationships of comradeship. The subversion of the bourgeois family meant a change in the purpose and form of home usage. In the bourgeois understanding of home, the house served as a showcase, with separate spaces for public display and private seclusion. Home was perceived as the site where members of a family, who were tied to each other by the fragile bond of love, exercised their intimacy for the growth and nourishment of this bond (Frykman and Löfgren 1987, 45). After the revolution, with the housing policies of government, this bond of love between wife and husband, parents and children was to be transformed into a bond of comradeship among all the dwellers of the communal house independent of their blood ties. The reconstruction and partitioning of already existing bourgeois quarters began at the end of the 1920s even as the building of house-communes still continued. The renewed houses came to be named with important designations like "dwelling comradeships" (Boym 1994). These reconstructed buildings were actually transitional communal arrangements later institutionalized as communal apartments. Communal apartments shared the utopian constructivist ideas with the house-commune in that they also had common areas of use such as the communal kitchens and bathrooms (Utekhin 2003).

Housing shortages, urban poverty, and various forms of collective living were part of Russian life before and after the revolution. However, collective living as a specific ideological institution became codified in the Soviet Union (Boym 1994). As such, the communal apartment incorporated a specific Soviet form of urban living, a utopian communist design, an institution of social control, and a dwelling for police informants between the 1920s and the 1980s (Boym 1994; Gerasimova 1999). In this context, privacy as it is understood today in the Western world was prohibited and, in a sense, reinvented.

THEORETICAL FRAMEWORK

Public and private are relational concepts; the definition of one does not make sense without the definition of the other. There are several definitions of public and private, ranging from liberal-economic models to republican virtue approaches, from socialization theories to feminist analyses (Weintraub 1997). In each case, the distinction between the two is projected to a spatial differentiation that finds its expression in a body, a building, a city, or another site (Madanipour 2003).

The projection of the dichotomous relationship between public and private to a spatial differentiation typically involves an idea of territoriality defined in terms of ownership of physical space. In this regard, ownership usually comes to be understood as a legal entitlement to control a property (Madanipour 2003, 50). I contend that the relationship between ownership and the public–private dichotomy is not necessarily grounded in universalist Enlightenment assumptions about privacy and the individual and, instead, point to the possibility of other explanations of the public–private dichotomy in other cultural contexts.

In seventeenth-century England, Hobbes cast aside traditional concepts of society, justice, and natural law and instead saw political rights and obligations as deriving from the interest and will of individuals. Accordingly, the individual was seen as the natural proprietor of his or her own person or capacities, owing nothing to society. In this context, society was argued to be the sum of relations of exchange between proprietors. In other words, "possessive equality" was assumed to be a fundamental feature of the individual (Macpherson 1964). Later, in the twentieth century, C.B. Macpherson (1964) has suggested, these assumptions about the nature of the individual and society correspond to a model or ideal type for the modern, post-feudal European societies he called "the possessive market society."

This idea of the individual and society as developed particularly in eighteenth-century French philosophy and in English and American tradition from the seventeenth to nineteenth century onward was very much related to the development of ideas of equality, liberty, universal humanity, and property in the West. Such an understanding of individualism based on property relations situated privacy in a non-changing universalistic context predicated on the possessive nature of human beings. Accordingly, private property was thought to organize personal and impersonal dimensions of dealing with space. It was one of the most widely used "vehicles of psychological development, expression of personal identity, and empowerment in social networks" (Madanipour 2003, 202). At the same time, it was thought to be an abstract commodity exchanged in the market and regulated by law. As also expressed by Hegel, private property was associated closely with personal freedom, the idea being that in the end, no community has as much right to property as a person has. This relationship between private property and individual development was elaborated as property ownership allowing a person to translate his or her freedom into an external sphere in the realm of things over which humans have the absolute right of appropriation (Hegel in Madanipour 2003, 57). In that respect, Enlightenment thinkers argued in favour of the institution of private property as an expression of the possessive individual self and, hence, of privacy. Conceiving of the individual as an empirical subject and a moral, independent, autonomous, and non-social being meant that the modern ideology was very much opposed to holism – that is, to the world view found in many non-Western parts of the world that privileges social totality and neglects or subordinates the individual (Dumont 1983, 303).

Given Enlightenment ideas of individualism based on the notion of private property, the "home" more or less became the epitome of the private realm. The concept of domestic space materialized in our "homes" and came to symbolize our private lives as these ideas evolved in a seventeenth-century European setting of rising urbanism (Coontz in Cieraad 1999). The "home" is thought to provide a personal space, a territory, a place protecting us from the natural elements as well as from the scrutiny of others. In this way, "home" becomes a location in the social world that demarcates a clear line between the intimate, cozy, secure indoor world and the public, perilous world outside (Cieraad 1999, 14). In a Western Enlightenment understanding, the home is the core institution in modern society, "sheltering the smallest viable unit of social organization" and enabling the basic patterns of social relations to be forged, reproduced, and changed within it (Madanipour 2003, 64). In this regard, the house is controlled by the household as its property – whether owned or rented – and thus is separated as a private realm from what is beyond the household's control.

Such an understanding of home and domesticity relates to the emergence of the modern family in the West. As the modern individuated self appeared in western Europe after the Middle Ages, the house emerged as the setting for the development of private life for both the individual and the nuclear family (Madanipour 2003). In the seventeenth and eighteenth centuries, the bourgeois house became more and more a residence separated from the workplace. By the eighteenth century, the modern family was being forged in a private space provided by the home. In the nineteenth century, urban space was divided into private and public domains. With the house of the bourgeois family becoming the place of intimate relations between parents and children, private family life was reinforced at the expense of older forms of neighbourly relations, friendships, and traditional contracts that used to take place at home (Madanipour 2003).

This concept of home embraces both a physical and a social space, and it carries an ideological burden; ideas of what constitute a proper family give shape to the ways in which individuals relate to one another in the intimacy of their domestic life (Munro and Madigan 1999). In that respect, the ideal of nineteenth-century housing reflected the ideal of the bourgeois family with its clearly demarcated boundaries of public and private.

Karl Marx and Friedrich Engels criticized this understanding of the private–public distinction based on private ownership of property and the notion of bourgeois family life as developed in the epitome of privacy – that is, the home. Arguing that private ownership of property is the source of "alienation," they called for its abolishment as the only possible means for the actual realization of the individual self (Marx and Engels 1930, 46–50). For them, abolishing private property and the bourgeois family life signified an escape from the Enlightenment assumption of the possessive individual. Following the ideas of Marx and Engels, revolutionaries in Russia tried to abolish private property and bourgeois family life in the aftermath of the 1917 Revolution. It was the idea of turning Enlightenment assumptions upside down that underlay their assumption of the utopias that could be achieved by creating socialism in one building, abolishing the private–public distinction, and replacing family ties with comradeship ties.

However, as demonstrated by the alternative means of expressing privacy that emerged in the communal apartments, the calculations of the revolutionaries were wrong as they tried to replace one universalist assumption with another in the name of extinguishing it. Assuming that the Enlightenment view of possessive individualism was false, they thought they could reveal authentic human nature by getting rid of the institutions that assume relations based on ownership of private property. However, these calculations were based on another universal claim about human nature that also disregarded the specific cultural and historical contexts in which individuals and the institutions regulating their relations develop. By doing so, they excluded the possible existence of other explanations of the public–private distinction. In other words, their attempt to abolish the public–private distinction in Russia took for granted that during the pre-revolutionary period the public–private distinction was based on the relations of ownership of private property suggested by the Enlightenment thinkers.

However, as argued by Boym (1994), the development of individualism did not follow the same path all around the world. In eighteenth-century Russia, there was no individual identity defined as separate from the social and religious roles of people. The Russian understanding of the individual was so different from its Western counterpart that the words "privacy," "self," "mentality," and "identity" in the Western sense did not exist in Russian at all. As Dostoevsky, writing in the nineteenth century, also put it, the Russian understanding of the individual at the time was more closely linked with unconditional sacrifices for society than with the individual rights that characterized western Europe (Boym 1994, 75). The distinct understanding of the individual in the Russian context produced a different notion of privacy, one that cannot be understood as solely based on private ownership of property. How could the Bolsheviks have so misunderstood their own culture? They were Marxists revolutionaries committed to the unfolding of a universal history, not to a culturally sensitive understanding of Russia. Thus, as ideology trumped culture in Bolsheviks' commitment to the unfolding of a universal history, overlooked cultural nuances gave way to unintended consequences that were visualized in the discrepancy between the goals and results of revolutionary housing policies.

As the discrepancy between the goals of the utopian housing policies and the actual results of their implementation also suggests, I believe, both the pre-revolutionary and the post-revolutionary public–private distinction in Soviet Russia requires a different outlook on the issue. The public–private distinction as it exists in non-Western societies needs an explanation other than the one based on ownership of private property, simply because all cultures have their own types of private and public spaces (Gerasimova 2002). Thus, I argue that we can only address the question of why Soviet utopian housing policies did not work out in the way they were intended through an alternate explanation of the public–private distinction.

To understand "privacy," we should start by recognizing that the individual is situated within his or her family, community, and nation as a bearer of a particular history and identity. Identities of people are shaped through communicative processes of socialization. The values of individuals come from their communities, their traditional understandings within which they are socialized. Moreover, toward these values individuals develop certain attitudes that are not predetermined by communities and traditions. In this way, people contribute to the reinterpretation and reinvention of meanings, norms, traditions, and narratives. This happens because individuals require recognition for their personalities (Goffman, Lemert, and Branaman 1997). Individuals, for the presentation of their personalities, require protection that would provide them a sense of control over their self-definitions through their communicative interactions with others. In fact, the normative nature of privacy lies precisely in this protection of what Erving Goffman has called "the territories of the self" (Goffman, Lemert, and Branaman 1997).

Accordingly, the ability to develop and maintain a coherent sense of self is a precondition of successful individuation, and the self is developed in the private. Hence, the reciprocal recognition of privacy is the condition of successful social interaction based on mutual recognition of the integrity of participants. In this normative conception of privacy, it is the sense of control over one's identity and over access to one's self, one's territory that is crucial (Goffman, Lemert, and Branaman 1997, 99). In this sense, we can evaluate the private as what is individual or what pertains only to an individual (Weintraub 1997, 5). Hence, "privacy" is a fundamental part of the complex social practices through which a social group recognizes and relates to the individual. It is a precondition of personhood. It is in this sense that one believes the concrete reality of him- or herself as belonging to him or her in a moral sense. It is through "individual privacy" that one develops and maintains a sense of selfhood, of agency, and of personal identity without perceiving them in the form of alienable property (Goffman, Lemert, and Branaman 1997). In this respect, public as the category defined in relation to the private becomes what is collective and what affects the interests of a collectivity of individuals as opposed to what is individual (Weintraub 1997, 5).

RUSSIAN PRIVACY

If it is the sense of control over one's identity and over access to one's self and one's territory that is crucial and empowering in the construction of individual privacy, then the "home" is the very territory of one's self as a site that protects and defines the individual. However, in the post-revolutionary Soviet context, when the regime was in need of "little people builders of socialism" who were supposed to be depersonalized and less individuated, people got taken out of their "homes" and placed in "semipublic/semiprivate," overcrowded communal apartments (Boym 1994, 129). Hence, the home, in our case the communal apartment, came to be an ambiguous sphere in terms of its definition as private.

Life in the communal apartments cannot be described as purely private, since it included social relations with those who were neither members of the household nor members of the family and everyday life was regulated from outside by the state (Gerasimova 2002, 208). In the aftermath of the revolution, everything physical was opened to the state and the collective with the aim of creating a collective identity. As a Russian writer put it: "the house is a Soviet fortress"

(Gerasimova 2002, 209). In this context, as the Soviets tried to turn the very private sphere of home into a public sphere by abolishing ownership of housing, private emerged at the centre of this new public space, giving way to two concepts developed by Gerasimova (2002, 207–30) – namely, "private publicity" and "public privacy."

The communal apartment was a forced collective united by shared space and equipment as well as mutual dependency among its inhabitants (Gerasimova 2002, 215). There were two major kinds of spaces in the communal apartments, places of common use, such as the kitchen, the hallway, and the bathroom, and the rooms for families (Gerasimova 2002, 215). Among the first type, we can distinguish between the simultaneously used spaces like the kitchen and the hallways and those that were used by turns like the toilet and the bathrooms (Gerasimova 2002, 215). While undesired company characterized kitchens and hallways used simultaneously by several tenants, the toilets and the bathrooms were marked by queues and posted schedules. In Svetlana Boym's words, these places were perceived as a kind of "no man's land" where the space belonged to nobody and to everybody (Boym 1994, 141).

The kitchen was a major setting for public use. It was multi-functional and accessible to both tenants and outsider guests. It was a place of "comrades" court where you had your tea or smoked with others. One barely could find static physical markers of personality in kitchens. There were no ornaments, no curtains on the windows (Utekhin, 2003). However, even though the kitchens lacked the usual signifiers of personality, people developed new forms of marking their own places within these common territories. The position of furniture and individual utensils like pots, pans, dishcloths, tables, and gas burners marked the boundaries between one's own and the others'. Violation of these open boundaries was common in the communal kitchens and frequently ended in significant disputes. In a sense, they were open places with traces of personality (Gerasimova 2002; Utekhin 2003).

The typical halls of communal apartments, on the other hand, were long, dark, transitional spaces that connected the main gate to the rooms of tenants, the kitchen, and the bathroom (Boym 1994, 141). Far from being an intermediate zone to protect the privacy of inhabitants (Eleb-Vidal and Debarre-Blanchard 1989, 82) or a zone easing transition from public to private (Rosselin 1999, 55) as in today's houses, it was a place where a tenant could encounter a stranger immediately after leaving her or his room. It was a place where the most unplanned encounters took place. Just like the communal apartment kitchens, hallways were marked by impersonality. People, afraid of theft, would not even leave their shoes in the hallway. Usually, these transitional spaces were lit by broken or personal light bulbs changed every time a tenant needed to light the hallway (Boym 1995, 148; Utekhin 2003).

Kitchens and hallways as places of a simultaneous communal use were both public and private places. Privacy as a territory of the self, where one protected his or her presentation of his or her personality, was invented in these places through individual light bulbs, separate kitchen tables and dishes, or personal doorbells, each with the name of the tenant on it. As opposed to the hidden or spatially demarcated privacies that are found in our everyday lives, in communal apartments "privacy was formed in a space of mutual visibility" and was therefore "always subject to intrusion and corrective controls of others" (Gerasimova 2002).

Bathrooms, another kind of collective place in communal apartments, were used in turns, and their cleansing was planned according to schedules (Boym 1994, 147). They were like signifiers of the long queues in Soviet life. While on the one hand, the sharing of space and equipment produced a common responsibility among inhabitants of the communal apartments, on the other, it was the very source of reluctance among tenants as it was visualized in the dirt and dust that marked the bathrooms. People washed in their own basins put inside the common bathtub and tried to avoid touching bathtub walls (Utekhin 2003). Toilet paper was kept in tenants' rooms and carried to the bathroom each time it was needed (Boym 1994, 147).

Following Goffman's argument that every person has spatial claims, the inhabitants constructed their identities through such claims (Gerasimova 2002). They were, however, not claims of ownership but rather an identification with specific objects or places within the commonly shared rooms, which were always open to intrusion. Tenants had their own places in the kitchen, the bathroom, or the hallway. Boundaries were drawn such that everyone marked his or her own place. In this sense, the kitchen tables, the different doorbells belonging to different inhabitants, separate gas burners, individual electric switches on the hallways, or the separate toilet covers were markers of one's own territory within communal spaces – that is to say, of one's "private publicity" (Gerasimova 2002). It was through these "territories of self" that inhabitants gained mutual recognition for their individual identities. Tendencies toward protection of individual objects were efforts to protect individual identities. In a sense, if there were no separate doors for inhabitants, then there were separate bells; if there were no separate kitchens, then there were separate gas burners; if there were no separate hallways, then there were separate light bulbs (Utekhin 2003).

In addition to the shared spaces of usage, there were also rooms of personal usage in communal apartments. These rooms were not the private property of tenants, and tenants were always subject to the possibility of being forced out of their rooms by the state's hand (Boym 1994; Fitzpatrick 1999). Nonetheless, their inhabitants turned these rooms into very private places of themselves. A home, as we understand it, was condensed into a single room shared by multiple members of the family. Light partitions, screens, curtains, wardrobes, and thin walls were used to partition the room, to draw boundaries, and to create zones of self. Rather than rooms with different functions, different functional zones were created by the presence of furniture and other domestic equipment. Examples include a bed for a "sleeping room," a desk for a "study," a dinner table for a "dining room," a children's bed and toys for a "children's room" (Gerasimova 2002, 219). Personal life in this context came to be closely connected to one's family, friends, and love relationships. However, even in these rooms the privacy of tenants was not secured. There was always the danger of a neighbour interrupting their privacy. In fact, all that might be considered as personal was actually open and controlled from outside by the sight and hearing of others, giving way to the development of a "public privacy" (Gerasimova 2002).

Privacy in tenants' rooms was also constructed through the formation of personal narratives by symbolic attachment to objects. These narratives were constructed in small spaces behind the partitions. Svetlana Boym (1994, 151) provides the example of an old and non-luxurious commode that served as a site of personal pride and the display of one's individuation. Similarly, she describes Aunt Liuba, whose overcrowded room was filled with personal memorabilia, personal objects such as postcards, baby pictures, and portraits displayed behind the glass of her bookshelves. These small spaces behind the glass, on the walls, and on the tables reflected the images of the residents. They mostly did not construct a linear narrative but still reflected the individual perceptions and histories. In fact, it was the stories that really mattered, which left traces and survived to the day for these people (Boym 1994, 153). In the Soviet Union, objects were treated as artifacts, and the individual territories of the self were preserved in these artifacts (Boym 1994, 153).

As exemplified in the attitudes of communal apartment tenants, these individuals developed privacies at the very centre of public spheres where the notion of private property was absent (Gerasimova 2002). In that respect, I argue that the discrepancy between the utopian housing policies and their outcome was grounded in the dominance of ideology over culture – in other words, in the ignorance of cultural nuances of pre-revolutionary conceptions of public and private spheres that significantly differed from Marxist assumptions of the public-private distinction. I believe, following Goffman, that the culturally and historically specific boundaries of the public–private distinction can only be understood by reference to processes of social interaction. Hence, the deviation of Soviet housing policies from their actual intentions resulted from the reliance of the revolutionaries on the universalistic claims of Enlightenment ideas that were actually born in the culturally and historically specific context of western Europe.

REFERENCES

Benjamin, Walter, and Michael William Jennings. 1999. *Selected Writings, vol. 2. 1927–1934.* Cambridge, MA: Harvard University Press
Boym, Svetlana. 1994. *Common Places: Mythologies of Everyday Life in Russia.* Cambridge, MA, and London: Harvard University Press
Cieraad, Irene. 1999. "Introduction." In *At Home: An Anthropology of Domestic Space*, edited by Irene Cieraad. Syracuse, NY: Syracuse University Press
Dumont, Louis. 1993. *Essai sur l'individualisme : une perspective anthropologique sur l'idéologie moderne.* Paris: Seuil
Eleb-Vidal, Monique, and Anne Debarre-Blanchard. 1989. *Architectures de la vie privée : maison et mentalité XVIIe–XIXe siècles.* Brussels: AAM Editions
Fitzpatrick, Sheila. 1999. *Everyday Stalinism.* Oxford: Oxford University Press

Frykman, Jonas, and Orvar Löfgren. 1987. *Culture Builders: A Historical Anthropology of Middle Class Life.* New Brunswick, N J: Rutgers University Press

Gerasimova, Katerina. 1999. "The Soviet Communal Apartment." In *Beyond the Limits: The Concept of Space in Russian History and Culture,* edited by Jeremy Smith. Helsinki: S H S

– 2002. "Public Privacy in the Soviet Communal Apartment." In *Socialist Spaces: Sites of Everyday Life in the Eastern Bloc,* edited by David Crowley and Susan E. Reid. London: Berg

Goffman, Erving, Charles Lemert, and Ann Branaman. 1997. *The Goffman Reader.* Oxford: Blackwell

Macpherson, Crawford, B. 1964. *The Political Theory of Possessive Individualism: Hobbes to Locke.* Oxford: Oxford University Press

Madanipour, Ali. 2003. *Public and Private Spaces of the City.* London and New York: Routledge

Marx, Karl, and Friedrich Engels. 1930. "The Communist Manifesto." In *The Communist Manifesto of Karl Marx and Friedrich Engels,* by D. Ryazanoff and Martin Lawrence. New York: International Publishers

Munro, Moria, and Ruth Madigan. 1999. "Negotiating Space in the Family Home." In *At Home: An Anthropology of Domestic Space,* edited by Irene Cieraad. Syracuse, N Y: Syracuse University Press

Rosselin, Celine. 1999. "The Ins and Outs of the Hall: A Parisian Example." In *At Home: An Anthropology of Domestic Space,* edited by Irene Cieraad. Syracuse, N Y: Syracuse University Press

Spagnolo, Rebecca. 2006. "When Private Home Meets Public Workplace: Service, Space and the Urban Domestic in 1920s Russia." In *Everyday Life in Early Soviet Russia,* edited by Christina Kiaer and Eric Naiman. Bloomington and Indianapolis: Indiana University Press

Stites, Richard. 1999. "Crowded on the Edge of Vastness: Observations on Russian Space and Place." In *Beyond the Limits: The Concept of Space in Russian History and Culture,* edited by Jeremy Smith. Helsinki: S H S

Uthekin, Ilia. 2003. "Essays on Communal life, Summary." http://utekhin. narod.ru/summary.htm

Weintraub, Jeff. 1997. "The Theory and Politics of the Public/Private Distinction." In *Public and Private in Thought and Practice,* edited by Jeff Weintraub and Krishan Kumar. Chicago: University Of Chicago Press

14

Urban Imagery, Tourism, and the Future of New Orleans

MARK HUTTER AND DeMOND S. MILLER

The image of the city is a result of how people perceive the city. Urban imagery also has consequences in shaping city life. Urban images have a symbolic function: images that help provide strong associations with a place facilitate interaction between people who share a common environment. Shared images of places and communities are the facilitator in the development of strong bonds among people. The urban social geographer Kevin Lynch (1960, 126) has pointed out that "[t]he landscape plays a social role as well. The named environment, familiar to all, furnishes material for common memories and symbols which bind the group together and allow them to communicate with one another. The landscape serves as a vast mnemonic system for the retention of group history and ideals." This vast collection of memories serves as the foundation of the lived experience common to many of the urban dwellers of the city of New Orleans.

URBAN IMAGERY AND THE CHICAGO SCHOOL

Lynch's perspective echoes that put forth by the Chicago School many years ago. Robert Park (1967 [1925]), in the opening remarks of his important essay, "The City: Suggestions for the Investigation of Human Behavior in the Urban Environment," states a basic premise of symbolic interaction thought on the nature of urban imagery and urban identification that the city is a "state of mind": "The city is ... a state of mind, a body of customs and traditions, and of the organized attitudes and sentiments that inhere in these customs and are transmitted with the tradition. The city is not, in other words, merely a physical mechanism and an artificial construction. It is involved in the vital processes of the people who compose it."

Park's statement emphasizes symbolic and psychological adjustments to the social organization of urban life influenced by shared sentiments and values. Park's work views the city as a product of the participation and communication of its inhabitants and not solely as a physical artifact or a collection of people. Park's intellectual interests centre on urban conditions that result in the breakdown of human interaction, decline of the primary group associations, breakdown of the community, and social disorganization.

Walter Firey (1945; 1947) examined land use patterns in Boston to build on Park's idea that "the city is a state of mind" and to test what he saw as the basic shortcomings of the urban ecology approach that was also articulated by Park and particularly favoured by his colleague Ernest Burgess. Firey argued that people respond not solely to the physical environment but to conceptions of that environment. He criticized the human ecologists for not stressing the moral or cultural side of society but instead focusing on the physical nature of the environment itself to determine urban spatial patterning. Firey argued that two social-psychological factors – sentiment and symbolism – were also at work, in addition to economic competition, in determining land use. Sentiment and symbolism, in fact, can supersede other considerations and can result in non-economic, "non-rational" use of land. They therefore must be considered as important cultural factors influencing locational processes and must be seen as additional ecological variables.

Firey's research emphasizes the power of place, the importance of social-psychological factors, and the emotional attachments and enduring connections between social groups and specific communities. His study of location choices in central Boston indicated that symbols and sentiments were at work in influencing land use patterns.

R. Richard Wohl and Anselm L. Strauss, building on the ideas of the Chicago School and particularly the ideas of Park and of Firey, extend the analysis on urban imagery. Strauss (1961), in his *Images of American Cities*, sets forth his intellectual agenda. "It is a framework of a social psychologist – which in this instance means a joining of sociological, psychological, and historical perspectives" (1961, x). His particular concern is the examination of American imagery with focus on the "spatial and temporal aspects of that imagery" and the "meaning" the city has for its inhabitants. By "urban imagery," Strauss refers to the symbolization of the city.

Wohl and Strauss first pick up on the theme articulated by Park that the city is "a state of mind." They comment on the nature of urban imagery and urban identification by informing us that given objects of the city become symbolically representative of the city as a whole. Thus, the New York skyline, San Francisco's Golden Gate Bridge, and the French Quarter of New Orleans are the identification symbol of the given city and serve as a source of personal identification for the inhabitants. They point out how the spatial complexity and the social diversity of a city often become integrated by the use of "sentimental" history in selected landscapes such as the Water Tower in Chicago or Telegraph Hill in San Francisco. They build on this observation by arguing that an invariable characteristic of city life is that people, in order to "see" the city, must employ certain stylized and symbolic objects. The streets, the people, the buildings, the changing scenes do not come already labelled. They require explanation and interpretation (Wohl and Strauss 1958, 527).

In *Images of the American City*, Strauss (1961) builds on his essay with Wohl. He observes that people know best ("see") those parts of a city with which they are intimately involved – where they go to school, shop, work, and meet friends. In Strauss's (1961, 67) words: "the various kinds of urban perspectives held by the residents of a city are constructed from spatial representations resulting from membership in particular social worlds." For Strauss, the images a person has of the city are based on relationships. Images can be seen as a spatial consequence of the different types of social relationship that people have with each other in different places. Strauss examined how the physical reality of cities is interpreted through the "images" that people have of them. The *feelings* that people have of cities influence how they perceive and act toward them.

Strauss also places these images in a historical context in that they are a result of understanding the rapid historical transformation of rural America to an urban society. Of essential interest to Strauss is how this social change is observed and felt by its citizens. When we ascertain how people "see" the city, we have a better understanding of how they experience it. "What Americans see and have seen in their towns, and what they say and have said about them, can tell us a great deal about how they lived in them, how they have felt about them, how they have managed to cope with the problems raised by the conditions of life there" (Strauss 1961, viii).

Strauss examined the writings of Americans on the different viewpoints that were held of rural, regional, and urban life, on the processes and consequences of rapid urbanization, on the attraction and fear that cities elicit. He investigated, through this examination of the writings on American cities, why some view the city as exciting and friendly, while others view it with fear and dread. Lyn Lofland (2003) observes that Strauss was interested not only in recording the symbolic representations historically attached to American cities but also in their consequences. "He wanted to grasp the form and themes of those representations in their own right, but he also viewed them as phenomena with serious consequences for other areas of social life; that is, he was interested in mapping the symbols and in tracing their uses and abuses" (Lofland 2003, 946).

What is not emphasized in the analyses of Lynch and Wohl and Strauss is the recognition that the image of the city is not based solely on the ease of perceptual readings of the city but is influenced by underlying political, economic, and social factors. Probably the strongest proponents of this viewpoint are the followers of the urban political economy perspective. The ideas of Mark Gottdiener, who combines political economy within a socio-spatial framework, are of particular relevance. Gottdiener is interested in the role of ideology in the structuring of urban space. In his essay (1986), "Culture, Ideology, and the Sign of the City," he takes issue with the socio-culturalist school of urban ecology represented by the work of Walter Firey and the communications model of urban planners such as Kevin Lynch and his followers (for a discussion of culture and city redevelopment, see Horgan, this volume). Gottdiener argues that urban imagery is not simply a visibility cognitive matter, as Lynch proclaims, but rather is a result of ideological factors.

Gottdiener's (1986; 1994; 1997) and Gottdiener and Hutchinson's (2000) approach was to incorporate and integrate an urban political economy perspective with Firey's socio-cultural perspective. They seek to broaden the political economy perspective by integrating it with sensibility to the symbolic nature of environments. Space is seen as another compositional factor in human behaviour along with the more traditional factors such as class, race, gender, age, and social status. Gottdiener (1994) refers to the broader parameters of this perspective as the new urban sociology, and his own term for it is the socio-spatial perspective (s s p).

He introduces the importance of symbolic processes within a political economy framework to analyze urban structures and the urban environment. Such an approach, he argues, overcomes the limitations of urban ecology. Urban ecology, while recognizing the importance of urban location, does so through a one-dimensional, technologically deterministic framework. The approach also overcomes the limitations of political economy. The socio-spatial perspective expands the political economy analytical framework that emphasizes space as a container of political and economic activities but tends to ignore the importance of the symbolic meaning of spatial relations (for a discussion of the primacy of economic capacities of space as a part of development, see Horgan, this volume). s s p emphasizes the social production and meaning of urban space.

Similarly, Christopher Mele (2000) takes issue with Anselm Strauss's conceptualization of urban imagery as a resultant of a public consensus that is formed by shared symbols and understanding of the meaning of place. Mele (2000, 14) draws on the new urban sociology and a socio-spatial approach; he argues that the meaning of place is a result of "social power and contestation rather than as ad hoc by-products of consensual place image making." Mele places the symbolic meaning of place in political, economic, and cultural stratification. Following Mele's work, we contend that the image of New Orleans, "seen" solely through tourist sites, has become a significant contributory factor in political and economic decisions on its future. In contrast and often in opposition are the images and the symbolic meaning held by the residents and "refugees" of such devastated areas as the Lower Ninth Ward.

THE SYMBOLIC ECONOMY AND COMMODIFICATION OF URBAN IMAGE

Sharon Zukin has noted similar processes in her analyses of contemporary *symbolic economies* in which culture has become an important urban economic commodification. Based on her observations, Zukin develops a point of view that ties a political economy perspective to what she sees as the emergence of a symbolic economy. This new symbolic economy is anchored on the economic importance of tourism, media, and entertainment for cities. She believes that with the disappearance of local manufacturing, culture is increasingly the business in cities. The cultural consumption of art, gourmet food, fashion, and music and tourism, which often packages them all, are the driving forces on which the city's symbolic economy rests. Zukin describes the symbolic economy created by cultural strategies of urban redevelopment and the privatization of public space. Zukin persuasively argues that the recent growth of the symbolic economy has tangible spatial repercussions: it "reshapes geography and ecology" (Zukin 1995, 8). It creates new types of workplaces, commercial areas, and residences and throws into turmoil conventional meanings of public versus private, local versus transnational, commodity versus culture: "The growth of the symbolic economy in finance, media, and entertainment ... has already forced the growth of towns and cities, created a vast new work force, and changed the way consumers and employees think ... The facilities where these employees work – hotels, restaurants, expanses of new construction and undeveloped land – are more than just workplaces. They reshape geography and ecology; they are places of creation and transformation" (Zukin 1995, 8).

The symbolic economy for Zukin is not a singular phenomenon; rather it involves a number of different ways in which the cultural symbols of a place are combined with capitalist activity: the "intertwining of cultural symbols and entrepreneurial capital" (Zukin 1995, 3). She suggests that over the course of history, this economy takes three main forms influencing how a place is seen and used for subsequent investment and economic development to regenerate a city. The first and most basic form of the symbolic economy implies profiting from its imagery – "the look and feel of a city" (Zukin 1995, 7). The second form of symbolic economy refers to the concerns for profit through real estate developments and jobs by "place entrepreneurs." She uses the concept developed by Harvey Molotch (1976) that refers to real estate developers, corporate organizations, and venture capitalism that sought the development of the private sector through investments in retail and office developments or the housing market. The third form of symbolic economy consists of what have been traditional "place entrepreneurs" whose investments in the city are through such cultural forms such as museums, parks, and monuments. These businesses and municipal authorities operate for civic and philanthropic reasons to promote the public good and indirectly to both reflect and promote economic prosperity. What gives this third form its power and its increased importance since the beginning of the last quarter of the twentieth century is the decline in the manufacturing and industrial sector and the concomitant rise of service-sector industries intertwined with the consumer culture industry associated with the arts, music, film, theatre, sports, and entertainment complexes combined with food and drink establishments, retailing, and tourism.

Zukin's major concern is how the power of the symbolic economy in cities affects "social inclusion or exclusion, depending on your point of view" (Zukin 1995, vii). She argues that the cultural constructs of a city delegates "who belongs where" through its images and symbols, regulates the economy by producing goods, and designs public space through planning backed by those in positions of power in the private sector. Images in the city are controlled for the benefit of the middle and affluent classes as well as tourists. Unsavory images are removed or concealed. According to Zukin (1995, 2), controlling the various cultures of cities suggests the possibility of controlling all sorts of urban ills, from violence and hate crimes to economic decline.

The symbolic economy becomes dependent upon the creation of attractions such as museums and entertainment zones that offer "family-friendly" venues, sports stadiums, parks, and festival marketplaces for the more affluent groups and reshapes the political economy of the place. The establishment of an expensive sidewalk cafe is one means of establishing presence and control: "A sidewalk cafe takes back the street from casual workers and homeless people" (Zukin 1995, 9). Zukin's dominating concern is not only on issues of who occupies "real" space but on the utilization of "symbolic" space as well. In an allied work, Zukin states: "To ask 'whose city?' suggests more than a politics of occupation; it also asks who has a right to inhabit the dominant image of the city" (Zukin 1996, 43). Now we would like to build on the importance of urban imagery and power and the role it is playing in the rebuilding of New Orleans. We examine how the physical space of New Orleans is being redefined in terms of "place" by those in positions of power and economic control.

POWER, POLITICS, AND THE RESHAPING OF THE URBAN IMAGE: NEW ORLEANS AFTER KATRINA

New Orleans is dependent upon both domestic and international tourism, ranking with New York, San Francisco, and Los Angeles as a popular tourist site. Daniel Libeskind, the architectural planner of the World Trade Center site in New York, sees an opportunity to rebuild New Orleans similar to the opportunity that arose in Berlin after World War II. He believes that the cultural heritage of New Orleans provides a great foundation for the rebirth of the city.

Many cities have used tourism as a strategy for urban redevelopment and revitalization, forcing local governments and the tourist industry to forge close institutional and fiscal ties to "sell" the city. Such alliances on the part of government and business interests to market New Orleans's environment by using imagery and themes have usually positively affected the economy by capitalizing on the city's cultural aspects (Gotham 2002). Former Mayor Nagin's plan for rebuilding the city contains a cultural redevelopment component aimed at re-establishing the city's musical, visual, culinary, architectural, literary, and graphic arts because of their ability to draw tourists to the area. The plan calls for approximately $648 million of investment over a three-year period to jumpstart the redevelopment of the city's culture over the next few decades. Components of the plan include rebuilding artistic talent pools, repairing and rebuilding cultural venues, teaching the city's cultural traditions to young people, attracting national and international investment, requiring shared public and private investment in the city's infrastructure, and "marketing New Orleans as a world-class cultural capital" (City of New Orleans 2006, 14). By adhering to the plan proposed by the mayor's office, many leaders believe that "[t]he proposed public and private investments will revive the City's cultural base, benefit businesses and residents of every neighborhood, ensure the return of displaced artists and cultural workers, restore leading cultural facilities and create new cultural venues that celebrate the City's unique musical history and the cultural traditions of its diverse neighborhoods, revitalize street life and performances, increase tourism, and lever other investments many times over" (City of New Orleans 2006, 14).

Since the storm, the loss of culture indicative of New Orleans has been one of the primary concerns of the city's residents. Culture is significant to the survivors, because it has shaped a sense of place and place attachment; however, with an emphasis on tourism and the outside workers that are bound to follow, how significant will the renewing of New Orleans culture be to them? There is no doubt that those material components and festive aspects of New Orleans's culture will remain significant to the workers who will flock to the city for employment opportunities in the tourist industry; however, the city's economic revival rests in the commodification and selling of the "traditional New Orleans experience" – complete with jazz, food, and fun – as opposed to its cultural value. Gotham (2002, 1,737) explains that the "concept of commodification refers to the dominance of commodity exchange-value over use-value and implies the development of a consumer society where market relations subsume and dominate social life."

Therefore, in the context of selling the city's culture and sense of place, local customs, rituals, festivals, and ethnic arts will become tourist attractions performed on cue when tourists want to be entertained (Gotham 2002), devaluing the traditional experiences in the eyes of traditional practitioners. Devaluation of traditional culture practised by residents will occur as traditional events become trivial and less significant in relation to annual events with cultural meaning; traditional events will give way to more financially motivated activities that can be "packaged" and sold as "culture on demand." Local concerns about the establishment of a dominant tourist sector will be exacerbated by a more commodified tourist industry centred on less culturally significant activities rooted in and connected with the landscape.

In the pursuit of economic success, the city and private businesses will attempt to exploit the city's image; however, this may have a detrimental effect on the city's culture in the long term. Because culture will be an economic stimulus, and possibly the most relied-upon sector in the region, business and city planners will have to avoid the Disneyification and a manufactured urban state of mind. With Disneyification, local traditions, famous buildings and landmarks, and other heritage sights and events become "hyper-real," causing people to lose the ability to distinguish between the "real" and the "illusion" (Gotham 2002) or between original culture and marketing/manufactured culture.

Additionally, Harvey (1989) and Holcomb (1993) explain that with the expansion of the tourist industry into a dominating sector, place promotion is no longer about informing or promoting in the ordinary sense (i.e., selling the original cultural characteristics of New Orleans) but rather is geared toward manipulating desires and tastes through imagery that may or may not have anything to do with the product being sold (New Orleans culture) (Harvey 1989; Gotham 2002). In essence, the tourist industry ceases to "sell" the "authentic" or "true" culture of New Orleans; instead, city leaders are manufacturing a new New Orleans by adapting, reshaping, and manipulating images to remake a sense of place for visitors from afar. Functioning within this economic and power environment, New Orleans's culture and demographics may change, because New Orleans's culture will develop directly in conjunction with tourism market forces. Moreover, Gotham (2002) has noted that shifts toward tourist-dominated economics in an urban setting have historically coincided with population decline, white flight to the suburbs, racial segregation, poverty, and a host of other social problems, including crime, fiscal austerity, poor schools, and decaying infrastructure, all of which were observable in New Orleans prior to Katrina. Therefore, in looking toward the future, one can foresee that an expansion of the service sector may aid the economic redevelopment of New Orleans in the immediate short term; in the long term, social conditions may also revert back to what they were prior to Katrina, and the cultural significance, place attachment, and sense of place that many of the residents held for New Orleans before the storm may be lost.

DISASTER TOURISM, URBAN IMAGERY, AND THE FUTURE OF NEW ORLEANS

Travellers are becoming increasingly interested in places marked by tragedy, death, and various atrocities. The most popular are sites that highlight mass destruction, cemeteries for the war dead or victims of genocide, concentration camps, or places of religious significance. In visiting the sites of long-ago battles where heroes died or places where massive human suffering occurred, the tourist feels closer to the tragic event. In the twenty-first century, bus tours to places of mass casualty and catastrophe are commodified, marketed, and sold in a voyeuristic, "reality-style" manner. Tour guides are prepared for those seeking to get as close to the "real" experience of local disasters and war zones as possible, with cameras flashing and souvenirs in hand – a natural extension of any itinerary (Potts 2006; also see Miller 2008).

In the midst of the devastation, debates arose over the role culture and tourism would play in the redevelopment of New Orleans as images of the once vibrant city were juxtaposed to images of a city on the decline. A sub-specialty of the tourism industry – disaster tourism – comes into play here. But how does the disaster tour affect the tourist? How can cultural resilience be used to draw tourists back into the city? And what is the tourism industry's role in shaping the urban image of New Orleans?

"[T]he uncertainty and devastation unleashed by Hurricane Katrina has reinvigorated old debates and stimulated new arguments about the meaning and definition of local culture. New conflicts and struggles ... emerg[ed] between local groups and neighbourhoods over what constitutes New Orleans culture, who should define what culture means, and how local culture should be expressed" (Gotham 2007, 825). Disaster tourism has a history of giving the traveller an opportunity to experience "first-hand" what the mass media so vividly portray or at least through the mediated scripts of the tour guide. However, the disaster tour allows the paying customer a chance to go beyond the mediated and experience the vivid, irrevocable, and authentic rawness of disaster zones, the sights and sounds of the actual disaster landscape (Miller and Rivera 2008). In essence, the New Orleans Lower Ninth Ward offers a place that is "somewhat free" of curators, ticket-takers, and media middlemen, giving the tourist the fullness of the grim reality such places speak (Potts, 2006). The disaster tourist travels to a disaster scene not to help but to look with interest at the devastation. Potts (2006) further notes: "After the flooding that followed Hurricane Katrina, however, the Lower Ninth Ward suddenly transformed into a tourist attraction. Visitors were coming to the Big Easy to watch Mardi Gras parades and drink mint juleps, sure – but many people also wanted to see the working-class neighbourhood that had become a symbol of human suffering in the dramatic images that filled TV screens after the storm."

Shortly after the storm in 2005 and early 2006, for $49 each, riders could get a three-hour tour that began with a detailed history of the French Quarter and ended at one of New Orleans's new attractions: an enormous red barge that broke through a levee breach and now sits on top of a small school bus and several crushed homes in the devastated Ninth Ward (Helgeson 2005; Miller 2008, 118). The Katrina disaster tours that are sold in New Orleans put suffering, years of government neglect, poor civic planning, a failed government response, and centuries of racial and environmental injustice on the map as a tourist destination for the world to see. In a news report titled "Even after the Storm, New Orleans Visitors Can't Stay Away – Disaster Tours Pass Ninth Ward and Fats Domino's House; 'It's Just Human Nature,'" Christopher Cooper (2005) wrote:

In 2005, on a guided tour, travellers came to the storm-wrecked [Lower] Ninth Ward neighbourhood. There, they gazed at one of New Orleans's latest attractions: a big steel barge that had come to rest on top of a yellow school bus ... The massive red craft, which spun through a levee breach following Hurricane Katrina, sits in a wasteland of buckled concrete, downed trees and rusted appliances, all of it covered with a fine patina of river mud. [Such a tour, according to Cooper, is offered by a local taking part in the new business in post-Katrina New Orleans and is evidence of the emergence of a grim new business in the city, disaster tourism] ...

One must-see landmark on her disaster tour is the sprawling, ruined white brick home of famous rhythm-and-blues pianist Fats Domino. Rolling past the manse on a block littered with moldy church pews and a ruined upright piano, Ms. Cossart pointed out the red graffiti a fan had painted on the side of the structure, stating "RIP Fats." But it's mistaken. Mr. Domino, 77, got away by boat. "It's a happy story," says Ms. Cossart, whose own West Bank property suffered some damage when two trees fell in her yard, crushing her canary-yellow Corvette. She has worked the fate of her car into the spiel on the $49-a-head tour.

Cooper's disaster tour could be seen in various forms as the Lower Ninth Ward became the destination to visit for sightseers (Miller 2008). While the disaster tourism market declined in the years following Hurricane Katrina, the Gray Line Company was still advertising its disaster tours in 2009 as "voted most creative tour by Gray Line worldwide." Nearly five years after Hurricane Katrina, the three-hour 2009 tour price was $35 for adults and $28 for children while the 2.5-hour tour was $32 for adults and $19 for children. However, the 2009 version of the tour was rebranded as a celebration of the rebirth and resurrection of a city seemingly doomed for disaster. Advertising for the tour sought to sell the city as a place that was safe, vibrant, and filled with historical characters – indeed, the central theme of the rebranded urban image was not only one of renewal and recovery but: "New Orleans: REBIRTH: Restoring the Soul of America."

CONCLUSION

In this chapter, we noted the importance of urban imagery and power and how it comes to define not only given sections of a city but a city itself. Through an examination of the impact of Hurricane Katrina on New Orleans, we examined how physical *space* is redefined in terms of *place* by those in positions of power and economic control. Power and economic factors, combined with concerns for the symbolic meaning of space, interact and have consequences on how people interpret their built environment. We began by observing Park's concept of "the city as a state of mind" and Firey's concern with "sentiment and symbolism" as ecological variables. This was followed by an examination of the works of Anselm Strauss, whose discussion of the importance of urban imagery influenced how cities are both conceptualized and acted upon.

Anselm Strauss (1961) examined how the physical reality of cities is interpreted through the "images" that people have of them. The *feelings* that people have for cities influence how they perceive and act toward them. Further, the spatial complexity and the social diversity of a city often becomes integrated by the use of "sentimental" history in selected landscapes, and an invariable characteristic of city life is that certain stylized and symbolic objects must be employed by people in order to "see" the city.

However, Wohl and Strauss fail to make explicit how that "labelling" process is affected by people in positions of power who can influence and control the "symbolic meaning" given to a community. Similarly, Kevin Lynch's work on the imagery of the city does not fully emphasize the importance of underlying political, economic, and social factors in articulating that imagery. Using the work of Mark Gottdiener as the conceptual model, we looked at the "new urban sociology" and the socio-spatial approach that emphasizes the importance of people acting on behalf of political and economic interests who mold the symbolic meaning of space.

The case in point for our discussion was the havoc wreaked on the city of New Orleans by Hurricane Katrina. In our presentation, we sought to emphasize how political and economic players working on behalf of those interests have sought to mold the future of the city in terms that would be of benefit to them and what they see as its economic future. Here we framed our discussion through the work of Sharon Zukin, who conceptually emphasizes the political economy perspective in the analysis of the emergence of a *symbolic economy*. The symbolic economy grounded on the economic importance of tourism, media, and entertainment was shown to be characteristic of New Orleans. In this discussion, we made use of the conceptual ideas of Disneyification and *rebranding* to emphasize the political and economic power utilization of symbols in articulating a new city imagery. The future of New Orleans will be shaped by the winners of the battle for control of the culture of the city and its symbolization through resultant urban imagery as the symbolic economy transforms both neighbourhoods (on the local level) and the city (on the metropolitan level). The problems of New Orleans being played out "symbolically" by disaster tourism, Disneyification, rebranding, and political fighting will ultimately determine the future of that city and its urban imagery.

The Chicago School's contribution to our understanding of the urban rebuilding, "rebranding," and re-identification of New Orleans clearly illustrates its relevance and modern-day applicability. The Chicago School's theoretical contributions and the more recent conceptual ideas of the socio-spatial and political economy perspectives help us to better understand community redevelopment in the aftermath of major urban disasters.

REFERENCES

City of New Orleans. 2006. *Rebuilding New Orleans*. http://www .bringneworleansback.org/Portals/bringNeworleansback/Resources Mayors%20Rebuilding%20Plan%20Final.pdf

Cooper, Christopher. 2005. "Even after the Storm, New Orleans Visitors Can't Stay Away: Disaster Tours Pass Ninth Ward and Fats Domino's House; 'It's Just Human Nature.' *Wall Street Journal* 27 December, A1

Firey, Walter. 1945. "Sentiment and Symbolism as Ecological Variables." *American Sociological Review* 10:140–8

– 1947. *Land Use in Central Boston*. Cambridge, MA: Harvard University Press

Gottdiener, Mark. 1986. "Culture, Ideology, and the Sign of the City." In *Capitalist Development and Crisis Theory: Accumulation, Regulation, and Spatial Restructuring*, edited by Mark Gottdiener and Nicos Komninos . London and New York: Macmillan

– 1994. *The New Urban Sociology*. New York: McGraw-Hill

– 1997. *The Theming of America: Dreams, Visions, and Commercial Spaces*. Boulder, CO: Westview Press

– and Ray Hutchinson. 2000. *The New Urban Sociology*. 2nd edition. New York: McGraw-Hill

Gotham, Kevin. F. 2002. "Marketing Mardi Gras: Commodification, Spectacle and the Political Economy of Tourism in New Orleans." *Urban Studies* 39:1,735–56

– 2007. "(Re)branding the Big Easy: Tourism Rebuilding in Post-Katrina New Orleans." *Urban Affairs Review* 42(6):823–50

Harvey, David. 1989. *The Condition of Postmodernity: An Enquiry into the Origins of Cultural Change*. New York: Blackwell

Helgeson, Baird. 2005. Disaster Tourism Begins to Thrive. *Tampa Tribune* online. http://www.tampatrib.com/MGB9ZZ90UHE.html

Holcomb, Briavel. 1993. "Revisioning Place: De- and Re-constructing the Image of the Industrial City." In *Selling Places: The City as Cultural Capital, Past and Present*, edited by Gerry Kearns and Chris Philo, 133–44. Oxford: Pergamon

Lofland, Lyn H. 2003. "Community and Urban Life." In *Handbook of Symbolic Interaction*, edited by Larry T. Reynolds and Nancy Herman-Kinney, chapter 39. Lanham, MD: Altamira Press

Lynch, Kevin. 1960. *The Image of the City*. Cambridge, MA: MIT Press

Mele, Christopher. 2000. *Selling the Lower East Side: Culture, Real Estate, and Resistance in New York, 1880–2000*. Minneapolis: University of Minnesota Press

Miller, DeMond S. 2008. "Disaster Tourism and Disaster Landscape Attractions after Hurricane Katrina: An Auto-Ethnographic Journey." *International Journal of Culture, Tourism and Hospitality Research* 2(2):115–31

– and Jason D. Rivera. 2008. *Hurricane Katrina and the Redefinition of Landscape*. Lanham, MD: Lexington Books

Molotch, Harvey. 1976. "The City as a Growth Machine." *American Journal of Sociology* 82(2):309–30

Park, Robert E. 1967 [1925]. "The City: Suggestions for the Investigation of Human Behavior in the City Environment." In *The City*, edited by Robert E. Park, Ernest W. Burgess, and Roderick D. McKenzie, 1–46. Chicago: University of Chicago Press

Potts, R. 2006. "In New Orleans: The Allure of Disaster Tourism." *Yahoo News*. http://travel.news.yahoo.com/b/rolf_potts/20060313/rolf_potts/rolf_potts2915

Strauss, Anselm L. 1961. *Images of the American City*. New York: Free Press; New Brunswick, NJ: Transaction

Wohl, R. Richard, and Anselm L. Strauss. 1958. "Symbolic Representation and the Urban Milieu." *American Journal of Sociology* 63:523–32

Zukin, Sharon. 1995. *The Culture of Cities*. Cambridge, MA: Blackwell

– "Space and Symbols in an Age of Decline." In *Re-Presenting the City*, edited by Anthony King, 43–59. London: Macmillan

SECTION IV
The Chicago School Diaspora:
Boundaries, Constructions, and Claims

The Second Chicago School, consisting of Blumer, Hughes, and an exceptional crop of post–World War II graduate students (e.g., Strauss, Becker, Goffman), is closely associated with the development of symbolic interactionism and, in particular, with detailed attention to social processes that create intersubjectively shared meaning. For some scholars, the integration of the various strands of early Chicago School sociology into a coherent theoretical perspective (symbolic interactionism) represents the true meaning of the Chicago School tradition. This section displays yet another aspect of the Chicago School Diaspora: engagement with the Chicago School legacy through the application of key concepts associated with the symbolic interactionist perspective in order to make sense of new empirical observations. In particular, the chapters in section IV exemplify the social processes of boundary maintenance, claims-making, and social constructionism that these scholars identify as key ideas within the Chicago School Diaspora.

How, for example, does a minority group maintain its unique cultural identity? One well established mechanism employed by intentional communities is to use physical isolation as a boundary mechanism to enforce social separation. In chapter 15, "Hassidim Confronting Modernity," William Shaffir explores the challenges of maintaining a cultural boundary between a traditional community and the modern world in the Internet era where physical isolation is increasingly impossible. In chapter 16, "What Is 'Genius' in Arts and 'Brain Drain' in Life Science?", Izabela Wagner examines the constructed meanings attached to the terms "genius" and "brain drain" and shows how the use and meaning of the terms differ among groups. For example, elite musicians use "genius" and related terms (talent, gift, virtuoso, prodigy) in discussions with outsiders but use completely different words in discussions with other elite musicians. Thus, Wagner's work provides a concrete illustration of the link between shared meanings and boundary maintenance. Shared meanings are not only the product of group process, they also become resources for use by group members. In chapter 17, "Situating *The Hobo*: Romancing the Road from Vagabondia to Hobohemia," Jeffrey Brown contextualizes Nels Anderson's classic work in terms of various historically constructed meanings associated with life on the road (e.g., the hobo as hero or as menace) and shows how Anderson's construction of the hobo's identity (as a unique, and historically evanescent, travelling worker and builder) differs from them. The emphasis on processes of meaning-making has also spawned a large literature that views social problems as the result of claims-making activities through which putative problems are defined as problems. In chapter 18, "Constructing Stockholm Syndrome: A Definitional History," Antony Christensen, Benjamin Kelly, Michael Adorjan, and Dorothy Pawluch examine how the Stockholm syndrome label has entered the popular and medical lexicon, how it became available as a resource to be used by social actors to define certain social situations, and how its use has grown to include an ever-widening array of situations.

Significantly, the chapters in section IV contain substantially fewer references to pre–World War II Chicago School sociology than are found in sections I–III. This is not because the authors see the insights of Park, Mead, and other early Chicago members as irrelevant but rather because they view the Chicago School tradition as an evolving one in which the early members laid the foundation for what was to become the real legacy of Chicago School sociology: the full blown symbolic interactionist/constructivist paradigm used to inform their work.

15

Hassidim Confronting Modernity

WILLIAM SHAFFIR

I knew virtually nothing about Hassidic Jews when I began research-
ing their lifestyle and community organization in the late 1960s. But
I still vividly recall how I was struck by their distinctive presence
along the Park Avenue area in the Mile End district of Montreal.
Many of my peers mockingly referred to them as the "Park Avenue
White Sox" (after the famous Chicago White Sox baseball team)
because some of the men in the community wore breeches tied below
the knee so that their white-stockinged calves were visible below their
long black coats and above their slipper-like shoes. These Hassidim
not only appeared out of place but, to my surprise, seemed untouched
by the secular influences of the wider society (Shaffir 1995a).

The Hassidim are a success story, if success is measured by the
ability to retain a distinctive way of life that includes not only religious beliefs but also an abiding commitment to the norms and sanc-
tions that characterize the Hassidic sect with which the individual
identifies (Mintz 1992). To be sure, total uniformity is hardly possible, and as any observer of Hassidic life will attest, the variability in
lifestyle within the Hassidic community is best seen as falling along
a continuum. That said, however, identification with, and commitment to, a Hassidic way of life in line with the culture and ideology
of any particular sect remains impressive.

In what could not have been imagined but a few decades earlier,
today's Hassidic communities enjoy burgeoning numbers and a
plethora of institutions to meet their needs and rank extremely high
on any scale of "institutional completeness" (Breton 1964). Among
North American Jewry, Hassidim enjoy the highest birth rate at a
time when demographic analyses show the overall Jewish birthrate

to be declining (Shahar 2003). Significantly, this sizeable population increment is not matched by a defection stream warranting serious concern for the time being. Moreover, there is little evidence to indicate that the younger generation's commitment to the traditional Hassidic lifestyle is diminished; in fact, the reverse may actually be the case. As evidenced by an explosive birthrate and the ability to attract financial resources to sustain a widely diverse institutional infrastructure, matched by a heightened awareness of the economic and political clout that their numbers can exert in political circles, the commitment of the younger generation has not faltered.

Nevertheless, change (in some manner or other) is inherent in human activity, and the Hassidim are not an exception to that general rule. All communities seeking to insulate themselves must contend with outside influences; in order to do so, they organize a series of boundary-maintaining mechanisms that are intended to influence, shape, and regulate the behaviour of their members (not unlike the management of public/private boundaries in the Soviet communal apartment discussed by Över, this volume). However, although the leaders of Hassidic communities may initially succeed in regulating the pace of inevitable change, it now seems increasingly unlikely that they will be able to maintain the physical and social boundaries that they have hitherto succeeded in imposing. These boundaries have become more porous, and the impact of social change is already apparent. While Hassidic communities are often portrayed as a picturesque reminder of yesteryear caught in a time warp, they "are very much part of the modern world, struggling in a variety of ways against powerful social forces that threaten either to sweep them away or else transform them into something radically different" (Heilman 1995, xii).

In 1997, I wrote on changes I documented among the Tasher Hassidim in the community of Boisbriand in Quebec (Shaffir 1997b). I had first studied that group in 1987 and wanted to discover whether there had been any changes. I focused in particular on several demographic and institutional changes as well as on the Tasher's use of the media to enhance their agenda (Shaffir 1987). I found that an increasing number of unrelated incidents had brought the theme of change into clearer relief. Although each incident, by itself, might be seen as not entirely unusual, taken together they seemed to suggest that the community was in the throes of change, to use Gladwell's (2000) phrase, even if the tipping point had not been reached. First, I was beginning to hear about people who had divorced, and I had to revise my opinion that these people would not consider divorce, even if they had to deal with marital difficulties of a serious nature. Second, I was surprised at the extent of the activities in which they now engaged – activities that in earlier years would have been quite inadmissible to them but that they now claimed not to be that unusual or reprehensible. Most notable of these were visits to local bars and to sporting events. In 2004, a Hassid asked me to meet him at a fast-food restaurant, and in the course of our conversation there, he mentioned in a matter-of-fact, casual manner that he attended sporting events on occasion and had visited the local casino, while conveying the impression that he remained as firmly committed to the Satmar lifestyle as any of his deeply religious peers. It has also become increasingly clear that despite rabbinic prohibition, numbers of Hassidim whom I met were spending considerable time surfing the Internet just for purposes of pure enjoyment. Moreover, many of them assured me they were far from unique, that many of their peers did the same. Meanwhile, there had been a major tax scandal involving some individuals and institutions affiliated with the Boisbriand Tasher.

METHODS

My method of choice in the study of Hassidic Jews is ethnography with the help of participant observation and informal interviews. It is an appropriate method for two reasons: primarily because it enables the researcher to fully understand how Hassidim organize and make sense of their everyday lives and also because, since Hassidim strictly cloister their communities, only ethnographical methods are likely to succeed – certainly not formal interviews or replies to questionnaires (Becker and Geer 1957; Pawluch, Shaffir, and Miall 2005). In this case, an unexpected turn of events may have helped to reveal aspects of lifestyle that have been traditionally hidden from outsiders. Hassidim residing in the Mile End and Outremont areas of Montreal had to provide concrete evidence to support their entitlement to assistance, and a Hassid was appointed to spearhead a drive to conduct a needs survey of the target population. The Coalition of Outremont Hassidic Organizations (COHO) survey showed that Hassidim are not immune to such problems as care for the elderly, poverty, learning and development problems, and bleak employment prospects (Shahar 2005). In the process, stereotypes about Hassidim began to unravel: not all of them are content with their lifestyle, a proportion of the community has to live well below the poverty line, and both as a group and as individuals, their insulation from the mainstream does not succeed in keeping them unaware of the social, economic, and political climates obtaining outside their gates.

In addition to this survey material, I conducted a series of unstructured interviews with Hassidim residing in that area. Apart from such numerous conversations, I also completed eight informal interviews, three of them with women. The conversations were unplanned and typically occurred as I walked along the streets of the area and wandered into Hassidic-owned businesses to survey the goods. An additional source of data was the publications advertising Hassidic businesses and services; I relied upon the 2005–06 *Montreal Community Directory* prepared by the Beth Jacob Teachers Seminary, which encompasses both the Hassidic and ultra-Orthodox non-Hassidic residents of Montreal (including the Tasher in Boisbriand), as well as a weekly publication, *Quality Shopping*, which features (but is not limited to) advertisements of Hassidic commercial enterprises.

MACRO ELEMENTS OF CHANGE

The report based on the 2005 COHO survey reveals that while the size of the total Montreal Jewish community has been diminishing over the past three decades, the Hassidic and ultra-Orthodox populations have shown definite growth, doubling every fifteen years owing to the high fertility rate (Shahar 2005). This indicates starkly that the Hassidic community, in Outremont and the surrounding area in Montreal, has experienced change if only by virtue of a dramatic increase in population between 1996 and 2004. However, the explosive population growth has also been consequential in terms of the community's ability to provide for its own in times of need. As well, the Hassidic population has been compelled to respond to ongoing allegations of municipal improprieties that have been brought to the attention of legal authorities (Shaffir 2002). For the outside observer, the most tangible reflection of change lies in the increased numbers of Hassidic-owned businesses that are sprinkled through the neighbourhood, including supermarkets, bakeries, and stores selling prepared foods, photography equipment, furniture, and clothing. By contrast, in the past most commercial ventures were located in people's homes, a form of commercial enterprise that remains to this day, as evidenced by advertisements appearing in weekly shopping circulars distributed in the Hassidic community. The organization responsible for this transformation is COHO – the Coalition of Outremont Hassidic Organizations – which has professionalized the process by which Hassidic-owned business ventures are initiated and co-ordinated.

COHO was founded in 1996 and is situated in the heart of an upscale area of Outremont where it occupies three rooms on the second floor of an office building. These rooms are decorated with various photographs of COHO officials meeting with influential leaders of government up to the ranks of provincial premier and prime minister as well as provincial and federal cabinet members – a testimony to the political links that have been successfully cultivated over the years. COHO estimates that since its inception, it has helped to establish approximately 150 businesses, enjoying a success rate of between 60 and 70 per cent. The businesses vary in scope and include, as examples, stores selling photo supplies, shoes, picture framing, baked goods, jewelry, travel, groceries, and wedding supplies. In the final analysis, a person closely connected with the organization said that COHO offers business advice and, in reference to a particular business it helped to establish, remarked: "First of all, we gave him advice. The guy didn't know one end of a stick from the other. We got him a grant of $5,000 ... We got him loans, we taught him how to go to the bank, how to operate a business ... You know something? When you get married and soon have three, four kids, you don't have time to fool around. You have to make money. Whenever somebody comes in with an idea, we, COHO, help them develop it. We send them to this organization, this foundation that would give them some money. We direct them because they would never know what to do."

On the employment side, the organization helps individuals to complete resumés and offers career counselling and job placements. "About half of the clients are in their early twenties for business start-ups ... If they are ready to work hard, and why shouldn't they be, and with our advice, they can't go wrong," offers one of the counsellors.

The surveys that COHO commissioned reflect changes in the Hassidic population as well as identifying members' perceptions of their needs and changing circumstances. As well, indications of change can be seen in the range of business ventures that Hassidic Jews have undertaken in recent years. However, such a snapshot of

Hassidic life fails to fully appreciate the dynamic tensions that are experienced on the day-to-day level in the Hassidic community and that expose the more tenuous than imagined social and cultural boundaries in place to combat unwelcome foreign influences.

SOCIAL CHANGE CLOSER UP

I have argued elsewhere that regardless of their ideological stripe, Hassidic communities attach supreme importance to preventing assimilation by insulating their members from unfavourable secular influences of the host culture (Shaffir 1995b). The notion of boundaries and how they are maintained serves as an appropriate metaphor as Hassidim strive to close the circle around their chosen lifestyle by imposing strict measures of social control. As Kanter (1972) has observed, boundaries do more than define the group by setting it off in its environment but, in giving it the sharp focus, also facilitate commitment to its norms and expectations. The persistence of boundaries requires not only criteria and signals for identification but, as important if not more so, a structuring of interaction that allows for the perpetuation of differences, be these cultural, social, or political or more likely combinations thereof (Barth 1969; Mintz 1968).

Here I suggest that Hassidic Jews' efforts at boundary maintenance are meeting with increased resistance. However, the issue is not whether Hassidic communities fail to establish viable institutions to effectively control permissible contacts with outsiders but, rather, the degree to which the playing field has tilted over the past decade or so. For example, Hassidic sects continue to maintain separate schools for boys and girls, as in the past, and, as before, the secular curricular content remains closely supervised and even censored. The dramatic shift, rather, lies in the relative ease with which younger persons can access and interact with the outside world. While such contacts were not unknown in the past, they had to be practised surreptitiously to avoid detection. Avoiding detection today has been eased dramatically by the presence of a relatively new and expanding technology – the Internet (Levy 2004).

THE INTERNET

"The Internet is a real danger," remarks a Hassidic woman with whom I met. "It's the high-tech stuff that's a real danger to our kids, and it's so difficult to control," she adds. Such underlying concern about the media, very generally, and advances in modern technology was reflected in my conversations with Hassidic respondents. Levy (2004, 134) confirms this concern, writing that the Internet "represents the largest worry for the Haredi community ... as it allows any user uncensored access to virtually anything, without even looking for it." Hassidic leaders, and Haredi ones more generally, have typically issued religious decrees (*psak din*) against media as a threat to Torah and family values (Cohen 2006). However, the ban on computers and the Internet has not been entirely successful, with an estimated 40 per cent of Haredi houses in Israel having personal computers. Cohen (2006) notes that the rapid speed at which technology evolves has compelled Haredi entrepreneurs to market computer filtering programs.

In 2003, the Vishnitzer rebbe instructed his Hassidim to avoid the Internet, identifying it as a *sakoness nefoshess* – a threat to life. In a *pashkevil* – a poster with religious and social information in the form of a public statement – eleven Montreal Hassidic leaders discouraged Internet use because "It's already well-known to most people how dangerous a computer is, how many have fallen victim to it, may we be spared. And how many kosher people from decent homes have fallen due to the Internet? While it may have begun unwittingly, to their regret, they were corrupted and entire families have been destroyed" (quoted in the poster).

A Hassid I spoke with remarked: "There are many things going on in the world today, cellphones, let alone computers." He then asks: "You know about the kosher cellphones? Kosher means it's just a phone. Kosher means they cannot get the Internet. It's a phone, and that's it. Today telephones can do everything." Such kosher phones limit access to text messaging, video applications, and the Internet. A list of cellphone models that are considered kosher (appropriate) circulates within the community. Reflecting on this general theme, a Hassidic mother and grandmother considers the enormous threat posed by recent technological innovation: "We have the same problems right now that all parents, all over the world, are having, and that's the high-tech stuff ... The Internet's a threat to our kids too. You know the kids don't have access to computers. They have phones. Phones today are enabled to access e-mail ... All of a sudden, there's a whole big wide world out there, and you don't have control." The community's ability to exercise control is now lessened;

indeed, access to the Internet is even more insidious in that it enables contact with outsiders from the privacy of one's home, or from a computer, without requiring the inquisitive Hassid to come into actual physical contact with outsiders. A Hassid stresses the significance of this point this way: "Before, if you wanted to do something that wasn't allowed, like a movie, you had to go to the theatre, or if you wanted to read something that questioned what the rabbis said, you went to the library. No more. Today, with the Internet, I know many people that do these things on their computer."

The Internet, then, has magnified the opportunities for deviance, and deviant-related activities can be pursued anonymously. Of course, it is not the Internet per se but the unsupervised access to it that offers a range of activities and social worlds that were previously beyond the ken of the majority of Hassidim, particularly the younger, unmarried members. A Hassid underscores the opportunity dimension in this manner: "The biggest thing is opportunity. You know what we say? The mouse is not a thief, the hole in the wall is a thief ... Which means if there's no girls around, or nothing to steal, or whatever, you're not going to do it. [But] if there's opportunity." It is not surprising that opponents of the Internet emphasize its anonymity, underscoring the freedom it offers to express views and feelings that would otherwise be kept to oneself.

"Our Sages tell us," a woman from Satmar remarks, "that it's impossible that a person should not be influenced by his environment ... Everybody absorbs their environment and a little bit of the goyish culture. And what's going on in the street today," her voice trails off. It is not difficult for her, and for the others with whom I spoke, to identify problems that are confronting the Hassidic community and whose impact cannot be avoided. Two such problems, divorce and defection, are not novel conditions that were unheard of in the past; however, the number of such occurrences appears to have intensified, and their visibility has been enhanced. Such visibility bears consequences: their widening presence increases the possibility that they may be considered suitable options for others.

DIVORCE

In simple terms, divorce among Hassidic Jews has risen because of their greater numbers today. However, one can argue that Hassidic-arranged marriages remain more durable than marriages in the non-religious world and, more to the point, that divorce remains rare. Nevertheless, in 1992 Mintz claimed that while small in absolute numbers, by Hassidic standards there has been a divorce explosion. Writing some two decades earlier, Rubin (1974, 132) acknowledged that "[a] divorcee, once a stigmatized person, seems to have lost her stigma and has no apparent difficulty remarrying." I would suggest that divorce is more frequent not solely because of an increased Hassidic population but also because of changing expectations concerning quality of life, particularly as this pertains to Hassidic females. I caution the reader however, that my analysis here is somewhat tentative because of the relatively few divorced persons I had time to meet. As well, this is typically a sensitive topic to discuss, requiring the respondent to bare details of a personal nature that might compromise both self and others.

Divorce struck a chord with respondents not only because its consequences are generally unpleasant but because it generally hit close to home. For the majority, it was not an abstract topic about which one might speculate theoretically but a situation that had been experienced in one's family. A few illustrations from the data follow. In the first, I am sitting with a woman from Belz who is outspoken on issues involving the Hassidic community and sensitive about understanding that changing mores in the wider culture have influenced the status quo among the Hassidim. When I inquire whether divorce is more prevalent today than it was twenty years earlier, she replies: "Now you've hit home because my son just got divorced. I would say, let's go back twenty years, divorce was horrible, horrible. You really had to be something to get divorced. Now my friend's daughter lived with her husband three months. She decided he wasn't quite as smart as she thought he was, and she just left. And this is happening. Divorces, I would say I would hear about one a week."

Another female, already divorced and raising four children, echoes this view: "It's certainly a lot more than before. It's a real problem in the community because it never happened like this before. Don't misunderstand me," she adds, "the vast majority of marriages last, but the option [of divorce] is no longer impossible." Yet a third female, a mother of five children aged seven to fourteen, offers this perspective: "The big difference is that people your age are getting divorced. I mean, you hear about it in New York, but it's also happening here. When it happens to someone you know, a friend, it's natural to begin comparing. You also see that people survive the experience even though it's usually very painful. I just hope the problem doesn't get worse."

One explanation for this developing phenomenon centres on the particular needs of the individuals concerned. From·this perspective, the individual considers his or her needs to be supreme even if the ensuing behaviour – marital separation and divorce – violates the mores of the insular community. An example from the data follows as a Hassidic woman reflects upon a divorce in her immediate family: "Because of the 'Me' generation and the entitlement that has filtered down to our kids. When we got married, I knew I'm getting married, and if I had a problem I had to work it out. Today they get married, if there's a problem, I'm out of here ... The trouble is that nobody is willing to tolerate anything ... My daughter-in-law was with my son for two years. She didn't have any kids. She said: "You know what? I have a plan of the way I want to live my life, and it's not working out, so I'm out of there."

On the other hand, an explanation that is individual-centred, in the opinion of several informants, masks attention to gender considerations, the impact of which figures importantly in the divorce outcome. The next informant skillfully draws the connections between gender, secular education, and decision-making: "I would say 90 per cent it's the girls that are leaving. I blame, I shouldn't say I blame, but I could write a thesis that's because of the way the kids are educated. The girls get much more secular education. They are capable of going out and getting jobs as secretaries or whatever. The boy sits with the Gemorah. So until the night of his wedding he's told that girls are something you don't think about, you don't look at, la la la la la. All of a sudden he's got this female. She's been out there for a year or two. She starts working right about seventeen or eighteen, gets married at about nineteen or twenty. He's coming straight from the Gemorah, right? ... You take these girls, they have social skills."

As several informants indicated, this differential exposure of males and females to the outside world, whether in actual practice owing to employment or to secular studies within the confines of the school, contributes to perceptions of marital incompatibility that, in more cases than in the past, culminates in the dissolution of the marriage. Of course, divorces did occur in earlier years, but they were uncommon. More recent exposures to secular influences have resulted in unexpected repercussions. However, divorce is not the main repercussion of estrangement or discontent. Discontent and disillusion may lead to a Hassid becoming increasingly unhappy and isolated until the decision is made to leave the Hassidic community and its distinctive lifestyle.

ABANDONING THE HASSIDIC LIFESTYLE

Ricky was given my address by someone in Montreal who was familiar with my interests in Hassidism. She introduced herself in an email, stating that she had left her Hassidic husband but was still residing in a Hassidic neighbourhood and raising her six children. She said that she thought that I would find her experiences "very interesting." Some three weeks later, we met for coffee in a restaurant in her neighbourhood. She was modestly dressed, but her hair was not covered. We spoke generally about the Hassidic lifestyle, and she recounted some of the hardships she had endured before her final decision to obtain a divorce. On a later occasion, I was invited to her house – in the heart of the Hassidic area I was studying – and she showed me her wedding album and commented on members of the wedding party. She said that she had been vilified for securing a divorce and that some Hassidic women telephoned her, or even came to her door, and she specified: "One woman yelled that I'll burn in hell because of what I've done" and that there was great pressure from Hassidim in the neighbourhood that knew her "to raise the children Hassidic."

She particularly resented male privileges among Hassidim and their occasional hypocrisy. She claimed that one of her ex-husband's friends had propositioned her while she was still married, commenting that no one would need to know. She has completely dissociated herself from her native community, though she remains in contact with her mother and siblings. She said that she used to cover her hair but obviously no longer did so and added "And I'll wear short sleeves if I want to." Her friends and her children's friends did not include Hassidim. Despite having lost contact with her Hassidic peers, she occasionally heard of their activities. "Some of them I know are probably very content. They have a Hassidic family, there's a good chemistry between the husband and wife, and all's well. But I know of others ... that were stuck in a relationship, and what could they do? Where could they turn? You never hear about these women," she said. As it happens, one increasingly hears about them.

Mrs K, a Hassidic mother and grandmother who is not only involved in the community's affairs but also unusually familiar with events in the larger society, acknowledges that the Hassidic community has experienced unexpected change that is too painful to ignore. To her dismay, the Hassidic community has recently become the focus of filmmakers and academics who, in her estimation, have failed to do it justice. In the midst of our conversation about social changes, she suddenly focuses on this issue: "And that's another thing that infuriates me. The Hassidim, we're considered a very exotic species that's being put under the microscope more and more these days. [There's] an explosion of things written about Hassidim. And about what's written, all of it ... is sensationalized. Nobody can do a sociological study without having a sexual component in it." From her perspective, as soon as someone leaves Satmar, or one of the more well-known sects, a book is written about them. She is horrified by blogs appearing on the Internet in which Hassidim share their concerns and misgivings about Hassidic life in such a public forum. She is particularly charged about the recently published *The Unchosen* that details the experiential trajectories of individuals who have sought to leave the Hassidic fold (Winston 2005). "You get the impression that there are so many that have left, but it isn't true," she says. "I'm not saying it doesn't happen, but you get the impression there's an exodus."

While the actual number of Hassidim who have chosen to leave and sever ties with their religious upbringing has likely risen over the past two decades, the numbers are probably more contained than the exposés, whether in print or on film, suggest. As far as I know, reliable figures are unavailable. Indirect measures, however, could be reflected in statistics collected by an organization such as Hillel, in Israel, which documents the number of people contacting the organization as well as those attending its programs or using services it provides. In the cases of New York and Montreal more specifically, impressions about numbers of defectors are based largely on hearsay. However, any low count of formerly Hassidic Jews masks a more insidious development that appears to be causing considerable concern: those who have become marginalized while pretending to remain connected to the Hassidic lifestyle. Two Hassidim who chose to emphasize this concern – the first a female and the other a male – offer these appraisals: "I'm not worried about the ones that are checking out, but those that stay, [that are] like a worm in a rotten apple. There's a guy on the net who's a Hassid and a heretic ... I'm worried about the ones that are staying in the community and

leading a double life" and "It's hard to know who's being influenced
in which way and what they're thinking inside. When you see someone in shul wearing a shtreimel, what are you supposed to think?
He's kosher right? But people who are giving in to doubts and exper-
imenting are not so easy to detect, and they are the ones that can
spread poison." Those leading "double lives" carry a stigma that, in
Goffman's terms, is discreditable (Goffman 1959). They must learn
to craft a self-presentation that turns on deception – successfully
convincing others to believe that they abide by the norms of the
community despite strong inner doubts as to their relevance and
even legitimacy (Shaffir 1997a).

Here I must stress that in my experience with Montreal Hassidim
over the decades since I started my fieldwork research, and more
recently, I found no such serious problems of defection. To the best
of my knowledge, the actual numbers are minuscule: I have heard of
only four cases. Further, how leaving is defined should be seen as
problematic. One important distinction, for example, is between
those who are Orthodox from birth or Hassidic, in this case, and
those who, having become *baalei tshuvah*, decide to revert to their
non-observant lifestyle or remain observant but outside the context
of the Hassidic framework. However, there are many tales in
Montreal about those who have left the fold, and it is clear that there
is now a growing concern about the matter. During a conversation I
had with a Hassidic woman, she told me: "I just got off the phone
with my son in New York. His doorbell rang, he opened the door,
and there standing was his close friend who had cut off his *payess*
[earlocks]. My son was in shock."

Another Hassidic woman, living in Montreal, commented on the
changes that had occurred during the past three decades. She
bemoaned the present disappearance of what she called "intact families" and insisted that such families had been common in the past:
"I hate to tell you, mister, but there is almost no family out there
today that is totally intact. [And there were such families earlier?]
Yes, there were. Nowadays you can have a family of ten kids, and
you're going to find nine kids, eight kids perfectly following the
path, and you're going to find one or two that are totally out ... I
cannot think of a family, and I'm talking about an extended family
now ... everybody's got someone. It didn't used to be that way."

A Hassid made similar comments and then added: "You hear
about people, younger people, almost always, that drop out. It's

happening more and more today, and it's very sad. But it's not a major problem. If it was on a graph, it wouldn't show up. But it's happening more in New York, and so we hope it won't spread here."

CONCLUSION

The boundaries that traditionally separated the Hassidim from mainstream culture are more porous now, as is evident from the cases cited in this paper. However, I still find it hard to accept philosophically the changes that are occurring. When I said so to a Hassid whom I had come to know and who casually remarked that some of his Hassidic acquaintances frequented local bars to watch sporting events, he retorted: "What do you think? We're not human? You'd be amazed at what some Hassidic Jews are ready to try these days." At times imperceptibly, but more visibly on other occasions, Hassidim are responding to social change, which is driven both by internal community needs and by external social influences that can no longer be contained effectively. They will no doubt attempt to continue doing what they have done for decades: devise, co-ordinate, and negotiate tactics and strategies to preserve a cherished lifestyle. An excellent example concerns a recent controversy involving the Satmar in Montreal. The following excerpt from the *Hamilton Spectator* (2006) tells the story: "Some members of a Montreal YMCA and leaders of a neighbouring synagogue are involved in a spat over windows and the state of dress, or rather undress, of gym users. The congregation was upset that young boys and teens studying at the synagogue could look across into the windows of the "Y," and see sweaty bodies, stretching and bouncing about. So members of the Hasidic Jewish community raised money to have the windows frosted. Now some people who use the gym are upset because they've lost the view and the daylight and have begun circulating a petition to restore the original transparent windows."

In order to succeed, they will have to display even more ingenuity and creativity, and researchers will need to be even more persistent and ingenious to discover whether Hassidic leaders have been resourceful and vigilant in their battle for the hearts and minds of their young members.

In addition to the challenges to the Hassidic lifestyle coming from within the community, there are challenges emanating from the larger society. Indeed, recent events in Quebec reflect upon challenges

Hassidim are encountering in the sphere of secular education. Nowhere is this more evident than in the recently introduced legislation mandating the compulsory Ethics and Religious Culture (ERC) course for all students, in both public and private schools, from Grade 1 to the end of high school. The ERC course explores religious tradition in Quebec so that students can learn more about key figures and events associated with those traditions. For the course to succeed, plentiful and diversified resources must be available to encourage ethical reflection, including reference works, periodicals, newspapers, encyclopedias, and sacred texts. As well, students should have access to websites, museums and art galleries, historical texts, and audio-visual documentation. The issue is particularly problematic, since Hassidim, in general, give little attention to secular studies, especially for boys (Shaffir 2004). They not only consider them of no inherent value but they also view them as having a deleterious effect on Torah observance. Officials at Montreal's Hassidic schools maintain that many of the objectives of this course are irreconcilable with their convictions and that it is practically impossible for them to meet them. As well, they are dismayed by the government's declaration that no exceptions will be allowed. The media have been quick to spotlight government interactions with Hassidic school officials, and one may reasonably expect that the previous Hassidic strategy of either ignoring provincial educational guidelines, or procrastinating on their implementation, will be increasingly challenged in the public sphere.

REFERENCES

Barth, Fredrik. 1969. *Ethnic Groups and Boundaries: The Social Organization of Culture Difference*. Boston: Little Brown

Becker, Howard S., and Blanche Geer. 1957. "Participant Observation and Interviewing: A Comparison." *Human Organization* 16:28–32

Breton, Raymond. 1964. "Institutional Completeness of Ethnic Communities and the Personal Relations of Immigrants." *American Journal of Sociology* 70:193–205

Cohen, Joel. 2006. "The Religion–News Media Nexus in Israel." *Sociological Papers* 11(2):9

Gladwell, Malcolm. 2000. *The Tipping Point: How Little Things Can Make a Big Difference*. New York: Back Bay Books

Goffman, Erving. 1959. *The Presentation of Self in Everyday Life*. New York: Doubleday Anchor Books

Hamilton Spectator. 2006. 8 November, A4

Heilman, Samuel. 1995. Foreword to *New World Hasidim: Ethnographic Studies of Hasidic Jews in America*, edited by Janet Belcove-Shalin. Albany: State University of New York Press

Kanter, Rosabeth M. 1972. *Commitment and Community: Communes and Utopias in Sociological Perspectives*. Cambridge, MA: Harvard University Press

Levy, J. 2004. "Deviance and Social Control among Haredi Adolescent Males." PHD dissertation, McGill University

Mintz, Jerome R. 1968. *Legends of the Hasidim*. Chicago: University of Chicago Press

– 1992. *Hasidic People: A Place in the New World*. Cambridge, MA: Harvard University Press

Pawluch, Dorothy, William Shaffir, and Charlene Miall. 2005. *Doing Ethnography: Studying Everyday Life*. Toronto: Canadian Scholars Press

Rubin, Israel. 1974. *Satmar: An Island in the City*. Chicago: Quadrangle Books

Shaffir, William. 1987. "Separation from the Mainstream in Canada: The Hassidic Community of Tash." *The Jewish Journal of Sociology* 29(1):19–35

– 1995a. "Some Reflections on Approaches to Fieldwork in Hassidic Communities." *The Jewish Journal of Sociology* 27(2):19–35

– 1995b. "Boundaries and Self-Presentation among Hasidim." In *New World Hasidim: Ethnographic Studies of Hasidic Jews in America*, edited by Janet Belcove Shalin, 31–68. Albany: State University of New York Press

– 1997a. "Disaffiliation: The Experience of Haredi Jews." In *Leaving Religion and Religious Life*, edited by Motti Bar Lev and William Shaffir, 205–28. Greenwich, CT: JAI Press

– 1997b. "Still Separated from the Mainstream: A Hassidic Community Revisited." *The Jewish Journal of Sociology* 39(1–2):46–62

– 2002. "Outremont's Hassidim and Their Neighbours." *The Jewish Journal of Sociology* 44(1–2):56–71

– 2004. "Secular Studies in a Hassidic Enclave: 'What Do We Need It For?'" *The Jewish Journal of Sociology* 46(1–2):59–77

Shahar, C. 2003. *A Comprehensive Study of the Frum Community of Greater Montreal*. Unpublished document, October

– 2005. *The Hassidim and Ultra-Orthodox of Greater Montreal: A Needs Assessment and Populations Projections of the Hassidic and Ultra-Orthodox Communities of Greater Montreal.* Montreal: Coalition of Outremont Hassidic Organizations

Winston, Hella. 2005. *The Unchosen: The Hidden Lives of Hasidic Rebels.* Boston: Beacon Press

16

What Is "Genius" in Arts and "Brain Drain" in Life Science?

IZABELA WAGNER

Sociologists working in the Chicago tradition are well known for their studies of complex as well as marginal worlds (Chapoulie 2001; Humphreys 1970; Becker 1963; Sutherland 1937; Anderson 1923; Whyte 1943). While the entrance into such specific worlds is difficult for an investigator, ethnography and observation are methods that allow the unique possibility to study these phenomena, deconstruct stereotypes, and bring to light hidden processes. Thus, these methods are useful to the study of the elite universe, because such a milieu presents similar characteristics to marginal worlds. For instance, illegal practices (the process of selection during a violin competition), specific behaviour seen as marginal (excessive instrumental practice by young children), and hidden knowledge are present in the world of the violin soloist and the life-science scientist (Wagner 2004; 2006a; 2006b). Doing sociology in that professional universe requires years of fieldwork in order to obtain the trust of informants. This trust is the basis for fruitful collaboration, which allows for an understanding of the informant's point of view, the values that they privilege, and their culture. The participant's point of view is the first step in Chicago tradition–inspired inquiry.

I first studied the musicians' world in 1996 in Paris. Even though I partly belonged to this universe (as a child of musicians, piano and theory teacher, and mother of a violinist), I had to learn the specific rules and language of "soloists class" – the small world that is part of the classical music elite. I conducted my research according the main place of participant observation, playing several roles: a young virtuoso's relative (my position as participant observer corresponds to Adler and Adler's [1991] "parent-as-researcher" role), a translator, a concert organizer, a member of the association for young talents, a member of a host family during the time of violin competitions, and a sociologist. These various roles gave me the opportunity to cross several perspectives emerging from research data.

In my fieldwork, I closely observed the lives of ninety violinists and had frequent contact with nine teachers and thirty parents of young virtuosos. I collected data on the activity of more than twenty violin teachers. I observed lessons, concerts, rehearsals, parties, and other events, as well as an ordinary day-in-the-life of a soloist student. I conducted more than 100 formal semi-open audio-taped interviews focused on the biography of participants. Because of my strong attachment to this field, I was able to conduct several hundred informal interviews lasting from some minutes to four and a half hours. I followed the careers of the young students, kept in touch with them, and asked about their projects, competitions, concerts, accompanists, and problems. Some of my respondents agreed to recorded follow-up interviews with me, usually two or three times (with at least one-year intervals). This research was carried out in France, Poland, Germany, Spain, and Italy, with some research done in Canada and the US. In 2006, I stopped the systematic data collection; however, I keep in touch with some of my participants, following their careers from a distance.

My second project concerned laboratories specializing in basic research in molecular biology, genetics, and photosynthesis. I started my fieldwork in 2003 in a French laboratory, and I opened a new site of intensive fieldwork in Poland in 2006. In the meantime, I held short-term ethnographic sessions in Germany, Canada, and the United States. I observed not only laboratory life but also conferences, activities after work, and the free-time activities of researchers. I conducted more than 200 interviews with different categories of researchers at each level of their careers: from young PhD candidates to retired professors. Among these, I interviewed persons with excellent reputations and worked in close collaboration with Nobel Prize winners.

Because my research concerns people whose careers require a high level of geographical mobility, I travelled in order to follow them in their work. Indeed, the international dimension is very important in the lives of researchers who live as pilgrims (Mahroum 1999, 176).

They maintain close connections between laboratories of similar reputation and maintain contacts with numerous sites, travelling frequently and changing workplaces for some days to some years (Shapin 1996). For musicians (soloists), the situation is similar: their careers also require a high level of mobility. The soloists class and famous concert halls, as well as "good" laboratories, are international places of work in which people from different countries and cultures, speaking different languages, collaborate. In order to preserve the spontaneity of the interviews, I conducted my interviews in four languages: French, Polish, Russian, and English. The inhabitants of these international and mobile universes of musicians and scientists, who are perceived in their narrow specialty as top elites (by themselves as well as by their colleagues), have a high level of inter-acquaintance (in their narrow discipline), despite the fact that they are active in several places in the world. These actors easily recognize each other and can very quickly place one another in their respective worlds. Using the ethnographical method allows me to formulate a new understanding of these elite worlds.

THE OBLIGATORY PRESENCE OF "GENIUS": THE OUTSIDER'S PERCEPTION

The conviction that genius is necessary for achievement of artistic works is widespread. Like other people, sociologists are not free of the influence of this common knowledge, and frequently, in public or private exchanges, I've been asked for my opinion on the supposed necessity of "genius" in musical production. Sociologists influenced by philosophy and semiotic inquiry who analyze musicians' work, especially in Europe, frequently play with the concept of genius, showing that among strong social factors such as family origin, level of education, and specific context, some influence of the "it is difficult to explain" plays an important role in a musician's career. Elias's essay about the sociology of genius based on the Mozart case exemplifies this perspective. However, his essay is not convincing. He states that the genius is a romantic, which is not at all a precise notion, and claims that a genius is a person able to do things that a normal person can't do as a result of social and psychological factors (including the relationships of father–son, master–disciple), as in Wolfgang Amadeus Mozart's development (Elias 1991, 93). Elias's approach is one that I would characterize as an "outsider's" perspective on the music world. However, the artistic community is a complex social world that is difficult for an outsider to understand. In contrast to Elias's work, Tia DeNora's (1995) analysis of Beethoven is much more sociological and thus convincing because it is premised on the assumption that in order to see whether "genius" exists and what it means, the insider's perspective is of first importance.

MUSICIANS AND GENIUS IN ART: THE INSIDER'S VIEW

Following the Chicago tradition, which posits starting the inquiry from insider's point of view, I focused on musicians' use of the concept of genius. As the results of my fieldwork show, the use of the word "genius" concerns specific situations and involves specific categories of people. Musicians never use this word in internal discussions (exchanges between people who are musicians) but always use that word when speaking to outsiders, people who do not belong to the world of musicians. Similar use applies in the extension of the concept of "genius" through powerful synonyms, words with lower emphasis: talent, gift, virtuoso, and prodigy. The soloist performance (by a violinist) is an excellent illustration of this finding.

A typical situation in the universe of the young violinist trained to be a soloist is to play a virtuoso piece before a professor (who has never worked with him or her) to be evaluated. If there are no outsiders (those not belonging to the musician world) present, the comments of evaluators, and the eventual discussions between other violinists present, goes as follows: it "was played with easiness," has "huge potential," "was well prepared," was "well done!", showed "extreme mastery of technique," was "an excellent work," was a "professional performance," or was simply "good work." The import of these comments is related to the reputation of the person who formulates them. No such words as genius, talent, and/or gift are used in this context. In contrast, if the performance took place before outsiders, a performer's parents typically hear after the last note the evaluative sentence: "Your child is very talented!" or, less frequently, "What genius!" This evaluation is formulated especially for the parents of the performer, but what does it mean? Answering this question requires contextual data – namely, the age of the performer. If the violinist is seven years old, that opinion after his or her performance means: "Parent! You have to do everything in order to prevent wasting your child's potential!" If the performer is twelve years old, that same comment means: "I will take care of your child's education; if I do not, it will be too late for a soloist career." If the performer is over eighteen, it means: "This violinist has potential, but now it is now too late to think of a professional career. This performance is not good enough!" The latter situation rarely arises, because at that stage of violin education, parents are seldom present during the "auditioning process" (Wagner 2006b).

In the first situation, the sentence is positive – the teacher is enthusiastic and proposes to take care of the child's professional education. In the second situation, the verdict is less positive – this is the last moment for this child to start violin education and training at a higher level if he or she hopes to play as a soloist one day. Such a career is possible only if the parents immediately dedicate various resources in order to make up for lost time. The third situation leads nowhere – the violinist has potential, but at that age, he or she must be able to play very well, and the performance only reflected a wasted potential. The same judgment is positive when given of the performance of a seven-year-old violinist but negative when given of the performance of a violinist ten years older.

THE STRATEGIC USE OF THE LABEL "GENIUS"

Why do musicians use these categories (and other synonyms of "genius": talent, gift, virtuoso, prodigy) in discussions with outsiders and use completely different words when talking with insiders? One explanation is the strict separation of professional language into two categories: within the professional milieu and in communication with outsiders. Musicians focus their discussions on very specific problems, such as technique of play, choice of a work's interpretation, or collaboration problems. Such discussions are based on a different kind of vocabulary that contains specific technical words and expressions. This language is too difficult for a non-expert in violin performance to follow. Outsiders lack the knowledge necessary for understanding these professional discussions.

The second explanation for the use of such strong words as "genius" lies in their power to mobilize resources. Indeed, parents have to mobilize various resources so that their children can pursue this special kind of education. They must pay for expensive violin lessons (in Europe, between 100 and at least €250 for a single lesson), master class (as much as €300 per week), competitions (registration fee of about €100), travel (for the regular activities of a young soloist, several thousand euros annually), living expenses, scores, CDs, recording fees, violin maintenance costs, insurance, and interest on loans or mortgages. Some parents make many additional "sacrifices" in order to give their child a better chance of succeeding in professional training. Among the sacrifices I observed in my European fieldwork was moving the entire family – parents and other children – to a new country in order to follow a particular teacher and selling the family home in order to acquire an expensive, prestigious violin. Parents who are convinced that their child is a "genius" and that they have to prevent the waste of his or her "unique talent" (in the words of the teacher) organize their family life around that "reality." For instance, they might focus family life exclusively on this particular educational path and spend all their savings on this long-term project. Other people in the young musician's entourage might help the person judged a "big talent" to further his or her career by providing supplementary funding, helping to organize concerts, and providing an audience for the performance of a young virtuoso. This is similar to the Hassidic community's educational strategy, which is aimed at protecting Hassidic youth from Western teenager culture (Shaffir, this volume).

The third reason for using the word "genius" is to keep day-to-day instrumental practice hidden from the public. Keeping the young musician's extreme, daily exertions backstage protects newcomers and introduces them gradually to intensive instrumental practice. The public is more likely to want to buy concert tickets if they believe that a musician's wonderful performance is the fruit of genius, not the consequence of long hours of hard and extremely difficult instrumental practice.

The final explanation for the use of "genius" is the mask that hides the professional's knowledge of the proportion of candidates who ever succeed in attaining a virtuoso career as a soloist. In fact, the vast majority never reach that goal. Teachers maintain the illusion that such a prestigious career is possible and that the main condition is that a given candidate have sufficient talent. Very rarely do teachers tell parents or students that the soloist market is saturated and that it is almost impossible for a candidate to reach the position of soloist. All professional discourse is oriented toward attracting young candidates and convincing them, and their parents, that this radiant future is theirs to possess. When the possibility of lessons is raised following the audition, students are always described as "full of talent" and "full of genius." Talent or genius or lack thereof is the official explanation for success or failure. This discourse accompanies students throughout much of their education (about twenty years), and the pursuit of virtuoso education depends on the persuasive power of this message. The strong belief that the candidate is endowed with a huge talent – genius – is indispensable in this long process of professional socialization. Because teachers know that the longevity of their relation with students is crucial for their own career, they maintain a quasi-religious belief in the presence of genius, which is also necessary for attaining and maintaining a high-quality instrumental performance from their students. Teachers count among their former students at least some soloists, because these students' success builds a teacher's own career success, according to the process of career coupling (Wagner 2006a). However, they know very well how hard it is for a student to be placed as soloist in the classical music market. That is why the main goal for these teachers is not so much a soloist career for their students but the longevity of their teacher–student relationship, or rather, as they prefer to say, master–disciple relationship, which is the source of their salary. These four factors contribute to perpetuation of the widespread belief in the presence of genius in a music virtuoso's performance.

BRAIN DRAIN: THE CAREER OF A CONCEPT

My second example of the efficacy of the Chicago tradition in contemporary sociology is in validating and deconstructing the concept of brain drain, which is commonly used within economics, politics, and sociology as well in popular discourse. Many important institutions that handle the production of global statistics, the OECD among others, produce data that concern the phenomenon of brain drain (Widmer and Schneider 2006). The concept goes back more than fifty years – dating from the 1950s when scientists from the British Royal Society first used it to point out the massive migration of scientists and technicians from Great Britain to North America. As Pierpaolo Giannoccolo indicates in his literature review on brain drain (more than 350 publications examined), the concept has various definitions and derivations, such as brain circulation (EU Commission, definition), brain drain, waste drain, brain exchange (Giannoccolo 2004), and even motility or brain motility (Kaufmann 2002).

With the exception of rare studies such as Stark, Helmenstein, and Prskawetz's (1997) "brain-gain" analysis, which indicates the positive side of brain drain, the majority of researchers perceive this process of high-skilled worker migration as a negative process for poor countries, with the economic consequence of the waste of human capital. For example, Beine, Docquier, and Rapoport (2003, 4) state that "[t]he term 'brain drain' designates the international transfer of resources in the form of human capital, i.e. the migration of relatively highly educated individuals from developing to developed countries. In the non-academic literature, the term may be used in the narrower sense, and relates more specifically to the emigration of engineers, physicians, scientists or other very highly skilled professionals." And for some professions and countries, it could be that such analyses are correct. However, for researchers working in basic life-science research, use of this concept and conceptualization of researcher mobility in terms of "winners/losers" (or push-pull – a common perspective for migration studies) is not accurate according to my analysis – analysis grounded in a main assumption of Chicago sociology, which is the close relationship between concepts and contexts.

BRAIN DRAIN IN LIFE SCIENCES

If brain drain concerns "international transfers of resources in the form of human capital," it requires that the human capital change the country. According to this logic, the vision of "international transfer" supposes that if a Polish scientist works in the United States, this transfer occurs from Polish science into American science. But for the life sciences – even if we can attribute to a given scientist one single nationality (and in my field I often met scientists with dual nationality) – how can we determine the nationality of "science"? Do life-science laboratories have a "nationality"? Is establishing the "national" origin of the educational capital of scientists even possible? Does the migration of scientists constitute a one-way movement, which we can analyze according to the push-pull arguments? Finally, is the brain drain a problem for life-science researchers?

I address these questions based on my analysis of researcher activity in molecular laboratories. Is it possible to determine a Polish biology, a French medicine, or an American physics? Who dares to do that now? It might have been possible before the end of the Cold War because of international politics and the isolation of American physics (see Pestre and Dahan 2004). However, French physicians in the nineteenth century travelled around the world and closely collaborated with physicians in other countries to improve their knowledge and deal more effectively with cholera epidemics (Bourdelais 1987). Similarly, biological scientists (except secret military researchers) have for centuries crossed the borders of their countries to do research. Also, the main paradigm concerning science underlines its universal character; as Robert Merton (2002 [1973], 584) wrote, "the criteria and the request for scientific knowledge are not a question of national taste or culture." Knowing that, how can we agree with such statements as "the brain drain produces irreparable damage for Polish science?"

Finally, the organization of science and the division of labour inside the life-science world is international. Nowadays it is impossible to establish a nationality not only for a discovery but even for a basic experiment. For example, in the molecular laboratory, the researchers purify proteins. In order to complete this task, they have to conduct several manipulations and work with several products, which are ordered from various countries. In observed laboratories, the products frequently come from Germany, Switzerland, the US, or Korea regardless of the location of the lab. Equipment is bought in different countries as well – spectroscopes from the US, electronic microscopes from Germany or Japan, spin dryers from Great Britain, refrigerators from Italy, and pipettes from Germany, France, or Poland. The financial side of research is also international, and it is difficult to attribute the unique national source of such support (except for countries like the US or Russia). In Europe, basic research in molecular biology is financed by European organizations supporting research and various other national funding bodies. But the specialization that increases constantly in these sciences, as well as the narrow expertise necessary for the pursuit of these research projects, leads scientists to collaborate not only with scientists within the same laboratory but also with scientists in other laboratories around the world. Moreover, collaboration is favoured by research policy, especially since the creation of the EU and in competition with American science. Also, researchers who are looking for the best quality for their work – excellent laboratories with high reputations – work in collaboration. How in this international network of researchers, who sign their articles and publications by the dozens, can we determine the nationality of the author? Who is the winner? Who is the loser?

If we analyze the composition of an average laboratory in molecular science, we will certainly have trouble determining the nationality of the team, because in the majority of laboratories the people who work there are employed for a short time (two-, three-, or five-year contracts). Moreover, scientists working in these laboratories, especially in those that are perceived as successful workplaces, were educated in various countries. For example, the team of the European molecular biology laboratory I observed is composed of: a lab leader who is British; three post-docs, one from Japan, another from Holland, and a third from Poland; and PhD students from Russia, Germany, Korea, China, Italy, the US, Australia, Argentina, and Israel (the origin of students in Europe differs from that in the US, where Asian scientists are much more numerous). In this context, Mahroum's (1999) definition of scientists as Highly Skilled Globetrotters seems appropriate. Additionally, this international picture converges with another important ethos of science – communitarianism. Merton (2002 [1973], 586) underlined that "fundamental discoveries in science are the product of social collaboration and are the propriety of community ... Scientific ethic limits the right of propriety in science to the absolute minimum."

As a consequence of the internationalization of the world of researchers, which in Europe was promoted by political changes after 1994, and with the creation and enlargement of the European Union, the training of young scientists also takes place in several countries. Starting from their third year of study at university (from the age of about twenty-one), young Europeans participate in the Erasmus program (exchange of students between universities in different European countries). After six months or a year of foreign experience, they come back to their country of origin in order to complete their education and get their BS and MA degrees. After this first step of theoretical and practical education, the young scientists engage within PhD programs, which are not always in their own country, and the number of Polish PhD students who pursue their education abroad, for example, increases each year. Some of these students (mostly workers in research laboratories) spend a part of their PhD training in a laboratory in a different country, often to learn a specific technique that is not available in their own country. Afterwards, they return again to complete their exams and receive their PhDs. Immediately after that achievement, young researchers have to go for a post-doc contract, usually in another country, meaning that they move and change countries yet again.

The following short CV could be an example of such a trajectory: Peter is biologist, who got his BS at Warsaw University in Poland; two years later he got his MA at the same university, but his MA was based on work done in a laboratory in a research institute in Cardiff, Wales in which Peter spent a year. It was his first important work in a laboratory, and there he learned techniques that were not used in Poland at that time. Peter's doctoral training included six years of experimental work shared between two research institutions – Dutch and Polish – and he was awarded his PhD degree from a prestigious Dutch university. A few months after that, he won a prestigious scholarship (offered by Polish "Fulbright," a Polish fund for science) for a post-doc position at one of the National Institutes of Health (NIH) in the United States. After this one-year contract, he continued his research project thanks to the NIH post-doc contract. After a long stay in US laboratories and several prestigious publications, he hopes to get another post-doc contract or lab leader position in Europe.

As illustrated in the above example, training lasts in general about fifteen years, during which researchers frequently experience life in more than three countries and visit many more (for conferences and short contracts lasting several weeks). In the 1980s in Europe, this kind of trajectory was rare and was perceived in the community of researchers as an exceptional pathway representative of elite members only; today it is the regular experience in life-sciences training. It is rare for anyone to receive a complete education in molecular biology (and in several other life-science specialties) in one country (except, again, in the US). Thus, the conceptualization of that kind of mobility as a matter of push-pull is completely inadequate. Rather, mobility is an ordinary pathway for scientists in the twenty-first century and not at all a pathology requiring correction. It is not possible to reverse this mobility – instead, it is better to consider improving the quality of researchers' lives and creating better conditions for their mobile lifestyle. The mobility of researchers is an ordinary and necessary aspect of their career and an integral part of their professional life – they cannot be trained appropriately and they cannot work if they stay in the same place. Moreover, it is important to understand the insider's point of view – what meaning researchers give to the concept of brain drain. Several interviews focused on this question – what do you think about it? And the responses were always accompanied by smiles and jokes: "With pleasure I will follow my brain when it is drained by Americans!" Several cartoons depicted the popular opinion of researchers about brain drain, often drawn by researchers themselves.

Certainly, brain drain is a very useful concept for politicians and for institutions that study migratory waves. It is also used by some researchers close to policy creation activities (e.g. OECD researchers). But according to my ethnographical research, which was conducted in several countries among the community of life-science researchers, brain drain is an inappropriate way of understanding their specific mobility. Researcher mobility is not a pathology that needs to be addressed by brain return programs; rather, it is an ordinary career pathway in such international areas as the life sciences.

DISCUSSION

Several points should be considered in assessing in detail the impact of the Chicago tradition on these studies of elite worlds. The first is related to Hughes's particular attention to and strong focus on deviant cases. Hughes, and later Becker, urged new sociologists to consider these cases with special attention, because they have a particular and relevant role in sociological analysis. In the choice of my research fields, I had this advice in mind, and I tried never to forget that my fields were specific. But thanks to this specificity regarding their elite characteristic (which has as a consequence the extreme clarity of observing processes occurring inside these milieus), I have had an excellent opportunity to investigate complex social processes. I study these worlds with the tools provided from studies of marginal worlds. After detailed comparisons, it appears that several social processes that take place within these elite groups are in fact similar to processes within other social worlds (e.g., career coupling, Wagner 2006a). On the other hand, as Becker underlined (1998), employing extreme cases allows the transition into the abstract level, which is particularly useful for the transposition of the original analysis into other fields and situations.

But abstract knowledge should never drift far from field reality, because abstract analysis and second-hand data produce several biases that are difficult to detect. Because these biases constitute the ordinary part of scientific research, sociologists have to employ several preventive actions. Applying vigilance and logical thinking in order to avoid the numerous traps that confine us in old, well-established concepts is certainly not sufficient. Rather, it is through the process of the verification of concepts in the field that researchers avoid repeating their old mistakes.

Fieldwork was the main rule of Chicago sociologists. It constitutes the second element of the Chicago tradition that influenced my research. The use of ethnography seems to me obvious in the study of hidden phenomena (genius in arts) and dynamic processes (researcher mobility). The power of ethnography lies in its tools, which allowed me to verify a concept such as brain drain in the world of science. Starting from the actor's point of view, completed with the study of contextual factors (organization of scientists' work), my research shows that what is perceived as a negative process, named brain drain, is on the contrary a positive, ordinary, and crucial or even indispensable element of researchers' careers. Moreover, it is an indispensable element because it directly relates to creative thinking, the core of researcher activity. Similarly, thanks to participant observation, one of the main techniques of inquiry practised by Chicago sociologists, I was able to deconstruct the notion of genius in arts and show how musicians use this concept to control their social world and to assure the longevity of their activity in the very difficult context of a saturated market.

Participant observation seems particularly adapted to studies of elite worlds, especially in a very complex context of multicultural groups, frequently composed of international work teams. The investigation of multicultural (or multi-ethnic) groups requires deep immersion into these specific organizations. It is impossible to understand people originating from various cultures, often immigrants, socialized in different ways, and working together in "international workplaces" without long-term observation, long informal talks, deep relationships, and trust.

Finally, how dangerous are the unexamined and unproved generalizations that are so deeply present in our mind that even sociologists take them for granted and treat them as indisputable reality? As Latour and Woolgar (1979) argue for life sciences, an important part of our knowledge is a social construction born in interactions and negotiations among experts. Sociologists following the Chicago tradition respect this critical attitude. For example, Hughes brought into the light the dark sides of prestigious professions, work that had never been done before. Following this approach allows for inquiry independent of obvious "truths" and obligatory paradigms. Sociologists of the Chicago tradition, through their impact on the development of sociology, offer a rich array of methods, perspectives, and theories and thus provide a basis for the next century of sociological research. Taking into account the longevity of the Chicago heritage and observing the rise of contemporary interest in Chicago sociology in the form of re-editions and translations of "classics," numerous works devoted to this tradition and its reception in various countries, and the growing interest among the new generation of sociologists in this literature – from Anderson's *The Hobo* to Duneier's *Sidewalks* (1999) – we can expect that sociology (as this volume shows) will be fertile, thanks to the direct and indirect influence of the Chicago heritage. Qualitative sociologists will not be seen as mere survivors who practise their culture, treasuring their Chicago heritage, as a minority community and fearing extermination because of the supremacy of other paradigms. Thanks to Chicago sociology, the scientific community is accepting of ethnography as an indispensable tool in sociological study. As Bronislaw Malinowski stated, we have to employ ethnography "because people respect the rules as often as they violate them. This is why the human life escapes the mathematical methods" (cited in Young 2004, 122).

REFERENCES

Adler, P.A., and P. Adler. 1991. *Backboards and Blackboards: College Athletes and Role Engulfment*. New York: Columbia University Press

Anderson, Nels. 1923. *The Hobo: The Sociology of the Homeless Man*. Chicago: University of Chicago Press

Becker, Howard S. 1963. *Outsiders: Studies in the Sociology of Deviance*. New York: Free Press

– 1998. *Tricks of the Trade: How to Think about Your Research While You're Doing It*. Chicago: University of Chicago Press

Beine, Michel, Frederic Docquier, and Hillel Rapoport. 2003. "Brain Drain and LDCs' Growth: Winners and Losers." IZA Discussion Paper 819, Institute for the Study of Labor (IZA). http://ideas.repec.org/p/iza/iza-dps/dp819.html

Bourdelais, Patrice. 1987. *Visages du choléra*. Paris: Belin

Chapoulie, Jean-Michel. 2001. *La tradition sociologique de Chicago 1892–1961*. Paris: Seuil

DeNora, Tia. 1995. *Beethoven and the Construction of Genius: Musical Politics in Vienna 1792–1803*. Berkeley: University of California Press

Duneier, Mitchell. 1999. *Sidewalks*. New York: Farrar, Straus and Giroux

Elias, Norbert. 1991. *The Society of Individuals*. Oxford: Blackwell

Giannoccolo, Pierpaolo. 2004. *The Brain Drain: A Survey of the Literature*. http://www.statistica.unimib.it/utenti/WorkingPapers/WorkingPapers/ 20060302.pdf

Humphreys, Laud. 1970. *Tearoom Trade: Impersonal Sex in Public Places*. London: Duckworth

Kaufmann, Vincent. 2002. *Re-thinking Mobility: Contemporary Sociology*. Aldershot, UK: Ashgate

Latour, Bruno, and Stephen Woolgar. 1979. *Laboratory Life: The Social Construction of Scientific Facts*. Los Angeles: Sage

Mahroum, Sami. 1999. "Highly Skilled Globetrotters: The International Migration of Human Capital." Seville: Joint Research Center of the European Commission

Merton Robert. 2002 [1973]. *The Sociology of Science: Theoretical and Empirical Investigations*. 2002 Polish edition, edited by Norman Storer. Chicago: University of Chicago Press

Pestre, Dominique, and Amy Dahan, eds. 2004. *Les sciences pour la guerre, 1940–1960*. Paris: Presses de l'EHESS

Shapin, Steven. 1996. *The Scientific Revolution*. Chicago: University Of Chicago Press

Stark, Oded, Christian Helmenstein, and Alexia Prskawetz. 1997. "A Brain Gain with a Brain Drain." *Economics Letters* 55:227–34

Sutherland, Edwin H., ed. 1937. *The Professional Thief*. Chicago: University of Chicago Press

Wagner, Izabela. 2004. "La formation de jeunes virtuoses : les réseaux de soutiens." *Sociétés contemporaines* 56

– 2006a. "Career Coupling: Career Making in the Elite World of Musicians and Scientists." *Qualitative Sociology Review* 2(3). http:// www.qualitativesociologyreview.org /ENG/archive_eng.php

– 2006b. "La production sociale des violonistes virtuoses." PhD dissertation, École Haute Étude Science Sociale

Whyte, William Foote. 1943. *Street Corner Society*. Chicago: University of Chicago Press

Widmer, Eric, and Norbert F. Schneider. 2006. "State-of-the-Art of Mobility Research: A Literature Analysis for Eight Countries." http// www.jobmob-and-famlives.eu

Young, Michael W. 2004. *Malinowski: Odyssey of an Anthropologist 1884–1920*. New Haven, CT, and London: Yale University Press

17

Situating *The Hobo*: Romancing the Road from Vagabondia to Hobohemia

JEFFREY BROWN

Nels Anderson did not publicly acknowledge his personal experience as a hobo until nearly forty years following the original 1923 publication of his landmark work on the subject. In an introduction prepared for the 1961 Phoenix edition of *The Hobo*, Anderson confessed that his research was even more unorthodox than the new method of participant observation "gaining a vogue" among sociologists at the time. Anderson, in fact, was a participant in the "hobo way of life" for years before having any notion of observing it systematically. Indeed, embarking on the study of sociology at Chicago in 1921 was an attempt to leave the "hobo world" behind for good, a rather ironic goal given the frequency with which he returned to it as a subject of investigation in subsequent years (Anderson 1961 [1923], xiii). In his 1975 autobiography, *The American Hobo*, Anderson offered an explanation for his long silence about his own life on the road:

> The reason for keeping my past anonymous is understandable. I could not talk to fellow students about my background. I could anticipate too well their reactions, like trying to describe a foreign civilization. I let them believe that all the material in *The Hobo* had been assembled in Chicago's Hobohemia ... Among those who knew better it was a credit item to have had acquaintance with hobos and their way of life. But most people above the working class level reacted otherwise to these men who came from God knows where. If, as often happened, after *The Hobo*

appeared, someone asked me about my own background, I found ways to evade the question (Anderson 1975, 2).

By 1961, however, the hobo, and the immoderate reactions the figure provoked, had receded into history. Anderson could safely recount the unconventional life that had led him to the University of Chicago and the thesis research that produced his first and most important work. He had been born, we learn, into a peripatetic family. His father had become a migratory worker in the United States after arriving from Sweden in 1882 and continued to move frequently, with a growing family in tow, after Anderson's birth. "In his own way," Anderson recalled, "he saw the road as adventure. He never heard of Walt Whitman, but his thinking about the open road was no different" (Anderson 1961 [1923], vii). Anderson followed in his father's footsteps, becoming a hobo mule skinner, railroad worker, tunnel digger, hard-rock miner, and lumberman, while travelling the country, as he put it, "in pursuit of experience" (Anderson 1961 [1923], viii–ix).

The anecdote suggests something of the ambivalence that attended the "the hobo" during Anderson's lifetime, represented, by turns, as a racially degenerate menace, a comic buffoon or rogue, a heroic individualist, a seeker and rebel, and a social problem amenable to rational amelioration. Anderson's experience on the road between 1906 and 1917, and his sociological analysis of hobos at Chicago in the early 1920s, were deeply informed by this fraught interpretive context. I'd like to explore the complex and contested image of the alienated wanderer in American intellectual and popular culture during the late nineteenth and early twentieth centuries. I will focus, particularly, on the dialectic of stigmatization and romanticization that pervaded interpretation of life on the road during these years. How did Anderson himself, and his monograph, *The Hobo*, construe and respond to this dialectic?

First reports of the rise of a dangerous new species of social outcast, the "tramp," came amidst the deluge of bad news that followed the financial panic of 1873. The production of the "tramp menace" – in the media, academia, and popular culture – reflected the anxiety of an established order for which vagrancy seemed a dire portent of social disintegration: "As we utter the word Tramp there arises ... before us the spectacle of a lazy, incorrigible, cowardly, utterly depraved savage ... insolent and aggressive when he dares, fawning and obsequious when he thinks it more prudent to conciliate, but false, treacherous, ungrateful and malignant always, [the tramp] wanders aimlessly from city to city, from town to town, from hamlet to hamlet, wherever he goes, a positive nuisance and a possible criminal" (in Seelye 1963, 541).

These words, uttered by Yale professor Francis Wayland in an address to the American Social Science Association in 1877, epitomize the hard line taken against unemployed drifters by arbiters of the dominant culture. From the first identification of the tramp menace in the 1870s through the Great Depression of the 1930s, the greater part of the mainstream discourse on homeless transients was saturated with derision. In the late nineteenth century especially, the hobo appeared as one of a host of threatening signs of working-class unrest. Reports of gangs of tramps hijacking freight trains added to mounting evidence of an epidemic of disrespect for property and authority among the "lower sorts." The rhetoric of the tramp menace emanated from the same fear that compelled the building of armouries in urban centres and the organization of citizen militias to protect affluent neighbourhoods from rioting workers (Lears 1981, 31). Wayland's diatribe was thus an aspect of a broader invective directed against the "dangerous classes" in general: tramps, criminals, strikers, political radicals, racial minorities, and foreign "elements." His portrayal of the tramp as a "depraved savage" exemplifies the theme of racial recidivism running through this discourse. Tramps and other undesirables were depicted as biologically defective – as evidenced by beady eyes and sloping foreheads. Not only were such types dangerous and despicable in their own right, they posed a threat to civilization itself.

Despite the zeal with which pundits attacked mobile workers and wanderers, there were inconsistencies embedded in the dominant rendering of the tramp as menace. One discrepancy derived from the economic changes that both generated and made indispensable a fluctuating population of migratory workers. The burgeoning industrial system of the United States both routinely uprooted masses of workers during the boom and bust years following the Civil War and demanded rapidly mobilized, temporary concentrations of labour for the expansion of its infrastructure. Hobos comprised the fodder of a highly mobile labour force. They laid the track, blasted the tunnels, graded the roads, cut and milled the timber, extracted the coal, oil, and other minerals, constructed the towns and factories, and harvested the crops. Paradoxically, the object of the scorn of respectable society was also, at least in part, the raw force behind its prosperity (Anderson 1961 [1923]; Allsop 1967).

The instrumentality of the itinerant worker was rarely acknowledged, however. Lapses in the general reprobation of the hobo were more frequently associated with the persistence of older and alternative models of adventurous or insouciant mobility. The 1877 account by Allan Pinkerton, *Strikers, Communists, Tramps, and Detectives*, illustrates this theme. The founder of the notorious strike-breaking detective agency, Pinkerton's descriptions of what he calls "the tramp in the offensive sense" are consistent with the rhetoric of the tramp menace. "They seemed to be a tired, dreary, wretched lot," he writes of a group of hobos, "most ... had fallen upon the ground for rest, and in all sorts of sluggish positions were dozing in a stupid, sodden way that told of brutish instincts and experiences" (Pinkerton 1969 [1877], 59–60). But Pinkerton also notes the positive aspects of wandering, attributing to it a mysterious enjoyment that he links to "natural beauty," "freedom from care," "adventure," and "the utter absence of responsibility." "No person," he proclaims, "can ever get a taste of the genuine pleasure of the road and not feel in some reckless way ... that he would like to become some sort of a tramp" (Pinkerton 1969 [1877], 26). Pinkerton identifies the American hobo with an earlier picaresque tradition of carefree wanderers and nature-lovers and even praises tramping for the vigour and independence it has the potential to instil. The tramp, he suggests, has a thing or two to teach those wealthy and educated men who "are utterly wanting in self-reliance and experience": "Take a man who has had to use his wits to fill his stomach, who has passed from one county ... to another in that painfully slow way that the tramp is compelled – who has had to brighten and quicken every faculty in his efforts to evade police, to keep clothed, to make roadside friends, to get work – for all tramps are not shiftless vagabonds – and often to sustain life, and he has obtained a self-reliance, a wonderful knowledge of the world, and a rare observation of men and things that gives him a peculiar advantage whenever he is in a position to use it" (Pinkerton 1969 [1877], 36).

Pinkerton's incongruous approbation hints at a certain discomfort with the civility and predictability of the settled life, a vague uneasiness increasingly common among the late Victorian bourgeoisie. The understanding of experience as something to be deliberately pursued by those who believed themselves insulated from "real life" was reflected in a complex range of cultural developments. These included the proliferation of a literature of action, including both the advent of an activist brand of social realism and a new romanticism of high chivalry and adventure; the drive for more honest and authentic ways of living, exemplified by the settlement house movement and a host of utopian and craft communitarian schemes; and the "cult of the strenuous life," manifest in tendencies as diverse as the surge in martial spirit accompanying American adventurism abroad, the allure of the Alaskan gold rush, and the vogue for rugged outdoor sports, leisure, and amusement. By the early twentieth century, the road, too, would figure, in some quarters at least, as another venue for bourgeois regeneration and masculine self-formation (Lears 1981; Lasch 1991).

Paralleling the road's rise as a means to intense experience was its elevation as a platform from which to expose the absurdities and pretensions of an America undergoing tumultuous material and social change yet strangely static in its everyday assumptions and conventions. While the tramp as menace continued to make regular appearances in the news and editorial sections of late-nineteenth-century American papers, a far different rendition of this figure found a home in the funny pages. In his cartoon version, the tramp gradually emerged as pitiful buffoon and comic rogue and acquired a mass audience and powerful cultural resonance in the process. The late-nineteenth-century comic tramp served primarily as an object of scorn and ridicule. Tramp cartoons, like comic representations of other categories of the "dangerous classes," conflated social subordination and biological inferiority. As with the ruthlessly stereotyped ethnic minorities with whom he shared the page, the comic tramp was racially defective as well as a fool and a failure; indeed, these attributes presupposed one another (Brasch 1988, 28–30; Cresswell 2001, 130–70). Yet while racial derogation tended to isolate the tramp from the sympathies of mainstream society, his portrayal as an innocuous buffoon – disagreeable perhaps, but ultimately harmless – softened the hard edge of hostility so pervasive in the discourse of the tramp menace.

Frederick Burr Opper's "Happy Hooligan," whose debut in *Puck* in 1900 inaugurated a thirty-year run in a variety of publications, introduced an element of pathos to the caricature of the hobo. The Hooligan, with his bizarre features, outlandish rags, and tomato can hat, cut an even more pathetic figure than the cartoon tramps who preceded him. He was the quintessential fall-guy, the victim of sadistic slapstick pranks and his own foolish misadventures. To be sure, the brutality with which the Hooligan was routinely visited delineated a dark side to the audience's commiseration. Behind sympathy for the Hooligan's victimization lurked deeper currents of superiority and sadism. Nonetheless, an essential component of the Hooligan's appeal transcended his cruel pummelling. Opper's strip rose above sadism because of the Hooligan's perpetually thwarted good intentions – admirable purposes that, tragically, seemed to make a beating more, rather than less, inevitable. As the archetypal victim of circumstances, the Hooligan, try as he might, always wound up the loser (Opper 1977). This was a new permutation in the evolving image of the comic tramp. Conceiving of the tramp as a victim was in itself a departure from previous formulations; conceiving of the tramp as an underdog was a direct confutation of dominant cultural forms.

Identification with the tramp-clown as underdog provided an element of reassurance to a mass audience confronting the confusions and frustrations of rapid economic and institutional modernization. These issues, of course, were faced directly by the Happy Hooligan's most celebrated successor, Charlie Chaplin's apotheosis of the tramp-clown underdog: the Little Tramp. Chaplin's film characterization of the Little Tramp, beginning in 1914, struck an essential cultural chord. In contrast to the Hooligan, who finished every episode in the "hoosegow" or with a bulldog hanging from the seat of his pants, the Little Tramp inevitably vanquished the villain and won the heart of the damsel in distress. Often prevailing over nefarious or dull-witted bosses and bureaucrats or surmounting the inanities of a bewildering urban-industrial landscape, Chaplin's tramp character engaged his audience in the surmounting of impossible odds. The Little Tramp's triumph, however, stemmed not only from his disarmingly charming brand of innocence but also from a surreptitious, at times even cunning, heroic agency. In this respect, Chaplin's character was prefigured less by the Happy Hooligan than by James Montgomery Flagg's Nervy Nat. Another icon of early twentieth-century graphic humour, Nat appeared in *Judge* between 1903 and 1907, was revived by other artists through 1916, and eventually featured in some early animated films. The mischievous antithesis of the Happy Hooligan, Nat engaged in a more volitional brand of escapade. Flagg's tramp was a no-account rogue whose adventures consisted in outsmarting more powerful, clever, well-bred, and beguiling adversaries: brutish cops, haughty plutocrats, venal politicians, and saucy shop-girls among them. The worldly Nat was distinguished especially by his command of the English language; he had a proclivity for upbraiding his opponents with a clever and elaborate turn of phrase (Horn 1980, 413). Nat was an instigator, not a victim, and in contrast to his comic counterparts, his exploits were more courageous than they were villainous or ingenuous.

In his tentative delineation as a heroic agent, the comic tramp contributed to the coalescence of an image radically out of step with the dominant representation of the hobo as menace, miscreant, and racial throwback. Enid Welsford, in her classic study of the fool in literature, elucidates the subversive vitality of the eccentric/absurd outsider: "whenever the clown baffles the policeman, whenever the fool makes the sage look silly, whenever the acrobat defeats the machine, there is a sudden sense of pressure relieved, of a birth of new joy and freedom" (Welsford 1935, 318–19). The trope of exultant liberation connects the comic tramp of popular culture to the iconoclastic rebel-hero beginning to emerge in avant-garde literary and political circles early in the new century. Anderson, for his part, was well aware both of the physical existence and of the cultural currency of this sort of intellectual vagabond. Indeed, in his description of Chicago's "Main Stem" district, Anderson presents him as a distinct type with a particular habitat: "Here a class of transients have drifted together, forming a group unlike any in either of the other areas of Hobohemia. This is the region of the hobo intellectuals. This area may be described as the rendezvous of the thinker, the dreamer, and the chronic agitator ... They alone come here who have time to think, patience to listen, or courage to talk ... To the 'bos' it is "Bughouse Square" ... quite as much the stronghold of the more or less vagabond poets, artists, writers, revolutionists of various types as of the go-abouts. Among themselves this region is known as the village" (Anderson 1961 [1923], 8–9).

The contrary epithets for this space, the "village" for its idealistic denizens, the "bughouse" for the hard-core vagrants on its outskirts, locates something of the social and cultural cleavage between the hobo and the intellectual vagabond. Yet there is a crucial interdependence here as well, for much of what was written of "Hobohemia" issued from the pens of those literate rovers who plumbed its depths. These writers were often not of the hobo mass at all, their forays on

the road temporary exercises in youthful defiance, romantic alienation, social protest, sociological study, or some combination thereof
(Brown 1992).

The best-known prototype of this figure originated from the popular *Songs from Vagabondia* series of Richard Hovey and Bliss
Carman. Highly educated sons of the upper bourgeoisie, Hovey and
Carman met in Boston in the summer of 1887 and bonded over their
common love of literature and hatred for the materialist temper of
the day. Literary realism, they believed, was the unfortunate corollary
of the latter, and both dedicated their creative powers to reinvigorat-
ing a romantic and ennobling literary aesthetic (MacDonald 1957,
29). Appearing between 1894 and 1900, *Songs from Vagabondia*
promoted vagabondage as a vigorous alternative to the enervating
domesticity of the late Victorian era: "Off with the fetters/That chafe
and restrain/Off with the chain!/Here Art and Letters/and Myrtle
and Wanda/and winsome witches/blithely combine/Here are true
riches/Here is Galconda/Here are the Indies/Here we are free/Free
as the wind is/Free as the sea/Free!/Houp-la!" (Carman and Hovey
1894, 1). Hovey and Carman sought to create a more virile persona
for the literary man. "We had become so over-nice in our feelings, so
restrained and formal, so bound to habit and use in our devotion to
the effeminate realists," complained Carman in 1894, "that one side
of our nature was starved ... We must have a revolt at any cost"
(in Lears 1981, 106). The protagonist of their rebellion was the
vagabond poet, a man who combined literature with the lustiest of
proclivities: wine, women, song, stout comradeship, and the carefree
joys of the open road. The wandering celebrated in these slim
volumes, however, was intended to be of an entirely different variety
than that of tramps. Indeed, when a British reviewer described Hovey
and Carman as "two American hobos," Hovey's wife Henrietta
fumed: "To think their taking Richard for a vagabond! Why, he is
without exception the most aristocratic nature I ever knew or heard
of! Only an aristocrat would write nonsense and play at vagabond
... Anyone would know [that the poems are the work of] intelligent
men in holiday mood ... Think of dubbing their plein air school mere
hoboism, with its Saxon lustiness, its gypsy freedom [and] the virility
of Carlyle, Henley, Stevenson, and Kipling in it!" (in Miller 1985,
127–8).

Romantic literary wanderers following Hovey and Carman discovered that "Vagabondia" was frequented less by rovers of "aristocratic

nature" than by transients engaged in the "mere hoboism" Henrietta Hovey decried. No doubt inspired as much by Whitman – whose verse celebrated the open road, in part, as an arena for encounters with common folk – as by Hovey and Carman, the young men who became vagabonds around the turn of the century viewed their journeys not only as geographic and imaginative excursions but also as *incursions* into an unfamiliar and perilous social world. The hobo's road held multiple possibilities for these adventurers: an escape from the limits and predictability of home and habit; a tonic against self-doubt, anxiety, lethargy, and other "nervous" ailments; an experience of "real-life" adversity expected to pay dividends both in the form of masculine vitalization and literary inspiration; and a transgressive education in the trials and tribulations of social and cultural others ostracized by bourgeois society. Such possibilities were explored in various ways by different individuals. There were proto-ethnographers, such as Walter Wyckoff and Josiah Flynt, who passed as "down and out" in order to investigate and describe, often in lurid detail, the life of the mobile "other half" (Higbie 1997; Pittinger 1997). There were adventure writers, Jack London most prominent among them, who used their experiences on the road as dramatic material for journalistic and fictional work. And there were tramp poets, such as Vachel Lindsay and Harry Kemp, intent on following a more strenuous road and producing more muscular verse than Hovey and Carman. The "hobofication" of the intellectual vagabond and its correlate, what Rolf Lindner calls "the bohemianisation of hobo existence," proceeded along the distinct, but frequently converging, trajectories laid down by these different sorts of writers (Lindner, this volume).

Significantly, whether producing poetry or putatively scientific social analysis, these intellectual vagabonds all embraced variants of the realism spurned by Hovey and Carman. Both the mildly bohemian neo-romanticism of the 1890s as well as the domestic realism it disclaimed had, by the turn of the century, been eclipsed by more socially engaged and naturalistic forms of the genre. The new realism challenged the proprieties and conventions of the dominant culture through its unvarnished depiction of the "reality of a world of struggle," a world customarily sanitized or obfuscated in "polite" society (Lears 1981). As a vivid signifier of this reality, and, conjointly, a subject proscribed from disinterested, much less sympathetic, mainstream discourse, the hobo was an obvious target for explication by cultural dissidents.

Walter Wyckoff was the first to exploit this prospect. Setting out from Connecticut, penniless, in the coarse dress of a migrant worker, Wyckoff tramped around the country for a year and a half, exploring the "labour problem" first-hand. He hopped freights and worked at factories, mines, lumber camps, railroads, and farms. Wyckoff's observations from the journey were gathered in two volumes appearing in 1897 and 1898: *The Workers: An Experiment in Reality, East and West*. Like Pinkerton, Wyckoff embraced the idea that the hardships of the voyage would result in positive gains in character, knowledge, and experience: "One week ago I shared the frictionless life of a country seat. Frictionless, I mean, in the movement of an elaborate system which ministers luxuriously to the physical needs of life ... Now I am out of all that, and am sharing instead the life of the humblest form of labour upon which that superstructure rests. And whatever may be its compensations, they are not of the nature of easy physical experience ... but there was promise of adventure and almost a certainty of solid gain in experience (Wyckoff 1903, 3).

The "compensations" of this new life are explicit in Wyckoff's narrative. Foremost are the psychic and physical benefits of meeting the protean challenges of a foreign environment. Throughout *The Workers* we are informed of the painful encounter with a milieu far more austere and unpredictable than either Wyckoff himself or his readers might have imagined. Hence, at the dramatic core of Wyckoff's account is a tale of the arduous adaptation to the hobo's road on the part of an over-civilized minister's son and Princeton graduate.

Wyckoff revels in the physical and emotional immediacy of survival on the margins of civilization. "When life is lived in its simplest terms," he reflects, "one is brought to marvellous intimacy with vital processes" (Wyckoff 1904, 41). Even despair tastes pristine, elemental: "Baffled and weakened, you are thrust back upon yourself and held down remorselessly to the cold naked fact that you, who in all the universe are of supremest importance to yourself, are yet of no importance to the universe ... There remains for you simply this alternative: Have you the physical and moral qualities which fit you to survive?" (Wyckoff 1904, 1–2). Here are the outlines of what would become, in London's work, the essence of the hobo's heroism: dogged triumph in the primal struggle for existence. Yet while Wyckoff clearly recognizes the cogency of this struggle, he fails to develop a heroic mode within it, either for himself or for the hobos he describes. Indeed, Wyckoff's tramps seem, for the most part, to deserve their misery and degradation: "How widely severed from all things human is the prevailing type! Their bloated, unwashed flesh and unkempt hair; their hideous ugliness of face, unreclaimed by marks of inner strength and force, but revealing rather, in the relaxation of sleep, a deepening of the lines of weakness, until you read in plainest characters the paralysis of the will" (Wyckoff 1904, 37).

There are exceptions to the biologically and morally defective "prevailing type," however. These more evolved hobos claim Wyckoff's unmitigated sympathy. Notably, it is not weakness of will or deficit of character that explains the exile and suffering of these men but the incomprehensible fluctuations of industrial capitalism. One may detect a marked indignation in Wyckoff's account of the blighted Chicago labour market and a keen awareness of his own dehumanization in the face of its determinations. Describing himself as a "hungry human body" with physical energy for hire within a "like multitude of unemployed," he is bewildered by the irony of want in the midst of "ceaseless productivity." "Everywhere there is work, stupendous, appalling, cumulative in its volume and intensity," and yet, at the same time, "men everywhere are staggering under burdens too grievous to be borne" (Wyckoff 1904, 47). Here again are the preconditions for a kind of heroic agency in the economic refugees of *The Workers*, in a political rather than a naturalistic sense. But Wyckoff is no more interested in the hobo as an agent of class conflict than as a fighter in the evolutionary struggle.

The same was true of Wyckoff's fellow "class-passing" proto-ethnographer, Josiah Flynt. Flynt's highly popular *Tramping with Tramps*, published in 1899, offers an even grimmer portrayal of hobo life than *The Workers*. He castigates the tramp as a "discouraged criminal" who "laughs at law, sneers at morality and gives free rein to appetite" (Flynt 1907, 108). Such depictions, however, serve mainly to bolster Flynt's own stature as intrepid explorer. He represents the "real road" as a kind of parallel dimension, invisible to the uninitiated of respectable society but existing nonetheless – shadowy, menacing, and seductive: "Such is the geographical nearness of Hoboland to Civilization, and yet when you start out to explore it a journey to Africa seems more easily accomplished. To those who know its highroads and byways, however, it can be entered and left by the very thoroughfares which traverse our towns and villages, where its inhabitants knock at the doors for alms, and a few minutes later have returned to their mysterious country" (Flynt 1968 [1902], 44).

The "mysterious country" Flynt delineates is fraught with danger and best avoided by all but the most savvy and stalwart middle-class adventurers. The naive or fainthearted, he warns, might easily succumb to the addictive "wanderlust" that makes "change and variety [seem] so essential that they are unable to settle down anywhere" or be lured into a life of drifting and dissipation by sexually predatory hobo "jockers" (Flynt 1907, 54).

Jack London dedicated his 1907 collection of tramp stories, *The Road*, to Josiah Flynt – "The Real Thing," London called him, "Blowed in the Glass" (London 1967 [1907]). In a 1901 letter to Cloudesley Johns, an aspiring writer and occasional vagabond, London discloses something of the rationale behind his admiration: "Wyckoff is not a tramp authority. He doesn't understand the real tramp. Josiah Flynt is the tramp authority. Wyckoff only knows the workingman, the stake-man, and the bindle-stiff. The profesh are unknown to him" (in Labor, Leitz, and Shepard 1988, 259–60). Flynt's credibility, for London, hinges on his authenticity as a "real tramp" or "profesh" – a tramp, that is, as one who specializes in evading work rather than seeking it. Wyckoff's preoccupation with those who work, and corresponding disdain for those who do not, was enough to earn London's disapprobation. A hard-drinking agnostic socialist, London was doubtless also irritated by Wyckoff's sanctimonious abstinence and Protestant reformism. And he found Wyckoff's "scientific" sociological style too dry – bloodless – for its subject matter. In another correspondence to Johns, London criticizes his friend's draft essay on "the philosophy of the road" by identifying it with Wyckoff's approach: "He treated it scientifically, and empirically scientifically ... Your style should be different. You are handling stirring life, romance, things of human life and death, humor and pathos, etc. But God, man, handle them as they should be" (in Labor, Leitz, and Shepard 1988, 191). London's search for a discursive mode capable of conveying the drama of life on the road would help to shape the "activist," or, as London himself termed it, "passionate," realism that became his stock and trade (Lears 1981; Wilson 1985, 101–2). By constructing the hobo's road as a testing wilderness, Flynt facilitated London's literary interpretation of his own tramping experience, while Wyckoff – in London's estimation – did nothing to advance the hobo as a dramatic protagonist.

Ironically, however, it was Wyckoff's work that came closest to positioning the hobo as an agent of evolutionary and political

struggle, precisely those spheres of action in which London elaborated
the hobo's heroic qualities. London's hobos are represented, on the
one hand, as victims of a sick society, cast into the social pit by the
blind forces of capitalism, and on the other as self-conscious rebels
against the system that oppresses them, chasing an ideal of freedom,
masculine self-determination, and the joys of mobility and conflict.
Their heroism lies not in their suffering but in their activism. Fittingly,
London's own social consciousness was awakened on the road. In the
1903 essay "How I Became a Socialist," he tells of riding "on rods and
blind baggages" to the "congested labor centers of the East," where he
learned to "look upon life from a new and totally different angle": "I
had dropped down from the proletariat into what sociologists love to
call the 'submerged tenth' ... I found there all sorts of men, many of
whom had once been as good as myself and just as blond-beastly;
sailormen, soldier-men, labor-men, all wrenched and distorted and
twisted out of shape by toil and hardship and accident, and cast adrift
by their masters like so many old horses. I battered on the drag and
slammed back gates with them, or shivered with them in box cars and
city parks, listening the while to life histories which began under aus-
pices as fair as mine, with digestions and bodies equal to and better
than mine, and which ended there before my eyes in the shambles at
the bottom of the Social Pit" (in Etulain 1979, 99). Those not defeated
by toil and poverty – the most vigorous and self-willed – chose hobo
activism over economic expendability. London sketches their trajectory in "The Tramp" (1904):

> If he be of a certain calibre, the effect of the social pit will be to
> discourage him from work. In his blood a rebellion will quicken,
> and he will elect to become either a felon or a tramp. If he has
> fought the hard fight, he is not unacquainted with the lure of the
> road. When out of work he has been forced to hit the road
> between large cities in his quest for a job. He has loafed, seen the
> country and green things, laughed in joy, laid on his back and lis-
> tened to the birds ... unannoyed by factory whistles and boss's
> harsh commands; and, most significant of all, *he has lived*. That
> is the point! Not only has he been carefree and happy, but he has
> lived! And from the knowledge that he has idled and is still alive,
> he achieves a new outlook on life; and the more he experiences
> the unenviable lot of the poor worker the more the blandish-
> ments of the road take hold of him. And finally he flings his

challenge in the face of society, imposes a valorous boycott on all work, and joins the far-wanderers of Hobo-land, the gypsy folk of this latter day (in Etulain 1979, 134).

London's "Hobo-land," though a fierce and turbulent domain, also contains the promise of liberation, its "blandishments" beckoning to all engaged in meaningless labour. Less sinister than Flynt's road, London portrays a wide open "wilderness of rails" on the fringes of organized society, hazardous, unsettled, and aleatory: "In Hobo Land the face of life is protean – an ever-changing phantasmagoria, where the impossible happens and the unexpected jumps out of the bushes at every turn of the road. The hobo never knows what is going to happen the next moment; hence, he lives only in the present moment. He has learned the futility of telic endeavour, and knows the delight of drifting along with the whimsicalities of Chance" (London 1967 [1907], 77).

The image of the Nietzschean "blond-beast" commingles with the Marxist motif of the downtrodden lumpenproletariat throughout London's tramp writing. It is not solidarity or organized struggle that liberates London's hobos from their oppression, however: it is combative autonomous individualism. In "Holding Her Down," a presumptively autobiographical account of a young hobo's victory over a train crew intent on "ditching" him, London's narrator glories in his superior skill and boldness: "And why not? Was I not blessed with strength, agility and youth? ... And didn't I have my 'nerve' with me? And furthermore, was I not a tramp-royal? Were not these other tramps mere dubs and 'gay cats' and amateurs alongside of me?" The last of fifteen hobos to evade expulsion, London's narrator revels in the "contest of skill and wits" on the speeding train: "My, but I was proud of myself! ... I was holding her down in spite of two brakemen, a conductor, a fireman, and an engineer ... It is five to one ... and the majesty of the law and the might of a great corporation behind them, and I am beating them out" (London 1967 [1907], 64–5). On the road, then, with skill and mettle, the individual can still triumph over the monolithic controlling forces of an increasingly mechanized society and live a free life of possibility. Yet the prospect of this, as the fourteen hobos thrown from the train attests, is far from certain. For London, it is only those who have best adapted to the hobo's road – the "profesh" – who truly thrive there. "Thousands of men on the road are unfit to be the 'profesh,'" London writes, but the few who reach this exalted status comprise "the aristocracy of their underworld. They are the lords and masters, the aggressive men, the blond beasts of Nietzsche, lustfully roving and conquering through sheer superiority and strength" (in Etulain 1970, 94–5).

The notion of the hobo as the consummate alienated proletarian, an emblem of the bankruptcy of the system and a model of defiance and resilience, played particularly well in the bohemian enclaves that had begun to take shape in American cities – Chicago and New York in particular – by the 1910s. The most militant rendering of this figure was disseminated by the Industrial Workers of the World (IWW), which had begun unionizing unskilled, often itinerant workers as early as 1905. IWW agitators proselytized at hobo congregation points – labour exchanges, "jungles," and boxcars – and the union opened meeting halls and reading rooms on urban "main stems." Hobo songs and poems were incorporated into the IWW's political culture; its *Little Red Song Book* included the lyrics of "Hallelujah I'm a Bum" as well as such revolutionary standards as "The Internationale" and "Solidarity Forever" (Milburn 1930, 85). "The nomadic worker," a 1914 issue of *Solidarity* proclaimed, embodied "the very spirit of the IWW": "His cheerful cynicism, his frank and outspoken contempt for most of the conventions of bourgeois society, including the more stringent conventions which masquerade under the name of morality, make him an admirable exemplar of the iconoclastic doctrine of revolutionary unionism … His anomalous position, half industrial slave, half vagabond adventurer, leaves him infinitely less servile than his fellow worker … Nowhere else can a section of the working class be found so admirably fitted to serve as the scouts and advance guards of the labor army. Rather they may become the guerrillas of the revolution – the francs-tireurs of the class struggle" (in Kornbluh 1964, 66–7).

As with London's road hero, the "Wobbly" hobo of the IWW was configured in radically individualistic terms, lone mobility suggesting a kind of exemplary purity in the revolt against bourgeois sociability and solidity. And while it is not known the extent to which the IWW's seemingly paradoxical effort to foster solidarity through the idealization of hobo alienation radicalized wandering workers themselves, it seems certain to have played a role in attracting the middle-class cultural radicals for whom the IWW became a *cause célèbre* in the early 1910s. This development reached its apex in the spring of 1913 with the famous collaboration of IWW militants and

Greenwich Village bohemians in the strike at the silk works of Paterson, New Jersey. This storied episode of cross-class solidarity saw bookish young radicals marching the picket line with unschooled immigrant strikers, hard-bitten Wobbly hobos feted in bohemian salons, and a "pageant" dramatizing the strike organized by Village artists and intellectuals and performed at Madison Square Garden by the workers themselves (Green 1988; Golin 1988).

The cultural radicals of bohemia seized upon the masculine image of the Wobbly nomad-militant because they "sensed an affinity," as historian Christopher Lasch notes, between it and "their own ideal of the emancipated individual, unburdened by the cultural baggage of the past" (Lasch 1991, 338). This ideal is perhaps best exemplified in the writings and exploits of "post-Vagabondia" tramp poets Vachel Lindsay and Harry Kemp. In his celebrated 1922 autobiography, *Tramping on Life*, Kemp describes setting out on his "peregrinations as blanket-stiff and bindle-bum," carrying "a second-hand Shakespeare, in one volume, of wretched print, with a much-abused school-copy of Caesar, in the Latin (of whose idiomatic Latin I never tired), an extra suit of khaki, a razor, tooth brush, and tooth-powder – and a cake of soap – all wrapped up in my army blankets" (Kemp 1922, 7). Caesar and Shakespeare notwithstanding, Kemp worked hard to fashion a fresh poetic idiom of "genuine vagabond moods," as he put it, "without [the] dilettantism" of Hovey and Carman (in Brevda 1986, 117). Claiming himself to be a "tramp for the sake of my art," he extolled "the rambling haphazard course of life" on the road as essential "for the freedom of mind and spirit that poets must preserve" (in Seelye 1963, 549). Combining elements of romanticism with the naturalistic realism of London, the poetry of Kemp's *The Cry of Youth* (1914) offers stark renditions of the hobo's road alongside celebrations of youth and rebellion.

Lindsay, for his part, viewed creative inspiration as of a piece with the spiritually transformative possibilities of vagabondage. His reflections on his 1906 journey through the southern states, exchanging verse for food and shelter, are reminiscent of Whitman: "I have taken back and forth in the world, yet feel as though I always stayed at home till I started South. That was living for the first time. It seems the beginning of wisdom to me, the first time I have really revered and followed the divine ... It is worthwhile to be alone. It is worthwhile to mix with one's fellows. It is worthwhile to be one's self on the road, and to study to be that ... The dust of the road shall make clay on my sweating face, and the eternal road shall lead me on, till I have travelled every foot of my ancient dwelling places, and gathered such wisdom as is there distilled from a thousand memories" (in Masters 1935, 169,172). Lindsay's idiosyncratic romantic travelogues and road poems were initially published in popular magazines under such titles as "The Man under the Yoke: An Episode in the Life of a Literary Tramp" (1907) and "A Religious Mendicant" (1912) but later collected in *The Tramp's Excuse and Other Poems* (1909), *Rhymes to be Traded for Bread* (1912), *Adventures While Preaching the Gospel of Beauty* (1914), and *A Handy Guide for Beggars: Especially Those of the Poetic Fraternity* (1916).

Anderson's research for *The Hobo* required, as Laura Browder observes, that he move in the opposite direction from the intellectual vagabonds who preceded him. Anderson, that is, had to *pass up*: "to assimilate into middle-class life in order to succeed as a graduate student" (Browder 2000, 179). Years of hoboing, however, had not prevented Anderson from acquiring a thorough familiarity with the work of those who "passed down." Indeed, Flynt's *Tramping with Tramps* provoked a fateful controversy in Anderson's very first undergraduate class at Brigham Young University. In contrast to London, Anderson faulted Flynt for focusing exclusively on tramps who avoided work. "Flynt had not included the hobos," Anderson recalls in his autobiography, "that large population of go-about workers found mostly in the Middle West and West." Anderson's professor and classmates rejected his critique and pigeonholed him "as a wise guy who thinks he knows more than the author of the book" (Anderson 1975, 128). Years later, Anderson mailed a copy of *The Hobo* to his old professor. "The humiliation could not be forgotten," he writes, "*The Hobo* was my answer to Flynt" (Anderson 1975, 170).

Indeed, *The Hobo* acknowledges, and occasionally comments upon and quotes from, the writings of all of the intellectual vagabonds considered here. Anderson was not only an experienced hobo, he was an experienced hobo steeped in the literary and sociological interpretation of the experience of hoboing. Much of this interpretation, in Anderson's view, was seriously flawed. In a satirical manual for tramps, published in 1931 as *The Milk and Honey Route* under the pseudonym "Dean Stiff," Anderson ridicules attempts by "class-passing" visitors to explain Hobohemia: "No fictionist can explore the hobo's province by riding across it as Stevenson explored Europe on a donkey. Bumping over the terrain ... may be as good a way as any to go slumming or sightseeing; but Hobohemia does not yield to such inspection." "The true reporter," Anderson continues, "must be of the blood, and they of the blood are few. He knows the truth because he lives it" (in Browder 2000, 181–2).

In *The Hobo*, of course, Anderson's imposture prevents him from claiming the authenticity of "living" his research. The text, on the contrary, eschews this sort of authority. It is a work of sociological analysis above all, conforming to the methodological and stylistic conventions of Chicago School urban studies. Accordingly, Anderson seeks to transcend the dialectic of stigmatization and romanticization by adopting the stance of objective participant-observer. Anderson's investigation, however, is hardly disinterested. He has an agenda, at the top of which is the refutation of the common conception of the hobo as biologically defective and socially pathological. Anderson's hobos, rather, are products of a particular historical environment who have, on the whole, adapted to it in ways commensurate to its challenges: "Hobos have a romantic place in our history. From the beginning they have numbered among the pioneers. They have played an important role in reclaiming the desert and in subduing the trackless forests. They have contributed more to the open, frank, and adventurous spirit of the Old West than we are always willing to admit. They are, as it were, belated frontiersmen" (Anderson 1961 [1923], 92).

Anderson carefully distinguishes the hobo, who wanders and works, from the tramp, who wanders and idles, and the stationary homeless: the home guard and the bum. It is the conflation of these types in the public mind, as Anderson had learned at Brigham Young, that accounts for the ignorance, fear, and animosity that greets itinerants of all stripes. As with Wyckoff, Anderson is most interested in the hobo as a worker in a uniquely American environment. European vagabonds, he observes, are primarily of the "psychopathic type." In the United States, however, the "tradition of pioneering, wanderlust, and seasonal employment attract into the group of wanderers and migratory workers a great many energetic and venturesome normal boys and men" (Anderson 1961 [1923], 70). These "heroic figures" not only played a pivotal role in building the society that followed the frontier, they produced a rich and colourful culture of their own (Anderson 1961 [1923], xxi). Anderson sympathetically surveys the varied "habitats," the organizations and institutions, the folkways and songs and poems, the politics, the intellectual life, and even the sexual practices of hobos. Yet Anderson does not shy from reporting the hobo's "weaknesses." Alcoholism, drug addiction, sexual "perversion," venereal disease, prostitution, and criminality are among the common problems of Hobohemia discussed by Anderson. *The Hobo* concludes with a set of "findings and recommendations" designed to be of use to social welfare organizations.

Anderson's *The Hobo*, in sum, is shaped by its interpretive context primarily in a negative sense. It rejects the heroic image of hobo propounded by intellectual vagabonds from Hovey and Carman to London and Kemp in all its permutations. Anderson is even more emphatic in his rejection of the pathological hobo disseminated in the mainstream discourse of the tramp menace. In its place he offers a new configuration: the hobo as a unique, and historically evanescent, travelling worker and builder.

REFERENCES

Allsop, Kenneth. 1967. *Hard Travellin': The Hobo and His History*. New York: American Library
Anderson, Nels. 1961 [1923]. *The Hobo: The Sociology of the Homeless Man*. Chicago: University of Chicago Press
– 1975. *The American Hobo: An Autobiography*. Leiden: E.J. Brill
Brasch, Walter M. 1988. *Zim: The Autobiography of Eugene Zimmerman*. Selinsgrove, PA: Susquehanna University Press
Brevda, William. 1986. *Harry Kemp: The Last Bohemian*. Lewisburg, PA.: Bucknell University Press
Browder, Laura. 2000. *Slippery Characters: Ethnic Impersonators and American Identities*. Chapel Hill: University of North Carolina Press
Brown, Jeffrey S. 1992. *Hobos and Vagabonds: The Cultural Construction of the American Road Hero*. MA thesis, SUNY College at Brockport
Carman, Bliss, and Richard Hovey. 1894. *Songs from Vagabondia*. Boston: Copeland and Day
Cresswell, Tim. 2001. *The Tramp in America*. London: Reaktion Books
Etulain, Richard W., ed. 1979. *Jack London on the Road: The Tramp Diary and Other Hobo Writings*. Logan: Utah State University Press
Flynt, Josiah. 1968 [1902]. *The Little Brother: A Story of Tramp Life*. Upper Saddle River, NJ: Gregg Press
– 1907. *Tramping with Tramps: Studies and Sketches of the Vagabond Life*. New York: Century
Golin, Steve. 1988. *The Fragile Bridge: Paterson Silk Strike, 1913*. Philadelphia: Temple University Press

Green, Martin. 1988. *New York 1913: The Armory Show and the Paterson Strike Pageant*. New York: Scribner

Higbie, Toby. 1997. "Crossing Class Boundaries: Tramp Ethnographers and Narratives of Class in Progressive Era America." *Social Science History* 21:4

Horn, Maurice. 1980. *The World Encyclopedia of Cartoons*. New York: Chelsea House

Kemp, Harry. 1922. *Tramping on Life*. New York: Garden City Publishing

Kornbluh, Joyce, ed. 1964. *Rebel Voices: An I.W.W. Anthology*. Ann Arbor: University of Michigan Press

Labor, Earl, Robert Leitz III, and Milo Shepard, eds. 1988. *The Letters of Jack London, vol. 1: 1896–1905*. Stanford, CA: Stanford University Press

Lasch, Christopher. 1991. *The True and Only Heaven: Progress and Its Critics*. New York: Norton

Lears, Jackson. 1981. *No Place of Grace: Antimodernism and the Transformation of American Culture, 1880–1920*. New York: Pantheon Books

London, Jack. 1967. *The Road*. London: Arco Publications

MacDonald, Allan. 1957. *Richard Hovey: Man and Craftsman*. Durham, NC: Duke University Press

Masters, Edgar Lee. 1935. *Vachel Lindsay: A Poet in America*. New York: Charles Scribner's Sons

Milburn, George. 1930. "Poesy in the Jungles." *American Mercury* xx (May)

Miller, Muriel. 1985. *Bliss Carman: Quest and Revolt*. St John's, NL: Jesperson Press

Opper, Frederick. 1977. *Happy Hooligan: A Complete Compilation, 1904–1905*. Westport, CT: Hyperion Press

Pinkerton, Allan. 1969 [1877]. *Strikers, Communists, Tramps and Detectives*. New York: Arno Press and the *New York Times*

Pittenger, Mark. 1997. "A World of Difference: Constructing the 'Underclass' in Progressive America." *American Quarterly* 49:1

Seeyle, John D. 1963. "The American Tramp: A Version of the Picaresque." *American Quarterly* 15:535–53

Welsford, Enid. 1935. *The Fool: His Social and Literary History*. London: Faber and Faber

Wilson, Christopher. 1985. *The Labor of Words: Literary Professionalism in the Progressive Era*. Athens: University of Georgia Press

Wyckoff, Walter. 1903. *The Workers: An Experiment in Reality, the East*. New York: Scribner's Sons

– 1904. *The Workers: An Experiment in Reality, the West*. New York: Scribner's Sons

18

Constructing Stockholm Syndrome: A Definitional History

ANTONY CHRISTENSEN, BENJAMIN KELLY,
MICHAEL ADORJAN, AND DOROTHY PAWLUCH

Over the past several decades, there have been several high-profile cases in which individuals who have been abducted and held hostage are rescued, only to turn on those who rescue them and side with their captors. Among the most recent cases making the news are those of Natascha Kampusch and Elizabeth Smart. Kampusch, an Austrian kidnapped in 1998 at ten years of age, was held by Wolfgang Priklopil for more than eight years. Priklopil eventually allowed the young girl to roam freely within the house while he was work, occasionally brought her out in public, and once took her on a ski trip. On the day Kampusch escaped, Priklopil committed suicide. Kampusch grieved his loss, asked to see his body, and lit a candle for him. A more recent case, in the US, involved Elizabeth Smart, who was kidnapped by Brian David Mitchell in 2002 at age fourteen. Though Smart too was eventually allowed to move about freely, she did not make an effort to escape. When police located her nine months later, she identified herself as Augustine Mitchell, adopting the surname of her abductor. When police insisted that she was Elizabeth Smart, she is reported to have replied: "Thou sayest" (*Chicago Tribune* 15 March 2003).

In each of these cases, the victims were said to be suffering from Stockholm syndrome, a psychiatric disorder whereby abductees bond with or express loyalty toward their captors in an effort to save their lives or make their ordeal more tolerable (Strentz 1980). The term Stockholm syndrome has also been used with reference to battered women, those who have experienced sexual or physical assaults,

abused children, incest victims, prisoners of war or political terrorism, cult members, concentration camp prisoners, slaves, and prosti-
tutes. Most recently, the term has come up in debates about everything
from gender and race politics to global and international relations.

Our interest in this paper is in tracking the emergence and expanding
use of the Stockholm syndrome as a diagnostic label. We are not interested in challenging the label or its application in any particular instance
or in offering an alternative explanation of what these responses are
"really" about, although it is perhaps worth mentioning that such
alternative explanations exist. Drawing on symbolic interactionist theory, Powell (1986) rejects the notion that sympathy for one's captors
represents a psychopathological reaction. He argues that not enough
attention has been paid to the interactional dynamics that lead hostages and captors to establish a sense of solidarity with each other and
that these responses represent a common working out of lines of action
and the development of unified standpoints.

Rather, our aim is to examine how the Stockholm syndrome label
has entered the popular and medical lexicon, how it became available as a resource to be used by social actors to define certain social
situations, and how its use has grown to include an ever-widening
array of situations. We consider the definitional history of the
Stockholm syndrome label in the context of debates in the social
constructionist literature on social problems claims-making and in
the sociology of health on medicalization. We start by briefly discussing the conceptual literature we use to frame the concerns of the
paper. We then turn to the history of the label – where it originated,
how it was defined and explained, and the situations, contexts, and
debates in which it has been used since. In the paper's conclusion, we
draw out the case study's implications for discussions of claims-
making and medicalization.

The chapter is based on an analysis of a wide array of materials
dealing with Stockholm syndrome. We looked at medical, psychiatric, and criminological literature, including FBI research reports. We
read newspapers, newsmagazines, Internet sources, and books about
high-profile cases. As we sharpened our questions, we focused on the
kinds of documents that would address our concerns and shed light
on the processes we were attempting to understand. In the same way
that field researchers use theoretical saturation to decide on the
points at which interviewing can stop, we continued our search until
we reached a point where we felt confident that we had a sufficiently

firm grasp of the discourse around the Stockholm syndrome label to develop our arguments.

CLAIMS-MAKING AND MEDICALIZATION

As we have seen throughout the previous three essays in this section, social problem categories, whether they be rampant divorce (Shaffir, this volume), the brain drain (Wagner, this volume), or the hobo (Brown, this volume), are the outcome of meaning-making activities. Reflecting common roots in symbolic interactionism and interpretive approaches in sociology, both the social constructionist perspective on social problems and those who study medicalization recognize this and are fundamentally interested in the meaning-making activities of social actors. Trained in the pragmatist tradition of the Chicago School and influenced particularly by the work of Herbert Blumer (1971), the first constructionists (Spector and Kitsuse 1977) redirected the study of social problems away from problematic conditions, their causes and solutions, to a study of the claims-making activities through which putative conditions are defined as problems. This development paralleled the shift in the study of deviance away from behaviours toward the labelling process through which deviance is constituted (Becker 1963; Brown, this volume; Shaffir, this volume). In the aftermath of the shift, attention in the sociology of social problems has focused on such issues as the definitional histories and changing meanings of behaviours/conditions and strategies used to typify conditions, people, and solutions in particular ways (Best 2008).

As definitional case studies proliferate, a persistent trend that has become obvious is the typification of problematic behaviours, situations, and conditions as medical or health-related problems. What was once thought of as madness has become mental illness. Problem drinking and gambling have become alcoholism and compulsive gambling. Family violence, once understood in moral terms, has become child abuse or spousal abuse syndrome (Conrad and Schneider 1980). The construction of medical meanings where they did not once exist has been a central concern for sociologists of health as well. The process of constructing these meanings and "the progressive annexation of nonillness into illness" (Sedgwick 1973, 37) is what defines medicalization. Starting with Freidson (1970), Zola (1972), and Illich (1976), there has been a long tradition in the area of looking at such issues as the contexts, degrees, and engines of medicalization, the pervasiveness of the trend to apply disease labels to so many aspects of human existence, and the consequences of medicalization, particularly in relation to the social control functions that disease labels perform (Conrad 2007). Our analysis builds on these related lines of research. We treat the emergence and promotion of the Stockholm syndrome label as an instance of claimsmaking and in our conclusion consider the ways in which this case study advances our understanding of both the social problems process and medicalization.

EARLY REFERENCES

While the concept of brainwashing has a long history (Schein, Scheier, and Barker 1961), the more specific label Stockholm syndrome was not developed until the 1970s. Its first usage can be traced back to 1973 when Nils Bejerot, a Swedish psychiatrist, was brought in to assist police with an incident involving the robbery of the Kreditbanken, one of the largest banks in Stockholm, Sweden. The robber, an escaped convict named Jan Olsson, had taken four bank employees hostage and demanded that his cellmate in a nearby penitentiary be brought to the bank. Together, the two convicts forced the hostages into the bank's vault where they strapped dynamite to their bodies, forced them to place nooses around their own necks, and held them for six days. After their release, the hostages defended their captors, refusing to testify against them. One of the hostages started a defence fund to assist the convicts. According to some reports, another hostage eventually married one of her captors (Strentz 1980). Bejerot, in discussing the hostages' reactions as part of a news broadcast after their release, described their response as a classic case of brainwashing, calling it the Stockholm syndrome.

The label was in the news again a year later when Patty Hearst attracted worldwide attention. Granddaughter of publishing magnate William Randolph Hearst, she was kidnapped in February 1974 by an urban guerilla group called the Symbionese Liberation Army (SLA). Shortly after the kidnapping, tapes were issued in which Hearst condemned her family and the police and expressed sympathy for the SLA. In April 1974, Hearst was photographed along with other SLA members, wielding an assault rifle while robbing a San Francisco bank. In September 1975, she was arrested for the robbery. Her defence lawyer, F. Lee Bailey, argued at her trial that she had been brainwashed and suffered from Stockholm syndrome. The defence was unsuccessful. In 1976, Hearst was convicted and received a seven-year prison term, though the sentence was commuted in 1979 by President Jimmy Carter, who was persuaded that Hearst had acted under duress. In 2001, a full pardon was granted by President Bill Clinton.

Since the 1970s, interest in the Stockholm syndrome has grown, fuelled by a steady stream of dramatic and well-publicized cases. In addition to the Kampusch and Smart cases, the label was invoked in a series of Mafia-related kidnappings in Italy through the 1970s and 1980s (Favaro et al. 2000) and hostage-taking incidents such as the hijacking of the cruise ship *Achille Lauro* in 1985 (McDuff 1992) and the storming of the Moscow Dubrovka House of Culture by Chechen terrorists in 2002 (Speckhard et al. 2005). Another highly publicized case involved a *Sunday Express* journalist, Yvonne Ridley, who was captured and held for eleven days in 2001 by the Taliban in Afghanistan. After her release, Ridley returned to London and became a full convert to Islam, adamantly denying charges that her conversion resulted from Stockholm syndrome (Bayman 2004).

SCIENTIFIC BUTTRESSING

As popular interest in the label grew, so too did professional attention and research, resulting in formal definitions, lists of symptoms, etiological theories, and prescribed treatment regimens. Stockholm syndrome was typified in the psychiatric and criminological literature as a condition resulting from situations where there is face-to-face contact between captors and captives, where captors induce extreme fright or terror in their victims in order to render them helpless, powerless, and totally submissive. Victims, according to psychiatric claims, see no means of escape and fear for their lives. Under such circumstances, any act of kindness on the part of the captors, or even the absence of beatings, abuse, or rape, leads victims to see their captors as "good guys" (Symonds 1980,138). Moreover, the symptoms of Stockholm syndrome, it is argued, may persist long after captives are free (Call 1999; Skurnik 1988).

Etiological theories generally posit a psychoanalytic explanation, emphasizing the idea of a survival mechanism adopted by an ego under stress. Strentz (1980, 148) explains that in a situation where individuals fear for their lives, "the victim's need to survive is stronger than his impulse to hate the person who has created the dilemma." This results in a particular form of pathological transference or identification whereby the victim becomes attached to the captor. More recent research claims that there may be an evolutionary basis to Stockholm syndrome. Pointing out that similar responses have been observed in reptiles and mammals, Cantor and Price (2007) argue that ethological concepts such as dominance hierarchies and submission strategies go a long way toward explaining the paradoxically positive relationships that develop.

The treatment typically recommended for Stockholm syndrome takes the form of counselling aimed at getting victims to recognize their experiences as pychopathological responses. If Stockholm syndrome creates false perceptions, emotions, and attachments, the argument goes, the goal is an "undoing and reversing [of] the factors that brought about the traumatic psychological infantilism" (Symonds 1980, 135).

EXPANDING RELEVANCE

While in the early years the Stockholm syndrome label was restricted to cases involving abductions and hostage-taking, during the late 1980s and early 1990s there was a broadening of the circumstances to which the label was applied. Picking up on the idea of power imbalances at the root of the syndrome and the false emotional bonds they were said to create, researchers increasingly claimed that Stockholm syndrome occurs in a range of situations that might not at first blush appear to be obvious cases of the syndrome.

One group to which the label has been applied is battered/abused women. Through the 1980s, Dee Graham, a feminist psychologist (Graham, Rawlings, and Rimini 1988), was instrumental in promoting the idea that the behaviours exhibited by battered women, particularly those who denied being battered or refused to leave their partners, were consistent with the symptoms of Stockholm syndrome. This typification has since come to permeate academic discourse about battered women (Bryan 1992; Dutton 1992; Follingstad, Neckerman, and Vormbrock 1988; Loring and Beaudoin 2000; Stark 1994) and is prevalent as well in materials aimed at service providers. For example, a training manual for certified domestic abuse advocates issued by the Iowa Coalition Against Domestic Violence (2006) describes battered women's syndrome as a manifestation of Stockholm syndrome and enumerates the "cognitive distortions" that serve as symptoms, including rationalizing the abuser's abuse, taking the abuser's perspective, and believing that the abuser's arousal and hyper-vigilance is love rather than terror. A book written for those involved in providing pastoral care advises: "Pastors can expect some members of their congregations who have been subjected to domestic violence to have coped through the psychological survival mechanism of Stockholm syndrome" (Rogers 2002, 8).

Stockholm syndrome has also been used to describe the reactions of victims of child abuse (Stanley and Goddard 1997) and child sexual abuse, particularly in those who resist reporting the abuse or assisting in the prosecution of its perpetrators. "The emotional bond between the survivors of child sexual abuse and the people who perpetrated the abuse against them," argues one author (Jülich 2005, 107), "is similar to that of the powerful bi-directional relationship central to Stockholm syndrome."

A number of authors have connected Stockholm syndrome to prostitution (Barry 1984; Card 2002; Farley 2003). Joseph Parker (2004, 14), the clinical director of a Portland treatment program for survivors of prostitution, explains that pimps invariably attempt to create Stockholm syndrome in those they prostitute, stating "Stockholm syndrome is often the real reason for what others see as the 'choice' to stay in the sex industry." The label has been applied to those who have experienced parental abductions (Lowenstein 2006), incest victims (Carver 2007), prisoners of war (Hunter 1988), political prisoners (Turner 1985; Wardlaw 1982), cult members (Tobias and Lalich 1994), suicidal terrorists (Speckhard et al. 2005), victims of sex trafficking (Freed 2007), victims of human trafficking more generally (Canada Department of Justice 2002), and victims of elder abuse (Scaletta 2006).

The label is appearing with greater frequency as well in everyday discourse, including at Internet sites, in chat room discussions, on personal blogs, and in popular media. Stockholm syndrome has been used to make sense of everything from employees who stay in abusive corporate environments (Bezroukov 2009) to the strong bonds that develop between household pets and their owners ("Kiz" 2007). A label that was coined and initially used in a fairly circumscribed set of circumstances (kidnappings and hostage-takings) can now potentially be used in any situation where mind control is seen to be involved.

There have been dissenting voices. Some law enforcement officials have expressed scepticism about the way Stockholm syndrome has been sensationalized and represented in the media and scholarly literature. Fuselier (1999, 22) has argued that Stockholm syndrome has been "overemphasized, overanalyzed, over psychologized and over publicized" and that its occurrence is much more rare than is typically believed. Some psychiatrists have questioned whether Stockholm syndrome is "real" or simply a media invention or "urban myth" (Namnyak et al. 2008). This puts the syndrome in the category of what Brown (1995) has called "contested illnesses," along with such conditions as autism, environmental disease, and chronic fatigue syndrome.

Despite these debates, the label continues to be widely employed by psychiatrists, researchers, clinicians, criminologists, advocates, victims, and the media, as well as in everyday discourse. Indeed, Stockholm syndrome may soon attain "official" status in the American Psychiatric Association's *Diagnostic and Statistical Manual* (DSM), the commonly used classification system for psychiatric disorders. The process of creating the fifth revision of the DSM (due to be completed by 2012) has started. Early reports indicate that the category of Post-Traumatic Stress Disorder (PTSD) will be replaced by the broader category Disorders of Extreme Stress Not Otherwise Specified (DESNOS), which will be divided into PTSD and Complex Post-Traumatic Stress Disorder (C-PTSD). In contrast to PTSD, which will describe reactions in the aftermath of a single and short-term traumatic incident, C-PTSD will describe the reactions of those who undergo prolonged periods of captivity and/or abuse. Besides Stockholm syndrome, C-PTSD may include battered woman syndrome and the reactions of those with long-term involvements with child exploitation rings, concentration camps, or prisoner of war camps.

STOCKHOLM SYNDROME AS A COLLECTIVE REACTION

Another significant development in the definitional history of the label has been its application to collective or group reactions. In a book published in 1994 called *Loving to Survive*, Graham, the psychologist who first applied the Stockholm syndrome label to battered women, introduced the term "societal Stockholm Syndrome" (Graham, Rawlings, and Rigsby 1994). Graham and her co-authors claimed that the key to understanding the psychology of not simply battered women but all women is the ever-present terror they experience in the face of men's violence. The fear that they might anger men or be sexually assaulted by them leads women to respond by trying to please men and exhibiting feminine behaviours of submission. Like the Stockholm hostages who bonded to their captors, the book argues that women bond to men in order to survive.

A similar argument has been made with respect to the putative reluctance among African Americans to take a stand against racism. Huddleston-Mattai and Mattai (1993) claim that as a direct result of the history of slavery, many African Americans, particularly those who have achieved positions of success or power, have developed a slave or "Sambo" mentality. They describe this response as a manifestation of Stockholm syndrome: "This manifestation of the Sambo mentality or the Stockholm syndrome may become externalized through attempts to mimic Euro-Americans, to dissociate from anything identifiably or perceived as identifiably African-American, and even to exhibit embarrassment when another African-American demonstrates behavior that is thought to be viewed negatively by Euro-Americans" (1993, 350).

Journalists and political commentators have used the label to explain political situations, international relations, and global conflicts. Pilevsky (1989), for example, analyzes political tensions during the 1980s between western Europe and its traditional ally, the United States, claiming that the former U S S R was responsible for the tensions in actively pursuing a policy that fostered a "hostage–captor" mentality among western Europeans. This, in turn, he insisted, generated a "Stockholm syndrome–type" response whereby western Europeans began distrusting the US and shifting either toward a nationalistic neutralism or a pro-Soviet position on many significant issues. Similarly, Stockholm syndrome has been invoked to explain the apparent willingness of the Indian government to appease Pakistani terrorists (Kaushal 2005), the alleged sympathy of the Israeli left for the Arab cause and the peace process (Levin 2005), the purported rise in conversions to Islam after 9/11 (Richardson 2006), and the resistance of some Taiwanese to reunification with China (Chu 1999).

DISCUSSION

The definitional history of the Stockholm syndrome label yields a number of interesting insights into processes of claims-making more generally and medicalization more specifically. First, medicalization is usually understood as a top-down process, with disease labels generated by experts filtering down and gaining currency among nonexperts (Conrad 2006). There are only a few cases in the literature in which the medical profession has not taken the lead and research has followed in the wake of, rather than preceded, the establishment of a new medical category. For instance, Alcoholics Anonymous was more important than the medical profession in promoting the disease concept of alcoholism (Schneider 1978); a small group of Vietnam War veterans organized themselves to spur research into post-traumatic stress disorder (Scott 1990); parent groups pushed scientists to take sudden infant death syndrome seriously (Johnson and Hufbauer 1982). An even closer analogous case to Stockholm syndrome would be sexual addiction (Levine and Troiden 1988), which seems to have received considerable mass media publicity before any scientific research was done. Together, these studies reinforce the need to ask about the variety of paths medicalization can take and how integral the medical profession and "scientific evidence" are to these processes (Conrad 2006; Furedi 2006; Pawluch and Vedadhir 2008).

Second, the expanding use of the Stockholm syndrome label, despite debates in certain circles, raises the question of what counts as "legitimate" medical diagnoses. Formal recognition, such as inclusion in the DSM, is often treated by sociologists as the sine qua non of medicalization. In other words, when medical labels are applied in the media or in popular culture but do not have the endorsement of the medical profession, the tendency is to treat these cases as instances of incomplete medicalization. We suggest that from its start, the sociology of medicalization has been more fundamentally interested in processes of medicalization than in the outcome of these processes in terms of how the medical profession or "experts" respond. Whether or not there is a consensus among psychiatrists and other medical experts about the legitimacy of the Stockholm syndrome label, and whether Stockholm syndrome is ever included in the DSM, are interesting questions but separate from the issue of how the Stockholm syndrome label is being promoted and used. Furthermore, Stockholm syndrome as a label is less contested within psychiatry than diagnoses such as seasonal affective disorder or premenstrual syndrome, though these labels have received formal recognition in the DSM (Brown 1995). These observations raise questions about whether official or formal recognition, however it might be operationalized, is necessary or sufficient in analyses of medicalization. Rather than setting some objective and arbitrary standard of legitimation or acceptance, we argue that a more fruitful approach involves treating legitimation as the prerogative of audiences and the social actors that constitute them, not simply official professional bodies or, for that matter, the sociologists or analysts who do these case studies. As well as asking whether a medical label or diagnosis has achieved recognition, there are sociological insights to be mined from asking questions about who recognizes medical labels (or contests them), under what circumstances, and with what consequences.

Finally, the definitional history of Stockholm syndrome demonstrates the potential for labels to grow, a phenomenon that social constructionists call domain expansion. Best (2008, 338) defines domain expansion as the "redefining of a troubling condition to encompass a broader array of cases." When a claim about a condition has gained acceptance, it is possible to build additional claims on that foundation. For example, since the 1950s there has been a steady expansion of the boundaries of what constitutes child abuse. A label that once described the beating of infants and young children has been expanded to include physical, emotional, and sexual abuse and now includes neglect as well as behaviours such as smoking in the presence of children, failing to strap children into car seats, or failing to insist on the use of bike helmets (Best 1990). Domain expansion has been observed as well in relation to medical labels whereby already existing labels are broadened and made more inclusive. For example, the concept of hyperactivity or attention deficit disorder (ADD), once understood as affecting only children, has recently been expanded to take in adults (Conrad and Potter 2000). Addiction has also expanded well beyond its original parameters (Peele 1995). The Stockholm syndrome label shows a similar pattern. A phenomenon that once did not exist, or at least had not been named, is now widely recognized and, as some would have it, fairly prevalent in one form or another.

But more significantly, the Stockholm syndrome label has become the rubric for an ever-widening range of responses at the societal level as well as at the individual level. The use of the label to describe broader social issues like gender, racial, and global relationships reflects domain expansion of a different order. While many labels have lent themselves to domain expansion, few have crossed the line in quite the same way as Stockholm syndrome has from discourses about individual behaviours to discourses about collective responses and those of entire nations, peoples, races, and genders. In another paper (Adorjan et al. 2009), we consider the representational appeal of a category like Stockholm syndrome to social problems claims-makers, arguing that the label functions as a rhetorical power play to neutralize the arguments of those with opposing viewpoints. Our point here is that the use of the label at this level represents the incursion of medical paradigms as explanatory frameworks into socio-political discourse. To the extent that medical labels such as Stockholm syndrome and others like it (e.g., historical or national trauma) are making their way into such discourse, there is a myriad of questions to be asked about the reframing of issues once treated explicitly as political into matters of pathology.

REFERENCES

Adorjan, Michael, Tony Christensen, Benjamin Kelly, and Dorothy Pawluch. 2009. "Stockholm Syndrome: Medicalizing the 'Senseless' in Social Problems Discourse." Unpublished manuscript, under review

Barry, Kathleen. 1984. *Female Sexual Slavery*. New York: New York University Press

Bayman, Hannah. 2004. "Yvonne Ridley: From Captive to Convert." *BBC News On-line*. http://news.bbc.co.uk/1/hi/england/3673730.stm

Becker, Howard S. 1963. *Outsiders: Studies in the Sociology of Deviance*. New York: Free Press

Best, Joel. 1990. *Threatened Children: Rhetoric and Concern about Child-Victims*. Chicago: University of Chicago Press

– 2008. *Social Problems*. New York: W.W. Norton

Bezroukov, Nikolai. 2009. "Traumatic Bonding with Corporate Psycho-paths, Office Stockholm Syndrome." http://www.softpanorama.org/Social/Toxic_managers/office_stockholm_syndrome.shtml

Blumer, Herbert. 1971. "Social Problems as Collective Behavior." *Social Problems* 18:289–306

Brown, P. 1995. "Naming and Framing: The Social Construction of Diagnosis and Illness." *Journal of Health and Social Behavior* 33:267–81

Bryan, Penelope. 1992. "Holding Women's Psyche Hostage: An Inter-pretative Analogy on the Thomas/Hill Hearings." *Denver University Law Review* 69(2):171–200

Call, John. 1999. "The Hostage Triad: Takers, Victims and Negotiators." In *Lethal Violence: A Sourcebook on Fatal Domestic, Acquaintance and*

Stranger Aggression, edited by Harold V. Hall, 561–88. Boca Raton, FL: CRC Press

Canada. Department of Justice. 2002. "Victims of Trafficking in Person: Perspectives from the Canadian Community Sector." Department of Justice research report. http://www.justice.gc.ca/eng/pi/rs/rep-rap/2006/rr06_3/p3.html

Cantor, Chris, and John Price. 2007. "Traumatic Entrapment, Appeasement and Complex Post-Traumatic Stress Disorder: Evolutionary Perspectives of Hostage Reactions, Domestic Abuse and the Stockholm Syndrome." *Australia and New Zealand Journal of Psychiatry* 41(5):377–84

Card, Claudia. 2002. *The Atrocity Paradigm: A Theory of Evil*. New York: Oxford University Press

Carver, Joseph. 2007. "Love and Stockholm Syndrome: The Mystery of Loving an Abuser." http://drjoecarver.makeswebsites.com/clients/49355/File/love_and_stockholm_syndrome.html

Chu, Ben. 1999. "Taiwan Independence and the Stockholm Syndrome." http://www.antiwar.com/chu/c091099.html

Conrad, Peter. 2006. "Up, Down and Sideways." *Society* 43(6):19–20

– 2007. *The Medicalization of Society: On the Transformation of Human Conditions into Treatable Disorders*. Baltimore, MD: John Hopkins University Press

– and Deborah Potter. 2000. "From Hyperactive Children to ADHD Adults: Observations on the Expansion of Medical Categories." *Social Problems* 47(4):559–82

Conrad, Peter, and Joseph Schneider. 1980. *Deviance and Medicalization: From Badness to Sickness*. St Louis: C.V. Mosby

Dutton, Mary. 1992. "Understanding Women's Responses to Domestic Violence: A Redefinition of Battered Woman Syndrome." *Hofstra Law Review* 21(1)191–242

Farley, Melissa, ed. 2003. *Prostitution, Trafficking and Traumatic Stress*. Binghamton, NY: Haworth Press

Favaro, A., D. Degortes, G. Colombo, and P. Santonastaso. 2000. "The Effects of Trauma among Kidnap Victims in Sardinia, Italy." *Psychological Medicine* 30(4):975–80

Follingstad, Diane, Ann Neckerman, and Julia Vormbrock. 1988. "Reactions to Victimization and Coping Strategies of Battered Women: The Ties That Bind." *Clinical Psychology Review* 8(4):373–90

Freed, Wendy. 2007. "Hidden in the Shadows: Sex Trafficking and Women's Health." bixbyprogram.ph.ucla.edu/lectureslides/freed_3.7.07.ppt

Freidson, Eliot. 1970. *Profession of Medicine*. New York: Dodd, Mead

Furedi, Frank. 2006. "The End of Professional Dominance." *Society* 43(6):14–18

Fuselier, Dwayne. 1999. "Placing the Stockholm Syndrome in Perspective." *FBI Law Enforcement Bulletin* 68(7):22–5

Graham, Dee, Edna Rawlings, and Roberta Rigsby. 1994. *Loving to Survive: Sexual Terror, Men's Violence and Women's Lives.* New York: New York University Press

Graham, Dee, Edna Rawlings, and Nelly Rimini. 1988. "Survivors of Terror: Battered Women, Hostages and Stockholm Syndrome." In *Feminist Perspectives on Wife Abuse,* edited by Kersti Yllö and Michele Bograd, 217–33. Newbury Park, CA: Sage

Huddleston-Mattai, Barbara, and P. Rudy Mattai. 1993. "The Sambo Mentality and the Stockholm Syndrome Revisited: Another Dimension to an Examination of the Plight of the African American." *Journal of Black Studies* 23(3):344–57

Hunter, Edna. 1988. "The Psychological Effects of Being a Prisoner of War." In *Human Adaptation to Extreme Stress: From the Holocaust to Vietnam,* edited by John Wilson, Zev Harel, and Boaz Kahana, 157–70. Berlin: Springer

Illich, Ivan. 1976. *Medical Nemesis.* New York: Pantheon

Iowa Coalition Against Domestic Violence. 2006. Training manual for certified domestic abuse advocates, Level II. www.icadv.org/lib/Resources/CDAA_Level_II/CDAAlevelIIintro.pdf

Johnson, Michael, and Karl Hufbauer. 1982. "Sudden Infant Death Syndrome as a Medical Research Problem since 1945." *Social Problems* 30(1):65–81

Jülich, Shirley. 2005. "Stockholm Syndrome and Child Sexual Abuse." *Journal of Child Sexual Abuse* 14(3):107–29

Kaushal, Vepa. 2005. "The Societal Stockholm Syndrome." http://vepa.us/diroo/SSS1.htm

"Kiz" [Blogger handle]. 2007. "'Pets,' Slavery & the Stockholm Syndrome." http://www.veggieboards.com/newvb/showthread.php?59838-quot-Pets-quot-slavery-amp-the-Stockholm-syndrome.&highlight=stockholm+syndrome

Levin, Kenneth. 2005. *The Oslo Syndrome: Delusions of a People under Siege.* New York: Smith and Kraus

Levine, Martin, and Richard Troiden. 1988. "The Myth of Sexual Compulsivity." *Journal of Sex Research* 25:347–63

Loring, Marti, and Pati Beaudoin. 2000. "Battered Women as Coerced Victim Perpetrators." *Journal of Emotional Abuse* 2(1):3–14

Lowenstein, L.F. 2006. "The Comparison of Parental Alienation to the 'Stockholm Syndrome.'" http://www.parental-alienation.info/ publications/46-thecomofparalitothestosyn.htm

McDuff, D.R. 1992. "Social Issues in the Management of Released Hostages." *Hospital and Community Psychiatry* 43:825–8

Namnyak, M., N. Tufton, R. Szekely, M. Toal, S. Worboys, and E.L. Sampson. 2008. "Stockholm Syndrome: Psychiatric Diagnosis or Urban Myth?" *Acta Psychiatrica Scandinavica* 117(1):4–11

Parker, Joseph. 2004. "How Prostitution Works." In *Not for Sale: Feminists Resisting Prostitution and Pornography*, edited by Rebecca Whisnant and Christine Stark, 3–15. North Melbourne, Victoria: Spinifex Press

Pawluch, D., and A. Vedadhir. 2008. "The Sociology of Medicalization: Getting Back to Basics." Paper presented at the International Sociological Association Research Committee on the Sociology of Health and the Canadian Medical Sociology Association Inaugural Meeting, 22 June, Montreal

Peele, Stanton. 1995. *Diseasing of America*. New York: Lexington

Pilevsky, Philip. 1989. *Captive Continent: The Stockholm Syndrome in European–Soviet Relations*. New York: Praeger

Powell, Joel. 1986. "Notes on the Stockholm Syndrome." *Studies in Symbolic Interaction* 7:353–65

Richardson, Joel. 2006. *Anti-Christ: Islam's Awaited Messiah*. Enumclaw, WA: Pleasant Word

Rogers, Dalene. 2002. *Pastoral Care for Post-Traumatic Stress Disorder: Healing the Shattered Soul*. Routledge

Scaletta, Giuseppe. 2006. "Hallmarks of Abuse: A Framework to Identify Abusers of Older Adults." *Newsletter of the British Columbia Psychogeriatric Association* 10(3):4–6

Schein, Edgar, I. Schneier, and C.H. Barker. 1961. *Coercive Persuasion*. New York: Norton

Schneider, Joseph. 1978. "Deviant Drinking as a Disease: Deviant Drinking as a Social Accomplishment." *Social Problems* 25:361–72

Scott, W.J. 1990. "PTSD in DSM III: A Case in the Politics of Diagnosis and Disease." *Social Problems* 37(3):294–310

Sedgwick, Peter. 1973. "Illness – Mental and Otherwise." *Hastings Center Studies* 1(3):19–40

Skurnik, N. 1988. "The Stockholm Syndrome: An Attempt to Study the Criteria." *Annales Médico Psychologiques* 146(1–2):174–81

Speckhard, Anne, Nadejda Tarabrina, Valery Krasnov, and Khapta Akhmedova. 2005. "Research Note: Observations of Suicidal Terrorists in Action." *Terrorism and Political Violence* 16(2):305–27

Spector, M., and J. Kitsuse. 1977. *Constructing Social Problems*. Menlo Park, CA: Cummings

Stanley, Janet, and Christopher Goddard. 1997. "Failures in Child Protection: A Case Study." *Child Abuse Review* 6(1):46–54

Stark, Evan. 1994. "Re-Presenting Woman Battering: From Battered Woman Syndrome to Coercive Control." *Albany Law Review* 58(4):973–1,026

Strentz, Thomas. 1980. "The Stockholm Syndrome: Law Enforcement Policy and Ego Defenses of the Hostage." *Annals of the New York Academy of Sciences* 347:137–50

Symonds, Martin. 1980. "Victim Responses to Terror." *Annals of the New York Academy of Sciences* 347(1):129–36

Tobias, Madeleine, and Janja Lalich. 1994. *Captive Hearts, Captive Minds: Freedom and Recovery from Cults and Other Abusive Relationships*. Alameda, CA: Hunter House

Turner, James. 1985. "Factors Influencing the Development of the Hostage Identification Syndrome." *Political Psychology* 6(4):705–11

Wardlaw, Grant. 1982. *Political Terrorism: Theory, Tactics and Counter Measures*. Cambridge: Cambridge University Press

Zola, Irving K. 1972. "Medicine as an Institution of Social Control." *Sociological Review* 20:487–504

SECTION V
The Chicago School Diaspora: New Directions

As foregrounded in the introduction to this volume, we understand the cultural object known as the "Chicago School" to be dynamic rather than fixed. In a manner parallel to the changing meanings ascribed to Stockholm syndrome (chapter 18), the meaning of the Chicago School itself can change over time. Thus, one aspect of the Swiss army knife–like character of the Chicago School involves the malleability of the tools themselves – a certain element associated with the school (metaphorically, one of the knife's tools, such as the leather punch) will no longer be associated with the school, and another tool (e.g., a bottle opener) may replace it.

The chapters in this section exemplify ways in which key ideas of the Chicago School Diaspora have been expanded and extended in ways not traditionally associated with the Chicago School. In relation to the book's overall argument, the process of enactment – that is, the manner in which scholars draw upon key ideas and key figures of the Chicago School Diaspora in unique and creative ways in order to further their own scholarly activity – is most dramatically evident in this section. It is through this process of appropriation and reinvention that the Chicago School tradition remains alive.

In chapter 19, "Aristotle's Theory of Education: Enduring Lessons in Pragmatist Scholarship," Robert Prus explores connections between Aristotle's theory of education and the pragmatists (e.g., Dewey) typically associated with the Chicago School. Thus, in contrast to the traditional account, which roots the Chicago School tradition in American pragmatic philosophy of the late 1800s, Prus traces the origins of the Chicago School tradition back to the

Greeks. In chapter 20, "Symbolic Interaction and Organizational Leadership: From Theory to Practice in University Settings," Scott Grills applies his understanding of the concept of generic social processes, a key idea of the Chicago School Diaspora, in analyzing his work as dean. In chapter 21, "The Emperor Has No Clothes: Waning Idealism and the Professionalization of Sociologists," Jacqueline Low uses insights from the novel method of analytic autoethnography to contextualize her experiences as a developing sociologist and serve as a corrective to classic Chicago School studies of professionalization. In Chapter 22, "Formal Grounded Theory, the Serious Leisure Perspective, and Positive Sociology," Robert A. Stebbins articulates the need for a new approach to sociology, which he labels positive sociology, and traces the roots of that approach to the serious leisure perspective that he developed through the use of formal grounded theory as expounded by individuals he associates with the "Chicago School."

Each of these contributions points to a potentially significant modification in the Chicago School toolkit: Prus reconceptualizes the school's origins; Grills translates the school's insights from scholarly analysis into a guide for practical action in everyday life; Low displays the utility (as well as the limitations) of a new methodology (autoethnography); and Stebbins articulates the need for an entirely new subfield of sociology (positive sociology, not to be confused with positivist sociology). Through their connection to the Chicago School tradition and the (re)enactment of that tradition in their scholarship, these individuals contribute to the ongoing dynamic that is the Chicago School tradition.

19

Aristotle's Theory of Education: Enduring Lessons in Pragmatist Scholarship

ROBERT PRUS

Aristotle (384–322 BCE) may have lived more than 2,000 years ago, but not only are the conceptual materials he developed on teaching and learning exceedingly relevant for comprehending education on a contemporary plane, but his "theory of education" also suggests some highly consequential directions for examining the roles that instructors as well as students may assume in these realms of community life. Still, before I address Aristotle's analysis of teaching and learning more directly, it is useful to comment on contemporary theory and research on education (including the contemporary era) and to establish some linkages of Aristotle's approach to the study of education with American pragmatism and its sociological extension, symbolic interactionism. Not only is Aristotle's consideration of education as a realm of humanly lived experience highly consistent with a contemporary pragmatist/ interactionist approach to the study of human group life, but Aristotle's materials also offer a sustained, conceptually astute, and exceptionally viable alternative to the rationalist and structuralist approaches that have dominated Western theory and research on education since the sixteenth century. Thus, although the terms of reference may have changed somewhat over time, along with the particular methods that academics have used for studying and analyzing education, most post-sixteenth-century theory and research has approached education as a phenomenon that is primarily contingent on the background characteristics and / or individual qualities of teachers and students.

Those who examine the twentieth- and twenty-first-century literature developed by social scientists and other academics working in
the area of education will see that these emphases pervade contemporary analysis of education. The predominant emphasis is on factors or variables thought to produce, generate, or affect student
achievement (typically measured by grades or program completion
rates). Most commonly, this is seen as a function of (a) inequality of
opportunities (as in class, race, ethnicity, and gender), (b) school differences and teaching styles, and (c) more individualized matters
such as student self-esteem, attitudes, and motivation. Although also
generally from a structuralist standpoint, some attention is given to
matters such as classroom order, student morals, behavioural problems, and protecting students from other students.

There seems to be an underlying assumption that if only the conditions were right – with students given the appropriate background
resources and opportunities – education would be readily accomplished and would proceed in a highly cooperative and efficient manner. A related assumption is that "appropriate instruction" will solve
the problems of education. Still, even though the focus is primarily
on the teacher as an instructor and motivator, not much research
focuses on what teachers actually do on a day-to-day basis. Likewise,
there is little recognition of the idea that students have capacities to
act as agents, as minded beings, who may tactically engage (cooper-
ate with, knowingly disregard, or resist) instructors. Whereas one
encounters some theory and research that more directly addresses
education as a field of human lived experience, survey research and
experimental psychology dominate the field. The emphasis, accordingly, is on antecedent conditions and outcomes.

Rather than reduce human group life to abstract sets of variables
signified by individual qualities and/or background categories (such
as class, race, gender) that are alleged (somewhat mysteriously – see
Grills and Prus 2008) to produce particular outcomes, the pragmatist viewpoint taken here envisions education as a social process "in
the making." It considers the ways that people collectively (and
knowingly) participate in the many, often notably varied instances
and theatres of operation in which educational ventures take place.
The pragmatist emphasis, thus, is on the ways that teachers and students engage the educational process as minded, reflective, adjustive
actors and interactors.

Given its focus on human activity and the ways that people relate to one another in their respective life-worlds, this chapter also provides us with an opportunity to look back over the development of Western social thought and to recognize our indebtedness to classical Greek scholarship (also see Durkheim 1977 [1904–05]). Still, before addressing Aristotle's theory of education more directly, it is important to comment on pragmatist scholarship as it has been envisioned on a more contemporary plane

THE PRAGMATIST STANDPOINT

As noted elsewhere (Prus 1999; 2003; 2004; 2006; 2007a), pragmatist philosophy, with its emphasis on the nature of human knowing and acting, can be traced back to the classical Greek era (circa 700–300 BCE) and most notably the work of Aristotle. However, our contemporaries (theorists in the social sciences included) are much more apt to be familiar with one of its more recent versions – American pragmatism. Accordingly, American pragmatism represents an instructive starting point for the ensuing discussion of education as a humanly engaged process.

Focusing on the meaningful, intentioned production of activity and purposive, adjustive interaction, American pragmatist philosophy is generally associated with an emphasis on the sharedness of meanings achieved through language or symbolic interchange. American pragmatism also attends to the related matters of reflectivity, self–other identities, interpersonal relations, and emergence, as well as the relativism of situated definitions and the intersubjective or group-based nature of humanly known reality.

Quite directly, American pragmatism can be seen as the study of human knowing and acting, as this takes place in process, linguistically enabled terms, within the community of the other. Because pragmatist thought is so notably at variance with most post-sixteenth-century philosophy and the structuralist theory and research that have dominated the social sciences, it has often been assumed that pragmatist philosophy represents the rather unique product of the American democratic, frontier mentality – with its seemingly pronounced emphasis on freedom, accomplishment, and individuality.

As well, despite some passing acknowledgment of their intellectual indebtedness to classical Greek scholarship, the early twentieth-century progenitors of American pragmatism (Charles Sanders Peirce, William James, John Dewey, and George Herbert Mead) also acted as if the theoretical viewpoints they were advancing were more entirely novel. Although one finds other instances of pragmatist scholarship among some European scholars in the intervening centuries (following Aristotle – see Prus 2004), the American pragmatists articulated an interrelated set of approaches that stand in stark contrast to the rationalist and structuralist emphases that had dominated philosophy over the several preceding centuries.

Rejecting both claims to an objective, rationalist, empirical reality that exists apart from human lived experience and notions of a subjective or individually realized reality, the pragmatists contend that *reality is intersubjectively accomplished*. Reality is generated as people develop, share, test out, and adjust meanings for particular phenomena. Thus, whereas they act toward particular things in terms of the meanings that they assign (and potentially reassign) to those things, the meanings that people assign to objects can be expected to change as people assess the viability of their earlier and ongoing lines of action for the purposes at hand (see Blumer 1969).

Still, and rather ironically, given the central relevance of pragmatist thought for comprehending and studying the educational process, the American pragmatists did not directly or systematically apply pragmatist theory to the study of education or any other particular substantive realm of community life. Thus, even though James and Dewey published materials on education and religion, for example, their statements are notably vague and largely void of pragmatist philosophy (also see Durkheim 1983 [1913–14]; Prus 2009b). Consequently, despite Dewey's extended commentaries on education, his discussions of education lack a clear pragmatist philosophic quality (see Biesta and Burbules 2003 for an instructive application of Dewey's pragmatist thought to education as a humanly engaged process). Likewise, Mead's writings on education have only recently been assembled in a more consistent and focused pragmatist manner (Biesta 1999).

Whereas Aristotle and his instructor Plato may be seen as the most enabling teachers of all time, Aristotle also addressed the fundamental features of education in much more direct and sustained pragmatist terms than did the twentieth-century American pragmatists. Nevertheless, the pragmatist philosophies of John Dewey (1859–1952) and George Herbert Mead (1863–1931) are highly consistent with Aristotle's conceptualization of education as a social process.

Given my exposure to mainstream sociological thought, I also had assumed that pragmatist philosophy was a relatively recent, largely independent American innovation. However, on examining Aristotle's *Rhetoric*, I began to question this commonplace academic assumption more intensively. After reading more literature from the classical Greek era and thinking about other materials I had earlier encountered from some scholars in the intervening centuries (especially the German scholar Wilhelm Dilthey [Ermarth 1978], with whom Mead had studied), I began to ask if there were more consequential connections between American pragmatist thought and classical Greek scholarship (Prus 2003; 2004).

This chapter emerged as part of a larger project that traces the development of Western social thought, particularly pragmatist scholarship, from the classical Greek era to the present time. In addition to developing a more extended familiarity with Aristotle's texts that most directly deal with the matters of human knowing and acting (e.g., *Nicomachean Ethics, Rhetoric, Politics, Poetics* – see Prus 2003; 2004; 2007a; 2008; 2009a; Prus and Camara 2010), I also have been examining the works of other scholars (e.g., Cicero, Augustine, Thomas Aquinas, Thomas Hobbes, and John Locke) involved in the development of Western social thought from the classical Greek era to our own time. This statement also has benefitted from J.J. Chambliss's (1987) *Educational Theory as Theory of Conduct: From Aristotle to Dewey*. However, as will become increasingly apparent, this consideration of Aristotle's "theory of education" has been developed primarily around Sister Mary Michael Spangler's (1998) *Aristotle on Teaching*.

Unlike some of Aristotle's related works on rhetoric, poetics, ethics, and politics, none of his surviving texts are more exclusively dedicated to education. Still, Aristotle addressed many pragmatist features of education in highly direct, focused terms. Thus, in developing her text, Sister Spangler has built extensively on materials from Aristotle's *De Anima* (The Soul or The Psyche), *Nicomachean Ethics*, and *Metaphysics* as well as his work on logic. Given the vast scope and depth of Aristotle's scholarship, there is much more to his analysis of education than can be covered in a single volume. Nevertheless, Spangler's text is an exceptionally instructive source for addressing Aristotle's thoughts on teaching and learning.

Because Spangler's volume is so detailed, stays so close to Aristotle's texts, and extensively cites materials from an array of his works, I will reference her text more exclusively. Moreover, since Spangler's text also covers a great deal of relatively complex and sophisticated conceptual material, I have focused primarily on the first chapter of her volume.

In presenting Aristotle's materials on teaching, Spangler assumes three tasks. Thus, she (a) provides a statement on the art of teaching, (b) discusses the natural acquisition of knowledge, and (c) considers the use of inductive and deductive logic in teaching. Relatedly, Spangler discusses the purposes, contingencies, and procedures involved in each of these aspects of the educational process.

DEFINING THE TEACHING ROLE

In discussing teaching, Spangler (1998, 3–9) first reminds us of Aristotle's emphasis on *teaching as activity* as well as his insistence that all instruction builds on what is already known. Thus, it is the role of the teacher to ascertain, comprehend, and build on students' existing capacities (and knowledge base). It is by using people's existing knowledge as a bridge that teachers may take students from the known to "the unknown." Second, for Aristotle, teaching involves both inductive and deductive reasoning. When invoking inductive reasoning, teachers attempt to foster an awareness of particular abstractions or generals by alerting students to commonalities among certain things. Subsequently, they encourage their students to search for similarities and differences across instances, and to consider the inferences thereof, so that students may develop more adequate abstractions on their own. Thus, whereas people experience things in instances, it is by locating the instances in more general or abstract terms that people develop notions of "whatness," or what things are or mean in relation to other things. In this way, instructors assist students in locating instances in broader, more meaningful contexts.

As a process, inductive instruction first focuses on communicating (via similarities, differences, implications) more simplistic and commonplace abstractions through the examinations and comparison of instances to the other. Once this base is established, this would be followed by the production of other abstractions on the part of instructors and students. Viewed thus, induction is the process of sharing reference points with the other and then using these notions to help the other comprehend and formulate categories, connections, functions, procedures, principles, or other abstractions. The teaching role, then, not only involves conveying specific abstractions to students and encouraging them to acknowledge particular abstractions as aspects of knowledge, but it also involves the matter of helping students develop capacities for, and tendencies toward, invoking inductive logic on their own. Therefore, in addition to teaching people about existing categories, connections, and principles that are used in the broader community or the setting at hand more specifically, it is the role of the teacher to encourage students to routinely engage the conceptualizing process.

When using *deductive reasoning*, instructors encourage students to make inferences about instances of things by locating these instances within the context of general principles (as in categories, abstractions, qualities, properties, and knowledge claims). The goal is to learn about the instances by applying existing principles or more abstract rules of association to the cases at hand. Relatedly, since people must learn categories, associations, and principles before they can draw inferences about instances from generals, deductive thinking or logic presupposes some fluency in inductive thinking. Because of its inferential qualities, deductive reasoning represents potent sets of practices or conceptual resources that can be brought to bear on particular circumstances. Nevertheless, Aristotle envisions induction as having a broader or more pervasive relevance. Since people first learn about things through their encounters with instances, induction or comparative reasoning is the starting point of the instructional process. Still, more is involved.

Because (a) inductive reasoning deals with instances (wherein notions of categories, comparisons, and similarities and differences are invoked and known) and (b) since things always take place in instances, it is (c) analytic induction that enables people to maintain closer contact with the "reality" of the particular situations they encounter (and experience). Thus, whereas deductive logic enables one to reach certain conclusions, it is inductive reasoning that more fundamentally enables people to define "whatness," to make sense of the instances of things they encounter.

The third element that defines teaching for Aristotle is the notion that teachers inform students of "the causes of things." Focusing on the authenticity and accuracy of conceptions of the parts, connections, and processes of one's subject matter, Aristotle deems it essential that instructors be able to explain the components of the things under consideration as well as their interlinkages. Knowing on the part of the instructor, thus, would include familiarity with the parts, forms, composition, associations, processes, directions, and effects of things as this pertains to both instances and generals of the subject matter under consideration. It also would encompass the use of, and instruction in, the comparative analyses (similarities, differences, and inferences) associated with inductive analysis as well as an extended familiarity with the logic or procedures of deductive reasoning.

Given the tendency on the part of many social scientists to restrict notions of causality to variable analysis, it should be noted that Aristotle is mindful of material (physical and biological) conceptions of causation as well as "the capacity of humans to enter into the causal process as agents" – both as linguistically informed, purposive solitary actors and through adjustive interchange with others (see Aristotle's *Nicomachean Ethics*, *Rhetoric*, *Poetics*, *Politics*; also Prus 2003; 2007a; 2008).

THE PURPOSE OF TEACHING

In discussing the purpose of teaching, Sister Spangler (1998, 9–13) engages Aristotle's notion of intellectual virtue. In contrast to one's moral virtues, which Aristotle envisions as constellations of habits, character dispositions, and emotional tendencies that people develop as active, biological beings from infancy onward, Aristotle defines intellectual virtues in reference to the learned, deliberative, and developmental qualities associated with knowledge, wisdom, judgment, and concerns with one's personal and community well-being.

Speaking mindfully of their roles in fostering the intellectual virtues, Aristotle encourages instructors to acquire a scientific, scholarly, or intellectual knowledge of all things or at least as many subject matters as possible. Because knowledge of this sort can only be developed through the sustained, analytic (vs. applied or practical) study of particular subject matters, it is the task of instructors to convey scholarly knowledge to their students and to encourage them, in turn, to engage particular subject matters through more rigorous inquiry and sustained comparative analysis.

Still, the more focused or active quest for knowing and wisdom presupposes that one's students will have absorbed some earlier instruction on "knowing about things" and are attentive to the processual and causal linkages between things more generally. As well, there is the yet prior matter of developing student characters (moral virtues) that foster receptivity to learning. As the preceding discussion suggests, the development of intellectual virtue is not to be understood as an isolated or singular process but becomes synthesized with one's developmental, active, interactive, deliberative, adjustive being.

It is instructive (Spangler 1998, 11–13), thus, to attend to Aristotle's delineation of three human powers or capacities for activity – vegetative or non-rational creature tendencies, appetitive or habitual and emotional capacities, and rational or reflective capacities. Education is primarily directed toward people's appetitive and rational capacities for activity. It is here that people (in differing manners and degrees) may be instructed and thereby become knowledgeable participants in community life. Noting that people's appetitive tendencies (also habits or "moral virtues") tend to take shape from infancy onward and are notably resistant to change, Aristotle acknowledges the importance of these earlier character dispositions and behavioural tendencies for people's subsequent capacities (i.e., abilities, receptivities, and resistances) for developing intellectual virtues.

Thus, while placing primary value on people's intellectual virtues, Aristotle also stresses the importance of people developing moral characters or patterns of habits that foster attentiveness, memory, receptivity, application, and dedication to learning. The development of people's intellectual virtues may be the ultimate good or goal to be pursued by the teacher, but considerable premium is placed on the roles that caretakers and other associates earlier assume in fostering qualities or habits that would contribute to people's subsequent intellectual development.

Having defined speech (and instruction-enabled reasoning) as the quality that most consequentially distinguishes people from other animals, and envisioning the intellectual virtues as the most desirable ends to which humans as reflective community creatures may aspire, Aristotle further insists that the life of study ("the contemplative life") is the single most worthwhile end for people to pursue. Insofar as instruction contributes to more sustained reasoning practices and the subsequent quest for intellectual virtue on the part of students, teaching attains its most noble objective as a productive art.

THE MATERIALS OF TEACHING

In contrast to those who invoke the (pitcher) metaphor of the teacher as someone who "pours knowledge into his or her students" in the manner that one might transfer liquid from one container to another, Aristotle envisions education as denoting realms of activity and interchange that build on student capacities, instructor knowledge, and the teacher–student relationship. Attending to these matters, Spangler (1998, 13–27) considers Aristotle's foundational materials of teaching.

Focusing first on student capacities, Spangler (1998, 14–18) draws attention to Aristotle's views of students as active participants in the instructional process. While clearly acknowledging the possible intellect or the human capacity to learn all manners of things, Aristotle draws particular attention to the active potential or agent intellect signified by people's involvements in the abstracting process – as in rudimentary conceptualizations of generals and then participation in more sophisticated instances of the abstracting processes.

Although knowledge is built up from people's encounters with instances, Aristotle explicitly observes that the abstracting processes do not exist within the instances themselves or in people's sensations thereof. Abstractions presume a biological readiness on the part of people to differentiate between sensations, but concepts (as modes of knowing) do not exist in things, motions, or sensations. Hence, people first acquire notions of generalities through direct linguistic (primarily verbal) instruction. Preliminary abstractions must be encouraged, taught, or conveyed to the child by a knowing other.

Still, linguistic instruction on its own is not enough. For humans to acquire abstractions, it is necessary that they actively experience, engage, or participate in the abstracting or conceptualizing process. This is what Aristotle means by the agent intellect and why this aspect of participation is so central to the instructional process. Without some attempt on the part of humans to attend to the other and focus on the words and other objects that instructors reference, there can be no meaningful or productive teaching. Further, as Aristotle also would remind us, teaching does not occur in general terms. Teaching and learning may be pervasive across all realms of community life, but, like all human activity, teaching and learning take place in instances as specific people do certain things.

The second type of material that Aristotle (Spangler 1998, 18–24) considers central to teaching as activity is the instructor's knowledge. Since it is the teacher who provides direction for the agent intellect and content for the possible intellect, Aristotle insists on the necessity of instructors knowing their subject matters. Whereas

Aristotle envisions people's abilities to teach as an indication that they know their particular subject matters, teachers are to pursue a scientific or scholarly knowledge of their more specific topics as well as possess a conceptual methodology for assessing the broader viability of all subject matters.

Thus, in addition to knowing the substantive contents and basic principles or premises of one's subject matters, as well as more exacting methods for dealing with these subjects, Aristotle also insists on the importance of teachers developing familiarity with a broader *philosophy of knowledge*. Relatedly, Aristotle emphasizes the importance of instructors learning logic as an analytic base for learning about the other sciences. Further, beyond instruction and learning of a more formalized sort, Aristotle stresses the importance of instructors continuously invoking reason (inductive and deductive) in dealing with all aspects of their subject matters. Mindful of the point that teaching, like learning, takes place in instances and involves particular people providing instruction to others, Aristotle also states that those who have experience as well as theory in their subject matter are considerably better prepared to assume roles as instructors than are those who have only formalized instruction. Indeed, Aristotle contends, extended experience in a field is likely to be considerably more consequential for achieving authenticity in the instructional process than is the reliance on formal education alone.

In discussing the teacher–student relationship, Spangler (1998, 24–7) observes that once people acquire capacities for abstraction and inference, they may be able to learn things "on their own." Still, instruction tends to be a more effective, accurate, and time-efficient mode of acquiring information about specific subject matters. Further, because (as Aristotle notes) people begin life as "blank tablets or slates" on which nothing is yet written, it is one's earlier instructors who provide one with the foundational materials for knowing about things. Indeed, until students develop a broader base of knowledge and reason for making more discerning judgments, they will proceed most effectively when they accept instruction (i.e., adopt the viewpoint of the instructor) on trust. Thus, teaching, for Aristotle, takes shape through a joint or mutually engaged process. To be effective, teaching assumes an ongoing series of developmental activities and interchanges that take place between attentive and knowledgeable instructors and students who exhibit trust and a readiness to learn.

TEACHING AS AN ART

After discussing "the materials of teaching," Spangler (1998, 27–34) next considers "teaching as practical activity." In contrast to what Aristotle defines as speculative or intellectual activity that is concerned with knowing and reasoning in more general and abstract terms, Aristotle's notions of practical activity focus on producing or making something in more direct or applied terms. Thus, whereas teaching builds on an array of intellectual materials (and practices), teaching is also concerned with helping others acquire capacities, knowledge, and intellectual virtue.

Albeit a practical activity, teaching also can be viewed as a productive art when it involves the application of the best available techniques or procedures to the task of educating and encouraging scholarship on the part of one's students. Still, Aristotle insists more generally that art or *techne* tends to be most viable when it imitates nature – when it is developed mindful of the ways things more typically take shape. Thus, instead of people resisting or ignoring the qualities and processes involved in the things with which they work, Aristotle encourages them to attend carefully to these matters (substances, resources, limitations, tendencies, and resistances) and to adjust their procedures mindful of these contingencies. Accordingly, in teaching as an art, the emphasis is on examining learning as a natural human process and adjusting one's instructional methods mindful of the ways that people know and act.

In the subsequent chapters of her text, Sister Spangler elaborates Aristotle's standpoints on the matters considered to this point. Because Aristotle's conceptualizations of these topics are, at once, so extensive, complex, and sophisticated, it is well beyond the scope of the present chapter to engage these matters in detail. Still, even a brief overview of the other chapters in Spangler's text may alert readers to the comparatively untapped resources available in *Aristotle on Teaching*. In chapter 2, "Natural Objects in Knowing," Spangler (1998, 35–65) addresses sense objects, sensory perception, human sense-making capacities, and people's notions of "whatness." Chapter 3, "Natural Way Knowing Occurs" (Spangler 1998, 67–97) not only deals with the problematics of knowing but also attends in more focused manners to possible and agent intellects, abstracting processes, and other basic intellectual processes.

The problematics of knowing and acting receive further consideration in chapter 4, "Natural Order in Knowing," wherein Spangler (1998, 99–129) discusses people's potentialities for knowing, the more rudimentary and more enabling aspects of the agent intellect, the transitions from instances to generals and from generals to particulars, and the implications of these reasoning processes for engaging the unknown. Chapter 5, "Inductive Process of Teaching" (Spangler 1998, 131–61), is an elaboration of the abstracting process, wherein more focused attention is given to knowing, categorization and differentiation, causality, sense perception, cognitive processes and memory, and the methods of articulating principles, generating divisions, and developing compositions. Focusing on the "Deductive Process of Teaching," chapter 6 (Spangler 1998, 163–93) deals more directly with the purposes, materials, and procedures of inferential reasoning and the ways in which deductive logic may be invoked in teaching contexts. Clearly, there is much to be gleaned from Sister Spangler's *Aristotle on Teaching*, as well as Aristotle's texts more broadly. Still, even this brief overview statement enables us to appreciate some of the exceptional potency of Aristotle's contributions to teaching, learning, and scholarship.

IN PERSPECTIVE

Informed by the contemporary pragmatist/interactionist scholarship of George Herbert Mead (1934) and Herbert Blumer (1969; also see Prus 1996; 2003; 2004), this chapter attests to the extended relevance of Aristotle's considerations of education for comprehending, studying, and analyzing education as a humanly engaged process. Locating the roots of pragmatist social thought in classical Greek scholarship, this chapter suggests some highly consequential directions for research on education as an actively engaged, intersubjectively accomplished realm of human lived experience. In contrast to the comparatively common tendency to view education as an essentially asymmetrical process, with students assuming passive roles and teachers assuming active roles with virtually totalizing control of the content, direction, and emphasis of learning, Aristotle not only envisions education (and communication more generally) as taking place within instances and realms of interchange but also insists on attending to students as *active co-participants* (agents and

interactants) in a collective process. Likewise, while placing considerable emphasis on knowing about things (as in the "whatness" of
form, content, components, directional and developmental flows,
interconnections and interdependencies, and sources of movement),
Aristotle stresses the importance of instructors helping their students
to develop more explicit, systematic, thorough reasoning practices.

Consistent with contemporary pragmatist philosophy, Aristotle
approaches *education as a series of developmental flows of activity*
characterized by meaningful interchange between teachers and students as linguistically enabled, purposive agents. Whereas Aristotle
is attentive to the sensate and emotional as well as the intellectual
aspects of teaching and learning, the primary focus is on activity,
interchange, and community-based concepts. Working with frames
of community-generated knowledge, teachers are to: establish points
of reference and categories; generate notions of whatness; provide
modes of thinking (as in encouraging recollection, understanding,
and analysis); foster deliberation and awareness of the other; encourage procedural competence; generate cooperation and independence
(within the context of the moral order of the community); and
encourage wisdom of thought and choice on the part of the other.
Still, these objectives can be achieved only insofar as students assume
roles as active (attentive, cooperative, inquiring, and adjusting) participants in the educational process.

Although physiologically enabled, teaching and learning are inter-
woven, intersubjectively accomplished processes. Education is *not*
an internal, individual cognitive phenomenon. Thus, in contrast to
the prevailing tendencies in psychology, sociology, and educational
pedagogy to search for variables thought to affect educational outcomes, the emphasis is on activity and minded, purposive interchange. Education cannot be reduced to the qualities of individual
instructors and/or students, abstract aspects of "social structure," or
some combination thereof – but should be examined historically and
ethnographically as a realm of linguistically informed interchange
(see Durkheim 1961 [1902–03]; 1977 [1904–05]; 1915 [1912]; Prus
2007b; 2007c; 2011). Learning not only involves matters of content,
categories, and connections, but it also entails an active, experiential
"sharing of whatness" through ongoing interchange with the com-
munity-informed other.

Moreover, because *education takes place within the context of
lived experience, in instances of human group life* rather than

through the abstract mathematical interplay of particular variables, it is essential to examine education as it takes place in instances and in terms that are attentive to the ways that people engage one another in actual practice. In this regard, there is no substitute for extended ethnographic inquiry and comparative analysis.

Even though there is an internal, developmental interfusing of speech, mind, body, sensation, and activity as people learn things in instructional contexts, the "learning of whatness" is first, and more or less continually, contingent on people achieving a "sense of oneness" or intersubjectivity with the instructor or community-based other. Humans achieve a sense of autonomy and judgment as they attend to community-based perspectives of "whatness" and subsequently become able to knowingly act, think, and learn on their own. However, the concepts (and associated definitions) that inform their thoughts and activities (however mundane or creative these may seem) reflect their linguistically enabled exposure to, and active, minded participation in, the whatness of community life (also see Durkheim 1961 [1902–03]; 1915 [1912]; Prus 2007b; 2007c; 2011). While this enabling function of education is what is desired at base, it also means that the capacity for people to be (in Mead's [1934] terms) "objects unto themselves" – to be able to take themselves and others into account as they think about and act toward other people and other objects – also needs to be recognized as a consequential feature of the interactive process that undergirds all realms of education.

Thus, in addition to any abilities, interests, intentions, and stocks of knowledge that particular teachers and students may bring into the setting, it is necessary to attend to the ways that people, as minded essences, act and interactively adjust to one another as instances of interchange take place. That is, because people act, interact, and act back on one another in adjustive, purposive terms, instances of human group life assume an emergent quality. As participants in unfolding, only partially predictable dramas of community life, people's experiences, senses of reality, and definitions of other people, self, and other objects can be expected to shift over time and within particular contexts as they deal with one another.

Still, by following instances of people's activities and interchanges and subjecting these to more sustained analytic comparisons (what Aristotle terms "analytic induction"), we not only may better appreciate what is unique about each instance, setting, or life-world but also may better comprehend those aspects of instances, settings, and life-worlds that have more generic or transsituational (transcontextual, transhistorical) qualities.

By examining education as a series of dynamic realms of community life – characterized by activity, interchange, intersubjectivity, deliberation, choice, and adjustment on the part of both instructors and students – as these emerge in instances within the broader developmental flows of community life, we may conceptualize education not only in more authentic, humanly engaged terms but also in ways that have much greater value for comprehending the future and the past as well as the ever-emerging present.

Four emphases define Chicago-style symbolic interactionism (Mead 1934; Blumer 1969; Strauss 1993; Prus 1996; 1997). They are: (a) a pragmatist philosophy of human knowing and acting; (b) ethnographic examinations of the nature of human lived experience; (c) an accumulation of a more conceptually consistent corpus of ethnographic research; and (d) a quest to define the basic features of human group life through sustained comparative analysis (as in generic social processes, grounded theory).

Developed more than 2,000 years ago, Aristotle's texts cannot be expected to fully match up with twentieth- and twenty-first-century interactionist scholarship. However, these materials still have the capacity to extend the boundaries of contemporary social thought (and pragmatist scholarship) in notably consequential ways. Thus, even this brief discussion of "Aristotle's theory of education" helps to draw attention to the importance of focusing on (a) the minded adjustive processes associated with activity, agency, and interchange, (b) the problematics of defining situations (developing and sharing conceptions of whatness, attending to particular instances, and participating in the categorizing process), (c) the development, instruction, acquisition, utilization, and transformation of reasoning practices, (d) people's conceptions of causation as this is implemented with respect to both material objects and humanly engaged matters, (e) character as an emergent, socially achieved process, and (f) the instructed, problematic, developmental cultural flows of human group life. Sustained consideration of these matters not only would contribute substantially to a pragmatist/interactionist analysis of human group life but also would help to establish the fundamental relevance of pragmatist/interactionist approaches for a more adequate analysis of community life.

As indicated in more detail elsewhere (Prus 2003; 2004; 2007a; 2008 2009a; Prus and Camara 2010), the pragmatist tradition associated with Charles Sanders Peirce, William James, John Dewey, and George Herbert Mead is most appropriately rooted in classical Greek thought – especially discussions of human knowing and acting developed by Aristotle. Like most social scientists, Herbert Blumer had very little direct familiarity with classical Greek scholarship. Still, having studied with George Herbert Mead and Robert Park, Herbert Blumer (1969) most effectively articulated the conceptual and methodological founda- tions of Chicago-style interactionism. This reflected Blumer's emphasis on (a) pragmatist philosophy, (b) ethnographic inquiry, and (c) the development of generic process-oriented concepts derived from the comparative analysis of ethnographic instances. Stressing the linguisti- cally enabled, reflective, purposive, enacted, interactive, and emergent nature of human group life, Herbert Blumer, in conjunction with George Herbert Mead, Robert Park, and Everett Hughes along with a corpus of ethnographers too numerous to list here, provided the intel- lectual core that was so central to the development of Chicago-style interactionism (Strauss 1993; Prus 1996; 1997; Prus and Grills 2003).

Whereas Chicago sociology – as suggested in the present volume – is much more multifaceted than implied in Chicago-style symbolic interactionism, the statements developed by William Shaffir (on reli- gion and change) and Izabela Wagner (on the careers of musicians and scientists) in the present volume help to illustrate an interaction- ist attentiveness to transitions and adjustments in the human com- munity. Like the transhistorical material provided in the statement on Aristotle and teaching, the papers developed by Shaffir and Wagner contribute to the more enduring pragmatist tradition.

REFERENCES

Aristotle. 1984. *The Complete Works of Aristotle*, edited by Jonathan
    Barnes. Princeton, NJ: Princeton University Press
Biesta, Gert J.J. 1998. "Mead, Intersubjectivity, and Education: The Early
    Writings." *Studies in Philosophy and Education* 17:73–99
– 1999. "Redefining the Subject, Redefining the Social, Reconsidering
    Education: George Herbert Mead's Course on Philosophy of Education
    at the University of Chicago." *Educational Theory* 49:475–92

– and Nicholas C. Burbules. 2003. *Pragmatism and Educational Research*. Lanham, MD: Rowman and Littlefield

Blumer, Herbert. 1969. *Symbolic Interactionism: Perspective and Method*. Englewood Cliffs, NJ: PrenticeHall

Chambliss, J.J. 1987. *Educational Theory as Theory of Conduct: From Aristotle to Dewey*. Albany: State University of New York Press

Durkheim, Emile. 1961 [1902–03]. *Moral Education*. Translated by Everett K. Wilson and Herman Schnurer. New York: Free Press

– 1977 [1904–05]. *The Evolution of Educational Thought*. Translated by Peter Collins. London: Routledge and Kegan Paul

– 1915 [1912]. *The Elementary Forms of the Religious Life*. Translated by Joseph Ward Swain. London: Allen and Unwin

– 1983 [1913–14]. *Pragmatism and Sociology*. Translated by J.C. Whitehouse. New York: Cambridge University Press

Ermarth, Michael. 1978. *Wilhelm Dilthey: The Critique of Historical Reason*. Chicago: University of Chicago Press

Grills, Scott, and Robert Prus. 2008. "The Myth of the Independent Variable: Reconceptualizing Class, Gender, Race, and Age as Subcultural Processes." *The American Sociologist* 39(1):19–37

Mead, George H. 1934. *Mind, Self and Society*. Chicago: University of Chicago Press

Plato. 1997. *Plato: The Collected Works*, edited by John M. Cooper. Indianapolis: Hackett

Prus, Robert. 1996. *Symbolic Interaction and Ethnographic Research: Intersubjectivity and the Study of Human Lived Experience*. Albany: State University of New York Press

– 1997. *Subcultural Mosaics and Intersubjective Realities: An Ethnographic Research Agenda for Pragmatizing the Social Sciences*. Albany: State University of New York Press

– 1999. *Beyond the Power Mystique: Power as Intersubjective Accomplishment*. Albany: State University of New York Press

– 2003. "Ancient Precursors." In *Handbook of Symbolic Interactionism*, edited by Larry T. Reynolds and Nancy J. Herman-Kinney, 19–38. Walnut Creek, CA: Altamira

– 2004. "Symbolic Interaction and Classical Greek Scholarship: Conceptual Foundations, Historical Continuities, and Transcontextual Relevancies." *The American Sociologist* 35 (1):5–33

– 2006. "In Defense of Knowing, in Defense of Doubting: Cicero Engages Totalizing Skepticism, Sensate Materialism, and Pragmatist Realism in Academica." *Qualitative Sociological Review* 2(3):21–47

- 2007a. "Aristotle's Nicomachean Ethics: Laying the Foundations for a Pragmatist Consideration of Human Knowing and Acting." *Qualitative Sociology Review* 3(2):5–45
- 2007b. "Human Memory, Social Process, and the Pragmatist Metamorphosis: Ethnological Foundations, Ethnographic Contributions, and Conceptual Challenges." *Journal of Contemporary Ethnography* 36(4):378–437
- 2007c. "On Studying Ethnologs (Not Just People, Societies in Miniature): The Necessities of Ethnography, History, and Comparative Analysis." *Journal of Contemporary Ethnography* 36(6):669–703
- 2008. "Aristotle's Rhetoric: A Pragmatist Analysis of Persuasive Interchange." *Qualitative Sociology Review* 4(2):24–62
- 2009a. "Poetic Expressions and Human Enacted Realities: Plato and Aristotle Engage Pragmatist Motifs in Greek Fictional Representations." *Qualitative Sociology Review* 5(1):3–27
- 2009b. "Reconceptualizing the Study of Community Life: Emile Durkheim's Pragmatism and Sociology." *The American Sociologist* 40:106–46
- 2011. "Examining Community Life 'in the Making': Emile Durkheim's *Moral Education.*" *The American Sociologist* 42:56–111
- and Fatima Camara. 2010. "Love, Friendship, and Disaffection in Plato and Aristotle: Toward a Pragmatist Analysis of Interpersonal Relationships." *Qualitative Sociology Review* 6(3):29–62
Prus, Robert, and Scott Grills. 2003. *The Deviant Mystique: Involvements, Realities, and Regulation.* Westport, CT: Praeger
Spangler, Sister Mary Michael. 1998. *Aristotle on Teaching.* Lanham, MD: University Press of America
Strauss, Anselm. 1993. *Continual Permutations of Action.* Hawthorne, NY: Aldine De Gruyter

20

Symbolic Interaction and Organizational Leadership: From Theory to Practice in University Settings

SCOTT GRILLS

For me as a graduate student, attending the Canadian-based Qualitative Research Conference (aka the Qualitatives) was the way to meet people like Carl Couch, Jackie Wiseman, Fred Davis, Helena Znaiecki Lopata, Virginia Olsen, Bob Stebbins, Robert Emerson, David Altheide, Spencer Cahill, and Stan Lyman and by so doing become connected to the narratives that make the history and development of interactionist traditions come alive. What has been remarkable is the extent to which some of the most important names in North American symbolic interactionism have made their way to these meetings and the extent to which they have given back to junior scholars. As time has passed, those very same people have become mentors of the next generation of dedicated students of the social world. These are the stories that are not always a part of the traditional literature, but they are the ones that can ground inquiry in innovative and passionate ways. These meetings have changed the degree of separation from our US-based colleagues that Canadian scholars experience – they have engendered a community of scholars that would simply not otherwise exist.

The "Canadian meetings" have allowed for an interchange of ideas, have facilitated conversations, and have allowed for relational dynamics that would not have otherwise been possible. The results can be transformative, as they were for me. At the meetings in 1986, I delivered a modest paper from my master's thesis. The paper included material about an undergraduate student who traded sex for grades, and it adopted a fairly standard social constructionist position. Carl Couch was in the room and heard the paper. At the time, he had recently completed his civilizations project (Couch 1984a), and he asked me privately, "so what will you do about the problem of tyranny?" This was an issue that marked his work and influenced his position on World War II, Vietnam, and the challenges of maintaining social order.

I had not previously made a connection between my work on the social process of writing in a university context and tyranny or any of its lesser conceptual cousins. But Couch, who was relentless about encouraging interactionists to study the joint act (or, more simply, people doing things together), pressed me to confront the abuse of power in the interaction. I was admonished that if I ever worked with a colleague who traded in academic prostitution, I should "fire his ass." As life has worked out, I occasionally find myself on the frontlines in the management of troublesome behaviour in university settings. Having served as an academic dean for eight years and as a vice-president (academic and research) for an additional five, I have experienced the problem of making decisions concerning organizationally defined wrongdoing, the abuse of power, and the inappropriate use of dominance strategies as part of my day-to-day work. This brings me to the purpose of this chapter. I wish to take up the question of how one's theoretical commitments to symbolic interactionism influence, inform, and otherwise modify an understanding of effective management in complex social organizations. While symbolic interactionism has been exceptionally productive in contributing to an understanding of how people accomplish social action, we have been less attentive to how our theoretical perspectives bring with them commitments that make one line of action preferable over another. In fairness, there are important exceptions here. Hurvitz, Araoz, and Fullmer (1975) anticipate a symbolic interactionist approach to family counselling, Meddin (1982) suggests a productive relationship between cognitive therapy and interactionist theory, and Becker's (1967) well-known and often cited "Whose Side Are We On?" addresses the sympathies and commitments we make in the field. However, my concern is not so much to engage the old argument that interactionism is value-laden as opposed to value-free but rather to argue that the commitments within interactionism lead one to select some lines of action over others.

For example, interactionist inclinations toward qualitative research are not mere preference but rather are an extension of a theoretical perspective that makes what people do a central part of the research enterprise. Once one takes the position that interaction is not a neutral medium through which external factors or variables pass, then one's methodological position must, in some way, attempt to take interaction into account. It is no wonder then that when symbolic interactionists do sociology, they tend to do it with people rather than upon the artifacts of human action. In this simple example, we see a clear indication as to how symbolic interactionist theory may influence and shape the choice between competing lines of action. That symbolic interactionists live out their sociology differently from their more positivistic colleagues is not an expression of mere preference but reflects the translation of theoretical commitment into social action (Grills 1998).

However, while the link between theory and method is an important issue, how does one move from a symbolic interactionist sociology to a symbolic interactionist position on the exercise of power? The problem of power, tyranny, and domination is a rather central problem for interactionists and social constructionists more generally (Athens 2002). In its most extreme forms, the problem of tyranny asks how interactionists find a meaningful voice in the face of the extended loss of human life, human dignity, and human security. Where is there to be found in our conceptual frameworks the words and the corresponding actions called for at specific moments in everyday life that we confront?

One can of course move back to Blumer (1969) and assert that there is no meaning inherent in the object, embrace social constructionism, reduce conflict to the observation that one person's insect is another person's god, and leave the whole thing up to interpretation. But to the extent that all of this is accurate enough, it is not really satisfying to the victim of a sexual assault. Human actors do not generally engage everyday life as though all there is to this life is interpretation. While persons engage their worlds perspectivally and engage in ongoing processes of sense-making, this interpretive work includes the development of a shared understanding of what is known, what is unknown, and that about which there is reasonable doubt (Berger and Luckmann 1966; Grills and Grills 2008; Schutz 1982). While notions of tyranny and evil are socially constructed by human actors, these very same actors imbue these constructions with an element of certainty, moral or otherwise, that allows for action.

Rather centrally, any adequate theory of the social world should be adequate for living in that world. How can we, as social scientists, endorse one theory for understanding the acts of others yet live our own lives as if those very same concepts, postulates, and theories have only partial relevance to our own choices? If one's theory of the social is different from the theories one employs for living in that world, there is a resultant problematic disjunction between the work of "theorizing" the social and the task of "living" in the social. Of all of the various theoretical commitments we may make, perhaps the most important are the ones that we use to engage one another in the paramount reality of everyday life.

A theory of the social world that is inadequate for living in that world may have extended merit within the finite province of meaning that gave rise to it, but if such notions are divorced from the empirical world, they can never serve as a reference point for selecting between lines of action in that world. On this point I need to make a careful distinction – the distinction between theories of how people live (theorizing about the essential qualities of the human condition) and theorizing that is prescriptive (e.g., theorizing that is explicitly moral entrepreneurial in its interests and character). My interest in this chapter is located much more fully in the former than in the latter, but I very much recognize that valuing an understanding of the human condition is in itself a moral position in that it privileges some questions over others and thereby makes a commitment to an inquiry for which the theorist is accountable.

For me, this argument is a very personal project. For the past decade, I have been working in labour relations and university administration in one form or another. This is morally charged work that includes processes and contexts that may bring people into various forms of conflict and competition. Universities are places marked by social processes of domination, dissent, organizational isolation, rites of passage, and degradation ceremonies of various sorts. My question is fairly simple: How does the conceptual framework of symbolic interaction contribute to developing a theory of administrative practice – of framing the practical accomplishment of power and of authority?

Given that doing university administration means selecting from competing lines of action and doing so in the context of scarce resources and incompatible demands, how does symbolic interaction contribute not only to acting but to acting well? That is, I wish to assert that a commitment to symbolic interactionist principles results in an exercise of authority different from various other commitments. To the extent that this is true, there is an implicit moral position within symbolic interactionism that recommends one set of decisions over another. To illustrate this point and to undertake an analysis of this problem, I will use several key root images of symbolic interaction as points of departure for understanding their relevance for administrative practice. Specifically, I will examine how attending to the perspectival, self-referential, and processual qualities of human group life may influence management work.

PERSPECTIVES AND THE PRAGMATIST IMPULSE TOWARD ACADEMIC FREEDOM

The notion that people act toward the world on the basis of meaning, and that these meanings are developed in relation to one another and are selectively employed in relation to others, is fundamental to symbolic interaction. William James (1893) demonstrated these themes in his cross-disciplinary *Principles of Psychology*, Dewey (1916) recognized the importance of meaning in his approach to educational reform, Goffman (1959) was attentive to this theme in the control one has on impressions given, Blumer (1969) joined more phenomenologically inclined theorists in asserting that meaning is never to be found in the social object itself but rather resides in the act of sense-making, and Wiley (1995) frames the social self in terms of the interpretive triad that hinges on the past, present, and future self. All have led to a strong interest in preserving the "symbolic" side of symbolic interaction through, in part, attending to how people make sense of things, how people employ signs and signifiers, and how they apply meaning to action.

Such a position makes meaning problematic. So how does one undertake the work of management or administration in the context of a diverse and multi-perspectival audience? A commitment to symbolic interactionism not only requires that multiple perspectives be recognized but also allows that there is no empirical reference point to turn to in order to resolve differences in perspective. A species may simultaneously be critically endangered from the perspective of a biologist and a food source to the parent of a hungry child.

I would suggest that the modern (as opposed to the medieval or classical) university has centrally entrenched a perspectivally oriented world view into its organizational life through the concept of academic freedom. There is a congruency between a symbolic interactionist world view and one that privileges the multi-perspectival world required to preserve academic freedom. There is a strong historical basis for this relationship. It was under Dewey's leadership as the president of the American Association of University Professors (AAUP) in 1915 that the "freedom of inquiry and research; freedom of teaching within the university or college; and freedom of extra-mural utterance and action" were adopted as organizing principles of the AAUP (a policy that arose out of joint meetings between the American Economic Association, the American Political Science Association, and the American Sociological Association two years earlier).

The very same pragmatist philosophical roots that supported the development of symbolic interactionism supported the entrenchment of modern notions of academic freedom in North America. As a direct result, university-level academic administrators work in a very different context from that of administrators within relatively closed organizational systems (e.g., law). The notion of academic freedom serves as something of a corrective to organizational practices that may produce the uniformity of world views found in some subcultural settings (Horn 1999).

Like other perspectivally attentive theorists, symbolic interactionists "must take other people's narrative analyses nearly as seriously as 'we' take our own" (Rosaldo 1989, 147). However, few individuals live as though the moral narratives that they hold are tentative, partial, or simply an expression of their academic freedom and therefore must be set aside in the interests of accommodating the protection of the academic freedom of another. In fact, the exercise of academic freedom requires that we profess what we hold to be the preferred understanding of the worlds we engage. In the very act of professing what we hold to be the case, we may directly, intentionally, and purposively impose on the academic freedoms of others.

In the context of multiple perspectives and an interest in the protection of academic freedom, how does one move forward to create a consensual/collegial understanding within a complex organization? Effective university administration is process-attentive.

THE POLITICAL IMPLICATIONS OF THE SELF

Like many strong theories that are born from intellectual conflict, symbolic interactionism is profitably framed relative to the interloculars

that situate its interests. In his important essays, "The Methodological Position of Symbolic Interactionism" and "The Sociological
Implications of the Thought of George Herbert Mead," Blumer (1969)
engages and resists the two reductionisms that he argues distort a
full understanding of the social world – the collectivist reductionism
that may deny the role of the human actor as an agent of anything
other than a collective consciousness and the individualist/behav-
ioural reductionism that adopts a biological basis for discounting
the self.

By so doing, Blumer articulates a non-reductionist version of the
social self. The self in symbolic interactionism requires the attribution of a great deal of autonomy to the human actor. Through a
synthesis of various interactionist thinkers (e.g., Blumer 1969;
Cooley 1956; Goffman 1959; James 1893; Mead 1934; Wiley 1995),
we gain a quick portrait of the symbolic interactionist self. Within
interactionism, human actors are capable of self-reflective thought
and are able to locate the self in past, present, and future contexts.
We are able to step back and forth through the "looking glass" to
view the self through multiple vantage points and are able to present
the self in multiple ways to multiple audiences. We are able to select
from competing lines of action (including the action of opting not to
act) and are able to reconsider, re-evaluate, and make adjustments
toward self and other on an ongoing basis. Therefore, persons are
autonomous actors who, when acting in a co-ordinated way, are
necessarily aligning their actions with other autonomous actors who
can and do act back against the intentions and directions of others.

I would suggest that the early pragmatists very much appreciated
the necessity of a clear theory of the self in relation to the social process of democratic decision-making and good governance (see also
Prus, this volume). One cannot embrace the idea of democracy without introducing a theory of the self. The foundational principles of
democratic practice require not only the concept of the discrete person but also a notion of personhood that allows for reflective, considered, free action. Were it otherwise, the principle of universal
enfranchisement would rest on very weak ground.

Correspondingly, an autonomous version of the self necessitates
governance practices that do not do violence to that notion. For
example, the Canadian Charter of Rights and Freedoms (1982)
states, "Everyone has the following fundamental freedoms: (a) freedom of conscience and religion; (b) freedom of thought, belief,

opinion and expression, including freedom of the press and other media of communication; (c) freedom of peaceful assembly; and (d) freedom of association." These rights reside at the level of the individual, and they are available to every person.

These freedoms belong to the person and are therefore made meaningful by an underlying theory of personhood – they are not a right conferred by citizenship or nationality, nor are they restricted by qualities of the person such as gender, race, ethnicity, and sexual orientation. While symbolic interactionists have articulated clearly the developmental nature of the self (Mead 1934) and the challenges that a relative absence of language holds for self in the context of deafness or limitations of the person (Evans 1984), these challenges to the formation and realization of the self do not subvert the status of the person. Why does this matter?

On the issue of governance and the democratic impulse, symbolic interactionism stands at a very different theoretical vantage point than do many other competing theories of the self. In fact, one of the most important features of the self as it is framed within symbolic interactionism is what is excluded. Many competing understandings of the self abandon the more abstract qualities of the interactionist self in favour of attributing to human actors specific motivations or intentionalities that are in some way taken to define the human experience. From various perspectives, the self, the person, and corresponding human action may be reduced to: (1) the pursuit of profit; (2) a series of exchange relations; (3) the innate goodness of the human person; (4) the pursuit of biological/evolutionary or sexual advantage; (5) conflict-based relationships; or (6) a rationalized understanding of human action. I would suggest that by very explicitly refusing to attribute to human action a particular motivational intentionality, the version of the self offered by symbolic interactionism is a particularly robust concept that allows for the full range of human experience. It is a version of the self that supports the notion of the autonomy of the person that is a requisite for democratic practice. And it is a version of the self that is consistent with the idea of collegial self-governance.

The modern university is built around the principle of this idea of collegial self-governance. This interest in self-regulation among professions such as law, medicine, and policing is fairly well established in the sociology of occupations (e.g., Lazega 2001). However, as an organizing principle, the notion of collegial self-governance is central to the idea of the university. As Newson (1998) argues, "With its prevailing doctrine of 'meritocracy,' the university of the 1960s and early 1970s could be viewed as having staged a contest between the two objectives of serving the needs of the economy, on the one hand, and contributing to the political project of advancing democratic sensibilities and practices on the other ... Together, these struggles contributed toward the relative success of institutionalizing the idea of collegial self-governance."

Just as democracy requires a theory of the self, so too does the organizational principle of collegial self-governance. Symbolic interactionism's cognitively situated self allows for the diversity of perspectives, beliefs, and values that define a university campus. As a framework for engaging the other, the absence of an assumed motive, morality, or emotive position on the part of the other provides for a genuine possibility of collegiality. However, without a means by which to effectively engage in collegial self-governance, we are left with principle devoid of practice. Symbolic interactionism's interest in process is a useful resource here.

ORGANIZATIONAL POLICY AND SOCIAL PROCESS

The conceptual fundamentals of symbolic interactionism are consistent with the conceptual requirements of academic freedom and collegial self-governance. However, these themes raise the organizational problem of multiple narratives, competing claims, a theory of the self that speaks to the equality of persons, and the practical need to navigate the waters of dissent and conflict. Fortunately, symbolic interactionism does not abandon the theorist to a position that leads to an infinite regress – to a world understood through a simple idealism where there is nothing left but interpretation. Blumer (1969) was exceptionally clear about this. While arguing for an interactional theory of meaning (and thereby rejecting realism and psychologism as theories of meaning), he allows for the reflective turn, the internal conversation, and, importantly, the existence of an obdurate reality that acts back against ideas of the world. But in all of this, it is the attention to interaction, to the act, to form over substance, to what Lofland (1976, 31) refers to as the "abstract, transcendent, formal and analytical aspects" of any human situation that provides an invaluable administrative resource.

It is through the joint act that meanings are modified, managed, and enacted. As Couch (1984b) has argued, the fundamental (but not exclusive) unit of analysis for symbolic interactionists is the joint act – for it is within the act that human group life is accomplished. By attending to joint acts, the theorist is encouraged to move away from simply attending to cultural content and personal experience toward a transsituational attentiveness to group relationships, identities, and activities (Prus 1996). Fine's (2007) study of the culture of prediction within meteorologists as an occupational group is illustrative of such work. While this text is a specific occupational study, it nevertheless speaks to the generic themes of judging the accuracy of claims and the problem of creating verification. Attentiveness to process allows for movement beyond the particular toward an understanding of the general, as well as away from the downward reductionism of private meaning to an understanding of the practical accomplishment of group life.

Two particularly important consequences for university administration and governance can be found in a process-centred theoretical position. First, it encourages those with some administrative responsibility in a given situation to move outside of the particular (e.g., a dispute about who teaches what, who receives a service increment, who gets to park where, or whether the image on an office wall is offensive to others) to the more generic aspects of the interactional sequence before them (e.g., Gawley 2008). It is particularly helpful to recognize processual themes such as: impression management, status contests, degradation ceremonies, influence work, careers of involvement, and associational or relational entanglements. By simply naming the process, the understanding of the social action may be reframed.

Second, an attention to process also reframes the organizational policies and structures within which university administrators operate. Universities are policy-rich environments. They have policies on themes as diverse as purchasing, hiring, conflict of interest, smoking, academic integrity, and access to information. What symbolic interactionism rather fundamentally teaches is that process matters. Interaction is not some neutral process through which preformed intentions pass to produce pre-formulated outcomes. Rather, it is through social process that people select from competing lines of action, engage in negotiation, make adjustments, throw their lot in with some and distance themselves from others, and engage in activities of coercion, dominance, and aggression. The necessity of social process for action helps to define the human condition. An interactionist approach to administration embraces the "doing" of administration not as some necessary evil that resides between goal and objective but as the means by which the very life of the community of scholars is realized. A symbolic interactionist administrator has an understanding of process very different from that of an administrator who accepts the concept of "false consciousness" into their intellectual commitments.

This chapter is necessarily somewhat partial and, some might suggest, overly hopeful. It is based upon a fairly simple premise – that a commitment to the fundamental principles of symbolic interactionism can have implications for effective practice. In this, I join feminist colleagues and Marxist ones, humanistic sociologists, and a wide range of other scholars who have sought to critically examine what their theoretical commitments required of them as principled actors. In this case, the work of everyday life that I turn my attention to is university administration and governance. I am arguing for an intersection between our theories of the social world and our life within it. Just as one can meaningfully speak of an interactionist approach to theorizing, one can also speak of an interactionist approach to teaching, or sales, or labour relations, or mentoring, or parenting.

There is a congruency between the root conceptual images of symbolic interaction and the cultural milieu that marks modern public university and administration. I argue that symbolic interactionism's interest in perspectives (e.g., world views, intersubjectivity, definitions of the situation, interpretations, a socially constructed reality) is compatible with and supportive of the principle of academic freedom. Likewise, the symbolic, interactionally realized self (the cognitive self of Mead and Peirce) is consistent with the version of self that is required of collegial self-governance or university governance as realized through a bicameral system. Further, social process stands as an important corrective to the possibility of irresolvable tensions between equally autonomous persons.

Importantly, effective interactionist-influenced administration does not give in to reification. The products of human action are recognized as such – not as "the way things are" or "the way things have always been" but as reflective of the decisions and processes undertaken by others that can be reconsidered, interpreted, set aside, or otherwise revised and revisited. Thus, opportunity is to be found in the possibility that the future of an organization is not determined by its past – for it is through negotiation with others that practices can be altered, previous relationship re-cast, and structures changed.

REFERENCES

American Association of University Professors. 1915. "Declaration of Principles on Academic Freedom and Academic Tenure." http://www.aaup.org/AAUP/pubsres/policydocs/contents/1915.htm

Athens, Lonnie. 2002. "Domination: The Blind Spot in Mead's Analysis of the Social Act." *Journal of Classical Sociology* 2(1):25–42

Becker, Howard S. 1967. "Whose Side Are We On?" *Social Problems* 14(3):239–47

Berger, Peter, and Thomas Luckmann. 1966. *The Social Construction of Reality*. New York: Anchor

Blumer, Herbert. 1969. *Symbolic Interactionism: Perspective and Method.* Englewood Cliffs, NJ: Prentice-Hall

Constitution Act. 1982. Part 1: Canadian Charter of Rights and Freedoms. http://laws.justice.gc.ca/en/charter/1.html#anchorbo-ga:l_I

Cooley, Charles Horton. 1956. *Two Major Works*. Glencoe, IL: Free Press.

Couch, Carl. 1984a. *Constructing Civilizations*. Greenwich: JAI Press

– 1984b. "Symbolic Interaction and Generic Social Principles." *Symbolic Interaction* 7:1–14

Dewey, John. 1916. *Democracy and Education: An Introduction to the Philosophy of Education*. New York: Macmillan

Evans, Donald. 1984. "Socialization into Deafness." In *Doing Everyday Life: Ethnography as Human Lived Experience*, edited by Mary Lorenz Dietz, Robert Prus, and William Shaffir, 129–42. Toronto: Copp Clark Longman

Fine, Gary Alan. 2007. *Authors of the Storm: Meteorologists and the Culture of Prediction*. Chicago: University of Chicago Press

Gawley, Tim. 2008. "University Administrators as Information Tacticians and Targets: Understanding Transparency as Selective Concealment and Instrumental Disclosure." *Symbolic Interaction* 31(2):183–204

Goffman, Erving. 1959. *The Presentation of Self in Everyday Life*. New York: Anchor

Grills, Scott. 1998. "An Invitation to the Field: Fieldwork and the Pragmatist's Lesson." In *Doing Ethnographic Research: Fieldwork Settings*, edited by Scott Grills, 3–20. Thousand Oaks, CA: Sage

Grills, Sheilagh, and Scott Grills. 2008. "The Social Construction of Doubt: Women's Accounts of Uncertainty and Chronic Illness." In *Dissonant Disabilities: Women with Chronic Illnesses Theorize Their Lives*, edited by Diane Driedger and Michelle Owen, 53–64. Toronto: Canadian Scholars Press

Horn, Michiel. 1999. *Academic Freedom in Canada: A History*. Toronto: University of Toronto Press

Hurvitz, Nathan, Daniel Araoz, and Dan Fullmer. 1975. "The Miller Family: Illustrating the Symbolic Interactionist Approach to Family Therapy." *The Counseling Psychologist* 5(3):57–105

James, William. 1893. *Principles of Psychology*, vol. 1. New York: Henry Holt and Company

Lazega, Emmanuel. 2001. *The Collegial Phenomenon: The Social Mechanisms of Cooperation among Peers in a Corporate Law Partnership*. Oxford: Oxford University Press

Lofland, John. 1976. *Doing Social Life*. New York: Wiley

Mead, George Herbert. 1934. *Mind, Self, and Society*. Chicago: University of Chicago Press

Meddin, Jay. 1982. "Cognitive Therapy and Symbolic Interactionism: Expanding Clinical Potential." *Cognitive Therapy and Research* 6(2):151–65

Newson, Janice. 1998. "The Corporate-Linked University: From Social Project to Market Force." *Canadian Journal of Culture and Communication* 23(1). http://www.cjc-online.ca/index.php/journal/article/view Article/1026/932

Peirce, Charles Sanders. 1998. *The Essential Peirce*, edited by Nathan Houser, Christian Kloesel, and the Peirce Edition Project. Bloomington: Indiana University Press

Prus, Robert. 1996. *Symbolic Interaction and Ethnographic Research: Intersubjectivity and the Study of Human Lived Experience*. Albany: State University of New York Press

Rosaldo, Renato. 1989. *Culture and Truth: The Remaking of Social Analysis*. Boston: Beacon Press

Schutz, Alfred. 1982. *The Problem of Social Reality*. The Hague: Martinus Nijhoff

Wiley, Norbert. 1995. *The Semiotic Self*. Chicago: University of Chicago Press

21

The Emperor Has No Clothes: Waning Idealism and the Professionalization of Sociologists

JACQUELINE LOW

While sociologists have written reams about the professionalization of doctors, midwives, lawyers, and others, they have been less enthusiastic about examining this social process within their own discipline – so unenthusiastic that the journal *The American Sociologist* devoted a special issue to the professionalization of sociologists (Nichols 2005). In the lead article, Shulman and Silver (2005, 5) maintain that a major goal of the issue is to encourage "sociologists to apply more of their own concepts to an analysis of their discipline." When the professionalization of sociologists is examined, attention tends to revolve around the practical issues faced by new sociologists, such as discovering how to maintain a balance between teaching and research or debates concerning the ethical questions of professional morality or public sociology (Leighninger, Leighninger, and Pankin 1973; Martindale 1976; Pescosolido 1991). Other studies have focused on the development of the professional identities of sociologists, including the professional values they develop (Adler and Adler 2005; Ferrales and Fine 2005), and while the issue of mentorship has been examined (Adler and Adler 2005; Ferrales and Fine 2005; Schnalberg 2005), of particular relevance to my analysis below, identification with a key thinker within sociology as an integral part of the professionalization of sociologists has not been included in such analyses. Moreover, the loss of idealism, a process seen as key to the professionalization of other occupational groups, has not been applied in studies of the professional socialization of sociologists. This is despite the fact that Haas and Shaffir (1984, 63) and others assert that "a shedding of prior, often lofty conceptions of how professionals ought to work" is "common to many – perhaps all – fields" (see also Watson, Deary, and Lea 1999). And while a very few have ventured that idealism first wanes then waxes (Hornosty 1989), or wanes, then waxes, then wanes again (Becker and Geer 1958), or never wanes at all in the first place (Freedman 1978), the vast majority have found that the loss of idealism is part of the process of professionalization (Becker et al. 1961; Fox 1985; 1989; Griffith and Wilson 2003; Haas and Shaffir 1984; 1991; Kuhnel, Heifen, and Sommerkorn 1986; Maher 2006; Manson 1994; Regoli, Poole, and Schrink 1979; Watson, Deary, and Lea 1999) and is at play in secondary socialization more generally (Levy and Churchill 1992; Wilson 2002).

THE WANING OF IDEALISM

The loss or waning of idealism has been most often addressed in studies of students training to enter the profession of medicine (Becker and Geer 1958; Becker et al. 1961; Bloom 1963; Bucher and Stelling 1977; Coombs 1978; de Brabander and Leon 1968; Eron 1955; 1958; Fox 1985; 1989; Griffith and Wilson 2003; Gordon and Mensh 1962; Gray, Moody, and Newman 1965; Haas and Shaffir 1984; 1991; Maher 2006; Manson 1994; Merton, Reader, and Kendall 1957; Olesen and Whittaker 1968; Smith and Weaver 2006). The waning of idealism here refers to the process by which neophytes, who begin their medical studies in an idealistic frame of mind, suffer a loss of idealism because of the rigours and demands of medical training. They must, as Becker et al. (1961, 52) argue, focus "their attention almost completely on their day-to-day activities in school," which "obscures or sidetracks their earlier or idealistic preoccupations." While a few assert that the loss of idealism is a consequence of the type of training program undergone, or the result of interaction with role models within the profession (Hornosty, Muzzin, and Brown 1992; Smith and Weaver 2006), most conclude, as Haas and Shaffir (1984, 64) point out, that such loss of idealism is not "situational and transitory" but rather something required by the demands of professionalization.

    Regardless of the occupation group under study, the waning of idealism is most often conceptualized as negative (Fox 1985; 1989; Haas and Shaffir 1991; Hornosty 1989; Hornosty, Muzzin, and Brown 1992; Maher 2006; Regoli, Poole, and Schrink 1979; Smith and Weaver 2006; Watson, Deary, and Lea 1999). In other words, it is seen as something lost, a thing to be regretted, and, as some argue, something that must be addressed by ameliorative action: idealism must be restored to the budding professional (Smith and Weaver 2006). Far fewer take the position that while the waning of idealism is a loss for the new professional, it also represents a gain for professional practice in terms of the development of a more realistic perspective (Kuhnel, Heifen, and Sommerkorn 1986) or the instrumental attitude Parsons (1951) termed affective neutrality (Haas and Shaffir 1984).

An experience I had in scholarly writing in the summer of 2007 led me to speculate that both the loss of idealism and the identification with a theoretical progenitor are part of the professionalization of sociologists and are thus issues worthy of deeper analysis. Therefore, in this chapter, using autoethnography, I focus on the sense of disillusionment I experienced while undertaking an indepth study of the work of Herbert Blumer and a critical review of commentary on those works. The analysis I present below serves as a corrective to the Chicago School's classic and others' studies of professionalization that foreground the losses and compromises associated with professionalization. It also enables me to comment on the efficacy of an autoethnographic approach to social analysis.

ANALYTIC AUTOETHNOGRAPHY

Autoethnography is a method whereby one makes use of one's own experience as a model in analysis. However, it is not my intent here to engage in what is often self-indulgent "mesearch" (Holt 2003; Ranson 2007); rather, it is to use my "key informant" status as a means by which lines of future research may be discovered and expanded upon (Voloder 2008). Citing Reed-Danahay (1997), Holt (2003, 2) points out that autoethnography can vary to the extent that "*graphy* (i.e., the research process), *ethnos* (i.e., culture), or *auto* (i.e., self)" are foregrounded. Thus, a few words about what I mean by autoethnographic analysis are in order. I follow Anderson's (2006) understanding of what he terms the analytic autoethnographic paradigm. Within this paradigm, the analysis is based on "self-narrative that places the self within a social context" (Reed-Danahay 1997, 9) and is thus more than merely a personal and autobiographical statement. Rigorous analytic autoethnography requires not only that the phenomena under study be something that autoethnographers have personal experience of (Voloder 2008) but also that researchers practise analytic reflexivity whereby they think critically about the sociological import of their experiences and display a "commitment to theoretical analysis" (Anderson 2006, 378). Finally, analytic auto-ethnographers must eventually enter into "dialogue with informants beyond the self" if they are to engage in fruitful sociological analysis (Anderson 2006, 378).

THE ANALYTIC AUTOETHNOGRAPHIC CASE

In the summer of 2007, I undertook revision for publication of a paper I presented at the 2006 Qualitative Analysis Conference in Niagara Falls, Canada. The paper in question was one in which I argued that while Mead no doubt had a manifest influence on the development of Blumerian symbolic interactionism, the perspective also owes much to the insights of Georg Simmel. In particular, a Simmelian flavour is evident in how Blumer addresses the core soci-ological issues of the nature of social reality, the nature of the rela-tionship between the individual and society, and the nature of social action (Low 2006). I concluded the paper by critiquing the failure of Blumer and Blumerian symbolic interactionists to acknowledge this influence. The revision of this conference paper for publication entailed a deep and critical reading of much of Blumer's writings as well as a review of a plethora of commentaries on those writings (cf. Low 2008). I emerged from that scholarly process disillusioned with Blumer (but not Blumerian symbolic interactionism). To understand my disillusionment, we first need to address "biographical context" in the form of salient facts from my personal biography – in particu-lar, those related to my academic career (Silverman 1998).

I began my bachelor's degree majoring in English and had finished half my program when I took a sociology course as one of my elec-tives. The course was social problems and was taught by Dorothy Pawluch, a sociologist noted for her work in social constructionist theory. I chose the course because I thought, like many undergradu-ates, that it would teach me how to solve the world's problems. Instead, what I learned about the constructionist perspective on social problems quite frankly blew my mind. I had what I can only describe as a conversion experience (Lofland and Stark 1965; Snow and Phillips 1980). The day after attending the first class, I began filling out the forms to change my major to sociology, and years later here I am, a tenured professor of sociology. Another key experience from my undergraduate years involved the iconic picture of Blumer (1969) that graces the original dust jacket of his opus *Symbolic Interactionism: Perspective and Method*. I ran across the copy of the book that I now own by chance at a book sale in the sociology lab at Concordia University where I was an undergraduate student in sociology. It was in holding that book and looking at that picture that my identification as a sociologist, not only with symbolic interactionism but also with Blumer himself, was actualized. So it is with no little idealism that I embarked on a career in sociology.

That idealism, based on a deep belief in the efficacy of a symbolic interactionist approach to the study of social life and an equally deep faith in the superiority of the Blumerian variant of the perspective, persisted unchallenged until my recent critical review of Blumer's work. While I did not lose faith in the principles of Blumerian symbolic interactionism or in Blumer as a social theorist, I did become disillusioned with Blumer's scholarly practice, including his failure to cite his sources, his dogmatic championing of Mead as the single progenitor of Blumerian symbolic interactionism, his failure to cite any textual evidence for almost all of his assertions in this regard (cf. Blumer 1966; 1967; 1969; 1978; 1980; 1981; 2004), and, finally, his defensive and vitriolic response to anyone who would dare to criticize or even disagree with him – a charge that Best (2006) has also recently levelled against Blumer (cf. Blumer 1966; 1967; 1978; 1980).

DISCUSSION

From the brief autoethnographic case I have just presented, it is clear that I have suffered a loss of idealism that is connected to my early identification with a key thinker who is also the progenitor of the theoretical perspective I most identify with as a sociologist. What is also clear to me is that the loss of idealism I experienced was inextricably tied to a maturing of my critical analytic abilities. Thus, it suggests to me that if a waning or loss of idealism is a generic social process involved in the professionalization of sociologists, it is also a process conducive to the good practice of sociology, because we need to be as critically reflective of our own discipline as we are of others.

Thus, the waning of idealism represents a gain in intellectual maturity and scholarly autonomy rather than a loss of scholarly ideals.

What this first level of autoethnography cannot tell us, however, is whether the loss of idealism I experienced is, on the one hand, merely an artifact of my personality and my personal, rather than social, biography or is, on the other hand, part of a generic social process of professionalization and maturation as a sociologist. A third possibility is that, as a colleague has suggested to me, my experiences represent neither and are rather indicative of the career path of a particular type of sociologist, one who adheres to a sociological school of thought that is ideologically driven, such as Marxism, and/or attached to an identifiable progenitor as in my case, Blumerian symbolic interactionism. To address these questions, we must move on to the next stage of autoethnographic analysis, and as Anderson (2006, 378) rightly concludes, seek out the experiences of informants "beyond the self."

REFERENCES

Adler, Patricia A., and Peter Adler. 2005. "The Identity Career of the Graduate Student: Professional Socialization to Academic Sociology." *The American Sociologist* 36(2):11–27

Anderson, Leon. 2006. "Analytic Ethnography." *Journal of Contemporary Ethnography* 35(4):373–95

Becker, Howard S., and Blanche Geer. 1958. "The Fate of Idealism in Medical School." *American Sociological Review* 23:50–6

– Everet C. Hughes, and Anselm Strauss. 1961. *Boys in White: Student Culture in Medical School.* Chicago: University of Chicago Press

Best, Joel. 2006. "Blumer's Dilemma: The Critic as a Tragic Figure." *The American Sociologist* 37(3):5–14

Bloom, Samuel W. 1963. *Power and Dissent in Medical School.* New York: Free Press

Blumer, Herbert. 1966. "Sociological Implications of the Thought of George Herbert Mead." *American Journal of Sociology* 71(5):535–44

– 1967. "Reply to Woelfel, Stone, and Faberman." *American Journal of Sociology* 72(4):411–12

– 1969. *Symbolic Interactionism: Perspective and Method.* Englewood Cliffs, NJ: Prentice Hall

– 1978. "Comments on George Herbert Mead and the Chicago Tradition of Sociology." *Symbolic Interaction* 2:21–2

- 1980. "Mead and Blumer: The Convergent Methodological Perspectives of Social Behaviorism and Symbolic Interactionism." *American Sociological Review* 45(3):409–19
- 1981. Review of *George Herbert Mead: Self, Language, and the World*, by David Miller. *American Journal of Sociology* 86(4):902–4
- 2004. *George Herbert Mead and Human Conduct*, edited by Thomas J. Morrione. Walnut Creek, CA: Altamira Press
Bucher, Rue, and Joan G. Stelling. 1977. *Becoming Professional*. Beverly Hills, CA: Sage
Coombs, Robert H. 1978. *Mastering Medicine: Professional Socialization in Medical School*. New York: Free Press
de Brabander, Bert, and Carlos A. Leon. 1968. "A Comparative Study of Attitudes among Columbian Medical and Nonmedical Students." *Journal of Medical Education* 43:912–14
Eron, Leonard D. 1955. "Effects of Medical Education on Medical Students." *Journal of Medical Education* 10:559–66
- 1958. "Effects of Medical Education on Attitudes: A Follow-up Study." *Journal of Medical Education* 33(2):25–33
Ferrales, Gabrielle, and Gary A. Fine. 2005. "Sociology as a Vocation: Reputations and Group Cultures in Graduate School." *The American Sociologist* 36(2):57–75
Fox, Rene. 1985. "Reflections and Opportunities in the Sociology of Medicine." *Journal of Health and Social Behaviour* 26(1):6–14
- 1989. *The Sociology of Medicine: A Participant Observer's View*. Englewood Cliffs, NJ: Prentice Hall
Freedman, Monroe H. 1978. "The Loss of Idealism – By Whom? And When?" *New York University Law Review* 53(592):658–62
Gordon, Leonard V., and Ivan N. Mensh. 1962. "Values of Medical Students at Different Levels of Training." *Journal of Educational Psychology* 53:48–51
Gray, R.M., P.M. Moody, and W.R.E. Newman. 1965. "An Analysis of Physicians: Attitudes of Cynicism and Humanitarianism before and after Entering Medical School." *Journal of Medical Education* 40:760–6
Griffith, Charles H., and John F. Wilson. 2003. "The Loss of Idealism through Internship." *Evaluation and the Health Professions* 26(4):415–26
Haas, Jack, and William Shaffir. 1984. "The Fate of Idealism Revisited." *Journal of Contemporary Ethnography* 13(1):63–81
- 1991. *Becoming Doctors: Adopting a Cloak of Competence*. Greenwich, CT: JAI Press

Holt, Nicholas L. 2003. "Representation, Legitimation, and Autoethnography: An Autoethnographic Writing Story." *International Journal of Qualitative Methods* 2(1):1–22

Hornosty, Roy. 1989. "The Development of Idealism in Pharmacy School." *Symbolic Interaction* 12(1):121–37

Hornosty, Roy, Linda Muzzin, and Gregory Brown. 1992. "Faith in the Ideal of Clinical Pharmacy among Practising Pharmacists Seven Years after Graduation from Pharmacy School." *Journal of Social and Administrative Pharmacy* 9(2):87–96

Kuhnel, Steffen M., Peter Heifen, and Ingrid N. Sommerkorn. 1986. "No Jump into Cold Water, yet No Easy Entry Either: Results of a Longitudinal Study of Medical Students in a One-Year Internship Program." *Sociologia Internationalis* 24(1):19–41

Leighninger, Robert D., Jr, Leslie H. Leighninger, and Robert M. Pankin. 1973. "Sociology and Social Work: Science and Art?" *Journal of Sociology and Social Welfare* 1(2):81–9

Levy, Gerald E., and Christina Churchill. 1992. "New Middle Class Youth in a College Town: Education for Life in the 1990s." *International Journal of Politics, Culture and Society* 6(2):229–67

Lofland, John, and Rodney Stark. 1965. "Becoming a World-Saver." *American Sociological Review* 30:862–75

Low, Jacqueline. 2006. "Structure, Agency, and Social Reality in Blumerian Symbolic Interactionism: The Influence of Georg Simmel." Paper presented at the Symbolic Interaction and Ethnographic Research Conference, Niagara Falls, Canada, 16–18 May

– 2008. "Structure, Agency, and Social Reality in Blumerian Symbolic Interactionism: The Influence of Georg Simmel." *Symbolic Interaction* 31(3):325–43

Maher, Kristy. 2006. "Physician Socialization and the Loss of Idealism." *Journal of the South Carolina Medical Association* 102:67–9

Manson, Aaron. 1994. "The Fate of Idealism in Modern Medicine." *Journal of Medical Humanities* 13(3):153–62

Martindale, Don. 1976. "Sociology Students and Teachers." *International Journal of Contemporary Sociology* 13(3 and 4):183–208

Merton, Robert K., George C. Reader, and Patricia L. Kendall. 1957. *The Student Physician*. Cambridge, MA: Harvard University Press

Nichols, Lawrence T. 2005. "Editor's Introduction: Reflections on Graduate Training in Sociology." *The American Sociologist* 36(2):1–3

Olesen, Virginia L., and Elvi W. Whittaker. 1968. *The Silent Dialogue: A Study in the Social Psychology of Professional Socialization*. San Francisco: Jossey-Bass

Parsons, Talcott. 1951. *The Social System*. Glencoe, IL: Free Press

Pescosolido, Bernice. 1991. "The Sociology of the Professions and the Profession of Sociology: Professional Responsibility, Teaching, and Graduate Training." *Teaching Sociology* 19(3):351–61

Ranson, Gillian. 2007. "Constructing the Methods Chapter." Paper presented at the 24th Qualitative Analysis Conference: Towards New Heights, St Thomas University and University of New Brunswick, Fredericton, NB, 16–19 May

Reed-Danahay, Deborah. 1997. *Auto/Ethnography: Rewriting the Self and the Social*. New York: Berg

Regoli, Robert M., Eric D. Poole, and Jeffrey L. Schrink. 1979. "Occupational Socialization and Career Development: A Look at Cynicism among Correctional Institution Workers. *Human Organization* 38(2):183–7

Schnalberg, Allan. 2005. "Mentoring Graduate Students: Going beyond the Formal Role Structure." *The American Sociologist* 36(2):28–42

Shulman, David, and Ira Silver. 2005. "Demystifying the Hidden Magic of Producing Sociologists." *The American Sociologist* 36(2):5–10

Silverman, D. 1998. "The Quality of Qualitative Health Research: The Open-Ended Interview and Its Alternative." *Social Sciences in Health* 4(2):104–18

Smith, Janice K., and Donna B. Weaver. 2006. "Capturing Medical Student's Idealism." *Annals of Family Medicine* 4(1):532–7

Snow, David, and Cynthia L. Phillips. 1980. "The Lofland Stark Conversion Model." *Social Problems* 27:430–47

Voloder, Lejla. 2008. "Autoethnographic Challenges: Confronting Self, Field, and Home." *Australian Journal of Anthropology* 19(1):27–40

Watson, Roger, Ian J. Deary, and Amandah Lea. 1999. "A Longitudinal Study into Perceptions of Caring and Nursing among Student Nurses." *Journal of Advanced Nursing* 29(5):1,228–37

Wilson, Brian. 2002. "The Canadian Rave Scene and Five Theses on Youth Resistance." *Canadian Journal of Sociology* 27(3):373–412

22

Formal Grounded Theory, the Serious Leisure Perspective, and Positive Sociology

ROBERT A. STEBBINS

Today, I believe it is accurate to qualify the serious leisure perspective as a formal grounded theory, a specimen of a rare entity in qualitative research. From the beginning, and for many years, work on the perspective has been exclusively conducted according to the procedures of constant comparison of data memos, memo sorting, and, from there, development of theoretic concepts that then became the basis for emergent theory. Throughout this process, to be eligible for inclusion in the emergent theory, all concepts had to be relevant to the leisure participants in question. Of note, in this interdisciplinary undertaking, is the fact that in addition to the large number of new concepts created directly from the data gathered, a significant number were imported into the perspective from a variety of disciplines and practices. Only a small proportion of the imported concepts came from symbolic interactionism, however, a branch of knowledge widely claimed as the paradigmatic home of all grounded theoretic efforts. Most recently, as an important extension of this formal theory, I have proposed a new field dubbed "positive sociology." This chapter traces the emergence of the serious leisure perspective to its present state as a formal grounded theory and then presents an *aperçu* of positive sociology.

THE SERIOUS LEISURE PERSPECTIVE

Leisure is defined here as uncoerced activity engaged in during free time, which people want to do and, in either a satisfying or a fulfilling way (or both), use their abilities and resources to succeed at. "Free time" is time away from unpleasant obligation, with pleasant obligation being treated here as essentially leisure, since *homo otiosus*, leisure man, feels no significant coercion to enact the activity in question. What people experience as leisure revolves around one or more "core activities," or distinctive sets of interrelated actions or steps that must be followed to achieve an outcome or product attractive to the participants.

The *serious leisure perspective* is a theoretic framework that synthesizes three main forms of leisure, showing at once their distinctive features, similarities, and interrelationships. Those forms are serious, casual, and project-based leisure, briefly defined as follows:

- Serious leisure: systematic pursuit of an amateur, hobbyist, or volunteer activity sufficiently substantial, interesting, and fulfilling for the participant to find a (leisure) career, acquiring and expressing a combination of its special skills, knowledge, and experience
- Casual leisure: immediately, intrinsically rewarding, relatively short-lived pleasurable activity, requiring little or no special training to enjoy it
- Project-based leisure: short-term, reasonably complicated, one-shot or occasional, though infrequent, creative undertaking carried out in free time or time free of disagreeable obligation

Although it was never my intention as I moved over the years from one study of free-time activity to another, my findings and theoretic musings have nevertheless evolved and coalesced into a typological map of the world of leisure. That is, as far as I can tell at present, all leisure (at least in Western society) can be classified according to one of these three forms and their several types and subtypes. More precisely, the serious leisure perspective offers a classification and explanation of all leisure activity and experience, since these two are framed in the social-psychological, social, cultural, and historical contexts in which the activity and experience take place.

Let us now add to the foregoing definition by noting that amateurs are distinguished from hobbyists by the fact that the former, who are found in the arts, science, sport, and entertainment, have a professional counterpart, whereas the latter do not. Hobbyists, some of whom have commercial counterparts, fall into five types: collectors; makers of, or tinkerers with, things; participants in activities

The Serious Leisure Perspective

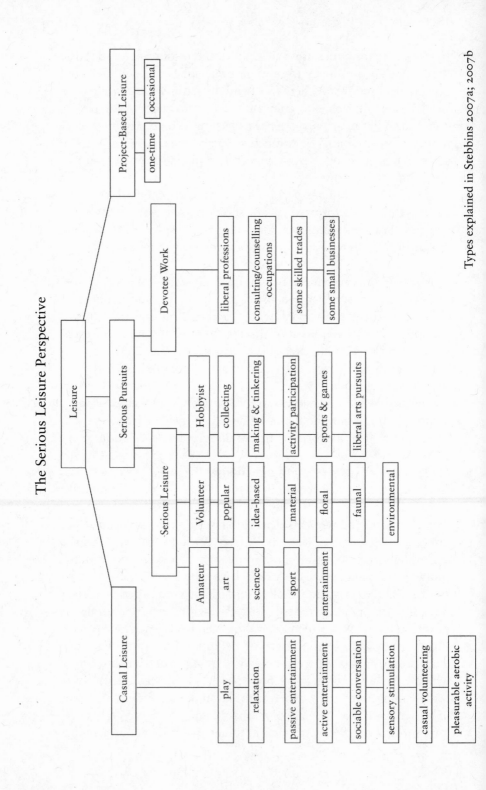

Types explained in Stebbins 2007a; 2007b

(e.g., hunting, mushroom-gathering, bird-watching, canoeing); players of sports and games (they lack professional counterparts); and the liberal arts hobbies (self-education in an area of life or literature). Serious leisure volunteers offer uncoerced, altruistic help either formally or informally with no or, at most, token pay and done for the benefit of both other people (beyond the volunteer's family) and the volunteer.

Serious leisure is further defined by six distinguishing qualities (Stebbins 2007a, 11–13), qualities found among amateurs, hobbyists, and volunteers alike. One is the occasional need to *persevere*, such as in learning how to be an effective museum guide. Yet it is clear that positive feelings about the activity come, to some extent, from sticking with it through thick and thin, from conquering adversity. A second quality is that of finding a *career* in the serious leisure role, shaped as it is by its own special contingencies, turning points, and stages of achievement or involvement (exemplified in Low, this volume, as the author moves through her student career). Careers in serious leisure commonly rest on a third quality: significant personal *effort* based on specially acquired *knowledge, training, experience,* or *skill* and, indeed, all four at times. Fourth, several *durable benefits,* or broad outcomes, of serious leisure have so far been identified, mostly from research on amateurs. They are self-development, self-enrichment, self-expression, regeneration or renewal of self, feelings of accomplishment, enhancement of self-image, social interaction and belongingness, and lasting physical products of the activity (e.g., a painting, scientific paper, or piece of furniture). A further outcome – self-gratification, or the combination of superficial enjoyment and deep fulfillment – is also one of the main benefits of casual leisure, in which, however, the enjoyment part dominates. But self-fulfillment – realizing, or the fact of having realized, one's gifts and character, one's potential, to the fullest – is the most powerful benefit of all (see Prus, this volume, on the fulfilling benefits of education).

A fifth quality of serious leisure is the *unique ethos* that grows up around each instance of it, a central component of which is a special social world where participants can pursue their free-time interests. Unruh (1979, 115) developed the following definition (a different conception of social world from that set out in Grills, this volume): "A *social world* must be seen as a unit of social organization which is diffuse and amorphous in character. Generally larger than groups or organizations, social worlds are not necessarily defined by formal boundaries, membership lists, or spatial territory ... A social world must be seen as an internally recognizable constellation of actors, organizations, events, and practices which have coalesced into a perceived sphere of interest and involvement for participants. Characteristically, a social world lacks a powerful centralized authority structure and is delimited by ... effective communication and not territory nor formal group membership."

The sixth quality revolves around the preceding five: participants in serious leisure tend to *identify* strongly with their chosen pursuits. In contrast, casual leisure, although hardly humiliating or despicable, is nonetheless too fleeting, mundane, and commonplace for most people to find a distinctive identity there.

THE PERSPECTIVE: EARLY YEARS

The term *serious leisure* was born between 1973 and 1976 while I was collecting data for what was to become the "fifteen-year project" of research on amateurs and professionals. Serious leisure is, in effect, a folk term, for, directly or indirectly, many of the amateur interviewees (autobiographers, in the case of my library study of classical musicians) decisively distanced themselves from the dominant conception of leisure as "simply a good time" (referred to here as casual leisure), doing so by underscoring the seriousness with which they approached their avocational passion.

The fifteen-year project, theoretically integrated in Stebbins (1992), consisted of studies of amateurs in archaeology, baseball, theatre, and classical music and of amateurs and professionals in astronomy, entertainment magic, stand-up comedy, and Canadian football. The object of the overall project was to amass exploratory data on two exemplars of each of the four subtypes of amateur (in the arts, science, sport, and entertainment). I collected data for these studies in Canada and the United States, mainly using participant observation and semi-structured interviews.

Publication of *Amateurs, Professionals, and Serious Leisure* in 1992 signalled the culmination of the project. It also served as the first stock-taking of the serious leisure part of the serious leisure perspective as the first had developed to that time. Just as important, that occasion also dramatically highlighted the need to explore, in similar open-ended fashion, the other two types of serious leisure. Stebbins 1995 started this exploration with the hobbies, turning first to the liberal arts variety in a study of cultural tourism in New Orleans. A field study of barbershop singing (in Calgary) followed shortly afterwards (Stebbins 1996a), which, as a hobby, is classifiable as activity participation. The first conceptual statement on volunteering from the serious leisure perspective appeared in Stebbins 1982; it was subsequently elaborated in Stebbins 1996b. This was followed by a participant-observer/semi-structured interview investigation of francophone volunteers in urban Alberta (Stebbins 1998).

Casual leisure got its start in the perspective at the same time as serious leisure, but it initially served only as a foil for the latter until I wrote a separate conceptual statement on it (Stebbins 1997). Central to that statement was the proposition that casual leisure is essentially and distinctively hedonic but, for all that, not without its own substantial benefits (Stebbins 2001a; Hutchinson and Kleiber 2005). Casual leisure certainly achieved a more prominent place in the developing perspective in the second stock-taking (Stebbins 2001b).

Project-based leisure joined the perspective much more recently (Stebbins 2005b). My observation of an instance of it was truly serendipitous but nonetheless sufficient to set in motion the wheels of conceptualization leading to the 2005 conceptual statement. More work on hobbies by me (Stebbins 2005a, on nature-challenge activities) and several other scholars as well as their work on amateurs and volunteers generated the need for yet another stock-taking. I (Stebbins 2007a) accomplished this by organizing the entire area under the heading of the serious leisure perspective. Together, the three forms have evolved and coalesced into the typological map of the world of leisure presented earlier.

THE PERSPECTIVE: RECENT DEVELOPMENTS

The reader should not leave this history with the impression (quite easily gained from the foregoing) that research in and theorizing about the serious leisure perspective is a one-man show. It was at the start, to be sure, but by the mid-1980s other scholars were beginning to use the ideas available in their day to guide and explain their own research. The two most recent stock-takings (Stebbins 2001b, 2007a) show just how many people have contributed, primarily empirically, to development of the perspective. Indeed, without their collaboration, talk of a perspective would be hollow, empirically wanting, and subject to accusations of intellectual imperialism on the part of its author.

That other scholars can contribute profoundly to the perspective is dramatically evident in two major additions by Daniel G. Yoder and James Gould. Yoder (1997) developed a model for commodity-intensive serious leisure. His study of tournament bass fishing in the United States resulted in an important modification of the original professional-amateur-public (P-A-P) model. He found, first, that fishers here are amateurs, not hobbyists, and second, that commodity producers serving both amateur and professional tournament fishers play a role significant enough to warrant changing, for some amateurs and professionals, the original triangular (P-A-P) system of relationships first set out in Stebbins (1979).

A serious leisure scale measuring the six distinguishing characteristics will soon be available for use by qualified researchers. James Gould is the principal author of this scale, which he has named the "Serious Leisure Inventory and Measure," or SLIM. The seventy-two-item scale – this is its long form (there is also a fifty-four-item short form) – and its development are described in Gould et al. 2008. It is the product of Gould's doctoral thesis research conducted at Clemson University. He used a q-sort, an expert panel (e.g., I was frequently consulted on the validity of his proposed measures of various serious leisure concepts), and confirmatory factor analysis to develop the scale, which, using several different samples, he subsequently demonstrated as having acceptable fit, reliability, and equivalence.

Development of a scale like SLIM is evidence of theoretic maturity of the part of the perspective it measures. It also stands as a model of the scientific process of research, wherein a field starts in exploration, develops inductively, and eventually matures by employing verificational procedures. Finally it helps to support the claim that the serious leisure perspective has developed to the point where it may be describe as formal theory.

KEY CONCEPTS

The essence of any grounded theory is its component concepts. In many such theories, some of these concepts have emerged from exploratory data, whereas others, already known, are imported by the researcher as useful sensitizing concepts. The three basic ideas conceptualizing the three forms – serious, casual, and project-based leisure – emerged from fieldwork. Other emergent theoretic codes include all the types and subtypes (except collecting) and the concepts of core activity, optimal leisure lifestyle, participant/devotee, marginality of serious leisure, and pleasurable aerobic activity. Some of the emergent concepts, like volunteering and obligation, root in common sense and therefore had to be reconceptualized to harmonize with field data.

There were also a number of imported theoretic codes. These codes included activity (general, phys. ed.), career (leisure), social world (Unruh 1979), identity (serious leisure), flow (psychology), commitment, professional (amateur), costs/rewards (exchange theory), satisfaction/self-fulfillment (psychology of leisure), human agency, play (anthropology), deviance, and sociable conversation (Simmel).

ACTIVITY AND ROLE

Activity and role are elementary concepts in the serious leisure perspective. An *activity* is a type of pursuit wherein participants mentally or physically (often both) think or do something, motivated by the hope of achieving a desired end. Life is filled with activities, both pleasant and unpleasant: sleeping, mowing the lawn, taking the train to work, having a tooth filled, eating lunch, playing tennis matches, running a meeting, and on and on. Activities, as this list illustrates, may be categorized as work, leisure, or non-work obligation. They are, furthermore, general. In some instances, they refer to the behavioural side of recognizable roles – for example, commuter, tennis player, and chair of a meeting. In others, we may recognize the activity but not conceive of it so formally as a role, exemplified in someone sleeping, mowing a lawn, or eating lunch (not as patron in a restaurant).

The concept of activity is an abstraction and, as such, is broader than that of role. In other words, roles are associated with particular statuses, or positions, in society, whereas with activities, some are status-based while others are not. For instance, sleeper is not a status, even though sleeping is an activity. It is the same with lawnmower (person). Sociologists, anthropologists, and psychologists tend to see social relations in terms of roles, and as a result overlook activities, whether aligned with a role or not. Meanwhile, certain important parts of life consist of engaging in activities not recognized as roles. Where would many of us be could we not routinely sleep or eat lunch?

Moreover, another dimension separates role and activity – namely, that of statics and dynamics. Roles are static, whereas activities are dynamic. Standard sociological theory conceives of roles as dynamic and statuses as static; however, compared with activities, roles are *relatively* static. Roles, as classically conceived, are relatively inactive expectations for behaviour, whereas in activities, people are actually behaving, mentally or physically thinking, or doing things to achieve certain ends. This dynamic quality provides a powerful explanatory link between an activity and a person's motivation to participate in it. Nevertheless, the idea of role *is* useful in positive sociology, since participants do encounter role expectations in certain activities (e.g., those in sport, work, volunteering). Although the concept of activity does not include these expectations, in its dynamism it can, much more effectively than role, account for invention and human agency.

POSITIVE SOCIOLOGY

In a recent book, I propose a new field called *positive sociology* (Stebbins 2009a). It looks into how, why, and when people pursue those things in life they desire, the things they do to make their existence attractive, worth living. Positive sociology is the study of what people do to organize their lives such that those lives become, in combination, substantially rewarding, satisfying, and fulfilling. As a complement to positive psychology, positive sociology centres on social meanings, interpersonal interaction, human agency, and the personal and social conditions in which these three unfold with reference to particular human activities. Positive sociology is one of many possible extensions of the serious leisure perspective, albeit one I consider crucial in the modern age.

Positive sociology, as defined here, is a new idea, even though traces of it have been around as long as sociology itself. Remember, for instance, that Max Weber (1947, 413–15) wrote on amateurs. Robert Dubin (1979, 405), writing more recently at a time when "relevance" was the reigning battle cry in American sociology, observed that a relevant sociology should do more than focus on the "disarticulations between the individual and society." He said it also needs theoretic models on how people construct "worthwhile lives." Such models, my book (Stebbins 2009a) stresses, are predominantly the province of the sociology of leisure, the principal wellspring of positive sociology. Unfortunately for positive sociology, the sociology of leisure has been a marginal branch throughout the history of its parent discipline (Stebbins 2007a, xiii). In the 2009 volume, I argue that sociology must become positive; that is, it must recognize the central place of the pursuit of those (mostly leisure) activities that make life rewarding, satisfying, and fulfilling, though in doing so, I also argue that it should certainly not abandon its long-standing interest in trying to understand and solve life's many difficult social problems, its disarticulations.

A positive sociology, if it is to plow any significant, new intellectual ground, must start in good measure from premises different from those of mainstream, problem-centred, sociology. That is, a large segment of sociology has focused and continues to focus on explaining and handling the various problematic aspects of life that many people dislike, which make their lives disagreeable (see also Jeffries et al. 2006). Controlling or even ameliorating these problems, to the extent this is truly effective, brings welcome relief to those people. Still, managing a community problem in this way, be the problem rampant drug addiction, growing domestic violence, persistent poverty, or enduring labour conflict, does not have the same effect on people as when they pursue something they like. Instead, control of or solutions to these problems brings, as it were, a level of tranquility to life – these efforts make life less disagreeable. This, in turn, gives those who benefit from them some time, energy, and inclination to search for what will now make their existence more agreeable, more worth living.

In other words, there is second major step to take, which is to find the positive, rewarding side of life, made possible after having accomplished the first major step of eliminating, or at least controlling as much as possible, conditions that undermine our basic tranquility. It is in this sense that much of sociology over the years can be said to have concentrated on the negative to the neglect, if not the detriment, of the positive. Nevertheless, let me be clear that I am in no way arguing that positiveness is completely absent during the first step, for obviously, some people manage to pursue leisure and other attractive aspects of life, at times quite effectively, while numerous social and personal problems rage about them. That is not my point. Instead, I want to underscore sociology's general neglect of the second step, including when it overlaps – as it indeed usually does – the first step.

Still, the control and solution of problems are complex processes. Some people pursue as leisure their contribution to the amelioration of certain social issues. Examples include volunteering to serve food to the needy, mentor juvenile delinquents, read to hospital patients, clean up beaches, and provide water filters and electrical lighting to Third World countries. Positive sociology recognizes these activities as leisure pursuits, whereas problem-oriented sociology tends to ignore the attractive, agreeable side of such pursuits. Instead, the latter favours study, control, and amelioration of the problems themselves, commonly referred to without reference to the volunteer component as poverty, juvenile delinquency, health care, environmental pollution, and Third World underdevelopment, respectively.

Moreover, many people face problems while trying to organize their leisure lives. We may refer to these as "positive problems" in that controlling or solving them helps to clear the road for positiveness in everyday life. Consider two examples: the wife who persuades her husband to prepare evening meals, thereby freeing her for community theatre rehearsals, and the father who reorganizes his volunteering at the food bank around the new schedule of soccer practices of his young children. Dealing with such problems is the province of positive sociology, not its problem-centred counterpart.

The distinctive premises of the positive sociology proposed in the book root primarily in the field of leisure studies and the serious leisure perspective, which are, however, expanded to apply to a larger swath of everyday life. That is, at the *activity* level, all of everyday life may be conceptualized as being experienced in one of three domains: work, leisure, and non-work obligation. One might ask whether our existence is not more complicated than this. Indeed it is, for each of the three is itself enormously complex and there is also some overlap in the domains. The novel claim of the book – that sociology can be, and also should be, positive and that positive attitudes and activities matter a great deal – rests on this, the domain approach. Considering the domain of non-work obligation, emphasizing the positive side of work, and viewing both from the angle of leisure and positiveness brings to sociology, anthropology, and psychology an uncommon orientation toward understanding contemporary life.

As just argued, the pursuit of activities in these three domains is framed in a wide range of social conditions, some of which, at that level of analysis, blur domainal boundaries. For example, if the state mandates that no one may work more than thirty-five hours a week, it will affect the amount of time spent in activities in the work domain vis-à-vis that spent in the domains of leisure and non-work obligation. As a second example, consider the impoverished, for whom hunger, disease, malnutrition, and unemployment largely efface the non-work and leisure domains, forcing these people into the full-time activity of survival (subsistence-level work). Third, on the cultural plane, some groups (e.g., religious, communal) stress the importance of altruism and its expression in volunteering. Volunteering here is leisure activity, which, however, loses this quality when experienced as coercion. The feeling of *having* to "volunteer" transforms such activity into a kind of non-work obligation. Examples of this nature are found throughout the book; they constitute a mechanism for facilitating understanding of the positive activities of life from the angle of the relevant social and personal conditions framing them.

CONCLUSION

My claim that the serious leisure perspective has reached the level of maturity of a formal grounded theory should certainly not be taken to mean that the perspective will undergo no further change. Nothing could be further from the truth. For example, many extensions to it remain to be made and elaborated (Stebbins 2007a, chapter 5). Moreover, we live in a world characterized by, among other ways, rapid social change, including a torrent of new and resurgent leisure activities (Stebbins 2009a). The perspective will have to incorporate these conceptual and empirical forces.

In parallel with this theoretic trajectory, let me observe that there has never been a better time in history than now for accentuating the positive. Here sociology should be leading the charge. Thích Nhat Hanh, Vietnamese Buddhist monk, poet, and peacemaker, holds that "people deal too much with the negative, with what is wrong. Why not try and see positive things, to just touch those things and make them bloom?" (source unknown). I agree. And this book offers a way of seeing and pursuing that which makes life worth living, a way of creating a worthwhile existence that is, in combination, rewarding, satisfying, and fulfilling.

REFERENCES

Dubin, Robert. 1979. "Central Life Interests: Self-Integrity in a Complex World." *Pacific Sociological Review* 22:404–26

Gould, James, Dewayne Moore, Francis McGuire, and Robert A. Stebbins. 2008. "Development of the Serious Leisure Inventory and Measure." *Journal of Leisure Research* 40:47–68

Hutchinson, S.L., and D.A. Kleiber. 2005. "Gifts of the Ordinary: Casual Leisure's Contributions to Health and Well-Being." *World Leisure Journal* 47(3):2–16

Jeffries, Vincent, Barry V. Johnston, Larry T. Nichols, Samuel P. Oliner, Edward Tiryakian, and Jay Weinstein. 2006. "Altruism and Social Solidarity: Envisioning a Field of Specialization." *American Sociologist* 37(3):67–83

Stebbins, Robert A. 1979. *Amateurs: On the Margin between Work and Leisure.* Beverly Hills, CA: Sage

– 1982. "Serious Leisure: A Conceptual Statement." *Pacific Sociological Review* 25:251–72

– 1992. *Amateurs, Professionals, and Serious Leisure.* Montreal and Kingston: McGill-Queen's University Press

– 1995. *The Connoisseur's New Orleans.* Calgary: University of Calgary Press

– 1996a. *The Barbershop Singer: Inside the Social World of a Musical Hobby.* Toronto: University of Toronto Press

– 1996b. "Volunteering: A Serious Leisure Perspective." *Nonprofit and Voluntary Action Quarterly* 25:211–24

– 1997. "Casual Leisure: A Conceptual Statement." *Leisure Studies* 16:17–25

– 1998. *The Urban Francophone Volunteer: Searching for Personal Meaning and Community Growth in a Linguistic Minority.* New Scholars–New Visions in Canadian Studies quarterly monographs series, vol. 3, no. 2. Seattle: University of Washington, Canadian Studies Centre

– 2001a. "The Costs and Benefits of Hedonism: Some Consequences of Taking Casual Leisure Seriously." *Leisure Studies* 20:305–9

– 2001b. "New Directions in the Theory and Research of Serious Leisure." *Mellen Studies in Sociology* vol. 28. Lewiston, NY: Edwin Mellen

– 2005a. *Challenging Mountain Nature: Risk, Motive, and Lifestyle in Three Hobbyist Sports.* Calgary: Detselig

– 2005b. "Project-Based Leisure: Theoretical Neglect of a Common Use of Free Time." *Leisure Studies* 24:1–11

– 2007a. *Serious Leisure: A Perspective for Our Time.* New Brunswick, NJ: Transaction

– 2007b. "A Leisure-Based, Theoretic Typology of Volunteers and Volunteering." *Leisure Studies Association Newsletter* 78 (November):9–12. www.seriousleisure.net – Digital Library, "Leisure Reflections No. 16"

- 2009a. "New Leisure and Leisure Customization." *World Leisure Journal* 51(2):78–84
- 2009b. *Personal Decisions in the Public Square: Beyond Problem Solving into a Positive Sociology*. New Brunswick, NJ: Transaction

Unruh, David R. 1979. "Characteristics and Types of Participation in Social Worlds." *Symbolic Interaction* 2:115–30

Weber, Max. 1947. *The Theory of Social and Economic Organization*, translated by Talcott Parsons. New York: Free Press

Yoder, Daniel G. 1997. "A Model for Commodity Intensive Serious Leisure." *Journal of Leisure Research* 29:407–29

Contributors

MICHAEL ADORJAN is assistant professor of sociology at the University of Calgary.

GARY BOWDEN is associate professor of sociology at the University of New Brunswick.

JEFFREY BROWN is associate professor of history at the University of New Brunswick.

TONY CHRISTENSEN is assistant professor of criminology at Wilfrid Laurier University – Brantford.

LUIS CISNEROS is a postdoctoral scholar in physics and at the Beyond Center at Arizona State University.

GARY A. COOK is emeritus professor of philosophy at Beloit College.

MARY JO DEEGAN is professor of sociology at the University of Nebraska – Lincoln.

SCOTT GRILLS is professor of sociology and vice-president academic and provost at Brandon University.

MERVYN HORGAN is assistant professor in the Department of Sociology and Anthropology at the University of Guelph.

MARK HUTTER is professor of sociology and anthropology at Rowan University.

BENJAMIN KELLY is assistant professor of sociology at Nipissing University.

ROLF LINDNER is professor emeritus of European ethnology at Humboldt University of Berlin and professor of urban anthropology at HafenCity University.

JACQUELINE LOW is professor of sociology at the University of New Brunswick.

MOURAD MJAHED completed his PhD in anthropology at the University of Arizona and is currently director of Arabic instruction for the Peace Corps in Rabat.

DeMOND S. MILLER is professor of sociology and anthropology at Rowan University.

EDWARD NELL is Malcolm B. Smith professor of economics at the New School for Social Research.

DAVID A. NOCK is professor emeritus of sociology at Lakehead University.

DEFNE ÖVER is a PhD candidate in sociology at Cornell University.

GEORGE PARK is professor of anthropology (retired) at Memorial University of Newfoundland and Labrador.

THOMAS K. PARK is associate professor of anthropology at the University of Arizona.

DOROTHY PAWLUCH is associate professor of sociology and director of the social psychology program at McMaster University.

ROBERT PRUS is professor of sociology at the University of Waterloo.

ANTONY J. PUDDEPHATT is associate professor of sociology at Lakehead University.

ISHER-PAUL SAHNI is instructor of sociology at Concordia University.

ROGER A. SALERNO is professor of sociology at Pace University.

WILLIAM SHAFFIR is professor of sociology at McMaster University.

GREG SMITH is professor of sociology at the University of Salford.

ROBERT A. STEBBINS is professor emeritus of sociology at the University of Calgary.

IZABELA WAGNER is associate professor of sociology at Warsaw University and associate researcher CEMS EHESS – School for Advanced Studies in Social Sciences – Paris, France.

YVES WINKIN is professor of anthropology and communication at the l'École Normale Supérieure de Lyon.

Index

Sociology

When the University of Chicago was founded in 1892 it established the first sociology department in the United States. The department grew rapidly and by the
1920s graduates of its program were heading newly formed sociology programs
across the country and determining the direction of thé discipline and its future
research. Their way of thinking about social relations – emphasizing an empirical
research method instead of the more philosophical "armchair" approach that
had long prevailed in American sociology – revolutionized the social sciences.

The Chicago School Diaspora presents works by Canadian and international scholars
who identify with the "Chicago School tradition." Broadly speaking, many of
the scholars affiliated with sociology at Chicago understood human behaviour
to be determined by social structures and environmental factors, rather than
personal and biological characteristics. Contributors highlight key thinkers
and epistemological issues associated with the Chicago School, as well as
contemporary empirical research.

Offering original theoretical explanations for the diversity and breadth of the
movement's scholarly traditions, *The Chicago School Diaspora* presents a new
perspective on the ideas, topics, and approaches associated with the origins of
North American sociology.

"Innovative and engaging, this book is animated by the conviction that the
Chicago School remains a vital sociological tradition, one that continues to
provide the basis and inspiration for a thriving scholarly community devoted
to devising an in-depth, nuanced, and broadly humanistic understanding of
social life."
PAUL COLOMY, Department of Sociology and Criminology, University of Denver

JACQUELINE LOW is a professor in the Department of Sociology at the
University of New Brunswick.

GARY BOWDEN is an associate professor in the Department of Sociology at
the University of New Brunswick.

McGill-Queen's University Press
www.mqup.ca

978-0-7735-4266-2

9 780773 542662